Sporting Sounds

Music and sport are both highly significant cultural forms, yet the substantial and long-standing connections between the two have largely been overlooked. *Sporting Sounds* addresses this oversight in an intriguing and innovative collection of essays.

With contributions from leading international psychologists, sociologists, historians, musicologists and specialists in sports and cultural studies, this book illuminates our understanding of the vital part music has played in the performance, reception and commodification of sport. It explores a fascinating range of topics and case studies, including:

*   the use of music to enhance sporting performance
*   professional applications of music in sport
*   sporting anthems as historical commemorations
*   music at the Olympics
*   supporter rock music in Swedish sport
*   Caribbean cricket and calypso music.

From local fan cultures to international mega-events, music and sport are inextricably entwined. *Sporting Sounds* is a stimulating and illuminating read for anybody with an interest in either of these cultural forms.

Anthony Bateman is an Honorary Visiting Research Fellow at the International Centre for Sports History and Culture, De Montfort University. He is also a former member of the Orchestra of Scottish Opera and the Hallé Orchestra. **John Bale** is Emeritus Professor of Sports Studies at Keele University. He has authored many books and articles on various aspects of sport, his most recent work being *Anti-Sport Sentiments in Literature*. He is an Honorary Professor at De Montfort University and the University of Queensland.

Sporting Sounds

Relationships between sport and music

Edited by Anthony Bateman and
John Bale

Routledge
Taylor & Francis Group

LONDON AND NEW YORK

First published 2009
by Routledge
2 Park Square, Milton Park, Abingdon, Oxon OX14 4RN

Simultaneously published in the USA and Canada
by Routledge
270 Madison Ave, New York, NY 10016

Routledge is an imprint of the Taylor & Francis Group, an informa business

© 2009 Selection and editorial matter, Anthony Bateman and John Bale;
individual chapters, the contributors

Typeset in Goudy by Wearset Ltd, Boldon, Tyne and Wear
Printed and bound in Great Britain by TJI Digital, Padstow, Cornwall

British Library Cataloguing in Publication Data
A catalogue record for this book is available from the British Library

Library of Congress Cataloging in Publication Data
Sporting sounds : relationships between sport and music / edited by
Anthony Bateman and John Bale.
p. cm.
Includes bibliographical references and index.
1. Music and sports. 2. Music–Social aspects. 3. Music–Psychological
aspects. I. Bateman, Anthony, 1966- II. Bale, John.
ML3916.S76 2008
780'.0796–dc22   2008020297

ISBN10: 0-415-44367-9 (hbk)
ISBN10: 0-203-88797-2 (ebk)

ISBN13: 978-0-415-44367-8 (hbk)
ISBN13: 978-0-203-88797-4 (ebk)

Contents

Figures

Tables

Contributors

John Bale is Emeritus Professor of Sports Studies at Keele University. He has authored a number of books on geographical aspects of sports, postcolonial perspectives on indigenous body culture, and relationships between sport and literature. His most recent work is *Anti-Sport Sentiments in Literature* (Routledge 2008).

Anthony Bateman is an Honorary Visiting Research Fellow at the International Centre for Sports History and Culture, De Montfort University. He is also a former member of the Orchestra of Scottish Opera and the Hallé Orchestra. His book *Cricket, Literature and Culture 1850–1965* is due to be published by Ashgate in 2009.

Daniel T. Bishop is a lecturer, researcher and member of the Centre for Cognition and Neuroimaging at Brunel University. He is also the psychologist for the Sutton Tennis Academy, UK. He has published and presented internationally on the use of music to manage emotions.

Mike Cronin is the Director of the Centre for Irish Programmes at Boston College in Dublin. He is the author of *Sport and Nationalism in Ireland: Gaelic Games, Soccer and Irish Identity Since 1884* (1999) and, with Daryl Adair, *Wearing the Green: A History of St Patrick's Day* (2002). He has published widely on the history of sport in Ireland. He is currently working on a history of major state spectacles in Ireland in the period after independence.

Henning Eichberg is a cultural sociologist and historian at the University of Southern Denmark in Odense. He specialises in the cultural sociology of body culture and sport, bodily and social movement and democracy, and movement and identity. He is the author of *Body Cultures* (1998) and *The People of Democracy* (2004).

David Forberg is a project manager who has worked extensively in the information technology field. He is an avid sports fan and has travelled the world attending numerous sporting events including figure skating. His figure skating video collection is especially extensive. He currently resides in South Florida.

Sonia Bianchetti Garbato served as an official of the International Skating Union for 25 years (from 1967 to 1992). During her time with the ISU she also officiated at several figure skating championships every year, including seven Olympic Winter Games, and moderated judges' seminars all over the world. She resides in Milan, Italy.

Glenn S. Harman, MD, is a medical oncologist and hematologist at Mayo Clinic in Minnesota. He has an active second career in music, having performed internationally as a solo and duo pianist. He also performs widely on oboe and cor anglais and is an active member of the International Double Reed Society. He has a nearly lifelong association with figure skating.

Jeffrey Hill is Professor of Historical and Cultural Studies at De Montfort University, Leicester. He was Director of the International Centre for Sport History and Culture between 2001 and 2007. His research is in sport as ideology.

Costas I. Karageorghis is Reader in Sport Psychology at Brunel University, West London. He is the author of more than 100 publications, most of which are in the area of the psychophysical and ergogenic effects of music on sport and exercise.

Georgios Loizou was recently awarded a PhD in Sport Psychology from Brunel University, West London and is currently a part-time lecturer at the University of Nicosia, Cyprus. His main research interest is the psychophysiological effects of video, priming and music in a sport context. His research is multi-cultural and multi-disciplined in nature.

Mike McGuinness is Senior Lecturer in Sports Studies at the University of Teesside, Middlesbrough. His principal research interests are cultural representations of sport, especially ephemera, and national identities through sport. He has previously published on the impact of European integration.

Malcolm MacLean teaches history at the University of Gloucestershire where he is Associate Dean, Academic Frameworks in the University's Academic Office. His principal area of research is sport in imperial and colonial settings, with a particular interest in indigenous peoples and colonial subalterns.

Dan Porsfelt is Senior Lecturer in Human Work Science/Sociology of Organisations at Växjö University, Sweden. His research focuses on organisational cultures, socialisation, alcohol at work and relations between home/leisure and work. Football and supporter culture is both a personal and professional interest for him.

Heinrich W. Schwab is Professor of Musicology at the University of Copenhagen. He has previously led a research group specialising in the culture of Scandinavia and the Baltic Sea area and has produced a work on the origins of the secular town musician in the Middle Ages.

Jeffrey O. Segrave currently serves as Interim Dean of Special Programmes at Skidmore College, Saratoga Springs, New York. A faculty member at Skidmore since 1978, he has also served as Director of Athletics, Chair of the Department of Exercise Science, Dance and Athletics, and women's tennis coach.

Peter C. Terry is Professor and Head of Psychology at the University of Southern Queensland. Author of more than 150 publications, he has worked at eight Olympic Games and over 50 other major international events as an applied practitioner.

Graham Welsh studied at the University of Cambridge and the Guildhall School of Music and Drama. He is currently a freelance pianist and translator and lives in Leipzig.

Claire Westall obtained her PhD in English and Comparative Literatures at the University of Warwick, where she also currently teaches. Her research is primarily concerned with English and Caribbean literatures, particularly their engagement with national and masculine identities in postcolonial contexts and as expressed through popular cultural practices such as sport.

Preface

The seeds of this book were sown while the two editors were affiliated to the Centre for Sports Research at the University of Aarhus in Denmark. We had both completed studies in literary representations of sport and discussed how music and sport might be similarly explored. It did not take long for us to discover that studies of the relationships between sport and music were relatively easy to track down in a wide range of publications that represented an equally wide range of academic disciplines. However, beyond the scattered literature there was no substantial text that reviewed and exemplified the ways in which music and sport are related. To fill this lacuna we set about editing this book, much of the contents of which were first presented at a conference at Aarhus in 2006.

We must acknowledge the help of Niels Kayser Nielsen, Michael Mann and Jens Behrend Christensen for their contributions to the conference and help with its organisation and funding. We are also grateful to other colleagues in Aarhus for their support. Additionally, Samantha Grant and Brian Guerin at Routledge have been fully supportive in nursing this book from proposal to completion. We are also grateful to the support of an anonymous referee. Finally, we must thank the authors who have contributed to the chapters that follow and hope that they have not suffered unduly from considerable nudging and occasional bullying from the editors.

Anthony Bateman
John Bale

Introduction

Sporting sounds

John Bale and Anthony Bateman

In 1993 a paper was published in the *Sociology of Sport Journal* stating that 'music has received very little attention among sports scholars'.[1] It is likely, though we have no proof, that a paper in a music journal has probably published the view that musicologists have ignored sports. But both claims are only partially true. Music has long been present in sport, while many musical works have been inspired by, or at least allude to, sporting matters. The chapters of this book confirm the nexus between the two cultural forms of sport and music. They are international in authorship and interdisciplinary in academic approach. Additionally, they span the imaginary spectrum between 'high' and 'low' cultures and between ancient and modern. To our knowledge, this is the first broad work of scholarship that brings sport and music together.

Sport engages many of the senses but the varied sensory aspects of sports that have been alluded to by students of sports studies (implicitly or explicitly) have been dominated by the sense of sight.[2] We tend to take for granted the centrality of sight in the activities and sporting experiences of players, sports-workers and spectators. Other senses are far from absent in the overall sporting experience and those of smell, touch and sound are often significant, as fans and players will testify. Chris Shilling notes that the dominance of visual representations 'underestimate the importance of sound to the environments in which we live'[3] and while we can shut out visual experiences by turning away or closing one's eyes, 'audition is a fairly passive sense; one cannot close one's earlids'.[4]

The sense of sound has been central in sports and has been studied from a variety of perspectives. Cheering, clapping, chanting, shouting and singing are commonplace, occupying a considerable amount of time at many sports events. Indeed, it is rare to find silence at sports events and the suggestion, made to fans in a 1907 football programme, 'that continued bellowing at the top of your voice ... gets on people's nerves and takes away a lot of the enjoyment of the game' has fallen on stony ground.[5] Sounds can, of course, be absent for part of the time in some sports because it is considered important that silence is required for concentration. Hence, in tennis the umpire traditionally calls for silence when a player is serving and the spectators usually politely obey. There is nothing in the official rules insisting that silence is required in these and other sports, and in tennis and cricket, for example, there has been a growing tendency for sounds to be added to what have traditionally been somewhat serene sporting environments. A 'carnivalisation' of cricket grounds has taken place, with all the sounds associated with festivity and, in the context of football clapping is increasingly replacing the one-minute silence before kickoff to honour someone's death.[6]

Sounds that are inside and outside the arena (be it stadium or sitting room) are evocative and often border on sentimentality. From inside the ground, cricket is evoked by the sound of leather against willow, but in some cases sounds external to the sport milieu can also come to symbolise a sense of sport and place. Such sounds led cricket writer John Arlott to comment that cricket played at Taunton evoked the sound 'of lowing cows in the cattle market punctuating the applause of the crowd'.[7] However, within the range of sporting sounds is 'noise', a word that carries negative connotations and is sometimes interpreted as 'unwanted sound' and 'out of place' in certain environments. In the 1990s, when the playing of pop music was introduced at English cricket grounds to accompany significant moments of the action during populist 'day/night games', the development led to impassioned debate between traditionalists and 'modernisers' around the sport.[8] As much as anywhere else, in the sports arena one person's music is another's noise. Similar issues are raised, for example, when noise impinges on residents living near sports stadiums when sport-induced noise becomes a nuisance or a 'negative spillover' – sound that is out of place.[9] However, we are more concerned in this book with sound within the arena or in its recorded form. The *roar* of the crowd, the *shouting* from spectators and the ripple of *applause* are familiar to sports fans. At the same time, of course, the very same sounds can produce in the sports fan senses of anticipation and excitement. Sports-sounds, therefore, are relative.

Music is one form of noise – wanted and unwanted – that occurs widely in sports and its milieu. Music in sport occurs in various ways and assumes various degrees of significance. It has been suggested that music 'is one of the primary phenomena associated with a sports event'[10] and in some sports such as ice skating, synchronised swimming and some forms of gymnastics, music is *essential*. These sports and leisure practices cannot exist without the presence of music and music is an integral part of the activity. In other sports, music is *important*. For example, the scientific and vernacular ways in which music is used to enhance performance is of considerable significance. Such music is used in the laboratory or during training, but it is also present at sports events in the form of terrace songs and chants. The music that accompanies goals in ice hockey, for example, has also become part of the sport though such music is not sanctioned in the rulebooks. 'Organised cheering' at college football games in the US was established as early as the 1860s[11] and fans have come to acknowledge that music is an almost essential part of the game with unwritten rules, but possessing choreographed qualities. The scientist too may see music in the laboratory and in training as an increasingly important, if not essential, part of the sporting experience of participants. In the field of exercise, aerobic step classes routinely rely on carefully formulated musical programmes which elicit a variety of physical responses from participants according to the tempo, texture, rhythmic and dynamic properties of the various pieces.[12]

Music was certainly seen as important by Pierre de Coubertin, the figure generally acknowledged as the founder of modern Olympism. A disciple of the British public school cult of athleticism, he nevertheless avoided the endemic philistinism of the creed, instead envisaging an 'athletic Ruskinism' in which sporting activity and immersion in the arts formed a holistic partnership. The athletic body, with its 'eurythmy' as he described it, would be particularly glorified by its fusion with music – the art he claimed most able 'to provide direct support for sports'.[13] Musical performances were thus integrated into the games from their inception in 1896, but Coubertin sought to increase the musicalisation of the games by integrating it and other art forms into the Olympic competitions themselves. The 1912 Stockholm Olympics were thus the first to include a 'Pentathlon of the Muses': competitions for music, literature, painting, sculpture and architecture. It was a short-lived experiment and 1948 saw the end of the Olympic arts competitions due to the difficulty of proving the amateur status of the participants (deeply ironic though that now seems). The quality and integrity of the music contests had been questionable but they had fulfilled Coubertin's ambition of enshrining music in Olympic culture. The Olympic arts exhibitions which took their place continued to honour his legacy by featuring musical performances and music still adorns Olympic rituals, encoding and transmitting Olympic ideology.[14]

In many sporting contexts, music is more *incidental*. Consider, for example, the place of national anthems in international sporting events, encouraging patriotism and nationalism among both spectators and players. Other incidental, but far from negligible niches for music in sport are in recorded 'football music' and the use of 'classical music' that may be relocated in 'popular' contexts. During the 1990 football World Cup the prominent role of the 'Three Tenors' became symbolic both of the tournament itself and of a broader postmodern blurring of cultural hierarchies. Other classical music has crossed over to the banal through its use as theme music for global sports events and works by Verdi and Elgar, for example, have been appropriated by football fans and reworked as terrace chants and songs. Additionally, Michael Nyman, whose opera is titled *a.e.t* (after extra time), incorporated football chants recorded during an actual game into his music.[15]

Of course, much music is mediated by written scores and by sound recordings. Musical scores that focus on sport have existed from at least the mid-nineteenth century, such as Franz Berwald's orchestral étude *Foot Race*. In the US a substantial number of music scores have focused on baseball and football.[16] Although such music can be experienced at sporting events, it can also be read as bringing sport into music through publication of sheet music and sound recordings, rather than placing music in sport. Music has also played a part in the making of sports heroes and in commemorating sporting achievements. For example, Irving Berlin's first hit song, 'Dorando', was written around the famous incident in the 1908 Olympic marathon in which Pietri Dorando lost the race but became the hero.[17] As David Rayvern Allen has shown, the achievements of famous cricketers such as Jack Hobbs were celebrated in specially composed popular songs[18] and, in economically depressed 1930s Australia, the song 'Our Don Bradman' eulogised this iconic sportsman while appealing to notions of patriotism and national solidarity.[19] Similarly, in 2001 an eponymous hit record lauded the American boxer Muhammad Ali. It is also possible to negate sports-workers in music, an example being Chumbawumba's critical song about the South African runner Zola Budd.[20] In such situations, sport appropriates music both through the world of commerce and more informally by fans. The huge number of variations based on the tune of the folk song 'The Wild Rover' and the popularity of the haunting Cuban song 'Guantanemera' among British foot-ball fans exemplify this.

As implied in the opening lines of this book, scholars have explored the important relationships between sport and the artistic and literary fields, but relatively little attention has been given to the long-standing links between organised sport and music. There are, of course, exceptions. Music has long been associated with Physical Education (PE) and PE manuals pay considerable attention to the place of music in the education of the body.[21] Also, during the 1980s, the pioneering work of Steve Redhead[22] saw music as part of the so-called 'transformation' of English football. Music was seen as 'carnivalising' a sport that had been seen as falling into decline and dominated by images of hooliganism. This is not to say that music has disappeared as being central to communicating malign (i.e. sexist, racist) aspects of the sports experience.[23] Generally, however, the relative absence of music in Sports Studies is a serious academic oversight given the central role of music in modern sport.

Before outlining the content of this book we should point out that we are concerned with both music in sport and with sport in music. However, we feel that it is beyond the scope of this book to explore the strong affinity that exists between music and the body per se, an affinity that has been well described by the writer and artist Wyndham Lewis:

> The coldest musician ... cannot help interfering with your body.... As you listen to music you find yourself dashing, gliding or perambulating about: you are hurried hither and thither, however rhythmically; your legs, your larynx, your heart are interfered with as much as is the membrane of the ear.[24]

While acknowledging that music affects the body and vice versa, we restrict our coverage to where these processes occur specifically *within sporting and musical contexts*.[25] Unfortunately, we also barely touch on other linkages such as the fact that forms of both sport and music rely to a considerable degree on notation.[26]

Plan of the book

In order to redress the relative lack of studies of music in sport the editors have selected a number of contributions by practitioners working in a diverse range of academic disciplines: Sports Science, Sports Sociology, Sports History and Music and Cultural Studies. All the contributors are experts on the relationship between music and sporting culture. Because of the multifaceted interface of music and sport the editors have encouraged a broad and pluralistic definition of music that includes opera, hymns, folk music, calypso and rock.

To an extent the structure of the book corresponds to its major (and often overlapping) themes of performance, reception and commodification. The first three chapters adopt an applied psychological approach to the issue of sporting performance. First, Costas I. Karageorghis and Peter C. Terry provide a detailed review and synthesis of recent theoretical developments, empirical research and applications pertaining to the psychophysical effects of music in sport. Their theoretical model emphasises that the principal benefits of music in sport – improved mood, pre-event activation or sedation, reduced perceived exertion, enhanced work output, improved skill acquisition, flow states, dissociation from feelings of pain and fatigue – are determined by the four factors of rhythm response, musicality, cultural impact and extra-musical associations. The chapter also addresses recent developments in the assessment of the motivational qualities of music – the Brunel Music Rating Inventory-2. Relevant literature is reviewed under three categories: asynchronous music, synchronous music and pre-task music. Asynchronous music is played as an adjunct to a task – in the background – and there is no conscious synchronisation between movement patterns and music tempo. The synchronous use of music entails performing repetitive movements in time with its rhythmical elements such as the beat or tempo. Pre-task music is used primarily for its stimulative or sedative properties, to activate or relax athletes prior to training or competition. A number of evidence-based examples of music-related interventions, drawn from the authors' applied work with World Championship and Olympic athletes are provided to assist practitioners to tap the psychophysical and ergogenic properties of music with greater precision.[27]

In Chapter 2 Georgios Loizou and Costas I. Karageorghis present a case study that examines the interactive effect of video, priming and music on emotions and motivation. The project is couched in extant theory and presents a critical appraisal of empirical research. Priming studies are concerned with temporary activation states and how environmental information interacts with internal readiness to produce perceptions and evaluations as well as motivations and behaviours. Priming can therefore act as a process to subconsciously alter an individual's psychological state prior to and during the execution of a task. Video has been used in psychosocial interventions as a feedback tool for behaviour modification strategies as well as to train communication skills and behaviours. Peak-performance videos, visualisation tapes and video clips set to musical accompaniment can be created for mental training and motivational purposes. Williams and Grant contended that video is one of the most efficacious perceptual motor training tools. In their review of psycho-musicological research, the authors conclude that motor performance could be facilitated by music in several ways. For example, music has the capacity to act as a legal stimulant or sedative and can enhance both pre-task and in-task affect (feelings of pleasure/displeasure). The chapter presents the state-of-the-art research for the use of video, priming and music in sport and suggests implications for theory development. The last quarter of the chapter is devoted to providing recommendations and applied examples for sport practitioners and researchers.

In Chapter 3 Daniel T. Bishop and Costas I. Karageorghis note that music listening as a pre-performance strategy in sport has received scant attention despite its ubiquity and evidence for its ability to elicit strong emotions and to modify one's affective response to visual stimuli. The objectives of this study were to gain an understanding of the phenomenon of music listening by young tennis players at a UK international tennis academy, and to propose a model to guide both future research and athletes' music use. Participants noted five personal pre-performance music selections on a bespoke pre-interview questionnaire, and brought these tracks to an interview in which they recorded their emotional responses to the music. Participants also adjusted the intensity of each track during the interview, to an intensity at which they would typically utilise the track.

Chapter 4 by Glenn S. Harman, Sonia Bianchetti Garbato and David Forberg shift the methodological approach away from the realm of 'hard' science to that of historical reconstruction. They address the sport of figure skating, one of the few where music is currently a part of every phase of competition. Largely because of this, it can be read as bridging the gap between sport and art. This chapter deals with many aspects of the use and interpretation of music in the competitive sport of figure skating. The history of competitive skating reveals the gradual diminution of the importance of figures and the increase in importance of free skating, which is judged not only for its technical merit but also for its presentation and artistry. This is followed by a discussion of how music came to have an impact on the judging of the sport. The chapter also deals with the selection and appropriateness of music and choreography for competition and of the factors used to pick music for a specific skater. Examples of the most effective uses of music in competitive skating are also discussed and the authors supply an overview of the music selections used by world and Olympic champions and an analysis of the genres most frequently represented.

In Chapter 5 Henning Eichberg moves the emphasis to the Danish national festival of gymnastics and sports that took place on the island of Bornholm in 2002. He focuses on the notion of 'energy', a term that has been used in the analysis of body culture from various angles – by Rudolf von Laban's dance theory, Wilhelm Reich's psychoanalysis and Eugenio Barba's anthropology of the theatrical actor. Also, as 'chi', energy is a keyword of the Chinese traditional movement culture. Eichberg stresses that 'energy' describes physical and physiological phenomena that have seriously troubled Western rationality as a result of its challenge to the reduction of the physical world to 'space, time, materiality and causality'. Energy is not only inside the individual but also between human beings, thus constituting a social-psychological 'aura'. It is in this field, between the physical and the psychical, that music also has its place. All this is related to a physical–psychical complex of intonation, where the bodily vocal expression plays together with emotional movement and social togetherness. Within this framework, the musical elements of the Danish sports festival were examined: joint singing as a folk tradition, the music of gymnastics, a certain fusion with the rock concert and the significance of clapping. Eichberg argues that the sports festival creates a form of rhythmic autohypnosis – self-orchestration being an important contribution to popular identity building.

Moving from Eichberg's anthropological view, Chapter 6 by Jeffrey O. Segrave explores the idea that music serves as sport history, or to be more precise, that opera serves as Olympic Games history. He argues that Pietro Metastasio's popular eighteenth century libretto, *L'Olimpiade*, publicised and transmitted a particular ideological and historicised conception of the Olympic Games that would ultimately contribute to the rationalisation and legitimisation of Pierre de Coubertin's own idiosyncratic Olympic ideology, a philosophico-religious doctrine that embraced a noble and honourable conception of sport at the same time as it served discrete class, race and gendered ends. Just as historians have increasingly employed anthropological questions to interrogate the organisation of gender and sexuality, notions of subjectivity, and how discourses operate to structure, reproduce and transform social reality, so Segrave interrogates Metastasio's *L'Olimpiade* and Coubertin's formulation of Olympism, and argues that the hegemony of the contemporary Olympic Games movement is grounded in part on the appropriation of the classicism and romanticism transmitted in Metastasio's work. Theoretically, his chapter borrows from musicological readings of opera, socio-linguistic conceptions of meaning, and postmodern social perspectives on material culture. Segrave contends that Metastasio's *L'Olimpiade*, in both narrative, music and production, sustained a particular image of the games, an image that nourished Coubertin's own ideological formulation at the same time as it paved the way for further musical representations of the Games that to this day lend authority to the hegemony of the Olympics by appealing to a musically transmitted, mythologised and Hellenised past.

In Chapter 7 the musicologist Heinrich W. Schwab examines the influence of sport on music by identifying and theorising the musical genre of 'tennis composition'. Defining the genre as 'each and every piece of music which makes any reference to the multifaceted event known as tennis', he provides an original contribution to both musicology and tennis historiography by identifying the different ways tennis entered music and how the sport inspired novel compositional procedures. While acknowledging that many of these works have been ephemeral in their impact, he nevertheless concludes that the genre includes one undoubted masterpiece, Claude Debussy's ballet score *Jeux*. In this work, Schwab argues, Debussy searched for new musical forms able to give a musical impression of the playful movements and volatile emotions of the ballet's three protagonists. In so doing, Debussy came up with a highly innovative 'wave form' – a technique hugely influential on later practitioners of the 'Neue Musik' such as Herbert Eimert and Karlheinz Stockhausen.

In Chapter 8 Anthony Bateman completes a trilogy of chapters concerned with so-called 'classical' music. Rather than adopting Schwab's single sport approach however, he focuses on a specific period of musical history – the years between 1910 and 1938 – when a number of modernist composers (Debussy among them) were drawn to sport as they attempted to break with the musical language and conventional extra-musical subject matters of the past. Considering the phenomenon of 'sports music' via the writings of that implacable opponent of organised sport, Theodor Adorno, Bateman's chapter is structured around three European case studies. The first examines a number of sports works which emerged from the highly adventurous artistic context of early twentieth-century Paris. The second section considers some critical responses to those and other sports compositions in the more culturally conservative context of inter-war England, where modernism was generally more temperate and slow to take hold. The final section explores the music/sport relationship in former Czecho-slovakia – then a newly independent nation. Here the analysis suggests how modernist musical engagement with organised body-cultural practices articulated with broader patterns of nation-building and cultural nationalism.

Jeffrey Hill, in Chapter 9, focuses on the English FA Cup Final, and in particular the singing of the hymn 'Abide With Me'. The match had been located at the new Empire Stadium, Wembley since 1923, and by 1927 a programme of pre-match music and singing had become an established feature of the proceedings. Drawing upon the work of recent British and French historians, Hill presents the Cup Final rituals of this period not simply as a form of entertainment for the assembled crowds. Rather, they are seen also as an aspect of the ideology of 'remembrance' and 'loss', a part of that movement which revealed an extensive and complex cultural response to the experience of the First World War in all the combatant countries. The construction of war memorials was perhaps its most potent symbol, but the expression of mourning came in many other forms. As with all manifestations of collective grief and remembrance, the singing of 'Abide With Me' was both an orchestrated public event and an occasion experienced at a more personal level, in the individual's innermost thoughts. In an attempt to understand the meanings of the event, Hill directs attention to both aspects, but places particular emphasis on the sensuous and 'indefinable' meanings associated with the hymn and its performance in a sporting crowd. As such, the social history of 'Abide With Me' is considered and the words of the hymn are subjected to a close reading. So too is the 'sound' of the first performance of 'Abide' in 1927. Though ultimately the atmosphere created on this occasion might defy conventional analysis, the chapter attempts to suggest why the experience was a moving occasion of collective grief. In this way Hill seeks to contribute to a discussion of some of the 'existential' aspects that make up the sporting experience – the sights, sounds and smells of the stadium – that have tended to be neglected because they are rarely registered in written sources.

Mike McGuinness, in Chapter 10, commences a group of chapters that focus on the 'popular' end of music production whose approach is more deconstructionist in approach. It considers whether such musical expressions should be seen as idiosyncratic and essentially ephemeral in nature, or as treasure troves of eccentricity. He supplies several examples to show these relationships. Football has tended to dominate the field of 'sports music' to a dramatic degree through the football record chronicling major events, being both celebratory and exploitative at the same time. To provide themselves with an identity fans have adopted anthems, or songs of loyalty, mainly taken from popular music. Popular music has been adopted to reflect mood in sport. There has also been a limited attempt by the music industry to engage with sport, and groups like Half Man Half Biscuit have offered witty observations across the sporting spectrum.

In Chapter 11, Dan Porsfelt provides the first analysis of the sub-genre of Swedish supporter rock music. In Sweden a number of rock bands and artists have symbiotic relationships with particular football clubs, making music and recordings about a club and its supporters and performing in pubs and other venues before home and away games. These musical expressions play an important part in the ongoing reconstruction of the club's respective supporter cultures and in the socialisation of new members. Porsfelt examines the music and lyrics of the three groups and explores a number of recurring themes in the lyrics of the different artists: love, joy, masculinity, alcohol consumption, the construction of the feminine and devaluation of the Other, city–countryside and more. The songs are thus shown to provide a good representation of Swedish supporter culture in general. He also shows that the three artists differ. In this respect four themes are identified and analysed in more depth: topophilia and the importance of the local, resistance against commercialisation, control of supporters and the self-ironic staging of the hooligan and the carnivalesque. These themes are shown to be more or less pronounced in the lyrics of the different bands, a contrast that is interpreted in terms of the particular histories and supporter cultures of the three clubs.

In the final three chapters, commencing with Chapter 12 by Mike Cronin, the emphasis shifts to postcolonial manifestations of sport and music. Cronin argues that the music attached to Ireland's sporting life has been centrally concerned with the idea of community. Building on long-standing Irish traditions of oral culture, singing, story telling and rural identities, sports related music has been focused on telling stories that root the narrative in a consideration of the local. Cronin examines the music that has specifically been associated with the Gaelic Athletic Association and demonstrates, through an analysis of club and county songs, that sports-related music sprang initially from nineteenth-century musical and story-telling forms, and were concerned with a narrative of locality and community-based heroism. While sports-related music has become more commercialised of late, especially in terms of the Saw Doctors, Folk Footballers and others, this transformation has developed a country style that is part of a normative transition from the oral form, a transition which has taken place across all Irish music.

In Chapter 13 Claire Westall reminds us that for more than half a century cricket has repeatedly featured in Caribbean calypso music and has, following Kitchener's 'Cricket Lovely Cricket', contributed to calypso's global popularity. Meanwhile, cricket has itself benefited from an engagement with calypso's flamboyant and assertive style of self-performance – a style which has helped to create popular cricketing heroes, individualise the West Indies crowd and negotiate the gap between players and spectators. Importantly, Caribbean scholars have established the aesthetic, political and economic commonalities between cricket, calypso and the Caribbean literary imagination. For example, it has been noted that calypsos in praise of the West Indies cricket team have constituted a special song-cycle or cluster through which Caribbean manhood has been 'affirmed' and 'reaffirmed'. Westall explores cricket and calypso as intersecting cultural practices that demonstrate the Caribbean's continual search for, and overinvestment in, the individual male hero. By considering calypsos that depict cricketing heroes and placing these alongside readings of similar cricket-focused poems, she suggests that the simultaneous construction and deconstruction of the cricketing hero is part of the region's inability to negotiate a path between 'the one' and 'the many', between island independence and regional collectivity. It concludes that an interrogation of traditional masculine identities, and particularly the hero of calypso-cricket, may aid a productive renegotiation of national discourses and collective Caribbean identities.

In conclusion, in Chapter 14 Malcolm MacLean returns to the phenomenon of music as often playing a key role in shaping the cultural understandings and affective relations of mediated sport. MacLean uses John Frow's notion of the literary frame to explore the role of music in the sport mediascape of Aotearoa/New Zealand during the late 1970s by examining 'Give 'em a Taste of Kiwi', a song used by Television New Zealand in its rugby union broadcasts in 1979 and 1980. This song is seen as articulating a particular version of national masculinity and as asserting rugby's role in this ideal.

An anonymous reviewer of the proposal for this book noted that most theoretical and empirical literature in sport and music is confined to the investigations of cognitions, behaviours and feelings. The underlying philosophy has usually reflected a positivistic, scientific and ultimately materialist perspective and the early chapters of this book reflect this approach. However, sound in sport in the form of music, singing and chanting has been relatively overlooked despite being a commonly encountered experience. For this reason we feel that there is a need to produce multi-disciplinary accounts of sport that approach the subject as both a science and an art. We feel that the study of sound in sport, and the role of music in particular, serve an important need that reminds us that sport cannot be adequately understood without reference to the transcendent and the spiritual. Music in sport and its place in sport for the performer as much as the fans, cannot be fully explained away by surveys, experimental procedures and statistical analysis, though these obviously have their place. To begin to make sense of this pervasive phenomenon there is a need to go beyond the cognitive representations and descriptions and to examine the experience from a multitude of perspectives, both scientific and philosophical.

Notes

1 Eldon Snyder, 'Responses to musical selections and sport: an auditory elicitation approach', *Sociology of Sport Journal*, 10, 2, 1993, 168–182.
2 For example, John Bale, *Landscapes of Modern Sport*, London: Leicester University Press, 1994.
3 Chris Shilling, *The Body in Culture, Technology and Society*, London: Sage, 2005, p. 127.
4 Douglas Porteous, *Environmental Aesthetics: Ideas, Politics and Planning*, London: Routledge, 1996, p. 33.
5 Quoted in Tony Mason, *Association Football and English Society, 1863–1915*, Brighton: Harvester, 1980, p. 232.
6 Simon Frith, 'Music and everyday life', in Martin Clayton, Trevor Herbert and Richard Middleton (eds), *The Cultural Study of Music: A Critical Introduction*, London: Routledge, 2003, p. 93.
7 John Arlott, *Arlott on Cricket* (edited by D. R. Allen), London: Collins, 1984, p. 57.
8 Colin Evans and Michael Kennedy, 'Bring on the dancing girls/stop that dreadful music' in *Lancashire County Cricket Yearbook 2001*, Manchester: L.C.C.C., 2001, pp. 35–37.
9 On this subject see John Bale, *Sport, Space and the City*, Caldwell, NJ: Blackburn Press, 2001 [1993], p. 119.
10 Snyder, 'Responses to musical selections and sport'.
11 M. Oriard, 'Professional football as cultural myth', *Journal of American Culture*, 4, 3, 1981, 27–41.
12 Tia DeNora, *Music in Everyday Life*, Cambridge: Cambridge University Press, 2000, pp. 90–91; see also Clayton, Herbert and Middleton (eds), *The Cultural Study of Music*, pp. 119–120.
13 Pierre de Coubertin, *Olympism – Selected Writings*, Lausanne: International Olympic Committee, 2000, pp. 605–633.
14 On this subject see, for example, Douglas Brown, 'Revisiting the discourse of art, beauty and sport from the 1906 consultative conference for the arts, literature and sport', *Olympika: The International Journal of Olympic Studies*, 5, 1996, 1–14.
15 Steve Redhead, *Post-Fandom and the Millennial Blues*, London: Routledge, 1997, p. 75.
16 Margaret M. Mott, 'A bibliography of song sheets. Sport and recreations in American popular songs: part 2', *Notes*, 7, 4, 1950, 522–561 and Margaret M. Mott, 'A bibliography of song sheets. Sport and recreations in American popular songs: part 3', *Notes*, 9, 1, 1951, 33–62. Part 2 mainly covers baseball and football (US version) and part 3 ranges over other sports including boxing and track and field athletics. For baseball and music see also Timothy A. Johnson, *Baseball and the Music Of Charles Ives: A Proving Ground*, Lanham, MD: Scarecrow Press, 2004.
17 Mott, 'A bibliography of song sheets', *Notes*, 9, 1.
18 David Rayvern Allen, *A Song for Cricket*, London: Pelham Books, 1981, p. 91.
19 Ibid, p. 89.
20 See John Bale, *Running Cultures*, London: Routledge, 2004.
21 See, for example, R. M. Thackray, *Music and Physical Education*, London: Bell, 1938.
22 Steve Redhead, *Sing When You're Winning*, London: Pluto, 1986; Steve Redhead, *Football with Attitude*, Manchester: Wordsmith, 1991; Steve Redhead, *Post-Fandom and the Millennial Blues*. See also Leanne McCrae, 'The Redhead review: popular

cultural studies and accelerated modernity', *History of Intellectual Culture*, 6, 1, 2006. Online, available at: www.ucalgary.ca/hic (accessed 5 March 2008).

23 See Tom Clark, '"I'm Scunthorpe 'til I die": constructing and (re)negotiating identity through the terrace chant', *Soccer and Society*, 7, 4, 2006, 492–507.

24 Wyndham Lewis, 'The credentials of the painter' in P. Edwards (ed.), *Creatures of Habit and Creatures of Change: Essays on Art, Literature and Culture 1914–1956*, Santa Rosa, CA: Black Sparrow Press, p. 70.

25 On the 'musical body' see Shilling, *The Body in Culture, Technology and Society*, pp. 127–147 and DeNora, *Music in Everyday Life*, pp. 75–108.

26 It is rare to see musical notation in academic work authored by sports historians and sports sociologists. A noteworthy exception is Les Back, Tim Crabbe and John Solomos, *The Changing Face of Football*, Oxford: Berg, 2001.

27 We should not ignore, of course, the malign aspects of music therapy such as the use of music as a form of bodily and social control.

1 The psychological, psychophysical and ergogenic effects of music in sport

A review and synthesis

Costas I. Karageorghis and Peter C. Terry

'In training build-ups for major races, I put together a playlist and listen to it during the run-in. It helps psych me up and remind me of times in the build-up when I've worked really hard, or felt good. With the right music, I do a much harder workout.'[1]

(Paula Radcliffe, marathon world record holder)

Introduction

Music has become almost omnipresent in sport and exercise environments. It blares out in gymnasiums, football stadiums and even in swimming pools through underwater speakers. Music is part-and-parcel of the modern-day sporting spectacle, while the advent of the *iPod*™ has better enabled athletes to cocoon themselves in their own auditory world. Does the use of music in sport actually yield higher performance levels or does it simply make sports participation and training more enjoyable? If music does indeed increase work output or enjoyment of a sporting activity, how can we go about maximising such benefits? These questions will be addressed within this chapter using the authors' research findings and examples from their applied work with elite athletes.

Any musical composition requires the organisation of five primary elements: *melody, harmony, rhythm, tempo* and *dynamics*. Melody is the tune of a piece of music – the part you might hum or whistle along to; harmony acts to shape the mood of the music to make you feel happy, sad, soulful or romantic through hearing different notes at the same time (e.g. the strum of a guitar chord); rhythm involves the distribution of notes over time and the way in which they are accented; tempo is the speed at which music is played, often measured in beats per minute (bpm); dynamics have to do with the energy transmitted by a musician through their touch or breath to impact on the loudness of their instrument. Rhythm and tempo are the elements of music most likely to prompt a physical reaction in the listener.[2] Wilson and Davey noted that even when people sit motionless, 'it is often very difficult to suppress the natural urge to tap the feet or strum the fingers along with the beat of the music'.[3]

In addition to a physical response, musical rhythm and tempo relate to the various periodicities of human functioning such as respiration, heart beat and walking.[4] Music and sport are purposefully intertwined at modern-day events, with professional disc jockeys often hired to make appropriate selections to rouse the players or engage the crowd. Most teams have adopted their own anthems or signature tunes which increase team identity and the sense of cohesion. For example, at West Ham United FC the home fans sing the classic 'I'm Forever Blowing Bubbles' while St Mary's Stadium at Southampton FC reverberates to the Dixieland favourite 'When The Saints Go Marching In', which was popularised by trumpeter Louis Armstrong in the 1930s.

Applied example 1.1: rugby music

The use of anthemic chanting that resonates around a rugby ground can be a huge source of inspiration to the players. Most teams have a signature chant or song. For example, England rugby fans sing the stirring hymn 'Swing Low, Sweet Chariot'. This recital, whether in the stands or the players' dressing room, serves to promote feelings of patriotism, unity and competitive drive. The All Blacks famously issue a Maori challenge known as the 'Haka' (Figure 1.1) just before the start of each game to reinforce their team identity. There is, however, an ancillary purpose to such collective bravado; in displaying unified strength, the All Blacks hope to intimidate their opposition.

Figure 1.1 All Blacks' 'Haka' (© PA Photos).

It is ironic that many governing bodies of sport are currently considering banning, or have already banned, the use of music in competition (e.g. the International Amateur Athletics Federation). As we write this chapter, UK Athletics is considering a recommendation by the UK Road Running Management Group to outlaw the use of personal music-playing devices at races. This is partly owing to the potential work-enhancing effects of music, but also to the fact that music can be so intoxicating that it places athletes in mass-participation events in danger – they might knock into each other, miss instructions from officials or, in more extreme cases, risk getting hit by a car.

It was for these exact reasons that the organisers of the New York Marathon banned the use of personal music players in the 2007 event which prompted considerable media debate on the effects of music in sport, but also provoked widespread condemnation from competitors. Nonetheless, banning *iPods*™ and other portable music devices in such large-scale events is almost impossible to enforce. Some race organisers, such as the International Management Group (UK), are organising half-marathon events with live bands lining the course. The music played is carefully selected to match the physiological demands of the event and the demographic profile of participants (see www.runtothebeat. co.uk).

How music affects the human organism

In the domain of sport and exercise, researchers have primarily explored the *psychological*, *psychophysical* and *ergogenic* effects of music. *Psychological* effects refer to how music influences mood, emotion, affect (feelings of pleasure or displeasure), cognition (thought processes) and behaviour. The *psychophysical* effects of music refer to the psychological perception of physical effort as measured by ratings of perceived exertion (RPE).[5] In the music and sport literature, the term psychophysical is often used synonymously with the *psychophysiological* effects of music which relate to the impact of music on physiological functioning. In the interests of parsimony, we will use the term psychophysical with reference to the perception of physical effort and a range of physiological outcome variables (e.g. blood pressure, heart rate, ventilation, etc.). Music engenders an *ergogenic* effect when it enhances work output or yields higher than expected levels of endurance, power, productivity or strength. In this regard, music can be seen as a type of legal drug that athletes can use in training. Sydney Olympics rowing gold medalist, Tim Foster, now a respected coach, uses music to regulate all of the indoor workouts that he leads. He finds that this increases the motivation of his rowers as well as making the sessions far more enjoyable.

In a sporting context, music is used in three main ways. First, as *asynchronous* music whereby it is played in the background to make the environment more pleasurable and where there is no conscious synchronisation between movement patterns and musical tempo. Second, as *synchronous* music, typified by athletes using the rhythmic or temporal aspects of music as a type of metronome that regulates their movement patterns. Third, as *pre-task* music which entails using a musical stimulus to arouse, relax or regulate the mood of an athlete or a team.

It is possible to use music in all three ways. For example, the Brazilian football team listens to stimulating Latin American music in their dressing room while they mentally prepare (pre-task) and when they step onto the pitch they are accompanied by a host of percussion musicians in the crowd. During play, the drums generally pound relentlessly in the background and thus exemplify the asynchronous use of music, though, on occasion, the team appear to lock into the lilting samba rhythm and it dictates the pace of play in a synchronous manner. No wonder then that the team is known as 'The Samba Boys'.

Music in sport – an overview of theoretical developments

Until our 1997 review paper, the approach taken to the study of music in sport or exercise was largely atheoretical in nature and unstructured.[6] We sought to provide researchers with a framework and methodological recommendations to guide their future scientific endeavours. In particular, we advocated greater rigour in the selection of music for experimental conditions with an emphasis on the age profile, preferences and socio-cultural background of experimental participants. We also provided recommendations on the design of music-related experiments with particular focus on the choice of appropriate dependent measures. Until the mid-1990s, the research in this area had yielded equivocal findings, making it difficult to gauge whether music had any meaningful effect when applied to sport-related tasks. Our review highlighted several methodological weaknesses that may have accounted for such varied findings and laid the foundations for the theoretical developments that followed.

The main weaknesses evident in past research were: (1) a failure to consider the socio-cultural background of experimental participants; (2) an imprecise approach to music selection or failure to report the music played; (3) inconsistencies regarding temporal factors such as the duration of music exposure and when it was played relative to the experimental task; (4) non-reporting of the intensity (volume) at which music was played and non-standardisation of this variable across tracks and experimental conditions; (5) inaccurate use of musical terminology by sports researchers; and (6) the use of performance measures that were either inappropriate or difficult to control.

In the decade since our review and accompanying methodological recommendations, there has been a significant improvement in the quality of published studies, complemented by increased interest from sport and exercise researchers. Our 1997 paper covered the 25-year period since the review of Lucaccini and Kreit and critically appraised just 13 related studies.[7] In the subsequent decade, at least 43 related studies have been published. The present chapter will focus primarily on theoretical advances and research conducted in the period since our 1997 review.

Our 1999 conceptual model

To address the paucity of relevant theory, we have published a number of conceptual frameworks over the past decade, two of which are reviewed here. Our original conceptual framework for predicting the psychophysical effects of asynchronous music in exercise and sport held that four factors contribute to the motivational qualities of a piece of music – rhythm response, musicality, cultural impact and association.[8] These factors were subject to empirical examination using both exploratory and confirmatory factor analyses.[9]

Rhythm response relates to natural responses to the rhythmical and temporal elements of music, especially tempo. Musicality refers to pitch-related (as opposed to rhythm-related) elements of music such as melody and harmony. Cultural impact draws upon the pervasiveness of music within society or a particular sub-cultural group, whereby frequent exposure to music increases its familiarity, which has an important role in determining preference. Finally, association pertains to the extra-musical associations that music may evoke, such as Vangelis's composition 'Chariots of Fire' and its connection with Olympic glory. Such associations are built up by repetition and powerful images in which cinema, television, radio and the internet play a pivotal role.

When an association between a piece of music and a sporting activity is promoted by the media, this may elicit a conditioned response that can trigger a particular state of mind; for example, the Rocky theme 'Gonna Fly Now' often evokes a state of optimism and excitement in the listener. Similarly, music can trigger a relaxation response to help ease an athlete's pre-competition nerves. Its therapeutic, anxiety-relieving properties have been used through the ages. To illustrate how music can trigger a relaxation response, think of Lou Reed's classic track 'Perfect Day' or go online to hear an excerpt on YouTube (www.youtube.com/watch?v=QYEC4TZsy-Y). The piece is so serene, so lyrical and so artfully structured that you will probably feel less tetchy and uptight, even by simply imagining the music in your mind.

Karageorghis *et al.* indicated that the four factors have a hierarchical structure in terms of determining the overall motivational score or *quotient* of a given piece of music.[10] The two most important factors, rhythm response and musicality, are called *internal* factors because they relate to the structure of the music itself, and the other two factors, cultural impact and association, are called *external* factors because they relate to how the listener interprets the music. Motivational music is generally higher tempo (more than 120 bpm), has catchy melodies, inspiring lyrics, an association with sporting endeavour and a bright, uplifting harmonic structure. Consider tracks such as 'Put Your Hands Up For Detroit' by Fedde Le Grand or 'I Feel Good' by James Brown, both of which typify motivational music in a sporting context. The relationship between internal and external factors, the motivational qualities of music and potential benefits can be seen in Figure 1.2.

The main benefit of listening to asynchronous music is that it can influence arousal or activation levels by acting like a stimulant or sedative. Research has

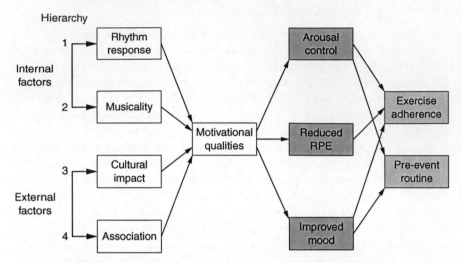

Figure 1.2 Conceptual framework for the prediction of responses to motivational asynchronous music in exercise and sport (adapted with permission from Taylor & Francis; *Journal of Sports Sciences*, 17, 713–724).

shown that loud, upbeat music functions as a stimulant (increases arousal) while soft, slow music functions as a sedative (reduces arousal).[11] Music can reduce ratings of perceived exertion (RPE) although this effect is most pronounced during submaximal work intensities. During high-intensity training activities, such as sprinting or weightlifting, physiological cues have the dominant influence on attention and, owing to an automatic switch from external cues to internal (bodily) cues, music has a negligible effect on perceived exertion.[12] Rejeski's parallel processing model is often mentioned with reference to the diminution of the effects of music as work intensity increases.[13] The aspect of the model most relevant to this phenomenon is known as the *load-dependent hypothesis*; when work intensity increases beyond anaerobic threshold, external cues such as music do not have any significant impact on perceived exertion.

Music can also enhance the positive aspects of mood such as vigour, excitement and happiness, and reduce the negative aspects such as boredom, tension, depression, anger, fatigue and confusion.[14] Collectively, such benefits can impact upon adherence to exercise or sports training by making such activities more pleasurable, or else be used as part of a pre-event routine to engender an optimal mindset (arousal control and improved mood).

In tandem with the development of our 1999 conceptual model, we developed an instrument to rate the motivational qualities of music: the Brunel Music Rating Inventory (BMRI).[15] Many subsequent studies have used the BMRI or its derivatives (e.g. the BMRI-2) to rate the motivational qualities of music used in experimental conditions objectively.[16] Such studies have demonstrated that if the age and socio-cultural background of participants is taken into account during the music selection process, and consideration is given to the congruence of music with the task, significant positive psychophysical and ergogenic effects are likely to ensue.

Our 2006 conceptual model

In 2006, we developed a conceptual framework that was focused primarily in a sport context to reflect the growing list of potential benefits that were coming to light through empirical studies (see Figure 1.3).[17] The model identified the potential benefits of music use for athletes as being: (1) increased positive moods and reduced negative moods; (2) pre-event activation or relaxation; (3) dissociation from unpleasant bodily sensations such as pain and fatigue; (4) reduced RPE; (5) increased work output through synchronisation of movement with musical tempo; (6) enhanced acquisition of motor skills when rhythm or association matches required movement patterns; (7) increased likelihood of athletes experiencing flow; and (8) enhanced performance levels via combinations of the above mechanisms. The literature that is reviewed and synthesised herein provides considerable support for these proposed benefits.

Asynchronous music

Most commonly, researchers have investigated the psychological and psychophysical effects of asynchronous music rather than its ergogenic effects. Tempo is postulated to be the most important determinant of the response to music and preference for different tempi may be affected by the physiological arousal of the listener and the context in which the music is heard.[18] Accordingly, there should be a stronger preference for high-tempo music during physical activity, although some research has indicated that slower tempi may increase physiological efficiency and thus prolong exercise performance.[19]

A body of work has investigated the relationship between working heart rate, usually during a training-related activity, and preference for music tempo.[20]

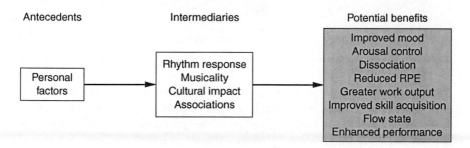

Figure 1.3 Conceptual framework for the benefits of music in sport and exercise contexts (reproduced with permission from Australian Psychological Society; 2006, *Proceedings of the Joint Conference of the Australian Psychological Society and the New Zealand Psychological Society*, 415–419).

Applied example 1.2: Sonja the swimmer

Sonja is an ambitious young swimmer on the fringe of the national squad. She makes a concerted effort to improve by swimming at least 15 miles in training each week. The lack of variation in her training and the early-morning slot during which she is required to train combine to make the task lonely and challenging, both mentally and physically. Her coach, Rob Robson, works hard to make Sonja a better swimmer. To progress, she needs to relax and avoid wasting energy through excessive muscular tension. To aid her improvement, Rob suggested that she wear a specially designed waterproof mp3 player (*Soundwaves*) in her swimming cap. Sonja listens to soulful ballads and energising R'n'B music sung by strong female role models like Beyoncé and Jennifer Lopez with whom she identifies. The harmonies within the music create a positive mood while the flowing rhythms and slower tempi help her to focus and maintain an efficient and regular stroke. The music also becomes a focus during long-distance swims and distracts her from the negative feelings associated with fatigue. In fact, the effects of the music can be quite hypnotic, and after a while she feels as though she is gliding effortlessly through the water.

Figure 1.4 The *Soundwaves* underwater mp3 player.

Such work stems from the recommendations of exercise practitioners indicating that music tempo should be matched closely to expected heart rate.[21] Also, work in the field of experimental aesthetics indicates that the *arousal potential* of stimuli determines preference.[22] Berlyne explained arousal potential in terms of the amount of activity that musical stimuli induce in areas of the brain such as the reticular activating system. Stimuli that have a moderate degree of arousal potential are liked most and preference decreases towards the extremes of arousal potential in a quadratic or inverted-U relationship.

Using experimental protocols that required participants to self-regulate a pure tone and subsequently a piece of music, Iwanaga predicted a positive and linear relationship between heart rate and music tempo preference.[23] However, these early findings were criticised by the psychomusicologist LeBlanc who argued that the methodologies used were unrepresentative of those employed in traditional music research and generally lacking in external validity.[24] Essentially, under normal circumstances, listeners are seldom able to self-regulate the tempo of a piece of music and most judgements of tempo preference are made after a piece has been heard. LeBlanc argued that in traditional music research it was evident that listeners preferred tempi slightly higher than their heart rate if at rest or while performing normal activity (i.e. not physical training).[25] LeBlanc also highlighted that younger listeners generally preferred higher tempi.[26] This notion was supported through subsequent work in an exercise context which showed large differences in tempo preference between young listeners (17–26 years old) and older adults (over 45 years old).[27]

It was evident that Iwanaga's findings could be validated by having the same participants select their preferred tempi for varying work intensities. If they preferred tempi close to their heart rates at a range of work intensities, it would lend support to Iwanaga's hypothesis concerning a positive, linear relationship.[28] Accordingly, the first author initiated two experiments that examined the relationship between heart rate and music tempo preference.[29]

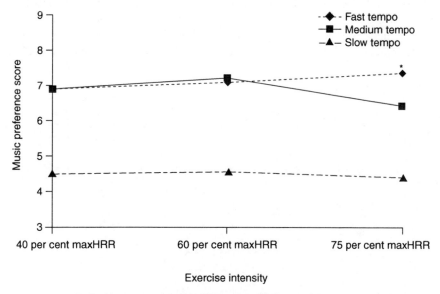

Figure 1.5 Significant two-way interaction for Exercise Intensity × Music Tempo (reproduced with permission from the American Alliance for Health, Physical Education, Recreation, and Dance; 2006, *Research Quarterly for Exercise and Sport*, 26, 240–250).

Note
* $p < 0.05$.

Karageorghis *et al.* investigated the relationship between exercise heart rate and preferred tempo.[30] Participants reported their preference for slow (80 bpm), medium- (120 bpm) and fast- (140 bpm) tempo music selections while working at 40 per cent, 60 per cent and 75 per cent of maximal heart rate reserve (maxHRR) on a treadmill. There was a significant effect for music tempo, wherein a strong preference for fast- and medium-tempo music over slow music was evident regardless of work intensity. An exercise intensity by tempo inter-action effect was also observed, with participants reporting a preference for either fast or medium-tempo music during low and moderate exercise intensi-ties, but for fast-tempo music during high-intensity exercise (see Figure 1.4).

Karageorghis *et al.* extended this line of investigation so that participants lis-tened to entire music programmes rather than just excerpts of music.[31] This study was predicated on a suggestion from the preceding study that although fast-tempo music was preferred at a high exercise intensity, continued exposure to such music during an exercise bout would result in negative psychological effects such as boredom and irritation.[32] Therefore, Karageorghis *et al.* tested medium tempi, fast tempi, mixed tempi (tracks arranged in the order medium, fast, fast, medium, fast, fast) conditions and a no-music control condition while participants worked at 70 per cent maxHRR on a treadmill.[33]

Measures of music preference, intrinsic motivation and global flow were taken. It was hypothesised that the mixed-tempi condition would yield the most positive psychological effects owing to the interspersion of medium and fast tempi. However, the findings did not support this hypothesis (see Figure 1.5) as it was actually the medium-tempi condition that elicited the most positive psy-chological effects. The authors suggested that there may be a step change in

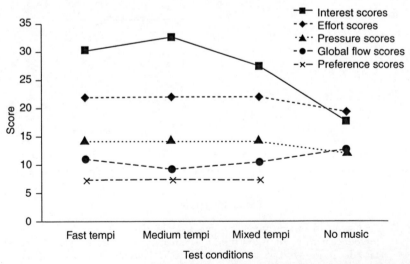

Figure 1.6 Combined male and female mean scores for IMI subscales, global flow and preference ratings (reproduced with permission from Thieme Publishers; in press, *International Journal of Sports Medicine*).

preference between 70 per cent and 75 per cent maxHRR in which participants express greater preference for fast-tempi music. This coincides with the point at which the body begins to rely more heavily upon anaerobic pathways for energy production and exercisers become more acutely aware of bodily cues associated with fatigue (cf. load-dependent hypothesis).[34]

The inconsistent findings derived from these two studies caused us to seriously question the positive and linear relationship proposed by Iwanaga.[35] Indeed, the extant findings have led us to hypothesise that the relationship between exercise heart rate and music tempo preference will display a quartic trajectory (with three points of inflection; see Figure 1.6). Specifically, during the early stages of an exercise bout, the relationship is linear, whereas during the moderate-to-high exercise intensities both fast- and medium-tempo music is preferred. Beyond 70 per cent maxHRR, fast tempi are preferred and the linearity of the relationship resumes. Once exercise intensity exceeds 80 per cent maxHRR, there will be a 'ceiling effect' for tempo preference as there are relatively few tracks recorded at tempi greater than 150 bpm. Considering the importance of familiarity in determining music preference, such high tempi are unlikely to be preferred regardless of work intensity.[36] Moreover, given the salience of physiological cues in determining attentional focus, it is unlikely that music at any tempo can be selectively attended to at high work intensities.[37]

Many athletes and practitioners struggle to determine the precise tempo of any given piece of music. To assist readers wishing to select music with reference to its tempo, we have included a table showing the tempi of a range of music selections that have proven popular in the sport and exercise domain

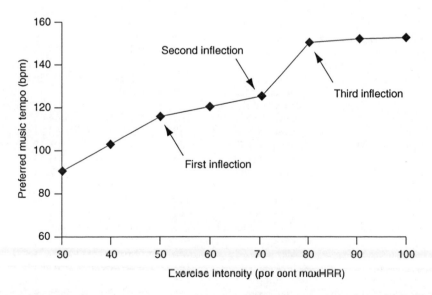

Figure 1.7 Hypothesised quartic relationship between exercise heart rate and preferred music tempo.

Table 1.1 Widely-used music selections in sport and exercise contexts

Track title	Artist(s)	Tempo (bpm)	Style	Length (minutes)
We Are The Champions	Queen	64	Rock	03:00
Beautiful Girls	Sean Kingston	65	R'n'B	03:45
Chariots Of Fire	Vangelis	68	Classical	03:26
Fix You	Coldplay	70	Pop/Rock	03:46
Milkshake	Kelis	75	R'n'B	03:05
Fly Away	Lenny Kravitz	80	Rock	04:32
Heads High	Mr Vegas	92	Reggae	03:31
Valerie	Mark Ronson featuring Amy Winehouse	94	R'n'B	04:20
Faith	George Michael	96	Pop	03:07
Hippychick	Soho	102	Pop	03:46
Wake Me Up When September Ends	Greenday	105	Rock	04:45
Flap Your Wings	Nelly	106	Hip hop	04:49
Gettin' Jiggy With It	Will Smith	108	Hip hop	03:51
The Power	Snap	112	Dance/Hip hop	04:05
Everybody Dance Now (Gonna Make You Sweat)	C & C Music Factory	113	Dance	04:10
The Way I Are	Timbaland	115	R'n'B/Hip hop	04:24
Umbrella	Rihanna featuring Jay-Z	116	Hip hop	04:11
My Love	Justin Timberlake	120	R'n'B/Pop	04:36
Lovestoned	Justin Timberlake	121	R'n'B	04:40
Proper Education	Eric Prydz featuring Pink Floyd	124	Dance	04:44
Let Me Entertain You	Robbie Williams	124	Pop/Rock	04:23
Get Ready For This	2 Unlimited	125	Dance	03:21
I Like The Way You Move	Bodyrockers	125	Dance	03:58
Brimful Of Asha (Norman Cook Remix)	Cornershop	126	Pop	03:56
Get Down	Groove Armada featuring Stush and Red Rat	127	Dance/ UK Garage	03:28
Hey Ya!	Outkast	127	R'n'B/Pop	04:00
This Love	Maroon 5	127	Rock/Pop	03:21
Ain't No Other Man	Christina Aguilera	128	Pop/R'n'B	03:25
Where's You Head At	Basement Jaxx	128	Dance	03:53
Put Your Hands Up For Detroit	Fedde Le Grande	129	Dance	02:33
Discoteka	Starkillers	130	Dance	04:45
Jump Around	House of Pain	134	Hip hop	03:22
Gotta Get Thru This	Daniel Beddingfield	135	Pop/R'n'B	04:31
Sandstorm	Da Rude	135	Dance	05:34
Firestarter	Prodigy	136	Dance	03:54
Ace Of Spades	Motörhead	142	Rock/Metal	03:45
Oh Yes (Mr Postman)	Juelz Santana	148	Hip hop	03:45
Danger Zone (from Top Gun movie soundtrack)	Kenny Loggins	154	Rock/Pop	03:14
Surfin' Safari	Beach Boys	156	Pop	02:05
Burn Baby Burn	Ash	162	Rock	03:29

(Table 1.1). There is also an applied example which follows that demonstrates how you might construct a music programme to accompany a typical training session. Should you wish to find out the tempi of your favourite musical selections, you might try internet sites such as www.thebpmbook.com, www.ez-tracks.com or in the case of dance and hip hop selections, www.jamglue.com. There are also various software packages such as Tangerine (www.potionfactory.com), which can assess the tempo of each track on your PC and automatically add this detail to an *iTunes™* library.

Szabo *et al.* found that a switch from slow-tempo to fast-tempo music yielded an ergogenic effect during static cycling.[38] The implication of this finding is that a change of music tempo from slow to fast may enhance participants' motivation and work output, especially when work level reaches a plateau or during the latter stages of an exercise bout. Similarly, Atkinson *et al.* indicated that the careful application of asynchronous music during a simulated 10 km cycle time-trial could be used to regulate work output.[39] The music was particularly effective in the early stages of the trial when perceived exertion was relatively low. Participants used the BMRI to assess the motivational qualities of accompanying music and their ratings supported the prediction that rhythmical components of music contribute more to its motivational qualities than melodic or harmonic components.[40]

A follow-up study by Lim *et al.* investigated the effects of an asynchronous music programme used in different half-segments of a 10 km cycle time-trial.[41] The music was played either for the first half (M1) or second half (M2) of the trial and the two experimental conditions were compared against a no-music control (C). It was expected that music would have a greater impact on power output when introduced during the latter half of the trial, although the results did not support this hypothesis (see Figure 1.8). In actuality, condition M2 yielded the highest power in the early stages of the trial when no music was played. A plausible explanation for this anomaly is that foreknowledge of the

---

Applied example 1.3: how musical selections can be moulded around the components of a typical training session

Table 1.2 Musical selections to accompany a workout

Workout component	Title	Artist(s)	Tempo (bpm)
Mental preparation	Survivor	Destiny's Child	92
Warm-up activity	Crazy	Gnarls Barkley	112
Stretching	Keep On Moving	Soul II Soul	100
Strength component	The Power	Snap	112
Endurance component	Move On Up	Curtis Mayfield	136
Warm-down activity	Lifted	Lighthouse Family	97

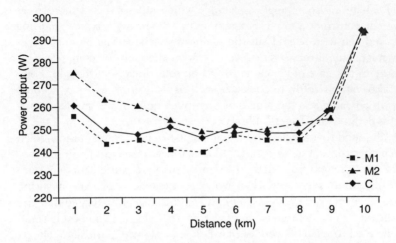

Figure 1.8 Impact of asynchronous music in the first half (M1) and second half of a 10 km stationary cycle time-trial, and a no-music control (C).

introduction or removal of music may have affected participants' pacing strategy. Notwithstanding this possible confound, Lim *et al.*'s methodology is representative of a fruitful new avenue of research that reflects the way in which music is used strategically in sporting settings.[42]

Karageorghis and Terry assessed affective and psychophysical responses to motivational and oudeterous music during treadmill running at 50 per cent $\dot{V}O_2$ max using RPE, affect, heart rate and post-exercise mood as dependent measures.[43] Motivational music had the most positive influence on affect, RPE and the vigour component of mood. Differences were found primarily between the motivational and control conditions with no differences between the oudeterous (neutral music) and control conditions. In a similar study, Szmedra and Bacharach showed that asynchronous music was associated with reduced heart rate, systolic blood pressure, exercise lactate, norepinephrine production and RPE during treadmill running at 70 per cent $\dot{V}O_2$ max.[44] The reduction in RPE for music versus the control condition was approximately 10 per cent, a figure replicated in a subsequent study by Nethery.[45] Szmedra and Bacharach suggested that music allowed participants to relax, reducing muscle tension, and thereby increasing blood flow and lactate clearance while decreasing lactate production in working muscle.[46]

Using a very novel approach, Crust and Clough tested the ergogenic effects of motivational music, drumbeat only, and no music on isometric muscular endurance (holding a weight at shoulder height for as long as possible).[47] The drumbeat used was the same as that used in the motivational track but without the remaining constituents of music (melody, harmony, lyrics). Participants endured for longer in the motivational music condition compared to the other two, which highlights the importance of all aspects of music structure in determining musical response. The researchers also administered Cattell's 16PF personality inventory to their participants and a small but statistically significant relationship between personality type and musical response was found. Specifically, the personality dimensions of liveliness and sensitivity were both positively associated with musical response.

It is evident that the beneficial effects of asynchronous music are diminished once exercise intensity approaches maximal levels. For example, a study of supramaximal performance using the Wingate test (an all-out cycle ergometer effort over 30 seconds) showed that music had no benefit on performance, supporting the load-dependent hypothesis.[48] This finding was corroborated in a subsequent study using a treadmill and outdoor running task at 90 per cent $\dot{V}O_2$ max, where the researchers demonstrated that while motivational asynchronous music did not influence perceptions of effort, it did shape interpretations of fatigue symptoms.[49]

Not all research has supported the benefits of motivational music. For example, Elliott *et al.* showed that, compared to a control condition, motivational music enhanced affect during submaximal cycle ergometry, but showed no benefits over oudeterous (neutral) music; and neither music condition impacted upon the distance cycled.[50] However, the authors acknowledged that the supposedly motivational music tracks had relatively low motivational quotients on the BMRI (M = 20.92 compared to BMRI maximum score of 33.33), which may well explain the lack of support for theoretical propositions.

There are a number of clear trends to emerge from the body of research that has investigated the use of asynchronous music. First, slow asynchronous music (under 100 bpm) is generally inappropriate for exercise or training contexts unless used to limit effort exertion or as an accompaniment for warm-up or warm-down activities. Second, fast-tempo asynchronous music (over 140 bpm) played during high-intensity activity results in high preference ratings and is likely to enhance in-task affect. Third, an increase in tempo from slow to fast can elicit an ergogenic effect in aerobic endurance activities. Fourth, asynchronous music played during submaximal exercise reduces RPE by approximately 10 per cent, although it remains unclear the degree to which this effect is mediated by the motivational qualities of music. Finally, asynchronous music has a negligible effect on psychological and psychophysical indices during very high-intensity activities, which substantiates the load-dependent hypothesis.[51]

Synchronous music

People have a strong tendency to respond to the rhythmical and temporal qualities of music. This tendency sometimes results in synchronisation between the tempo or speed of music and an athlete's movement patterns. A much-cited example concerns the celebrated Ethiopian distance runner, Haile Gebrselassie, who, in February 1998, smashed the indoor world record for 2,000 metres while synchronising his stride rate to the rhythmical pop song 'Scatman', which was played over loudspeakers.

Synchronous music is closely associated with sports such as figure skating, rhythmic gymnastics and synchronised swimming. Researchers have explained the synchronisation between musical tempo and human movement in terms of the natural predisposition of humans to respond to the rhythmical and temporal qualities of music.[52] Ostensibly, musical rhythm can replicate natural movement-based rhythms. Despite the intuitive appeal of this notion, relatively few studies have investigated the impact of synchronous music.[53]

Researchers have consistently shown that synchronous music yields significant ergogenic effects in non-highly-trained participants. Such effects have been demonstrated in bench-stepping, cycle ergometry, callisthenic-type exercises, 400-metre running and in a multi-activity circuit task.[54] Independent of such research, there has been a wave of commercial activity focused on the development and promotion of walking programmes that use synchronous music either to enhance fitness (e.g. www.run2r.com) or as part of a cardiac rehabilitation programme (e.g. www.positiveworkouts.com).

A landmark study by Anshel and Marisi compared synchronous and asynchronous music using a cycle ergometer endurance task.[55] Synchronous music elicited longer endurance than either asynchronous music or a no-music control (Cohen's $d = 0.6$ for synchronous versus control). However, the music was chosen somewhat arbitrarily from the 'popular rock' category without due consideration of the musical preferences and socio-cultural background of the participants, suggesting that the potential effect may have been even greater.[56]

Hayakawa et al. compared the effects of synchronous and asynchronous music on mood during step-aerobics classes of 30 minutes duration.[57] Aerobic dance music was used for the synchronous condition while, unusually, traditional Japanese folk music was used in the asynchronous condition. Participants reported more positive moods when classes were conducted with synchronous music compared to asynchronous music and a no-music control. However, it remains unclear whether the purported benefits of synchronous music were associated with the music itself or the physiological demands of the class (e.g. thermoregulation or oxygen uptake). Moreover, it is also not apparent to what extent the results can be attributed to the style of music used or its synchronicity with the bench-stepping exercise.

In addition to the benefits associated with asynchronous music detailed within the conceptual framework of Karageorghis et al., it has been proposed that the synchronous use of music results in a reduced metabolic cost of exercise by promoting greater neuromuscular or metabolic efficiency.[58] This proposition was the subject of a very recent study by Bacon et al.[59] Participants performing a submaximal cycle ergometry task were able to maintain a constant exercise intensity (60 per cent of their maximum heart rate) using 7.4 per cent less oxygen when listening to a selection of synchronous music compared to music that was asynchronous (slightly slower than the movement tempo). This study also showed that there were no differences in heart rate and RPE measures between synchronous and asynchronous cycling conditions.

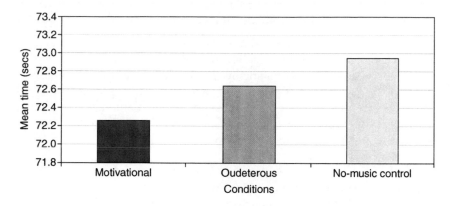

Figure 1.9 Mean 400-metre times for synchronous motivational music, synchronous oudeterous music and a no-music control.

Until recently, there had been scant research into the effects of synchronous music on anaerobic endurance performance. Simpson and Karageorghis sought to address this gap in the literature by examining the effects of synchronous music during 400-metre track running using an externally valid, race-like protocol.[60] Their findings showed that both motivational and oudeterous (neutral) music conditions elicited faster times than a no-music control condition (see Figure 1.9) and that the times associated with the two experimental conditions did not differ. This latter finding indicates that the motivational quality of music may not be of critical importance when it is used synchronously for an anaerobic endurance task; a notion that is entirely consistent with the load-dependent hypothesis.[61] Nonetheless, there is considerable scope for further investigation of the ergogenic effects of music in anaerobic and rhythmical sports (e.g. canoeing/kayaking, cycling and rowing).

In summary, the limited evidence that is available suggests that synchronous music can be applied to aerobic and anaerobic endurance performance among non-elite athletes to produce positive psychological, psychophysical and ergogenic effects. Very recent findings have indicated that synchronous music applied to submaximal repetitive activity can result in approximately a 7 per cent decrease in oxygen uptake.[62] However, there is insufficient research and specific theory underlying the use of synchronous music, especially among elite athletes, rendering this a particularly fruitful area for future research.

Pre-task music

A few studies have examined the use of music as a pre-task stimulant or sedative. Building upon an earlier study by Pearce, we tested the effects of fast tempo, energising music and slow tempo, relaxing music on grip strength.[63] Participants produced significantly higher hand-grip dynamometer scores after

Applied example 1.4: Khalida and the musical pacing method

Khalida is an 800-metre runner who has just completed her first season on the European grand prix circuit following a very successful international career as a junior. While attending her *Lycées d'Enseignement* (Technical School) in Algiers, her training was inconsistent in terms of quality although she was able to get by quite comfortably on natural ability. The demands of grand prix races and major championships necessitated a far more structured approach and she found the transition from the junior to the senior ranks very challenging.

While Khalida was growing up in Algeria, she noticed that on occasions when music was played over the public address system of her local stadium, it made her feel as though she was running on air. Pace judgement was always a problem for Khalida both in training and competition. Frequently, she would start too fast, but musical accompaniment helped to regulate her pace. Following a consultation with a performance specialist in London, it was suggested that Khalida should apply synchronous music to her interval training; music that would coincide in tempo with her cadence at different running intensities.

Thus, when Khalida was performing 400-metre intervals at 60-second pace, using video analysis she worked out that she took 200 strides on average. This coincided with musical selections that had a tempo of 100 bpm as Khalida took two strides to each beat. Appropriate musical selections included the bright dance track 'A Little Bit Of Ecstasy' by Jocelyn Enriquez and the energising 'Out Of Space' by The Prodigy. Khalida made similar calculations for other common interval distances that she completed in training – 600 metres, 800 metres and so on. She used an mp3 player attached to her upper arm to ensure that the audio equipment did not inhibit her smooth style and even used music editing software to adjust the tempo of some of her favourite tracks such as 'Beat It' by Michael Jackson.

Use of music is not permitted in competition so Khalida sang a song to herself that corresponded with her time goal and this helped her to pace each race evenly. Also, the music distracted her from the internal sensations of hard running while the inspirational lyrics also gave her a competitive edge: 'Beat it, no one wants to be defeated.'

listening to stimulative music compared to sedative music or a white noise control. Sedative music yielded lower scores than white noise. This study demonstrated the powerful effects of music on even the most basic of strength tasks and showed that simple motoric tasks such as grip strength provide an effective means by which to test the ergogenic properties of music.

Karageorghis and Lee tested the effects of pre-task motivational music and imagery on isometric muscular endurance by requiring participants to hold dumbbells weighing 15 per cent of their body mass in a crucifix position until they reached voluntary exhaustion.[64] The combination of music and imagery significantly enhanced muscular endurance performance compared to imagery only. This finding contrasted with an earlier study conducted by Gluch, a discrepancy that might be explained by the highly motoric nature of the endurance task, especially considering that imagery has typically proven effective in relation to cognitive tasks.[65]

Using an idiographic, single-subject, multiple-baselines, across-subjects design, Pates *et al.* examined the effects of pre-task music on flow states and netball shooting performance using three collegiate players.[66] Two participants reported an increase in their perception of flow and all three showed considerable improvements in shooting performance. Participants also reported that the intervention enabled them to control the emotions and cognitions that impacted upon their performance. The authors concluded that interventions including self-selected music and imagery could enhance athletic performance by triggering emotions and cognitions associated with flow. One potential limitation of this study is that the mental rehearsal and recall of flow states, which constituted part of the intervention, may have elicited the improvements in performance, rather than the music itself.

Along similar lines, Lanzillo *et al.* examined the impact of pre-event music on competition anxiety and self-confidence among intercollegiate athletes from a wide variety of sports.[67] One group of athletes listened to a three minute selection of their preferred music prior to competition while a control group had no music intervention. The experimental group reported higher state self-confidence than the control group although there were no differences found in competition anxiety.

In summary, research has shown that pre-task music can be used to: (1) manipulate activation states through its arousal control qualities; (2) facilitate

---

Applied example 1.5: Olympic double-trap shooting champion Richard Faulds

Peter Terry worked as team psychologist with British double-trap shooter Richard Faulds at the 2000 Sydney Olympic Games. As they approached the shooting range each day for training, and on the day of competition, Terry would play Whitney Houston's 'One Moment In Time' on the car stereo while Faulds would close his eyes and mentally rehearse how he would calmly and decisively seize his moment in time. On the final day of competition, that's exactly what Faulds did in an enthralling contest in which he won gold by the slimmest of margins, edging out the 1996 Olympic champion and pre-competition favourite, Russell Mark of Australia.

Applied example 1.6: strange choices also work, but for strange reasons....

In March 2006, prior to their final test against India in Mumbai, the England cricket team led by their charismatic captain Andrew 'Freddie' Flintoff, sang the Johnny Cash classic 'Ring Of Fire' before stepping out onto the pitch. When asked by an Indian reporter to explain the meaning behind the use of the song, Flintoff could barely keep a straight face: 'It's just a song that the boys like', he pronounced.

Flintoff knew the real connection, but it would have been distinctly impolite to explain that the song's title is an unintended reference to the after-effects of eating spicy food; indeed, most of the team had been dogged by tummy upsets during the test series. It was said that the atmosphere in the England dressing room during the lunch interval on the final day was akin to a rugby match. With 'Ring Of Fire' blaring out at full blast, the players whipped themselves up into a hand-clapping, feet-stomping frenzy.

Similarly, during the 2007 Rugby World Cup in France, England's rugby stars sang Kenny Rogers' song 'The Gambler' to boost morale before matches after prop Matt Stevens began strumming it on his guitar in their hotel lounge. The song became a regular part of the team's evening social gatherings and their pre-match build-up as they made unexpected progress through the tournament into the final. Martin Corry, the England captain, told *The Sunday Telegraph* that: 'Given where we are as a team, the lyrics seem to have struck a chord with us.' He highlighted the chorus: 'You've got to know when to hold 'em, know when to fold 'em, know when to walk away and know when to run.' Team veteran Mike Catt told the same newspaper that the song had become the squad's 'lucky charm'. The players clearly identified with the underlying message of the song: it's not the hand you have but the way that you play it.

---

task-relevant imagery/mental rehearsal; (3) promote flow; and (4) enhance perceptions of self-confidence. There is limited research in this area, which indicates considerable scope for further examination of the role of music in eliciting optimal pre-performance states and priming athletes in order to facilitate peak performance (see also Chapters 2 and 3).

Summary

We have presented two complementary conceptual approaches underlying the study and application of music in sport and exercise contexts.[68] We have also established that music can be applied to sports training and competition in many different ways, and have provided initial evidence for a quartic relationship between exercise heart rate and music tempo preference. One of the main demonstrated benefits of music is that it enhances psychological state, which has implications for optimising pre-competition mental state and increasing the enjoyment of training activities. Used synchronously, music can boost work output and makes repetitive tasks such as cycling or running more energy efficient. When we embarked upon our programme of research almost two decades ago, our intention was to promote more judicious use of music. The evidence that we have accumulated, coupled with the findings of many other researchers from around the world, should allow athletes and practitioners to tap the psychological, psychophysical and ergogenic effects of music with greater precision.

Notes

1 'Breaking the sound barrier', *Athletics Weekly*, 25 January 2007, 36.
2 C. I. Karageorghis, P. C. Terry and A. M. Lane, 'Development and initial validation of an instrument to assess the motivational qualities of music in exercise and sport: the Brunel Music Rating Inventory', *Journal of Sports Sciences*, 17, 1999, 713–724; C. I. Karageorghis, D. L. Priest, P. C. Terry, N. L. D. Chatzisarantis and A. M. Lane, 'Redesign and initial validation of an instrument to assess the motivational qualities of music in exercise: the Brunel Music Rating Inventory-2', *Journal of Sports Sciences*, 24, 2006, 899–909.
3 R. M. F. Wilson and N. J. Davey, 'Musical beat influences corticospinal drive to ankle flexor and extensor muscles in man', *International Journal of Psychophysiology*, 44, 2002, 177.
4 H. L. Bonny, 'Music, the language of immediacy', *Arts in Psychotherapy*, 14, 1987, 255–261.
5 J. Edworthy and H. Waring, 'The effects of music tempo and loudness level on treadmill exercise', *Ergonomics*, 49, 2006, 1597–1610; D. Elliott, S. Carr and D. Savage, 'Effects of motivational music on work output and affective responses during submaximal cycling of a standardized perceived intensity', *Journal of Sport Behavior*, 27, 2004, 134–147.
6 C. I. Karageorghis and P. C. Terry, 'The psychophysical effects of music in sport and exercise: a review', *Journal of Sport Behavior*, 20, 1997, 54–68.
7 L. F. Lucaccini and L. H. Kreit, 'Music', in W. P. Morgan (ed.), *Ergogenic Aids and Muscular Performance*, New York: Academic Press, 1972, pp. 240–245.
8 Karageorghis, Terry and Lane, 'Development and initial validation of an instrument to assess the motivational qualities of music in exercise and sport'.
9 Ibid.
10 Ibid.
11 B. L. Copeland and B. D. Franks, 'Effects of types and intensities of background music on treadmill endurance', *Journal of Sports Medicine and Physical Fitness*, 31, 1991, 100–103; C. I. Karageorghis, K. M. Drew and P. C. Terry, 'Effects of pretest stimulative and sedative music on grip strength', *Perceptual and Motor Skills*, 83, 1996, 1347–1352.
12 R. Hernandez-Peon, 'The efferent control of afferent signals entering the central nervous system', *Annals of New York Academy of Science*, 89, 1961, 866–882; W. J. Rejeski, 'Perceived exertion: an active or passive process?', *Journal of Sport Psychology*, 75, 1985, 371–378; G. Tenenbaum, 'A social-cognitive perspective of perceived exertion and exercise tolerance', in R. N. Singer, H. A. Hausenblas and C. Janelle (eds), *Handbook of Sport Psychology*, New York: Wiley, 2001, pp. 810–822.
13 Ibid.
14 Ibid.; R. Hewston, A. M. Lane, C. I. Karageorghis and A. M. Nevill, 'The effectiveness of music as a strategy to regulate mood [Abstract]', *Journal of Sports Sciences*, 22, 2005, 181–182; P. C. Terry, S. L. Dinsdale, C. I. Karageorghis and A. M. Lane, 'Use

and perceived effectiveness of pre-competition mood regulation strategies among athletes', in M. Katsikitis (ed.), *Proceedings of the Joint Conference of the Australian Psychological Society and the New Zealand Psychological Society*, Melbourne: Australian Psychological Society, 2006, pp. 420–424.

15 Karageorghis, Terry and Lane, 'Development and initial validation of an instrument to assess the motivational qualities of music in exercise and sport'.

16 L. Crust and P. J. Clough, 'The influence of rhythm and personality in the endurance response to motivational asynchronous music', *Journal of Sports Sciences*, 24, 2006, 187–195; C. I. Karageorghis, L. Jones and D. C. Low, 'Relationship between exercise heart rate and music tempo preference', *Research Quarterly for Exercise and Sport*, 26, 2006, 240–250; C. I. Karageorghis, L. Jones and D. P. Stuart, 'Psychological effects of music tempi during exercise', *International Journal of Sports Medicine*, 29, 2008, 613–619; S. D. Simpson and C. I. Karageorghis, 'The effects of synchronous music on 400-m sprint performance', *Journal of Sports Sciences*, 24, 2006, 1095–1102.

17 P. C. Terry and C. I. Karageorghis, 'Psychophysical effects of music in sport and exercise: an update on theory, research and application', in M. Katsikitis (ed.), *Proceedings of the Joint Conference of the Australian Psychological Society and the New Zealand Psychological Society*, Melbourne: Australian Psychological Society, 2006, pp. 415–419.

18 P. Brown, 'An enquiry into the origins and nature of tempo behaviour: II. experimental work', *Psychology of Music*, 9, 1979, 32–43; D. E. Berlyne, *Aesthetics and Psychobiology*, New York: Appleton Century Crofts, 1971; A. C. North and D. J. Hargreaves, 'The musical milieu: studies of listening in everyday life', *The Psychologist*, 10, 1997, 309–312.

19 Copeland and Franks, 'Effects of types and intensities of background music on treadmill endurance'.

20 Karageorghis, Jones and Low, 'Relationship between exercise heart rate and music tempo preference'; Karageorghis, Jones and Stuart, 'Psychological effects of music tempi during exercise'.

21 K. Gfeller, 'Musical components and styles preferred by young adults for aerobic fitness activities', *Journal of Music Therapy*, 25, 1988, 28–43.

22 D. E. Berlyne, *Aesthetics and Psychobiology*.

23 I. Iwanaga, 'Relationship between heart rate and preference for tempo of music', *Perceptual and Motor Skills*, 81, 1995a, 435–440; I. Iwanaga, 'Harmonic relationship between preferred tempi and heart rate', *Perceptual and Motor Skills*, 81, 1995b, 67–71.

24 A. LeBlanc, 'Differing results in research in preference for music tempo', *Perceptual and Motor Skills*, 81, 1995, 1253–1254.

25 A. LeBlanc, J. Coleman, J. McCrary, L. Sherrill and S. Malin, 'Tempo preference of different age listeners', *Journal of Research in Music Education*, 36, 1988, 156–168.

26 A. LeBlanc, 'An interactive theory of music preference', *Journal of Music Therapy*, 19, 1982, 28–45.

27 D. L. Priest, C. I. Karageorghis and N. C. C. Sharp, 'The characteristics and effects of motivational music in exercise settings: the possible influence of gender, age, frequency of attendance, and time of attendance', *Journal of Sports Medicine and Physical Fitness*, 44, 2004, 77–86.

28 Iwanaga, 'Relationship between heart rate and preference for tempo of music'; Iwanaga, 'Harmonic relationship between preferred tempi and heart rate'.

29 Karageorghis, Jones and Low, 'Relationship between exercise heart rate and music tempo preference'; Karageorghis, Jones and Stuart, 'Psychological effects of music tempi during exercise'.

30 Ibid.

31 Karageorghis, Jones and Stuart, 'Psychological effects of music tempi during exercise'.

32 Karageorghis, Jones and Low, 'Relationship between exercise heart rate and music tempo preference'.

33 Karageorghis, Jones and Stuart, 'Psychological effects of music tempi during exercise'.
34 Rejeski, 'Perceived exertion: an active or passive process?'.
35 Iwanaga, 'Relationship between heart rate and preference for tempo of music'; Iwanaga, 'Harmonic relationship between preferred tempi and heart rate'.
36 Berlyne, *Aesthetics and Psychobiology*; Karageorghis, Terry and Lane, 'Development and initial validation of an instrument to assess the motivational qualities of music in exercise and sport'.
37 Hernandez-Peon, 'The efferent control of afferent signals entering the central nervous system'; Rejeski, 'Perceived exertion: an active or passive process?'; Tenenbaum, 'A social-cognitive perspective of perceived exertion and exercise tolerance'.
38 A. Szabo, A. Small and M. Leigh, 'The effects of slow- and fast-rhythm classical music on progressive cycling to physical exhaustion', *Journal of Sports Medicine and Physical Fitness*, 39, 1999, 220–225.
39 G. Atkinson, D. Wilson and M. Eubank, 'Effects of music on work-rate distribution during a cycle time trial', *International Journal of Sports Medicine*, 62, 2004, 413–419.
40 Karageorghis, Terry and Lane, 'Development and initial validation of an instrument to assess the motivational qualities of music in exercise and sport'.
41 H. Lim, G. Atkinson, M. Eubank and C. I. Karageorghis, 'The effect of timing exposure on performance, perceived exertion and psychological affect during a 10-km cycling time trial', in T. Reilly and G. Atkinson (eds), *Sixth International Conference on Sport, Leisure and Ergonomics*, Liverpool: The Ergonomics Society, 2007, p. 46.
42 Ibid.
43 C. I. Karageorghis and P. C. Terry, 'Affective and psychophysical responses to asynchronous music during submaximal treadmill running', *Proceedings of the 1999 European College of Sport Science Congress*, Rome: European College of Sport Science, 1999, p. 218.
44 L. Szmedra and D. W. Bacharach, 'Effect of music on perceived exertion, plasma lactate, norepinephrine and cardiovascular hemodynamics during treadmill running', *International Journal of Sports Medicine*, 19, 1998, 32–37.
45 V. M. Nethery, 'Competition between internal and external sources of information during exercise: influence on RPE and the impact of the exercise load', *Journal of Sports Medicine and Physical Fitness*, 42, 2002, 172–178.
46 Szmedra and Bacharach, 'Effect of music on perceived exertion, plasma lactate, norepinephrine and cardiovascular hemodynamics during treadmill running'.
47 Crust and Clough, 'The influence of rhythm and personality in the endurance response to motivational asynchronous music'.
48 T. J. Pujol and M. E. Langenfeld, 'Influence of music on Wingate anaerobic test performance', *Perceptual and Motor Skills*, 88, 1999, 292–296.
49 G. Tenenbaum, R. Lidor, N. Lavyan, K. Morrow, S. Tonnel, A. Gershgoren, J. Meis and M. Johnson, 'The effect of music type on running perseverance and coping with effort sensations', *Psychology of Sport and Exercise*, 5, 2004, 89–109.
50 Elliott, Carr and Savage, 'Effects of motivational music on work output and affective responses during submaximal cycling of a standardized perceived intensity'.
51 Rejeski, 'Perceived exertion: an active or passive process?'.
52 Brown, 'An enquiry into the origins and nature of tempo behaviour'; Karageorghis and Terry, 'The psychophysical effects of music in sport and exercise; Karageorghis, Terry and Lane, 'Development and initial validation of an instrument to assess the motivational qualities of music in exercise and sport'.
53 M. H. Anshel and D. Q. Marisi, 'Effects of music and rhythm on physical performance', *Research Quarterly*, 49, 1978, 109–113; C. Bacon, T. Myers and C. I. Karageorghis, 'Effect of movement–music synchrony and tempo on exercise oxygen consumption', under review; Y. Hayakawa, H. Miki, K. Takada and K. Tanaka, 'Effects of music on mood during bench stepping exercise', *Perceptual and Motor Skills*, 90, 1990, 307–314.

54 A. K. Uppal and U. Datta, 'Cardiorespiratory response of junior high school girls to exercise performed with and without music', *Journal of Physical Education and Sport Science*, 2, 1990, 52–56; W. Michel and H. U. Wanner, 'Einfuss der musik auf die sportliche leistung [Effect of music on sports performance]', *Schweizerische Zeitschrift für Sportmedizin*, 23, 1975, 141–159.

55 Ibid.

56 Ibid.

57 Hayakawa, Miki, Takada and Tanaka, 'Effects of music on mood during bench stepping exercise'.

58 F. L. Smoll and R. W. Schultz, 'Relationships among measures of preferred tempo and motor rhythm', *Perceptual and Motor Skills*, 46, 1978, 883–894.

59 Bacon, Myers and Karageorghis, 'Effect of movement–music synchrony and tempo on exercise oxygen consumption'.

60 Simpson and Karageorghis, 'The effects of synchronous music on 400-m sprint performance'.

61 Rejeski, 'Perceived exertion: an active or passive process?'.

62 Bacon, Myers and Karageorghis, 'Effect of movement–music synchrony and tempo on exercise oxygen consumption'.

63 K. A. Pearce, 'Effects of different types of music on physical strength', *Perceptual and Motor Skills*, 53, 1981, 351–352.

64 C. I. Karageorghis and J. Lee, 'Effects of asynchronous music and imagery on an isometric endurance task', *Proceedings of the World Congress of Sport Psychology*, Vol. 4, Skiathos, Greece: International Society of Sport Psychology, 2001, pp. 37–39.

65 P. D. Gluch, 'The use of music in preparing for sport performance', *Contemporary Thought*, 2, 1993, 33–53; A. White and L. Hardy, 'Use of different imagery perspectives on the learning and performance of different motor skills', *British Journal of Psychology*, 86, 1995, 191–216.

66 J. Pates, C. I. Karageorghis, R. Fryer and I. Maynard, 'Effects of asynchronous music on flow states and shooting performance among netball players', *Psychology of Sport and Exercise*, 4, 2003, 413–427.

67 J. J. Lanzillo, K. L. Burke, A. B. Joyner and C. J. Hardy, 'The effects of music on the intensity and direction of pre-competitive cognitive and somatic state anxiety and state self-confidence in collegiate athletes', *International Sports Journal*, 5, 2001, 101–110.

68 Karageorghis, Terry and Lane, 'Development and initial validation of an instrument to assess the motivational qualities of music in exercise and sport'; Terry and Karageorghis, 'Psychophysical effects of music in sport and exercise: an update on theory, research and application'.

2 Video, priming and music

Effects on emotions and motivation

Georgios Loizou and Costas I. Karageorghis

Ἄνδρα μοι ἔννεπε, Μοῦσα, πολύτροπον, ὃς μάλα πολλά πλάγχθη, ἐπεὶ Τροίης ἱερὸν πτολίεθρον ἔπερσε·

Tell me, O Muse, of the man of many devices, who wandered full many ways after he had sacked the sacred citadel of Troy.

Homer[1]

In the oral tradition of ancient Greece, poems were composed by individuals known as αηδός (aedos) or ραψωδός (rhapsodos), meaning singer. At the beginning of the *Odyssey*, Homer refers to the Muse, one of the nine ancient Greek deities of the arts, who tells him the epic story of Odysseus in the form of a song. The word 'music' originates from the Greek μουσική (mousike), which is itself derived from the ancient Greek word μούσα (musa), meaning *art of the Muses*. Since ancient times, Muses have been a source of inspiration for artists in their creative endeavours. Video on the other hand originates from the Latin word *video* or *videre* which means *to see* and is a relatively new phenomenon by comparison.

In the western world, both music and video have become almost ubiquitous in everyday life. During the last two decades, the applications of music and video have been developed extensively within the leisure and recreation industries. They are played in gymnasiums and athletic stadiums before, during and after competitions and training.

A strong association has been formed between music, video and athletic endeavour during the twentieth century. Music and video have been used extensively during the opening and closing ceremonies of Olympic Games. A recent example is the Athens 2004 Olympic Games, in which the opening and closing ceremonies featured a dazzling combination of video effects with live music. Music is also incorporated in individual Olympic events such as gymnastics and synchronised swimming. In addition, the national anthem of the winning athlete is played at each medal ceremony, often reducing seasoned competitors to tears.

In ancient Greece, music was thought to have significant healing powers.

Indeed, in Greek mythology, Apollo was the god of both music and medicine. Greeks still use the ancient Greek maxim 'νούς υγιής εν σώματι υγιεί', meaning 'a healthy mind in a healthy body'. Further, music was thought to have distractive properties. On his way to Ithaca, Odysseus had to avoid the songs of the Sirens, creatures that were half-woman, half-bird, whose song attracted sailors' attention to the degree that their ships were dashed against the rocks. Odysseus ordered his men to place wax in their ears so they could not hear the song, and he himself was tied to the mast of his ship so as not to succumb to the musical spell of the Sirens.

Music was also used during the era of slavery as a tool that facilitated synchronisation of the slaves' collective efforts. As Farnsworth noted, 'their morale has been lifted and their work movements have been made smoother and more efficient by the directing force of group singing'.[2] Since the development of early civilisation, humans have combined sound and pictures in ways that have influenced their mental state. The development of technology has allowed music and pictures to evolve into ever more artistically pleasing arrangements. In this chapter we will review some of the key areas in psychology (e.g. the nature of emotion, types of motivation, etc.) that underlie our work into video, priming and music, before presenting some recent findings that illustrate the effects of these stimuli on emotions and motivation.

Emotion

Psychologists rely on self-report measures to help them in describing how people feel. Years of behavioural, cognitive and psychophysiological research have failed to solve the problem of ambiguity; clear and consistent measures to distinguish between the categories of experienced emotions have yet to be provided.[3] In self-report questionnaires, responses are treated as insights into an individual's inner psyche that can be further investigated. Responses vary on an intra-individual basis both in terms of the length and context of emotion. Some individuals will reply to a question with a single word, whereas others will describe an entire constellation of feelings and emotional information. Diener noted that research into the structure of affect is fundamental to the scientific analysis of emotions given that the structure of affect reveals a great deal about the nature of emotion.[4] Affect can be defined as 'a general term which describes mental processes that involve feeling, such as emotional experience or mood'.[5]

Sport can be described as an emotional experience since emotion is widely accepted as an integral part of the competitive experience.[6] One of the most important considerations to coaches, athletes and sport psychologists is the elicitation of an athlete's optimal state of mind before and during competition, which might well have an impact on the outcome of a sporting contest.[7]

Winkielman and Berridge stated that many psychologists share the traditional view that conscious awareness is a necessary ingredient of affect and emotion.[8] However, they also argued that affective states and cognitive processes might be occurring below awareness (unconsciously) or without attention (implicitly). They claimed that emotion is intrinsically unconscious yet it can be brought into full awareness through relevant motivational and attentional states.[9] Moreover, an emotional process may remain entirely unconscious under some conditions, even when the person is *attentive* and sufficiently motivated to describe his or her feelings correctly.[10] They also contended that an emotional process may drive one's behaviour as well as one's physiological reactions 'even while remaining inaccessible to conscious awareness'.[11] Winkielman and Berridge concluded that subliminally presented facial expressions could influence emotional behaviour without eliciting conscious feelings.[12]

Impact of emotions on sports performance

Research has shown that there is a strong connection between emotions and performance levels in sport.[13] A number of authors have outlined the mechanisms by which emotions might influence performance, indicating that an individual's emotional state could impact upon cognitive and physical functioning and therefore motivation.[14] Physical functioning is affected by changes in arousal that are accompanied by emotional states, while patterns of cognitive functioning are influenced by changes in arousal and existing thoughts.[15]

Optimal emotions generate sufficient effort towards the accomplishment of a task, whereas dysfunctional emotions are those which generate either too much or very little effort, causing a debilitative effect on performance. Further, optimal emotions ensure the appropriate use of resources in the completion of a sport-related task. Conversely, dysfunctional emotions lead to the inappropriate use of resources which invariably leads to failure. It should be noted however, that optimal emotions will vary from individual to individual for any given task or situation.[16]

Emotions enhance motivation towards a particular goal.[17] Indeed, there is a strong link between emotions and performance.[18] The extent to which feelings are activated depends on the importance of the goal together with its perceived difficulty.[19] According to Brehm, the intensity of the emotional response will be proportional to the perceived difficulty of the goal, provided the individual is willing to expand the effort needed to achieve it.[20] Given that an individual's emotional state can affect sports performance, and that there are several ways by which emotion might influence performance, the need for interventions that suit the needs of individual athletes is patent. Ostensibly, the relationship between emotional state and sporting performance is idiosyncratic in nature.

Human motivation

Motivation is a powerful inner force that can direct, spark and maintain human behaviour.[21] Research into motivation has involved detailed study of the energisation, direction and regulation of behaviour.[22] Deci and Ryan asserted that behaviour is influenced by three primary motivational factors: intrinsic motivation, extrinsic motivation and amotivation.[23] Intrinsic motivation is characterised by participation in an activity for the pleasure and satisfaction that one derives from it, whereas participation for the purpose of gaining external rewards characterises extrinsically motivated behaviour. A lack of perceived competence coupled with low expectations is associated with the absence of either intrinsic or extrinsic motivation. This is known as the state of amotivation.

Intrinsic motivation

Motivation involves the identification of personal and social factors that involve some form of valued reward or encouragement. Therefore, the desire to success-fully execute skill challenges in sport settings determines intrinsic motives.[24] The degree to which intrinsic motivation will be experienced involves the extent to which the needs for self-determination, competence and relatedness are satis-fied.[25] Vallerand et al. suggested that intrinsic motivation should be separated into three categories: intrinsic motivation to know, intrinsic motivation towards accomplishments and intrinsic motivation to experience stimulation.[26]

Intrinsic motivation to know entails a situation in which an individual is introduced to something new and consequently a learning process takes place. It relates to an inner desire to seek new knowledge or information. Intrinsic motivation towards accomplishment involves participation in an activity for the pleasure and satisfaction involved in completing a task or reaching a goal. Finally, the intrinsic motivation to experience stimulation involves engagement in an activity for the fun and excitement associated with it.

Extrinsic motivation

Extrinsic motivation includes external regulation, introjected regulation, iden-tified regulation and integrated regulation.[27] External regulation refers to behav-iours that are controlled by external factors such as payments, rewards and threats. Introjected regulation refers to actions performed by individuals when they feel they should accept and adopt the situation they find themselves in. They are influenced by external factors such as guilt and the rules controlling the activity. Identified regulation refers to actions performed freely, but as a means to an end. Such actions are adopted for reasons of pleasure or satisfaction and are engaged in as a result of beneficial consequences (e.g. weight loss). Finally, integrated regulation, although primarily self-determined, is considered extrinsic, as it is performed to reach personal goals.[28]

Amotivation

Amotivation is neither intrinsically nor extrinsically associated.[29] It refers to the individual's failure to act towards an accomplishment since there are neither intrinsic nor extrinsic motives present. According to Deci and Ryan, motives lie on a self-determination continuum with intrinsic motives being the most self-determined and amotivation the least self-determined (see Figure 2.1).[30]

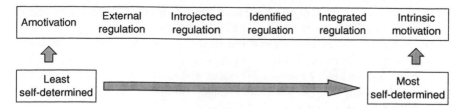

Figure 2.1 The self-determination continuum.

For sport psychologists, video can act as a means by which to facilitate modelling. It allows them to build personal relationships with their athletes through a highly positive form of interaction.[31] Through video and music, information can be presented to the athletes in a pleasant and interactive manner. Bandura asserted that modelling was 'one of the most powerful means of transmitting values, attitudes and patterns of thought and behaviour'.[32] Therefore, video coupled with music and priming could potentially act as a potent stimulant to engender greater levels of motivation.

Emotions and motivation

Emotions describe a meshing of evaluative and expressive languages, physiological events and behaviours. It has been suggested that this complexity inherent in emotions is coordinated by simpler underlying motivational parameters, given that emotions result when actions are either inhibited or delayed.[33] Affective states are determined by two opposing motivational systems in the brain, namely appetitive and aversive. The appetitive system (pleasant/consumatory) is primarily expressed through the behaviour or approach, while the aversive system (unpleasant/protective) is primarily expressed by behavioural escape and avoidance.[34] Arousal reflects variations in the activation of either or both systems rather than being a separate substrate.[35]

Priming and motivation

Human action is motivated by goals. It is widely accepted that both striving towards goals and goal setting are characterised by conscious processes. However, this view has led researchers to ignore the important issue of how these goals are actually emerging. Although individuals might be conscious of their goals, the resultant thoughts and actions are underpinned by brain processes that are not open to examination (introspection). Therefore, the individual is often unconscious of the processes underlying their motivated behaviours and thoughts.[36] This perspective provides support to the contention that motives and goals can be activated automatically by unconscious processes without the involvement of conscious guidance or choice.[37]

Researchers investigating social cognition have demonstrated that individuals are unaware of the processes underlying their perceptions, goal pursuits and behaviours.[38] These processes may play a vital role in behaviour and cognitions. According to Bargh, motives and goals can be activated automatically, without the involvement of conscious guidance or choice.[39] Priming studies are concerned with temporary activation states and how environmental information together with states of internal readiness interact to produce perceptions and evaluations as motivations and behaviour.[40] Priming can therefore act as a process by which to unconsciously alter an individual's psychological state prior to and during the execution of a task.

Motivational priming

It is widely agreed that emotions play a significant role in influencing behaviours and action.[41] The universal spread of emotions across a range of behaviours is motivationally mediated, as each emotion engages neural pathways and structures in either the appetitive or aversive motivation systems.[42] Responses to unconditioned stimuli are regulated according to: (a) the classification of the reflex; and (b) the affective valence of the individual's ongoing emotional state. Therefore, defensive reflexes increase in amplitude when an individual is negatively motivated and reduce in amplitude when the motivational state is positive.[43]

The circumplex model of affect

Early work analysing self-reported affective states concluded that there were between six and 12 independent monopolar factors of affect including anxiety, sadness and tension.[44] Self-report affective measurement used in clinical, personality and social psychology are based on the assumption that affective factors are separate dimensions. However, there is a contrasting concept which posits that affective states are related to one another in a highly systematic fashion and are not independent. This view was originally proposed by Schlosberg[45] who asserted that emotions could be arranged in a circular fashion, represented on two bipolar dimensions. This theory was later supported by Russell who developed the circumplex model of affect.[46]

The circumplex model of affect forms the basis for the circumplex theory of emotion. It illustrates how most emotional experiences can be arranged in a circular fashion around the perimeter of two independent bipolar dimensions that intersect each other, namely pleasant/unpleasant and aroused/sleepy. The present authors provided support for the use of the circumplex model of affect and its dimensions in sport, both in English and Greek cultures.[47]

North and Hargreaves used a modified version of the circumplex model to investigate the relationship between liking and the arousal potential of musical stimuli. They found that the emotions expressed through musical pieces may be predicted using liking and arousal ratings.[48] Despite evidence that music-based strategies could be used to alter mood regulation,[49] music has received limited attention as a pre-performance strategy in sport.[50] Music, video and priming techniques could potentially have a significant influence on an athlete's pre-competitive emotional and motivational states. Therefore, the need to investigate the circumplex model in different domains such as sport and exercise and with different stimuli such as music, video and priming, may be a valuable pursuit for researchers. This was one of the principal foci of the research presented later in this chapter.

Music and sport

Psychomusicological research has broadened during the last two decades to include research in a variety of social contexts.[51] One such social context that has attracted a considerable amount of interest is sport and exercise. There is burgeoning amount of evidence to suggest that music can have significant psychophysical effects and act as an ergogenic aid if certain conditions are satisfied.[52] Indeed, Karageorghis and Terry contended that, 'music is an untapped source of both motivation and inspiration for sport and exercise participants'.[53] The same authors suggested that motor performance could be facilitated by music in a number of ways.[54] For example, music has the capacity to act as a legal stimulant or sedative and can enhance both pre-task and in-task affect (i.e. feelings of pleasure/displeasure). Further, music stimulates the right hemisphere of the brain, which facilitates cognitive tasks such as imagery and mental rehearsal. According to Karageorghis *et al.* factors that contribute to the motivational qualities of music include *rhythm response*, *musicality*, *cultural impact*, and *association*.[55] For an extensive review and synthesis of the theory and research underlying the use of music in sport see Chapter 1 in this volume.

Video and sport

Video has been used in psychosocial interventions as a feedback tool for behaviour modification strategies as well as to teach communication skills and behaviours. Peak-performance videos, visualisation tapes and video clips accompanied by music can be created for mental and motivational training purposes.[56] Williams and Grant indicated that video is one of the most appropriate perceptual and motor-training tools.[57] Further, it can be used to train decision-making skills and sport-specific anticipatory skills.[58]

Leavitt *et al.* investigated the effects of videotaped highlights on state self-confidence in volleyball players.[59] This research was prompted by the notion that a lack of confidence is often related to poor performance.[60] The results revealed a significant increase in state self-confidence and self-efficacy levels when video highlights were used.[61] Video highlights included images of the players during training and previous matches coupled with motivational music playing in the background alongside verbal persuasion through lyrics such as 'I live to be the very best, I want it all, no time for less'.[62]

Mental training videos can heighten motivation and can be used for teaching behaviours as well as mental rehearsal.[63] Halliwell also noted that video coupled with visualisation techniques led to 'remarkable performance changes' and provided examples of how highlight videos can enhance confidence and motivation.[64] Further, Ives et al. reported that video can be used to enhance the communication and relationships between athletes and coaches, rather than eliminating the human element in sport psychology as has been suggested.

Researchers have explored the ergogenic and psychophysical effects of music,[65] and the use of video as a training and motivational tool.[66] Priming has been framed as a process by which an individual's motives and goals can be activated.[67] Yet no study to date has entailed an examination of the effects of all three stimuli when used in combination. This is the main focus of the research presented in the remainder of this chapter.

Effects of video, priming and music on emotions and motivation

In a recent research project[68] the present authors examined the interactive effects of video, priming and music on emotions and motivation with reference to the circumplex model of affect[69] and self-determination theory.[70]

A convenience sample of 210 volunteers (128 English and 82 Greek) who were heterogeneous in terms of their level of sports participation and their degree of involvement were recruited. Participants were asked to state how they felt in response to listening to/watching a particular piece of music/video using an 11-point Likert-type scale anchored by 0 (not at all) and 10 (very much so). Ten words describing emotional states, two from each quadrant of the circumplex model (quadrant 1: excited, delighted; quadrant 2: contented, relaxed; quadrant 3: depressed, bored; quadrant 4: distressed, frustrated) and two representing the main axes of the circumplex model (arousal, pleasure) were presented to them. Using the same scale, participants rated how much they liked the presented condition. At the end of the sixth condition, participants were asked to place the different conditions in their preferred order with the most liked first and the least liked last.

The Activity-Feeling State scales questionnaire (AFS) was used to assess the satisfaction of the needs underlying intrinsic motivation.[71] The AFS is a psychological state measure of the three psychological needs underlying intrinsic motivation (self-determination: the need to experience choice; competence: the need to be effective in one's environmental transactions; and relatedness: the need to establish close emotional bonds and attachments with other persons) and tension. Tension is considered to be an emotional marker of psychological states that are antagonistic to intrinsic motivation.[72] Participants were asked to state how they felt in response to listening to/watching the particular piece of music/video using a five-point Likert-type scale anchored by 1 (strongly disagree) and 5 (strongly agree).

The experimental conditions comprised of video footage of 148 seconds duration from past Olympic Games coupled with either music and/or primes. Video footage that could be directly related to either English or Greek culture was excluded. Further, Vangelis's 'Chariots Of Fire' was chosen to accompany the video clips. This particular piece of music was chosen as it is well known in both cultures as it was written by a Greek composer with reference to the British Olympic team. Primes consisted of the Olympic motto, 'Stronger, Higher, Faster', which is widely known by both the English and the Greek. Conditions included a control condition and five different experimental conditions that comprised of (1) video only, (2) music only, (3) video and music, (4) video with motivational priming and (5) video with motivational priming and music.

Preparing a video–music–primes intervention

Video footage
Select video footage that is directly related to the purpose of the intervention.
Select footage that is associated with the athletes. (e.g. if working with individual athletes, video footage from individual sports would be preferable. If working with a team, video footage of the specific sport of the team or relevant footage from different sport teams could be used according to the purposes of the intervention).

Music selection
Music can be selected either by the athletes or the sport practitioner with reference to the motivational qualities of music, namely: *rhythm response, musicality, cultural impact* and *association*.
Valid and reliable instruments such as the Brunel Music Rating Inventory-2 (BMRI-2) can be used for the selection of appropriate motivational music.[*]

Primes selection
Primes should be short in length and duration (40 ms) and directly related to the purpose of the intervention.
How often each prime is used should be considered with care, since too much information could lead to slower information processing and debilitate performance.[**]

---

[*] C. I. Karageorghis, D. L. Priest, P. C. Terry, N. L. D. Chatzisarantis and A. M. Lane, 'Redesign and initial validation of an instrument to assess the motivational qualities of music and exercise: the Brunel Music Rating Inventory-2', *Journal of Sports Sciences*, 24, 2006, 899–909.
[**] G. Tzetzis, E. Kioumourtzoglou and G. Mavromatis, 'Goal setting and feedback for the development of instructional strategies', *Perceptual and Motor Skills*, 84, 1997, 1411–1427.

Participants were instructed to sit comfortably, and carefully attend to each condition. They were administered two questionnaires immediately after each presented condition. Sound intensity was adjusted to 75 dBA at ear level. The conditions were presented in counterbalanced order to minimise any effects caused by the order of presentation. Primes were presented on the screen randomly at different time intervals and lasted for 40 ms. Figure 2.2 illustrates what the participants were actually viewing and how primes were presented to them through the video footage. In between conditions, a mental arithmetic task was used as a filler so that the impact of one condition did not carry over into the next.

Music exerted a positive influence on affective states and the needs underlying intrinsic motivation. The results also lent support to the proposition that priming facilitates the effects of psychological interventions. When combined with music, the effects of priming were considerably greater. Specifically, the

Figure 2.2 Video footage with primes above, and what the participants consciously viewed on the screen below.

music, video and priming condition exerted a positive impact on liking and also the arousal and pleasure dimensions of the circumplex model of affect (see Figures 2.3 and 2.4). This finding supports the efficacy of the circumplex model of affect in predicting the hedonic response to multiple stimuli.[73] In addition, the results supported the proposition that the emotional responses to a musical piece can be predicted by the degree of preference which the listener holds.[74]

The combination of video, priming and music led to increased perceptions of competence and self-determination together with a corresponding decrease in tension, resulting in an overall increase in intrinsic motivation (see Figure 2.5).

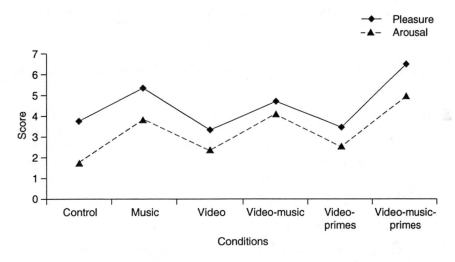

Figure 2.3 Pleasure and arousal changes across control and experimental conditions.

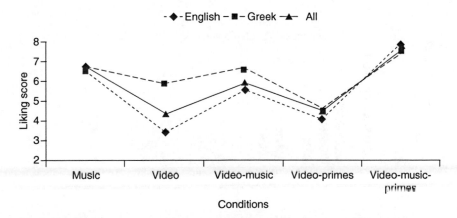

Figure 2.4 Changes of liking scores across experimental conditions.

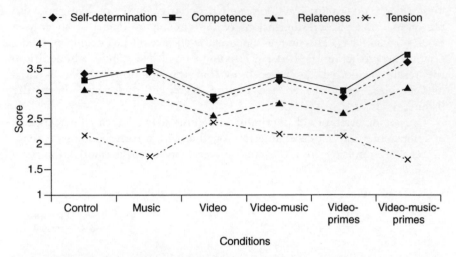

Figure 2.5 Changes in the needs underlying intrinsic motivation and tension across control and experimental conditions.

In terms of cultural differences, both the English and Greek participants ranked the video-music-primes condition as their most preferred (see Figure 2.6). The English preferred the music condition to the video-music condition, as an alternative to video-music-primes condition. Conversely, the Greeks preferred the video-music condition to the music condition (see Figures 2.7 and 2.8).

Effects of video, priming and music on performance

The next logical stage was to investigate the effects of video, priming and music on supramaximal exercise performance. Participants were asked to perform at maximal intensity on a cycle ergometer for 30 seconds across a series of four

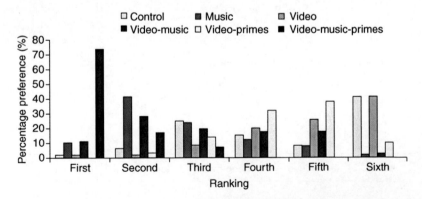

Figure 2.6 Preference ranking of the different experimental conditions for the whole sample.

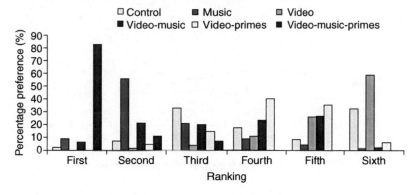

Figure 2.7 Preference ranking of the different experimental conditions in the English sample.

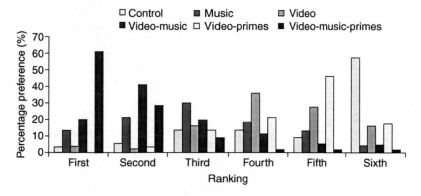

Figure 2.8 Preference ranking of the different experimental conditions in the Greek sample.

conditions that were separated by at least two days. The experimental conditions comprised of a music-only condition, a video with music condition, a video with music and primes condition and a control condition. The Wingate anaerobic test was used in the testing protocol. The Wingate test has been used to assess muscle power, muscle endurance and fatigue responses. It is regarded as a reproducible, standardised task for the examination of physiological and cognitive responses to supramaximal exercise.[75]

Results indicated significant improvements in anaerobic performance following exposure to the video-music-primes condition. Specifically, the peak power output and the mean power output produced during the video-music-primes condition were significantly higher when compared with the remaining conditions (see Figures 2.9 and 2.10). The results indicate that priming techniques can be used to subconsciously alter an individual's state prior to a task[76] and that this alteration may have a subsequent positive impact on performance.

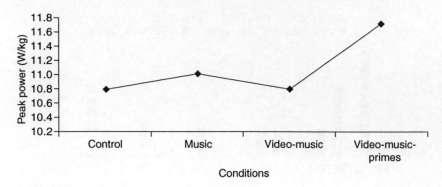

Figure 2.9 Changes in peak power (W/kg) across control and experimental conditions.

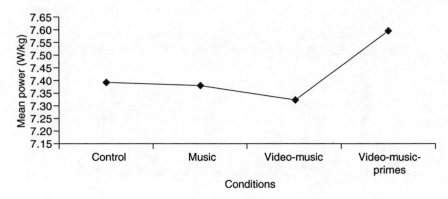

Figure 2.10   Changes in mean power (W/kg) across control and experimental conditions.

Effects of video, priming and music on heart rate variability

Changes in heart rate variability (HRV) have been related to coronary artery disease and increased mortality.[77] Further, Berntson *et al.* proposed that measures of HRV can serve as valuable tools in the assessment of relationships between physiological and psychological processes.[78] HRV parameters have been linked to sympathetic and parasympathetic nervous system activities. It has been suggested that indices relating to sympathetic activity increase during physical and psychological stress, while indices relating to parasympathetic activity decrease.[79]

Boutcher *et al.* investigated the HRV of trained and untrained men at rest and during mental challenge tasks (arithmetic tasks and the Stroop test).[80] They suggested that during mental challenges, a decrease in parasympathetic activity should be expected. Increases in sympathetic activity are thought to be related to an increase in low-frequency (LF) response and a corresponding decrease in high-frequency (HF) response,[81] while increases in parasympathetic activity are associated with reduced LF and increased HF response.[82] Rainville *et al.* indicated that distinct patterns of peripheral physiological activity are associated with emotions.[83] Indeed, McCraty *et al.* found that increases in heart rate during anger reflect sympathetic activation with an associated rise in LF response, whereas positive emotions are associated with similar increases in HF response.[84]

Etzel *et al.* investigated cardiovascular and respiratory responses during a musical induction.[85] Their results were contradictory, thus highlighting the difficulty of detecting the psychophysiological correlates of mood induction. They suggested that part of this difficulty might have been due to the tempo-related contributions of music when used as an inducer.[86] Further, Sokhadze investigated the effects of music and white noise on the recovery of physiological measures after a stressful visual stimulation. He found that both pleasant and sad music elicited a significantly lower level of HF response when compared with visual stimulation and white noise.[87]

In two subsequent studies investigating the effect of video, priming and music on HRV, the present authors observed an increase in the LF component and a corresponding decrease in the HF component (see Figures 2.11 and 2.12).[88] These results, in combination with the affective changes described earlier in this chapter, lend support to the contention that changes in HRV might reflect the physiological and psychological readiness of an individual to execute a particular task or activity.

Friedman suggested that during physical and psychological stress, sympathetic nervous activity (LF) increases and parasympathetic activity (HF) decreases.[89] As a result, during mental challenges, the HF component is expected to decrease with a corresponding increase in LF occurring.[90] Conversely, it has been suggested that positive emotions are associated with increases in HF and negative emotions with increases in LF and heart rate.[91] Further investigation of these phenomena and their causes is warranted in order to resolve such inconsistencies.[92]

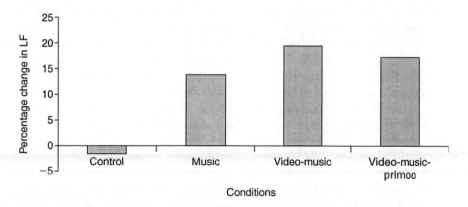

Figure 2.11 Percentage changes in LF across control and experimental conditions.

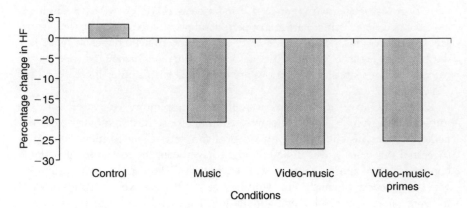

Figure 2.12 Percentage changes in HF across control and experimental conditions.

The results of the authors' study indicated an increase in LF response and a decrease in HF response during the experimental conditions. These findings supported those of Sokhadze who found that either sad or pleasant music decreases HF response.[93] However, the results do not concur with those of Friedman and McCraty *et al.*, given that a significant increase in positive emotions resulted during the video-music and video-music-primes conditions. It is possible that the increase in LF response and decrease in HF response during the experimental conditions might have been indicative of the participants' psychological and physiological readiness to initiate the physical task.

Conclusions and recommendations

The findings presented illustrate the potential benefits that might be derived through the use of video and music in psychological interventions. It is apparent that music can be a source of motivation and inspiration in sporting settings.[94] Video, on the other hand, serves as a behaviour modification and motivation tool.[95] Combining the two with priming techniques is particularly effectual as both a motivational and emotional intervention.

The findings presented in this chapter provide support for the proposition that music has positive effects on emotional states and the needs underlying intrinsic motivation. Further, support was found for the application of priming techniques in sport psychology interventions; these techniques had a considerably higher impact when coupled with music. Future work might include the application of priming techniques in both individual and team sports using a variety of musical pieces and videos. Also, the effects of priming, video and music on the physiological indices of performance (e.g. heart rate, HRV) should be more extensively examined.

Researchers working in this area of psychophysiology should seek to examine the effects of video, priming and music techniques on different indices of cardiovascular functioning such as respiratory sinus arrhythmia, which is considered to be a marker of vagal (parasympathetic) control of the heart.[96] They might also employ electroencephalography (EEG) and functional magnetic resonance imaging (fMRI) techniques in order to clarify the exact mechanisms underlying the psychophysiological effects of video, priming and music. Future studies might entail the investigation of video, priming and music effects on a range of endurance activities. The effects of such techniques on psychological states and physiological parameters post-exercise, during the recovery phase and in sport injury rehabilitation programmes might also be investigated. Further, the application of priming techniques in the cardiovascular training programmes that take place in health and exercise centres would be a valuable extension to the research presented in this chapter.

The present findings are particularly relevant for public health practitioners given the extensive use of music and video in everyday life. Musical excerpts and video clips coupled with primes could be used in public places to promote physical activity and exercise. Such techniques could also be used in rehabilitation programmes to enhance participants' motivation and reduce boredom.

The application and effects of video, priming and music techniques in sport and exercise settings warrant further investigation. Motivational videos coupled with primes and music could be used during pre-performance routines and team meetings. Such techniques boost intrinsic motivation and self-confidence and decrease pre-performance anxiety and tension. However, the delivery of music, video and primes should be undertaken with consideration to the cultural background of athletes and their individual preferences. The results presented herein are by no means conclusive, but provide a useful springboard for further psychophysiological research. The main contributions of this body of work have been empirical support for the use of priming, video and music delivery techniques on performance and the identification of links between video, priming, music and psychophysiological (HRV) changes during a sport-related task.

Notes

1 Homer, *Odyssey*, trans. A.T. Murray, Cambridge, MA: Harvard University Press, 1919. Online, available at www.odyssey.com.mx/Text_and_Commentaries/Book_i/Book_i.html (accessed 20 December 2007).
2 P. R. Farnsworth, *The Social Psychology of Music*, Iowa: Iowa State University Press, 1969, p. 217.
3 L. F. Barrett, 'Feelings or words? Understanding the content in self-report ratings of experienced emotion', *Journal of Personality and Social Psychology*, 87, 2004, 266–281.
4 E. Diener, 'Introduction to the special section on the structure of emotion', *Journal of Personality and Social Psychology*, 76, 1999, 803–804.
5 W. G. Parrot, 'Affect', in A. S. R. Manstead and M. Hewstone (eds), *The Blackwell Encyclopaedia of Social Psychology*, Oxford: Blackwell Publishers, 1996, pp. 15–16.
6 S. Boutcher, 'Emotion and aerobic exercise', in R. N. Singer, M. Murphey and L. K. Tennant (eds), *Handbook of Research on Sport Psychology*, New York: Macmillan, 1993, pp. 799–814; M. V. Jones, 'Controlling emotions in sport', *The Sport Psychologist*, 17, 2003, 471–486.
7 R. J. Butler, *Sport Psychology in Action*, Oxford: Butterworth-Heinemann, 1996; Y. L. Hanin, *Emotions in Sport*, Champaign, IL: Human Kinetics, 2000; L. Hardy, G. Jones

and D. Gould, *Understanding Psychological Preparation for Sport: Theory and Practice of Elite Performers*, Chichester: Wiley, 1996; J. G. Jones and L. Hardy, *Stress and Performance in Sport*, New York: Wiley, 1990.

8 P. Winkielman and K. C. Berridge, 'Unconcious emotion', *Current Directions in Psychological Science*, 13, 2004, 120–123.

9 Ibid.

10 Ibid.; K. C. Berridge and P. Winkielman, 'What is an unconscious emotion? The case for unconscious "liking"', *Cognition and Emotion*, 17, 2003, 181–211; P. Winkielman, K. C. Berridge and J. Wilbarger. 'Unconscious affective reactions to masked happy versus angry faces influence consumption behaviour and judgments of value', *Personality and Social Psychology Bulletin*, 31, 2005, 121–135.

11 Winkielman and Berridge, 'Unconscious emotion', 120.

12 Ibid.

13 Hanin, *Emotions in Sport*; M. V. Jones, R. D. Mace and S. William, 'Relationship between emotional state and performance during international field hockey matches', *Perceptual and Motor Skills*, 90, 2000, 691–701.

14 Hanin, *Emotions in Sport*; R. S. Lazarus, 'How emotions influence performance in competitive sports', *The Sport Psychologist*, 14, 2000, 229–252; R. J. Vallerand and C. M. Blanchard, 'The study of emotion in sport and exercise: historical, definitional, and conceptual perspectives', in Hanin, *Emotions in Sport*, Champaign, IL: Human Kinetics, 2000, pp. 3–37.

15 M. V. Jones, 'Controlling emotions in sport'.

16 Hanin, *Emotions in Sport*.

17 J. W. Brehm, 'The intensity of emotion', *Personality and Social Psychology Review*, 3, 1999, 2–22.

18 Hanin, *Emotions in Sport*; Jones, Mace and William, 'Relationship between emotional state and performance'.

19 Brehm, 'The intensity of emotion'.

20 Ibid.

21 S. J. Virgilio, *Fitness Education for Children. A Team Approach*, Champaign, IL: Human Kinetics, 1997.

22 G. C. Roberts, *Advances in Motivation, in Sport and Exercise*, Champaign, IL: Human Kinetics, 2001.

23 E. L. Deci and R. M. Ryan, *Intrinsic Motivation and Self-determination in Human Behavior*, New York: Plenum Publishing Co., 1985.

24 J. G. Clews and B. J. Gross, 'Individual and social motivation in Australian sport', in T. Morris and J. Summers (eds), *Sport Psychology, Theory and Application and Issues*, Brisbane: Wiley, 1995, pp. 90–121.

25 Deci and Ryan, *Intrinsic Motivation and Self-determination in Human Behavior*; R. M. Ryan, 'Psychological needs and facilitation of integrative processes', *Journal of Personality*, 63, 1995, 397–427; R. M. Ryan and E. L. Deci, 'Self-determination theory and facilitation of intrinsic motivation, social development and well-being', *American Psychologist*, 55, 2000, 68–78.

26 R. J. Vallerand, L. G. Pelletier, M. Blais, N. M. Briere, C. Senecal and E. F. Vallieres, 'On the assessment of intrinsic, extrinsic, and amotivation in education: evidence on the concurrent and construct validity of the academic motivational scale', *Educational and Psychological Measurement*, 53, 1993, 159–172.

27 Ibid.; M. Standage, J. L. Duda and N. Ntoumanis, 'A model of conceptual motivation in physical education: using constructs from self-determination and achievement goal theories to predict physical activity intentions', *Journal of Educational Psychology*, 95, 2003, 97–110.

28 Deci and Ryan, *Intrinsic Motivation and Self-determination in Human Behavior*; Standage, Duda and Ntoumanis, 'A model of conceptual motivation in physical education'.

29 Ibid.
30 Deci and Ryan, *Intrinsic Motivation and Self-determination in Human Behavior*.
31 W. Halliwell, 'Providing sport psychology consulting services in professional hockey', *The Sport Psychologist*, 4, 1990, 369–377; J. C. Ives, W. F. Straub and G. A. Shelley, 'Enhancing athletic performance using digital video in consulting', *Journal of Applied Sport Psychology*, 14, 2002, 237–245.
32 A. Bandura, *Social Foundations of Thought and Action*, Englewood Cliffs, NJ: Prentice-Hall, 1986, p. 47.
33 P. J. Lang, 'The emotion probe. Studies of motivation and attention', *American Psychologist*, 50, 1995, 372–385.
34 Ibid.; A. Dickinson and M. F. Dearing, 'Appetitive–aversive interactions and inhibitory processes', in A. Dickinson and R. A. Boakes (eds), *Mechanisms of Learning and Motivation*, Hillsdale, NJ: Erlbaum, 1979, pp. 203–233; J. Konorski, *Integrative Activity of the Brain: An Interdisciplinary Approach*, Chicago: University of Chicago Press, 1967; R. L. Solomon and J. D. Corbit, 'An opponent-process theory of motivation: I. temporal dynamics of affects', *Psychological Review*, 78, 1974, 3–43.
35 J. T. Cacioppo and G. G. Bernston, 'Relationships between attitudes and evaluative space: a critical review with emphasis on the separability of positive and negative substrates', *Psychological Bulletin*, 115, 1994, 401–423.
36 S. Blackmore, *Consciousness: An introduction*. New York: Oxford University Press, 2003; R. E. Nisbett and T. D. Wilson, 'Telling more than we can know: verbal reports on mental processes', *Psychological Review*, 84, 1977, 231–259; T. Nørretranders, *The User Illusion: Cutting Consciousness Down to Size*, New York: Penguin, 1991.
37 J. A. Bargh, 'Auto-motives: pre-conscious determinants of thoughts and behavior', in E. T. Higgins and R. M. Sorrentino (eds), *Handbook of Motivation and Cognition*, Vol. 2, New York: Guildford, 1990, pp. 93–130.
38 C. Levesque and L. G. Pelletier, 'On the investigation of primed and chronic autonomous and heteronomous motivational orientations', *Personality and Social Psychology Bulletin*, 29, 2003, 1570–1584.
39 Bargh, 'Auto-motives'.
40 J. A. Bargh, 'The automaticity of everyday life', in R. S. Wyer and T. K. Srull (eds), *Advances in Social Cognition*, Vol. 10 Mahwah, NJ: Lawrence Erlbaum, 1997, pp. 1–61.
41 Lang, 'The emotion probe'.
42 Ibid.
43 Ibid.
44 V. Nowlis and H. H. Nowlis, 'The description and analysis of mood', *Annals of the New York Academy of Sciences*, 65, 1956, 345–355.
45 H. Scholsberg, 'The description of facial expressions in terms of two dimensions', *Journal of Experimental Psychology*, 44, 1952, 229–237.
46 J. A. Russell, 'A circumplex model of affect', *Journal of Personality and Social Psychology*, 39, 1980, 1161–1178.
47 G. Loizou and C. I. Karageorghis, 'The circumplex model of affect: a bi-cultural study', *Journal of Sports Sciences*, 25, 2007, 316.
48 A. C. North and D. J. Hargreaves, 'Liking arousal potential, and the emotions expressed by music', *Scandinavian Journal of Psychology*, 38, 1997, 45–53.
49 S. Saarikallio and J. Erkkila, 'The role of music in adolescents' mood regulation', *Psychology of Music*, 35, 1, 2007, 88–109.
50 For an example of the use of music as a pre-performance strategy in sports see C. I. Karageorghis, K. M. Drew and P. C. Terry, 'Effects of pretest stimulative and sedative music on grip strength', *Perceptual and Motor Skills*, 83, 1996, 1347–1352.
51 D. J. Hargreaves and A. C. North, 'The functions of music in everyday life: redefining the social in music psychology', *Psychology of Music*, 27, 1999, 84–95; A. C. North and D. J. Hargreaves, 'Uses of music in everyday life', *Music Perception* 22, 2004, 41–77.

52 For an initial review on psychomusicological research in sport see C. I. Karageorghis and P. C. Terry, 'The psychological effects of music in sport and exercise: a review', *Journal of Sport Behavior*, 20, 1997, 54–68. For an up-to-date review on psychomusicology research in sport see P. C. Terry and C. I. Karageorghis, 'Psychophysical effects of music in sport and exercise: an update on theory, research and application', in M. Katsikitis (ed.), *Psychology Bridging in the Tasman: Science, Culture, and Practice*, Proceedings of the 2006 Joint Conference of the Australian Psychological Society and the New Zealand Psychological Society, Melbourne: Australian Psychological Society, 2006, pp. 415–419.

53 C. I. Karageorghis and P. C. Terry, 'The magic of music in movement', *Sport and Medicine Today*, 5, 2001, 38–41.

54 C. I. Karageorghis and P. C. Terry, 'The psychological effects of music in sport and exercise'.

55 C. I. Karageorghis, P. C. Terry and A. M. Lane, 'Development and initial validation of an instrument to assess the motivational qualities of music in exercise and sport: the Brunel Music Rating Inventory', *Journal of Sports Sciences*, 17, 1999, 713–724.

56 Ives, Straub and Shelley, 'Enhancing athletic performance using digital video in consulting'.

57 A. M. Williams and A. Grant, 'Training perceptual skills in sport', *International Journal of Sport Psychology*, 30, 1999, 194–220.

58 Ives, Straub and Shelley, 'Enhancing athletic performance using digital video in consulting'.

59 J. Leavitt, J. Young and D. Connelly, 'The effects of videotape highlights on state self-confidence', *Journal of Applied Research in Coaching and Athletics*, 4, 1989, 225–232.

60 A. Bandura, 'Self-efficacy: toward a unifying theory of behavioral change', *Psychological Review*, 84, 1977, 191–215.

61 Leavitt, Young and Connelly, 'The effects of videotape highlights on state self-confidence'.

62 W. Houston, *One Moment In Time*, Arista Records, New York: Perfection Light Productions, 1998.

63 Ives, Straub and Shelley, 'Enhancing athletic performance using digital video in consulting'.

64 W. Halliwell, 'Providing sport psychology consulting services in professional hockey', *The Sport Psychologist*, 4, 1990, 369–377.

65 For a more extensive review of the use of music in sports see the Chapter 1 in this volume.

66 Ives, Straub and Shelley, 'Enhancing athletic performance using digital video in consulting'; Williams and Grant, 'Training perceptual skills in sport'.

67 Bargh, 'Auto-motives'.

68 The research presented herein is derived from the first author's PhD thesis entitled 'The psychophysiological effects of video, priming and music on state motivation and performance', unpublished thesis, Brunel University, 2008.

69 Russell, 'A circumplex model of affect'; Loizou and Karageorghis, 'The circumplex model of affect'.

70 Deci and Ryan, *Intrinsic Motivation and Self-determination in Human Behaviour*; Ryan and Deci, 'Self-determination theory and facilitation of intrinsic motivation, social development and well-being'.

71 J. Reeve and B. Sickenius, 'Development and validation of a brief measure of the three psychological needs underlying intrinsic motivation: the AFS scales', *Educational and Psychological Measurement*, 54, 1994, 506–515.

72 R. M. Ryan, R. Koenster and E. L. Deci, 'Ego-involved persistence: when free-choice behavior is not intrinsically motivated', *Motivation and Emotion*, 15, 1991, 185–205.

73 J. A. Russell and G. Pratt, 'A description of affective quality attributed to environ-
    ments', *Journal of Personality and Social Psychology*, 38, 1980, 311–322; J. A. Russell,
    M. Lewicka, and T. Niit, 'A cross-cultural study of a circumplex model of affect',
    Journal of Personality and Social Psychology, 57, 1989, 848–856.
74 North and Hargreaves, 'Uses of music in everyday life'.
75 The Wingate Anaerobic Test was developed at the Department of Research and
    Sport Medicine of the Wingate Institute for Physical Education and Sport during the
    1970s. For more details on the Wingate Anaerobic Test see O. Inbar, O. Bar-Or and
    J. M. Skinner, *The Wingate Anaerobic Test*, Champaign, IL: Human Kinetics, 1996.
76 Bargh, 'Auto-motives'.
77 G. J. Martin, N. M. Magid and G. Myers, 'Heart rate variability and sudden death
    secondary to coronary artery disease during ambulatory electrographic monitoring',
    American Journal of Cardiology, 60, 1987, 86–89; R. E. Kleiger, J. P. Miller and J. T.
    Bigger, 'Decreased heart rate variability and its association with increased mortality
    after acute myocardial infarction', *American Journal of Cardiology*, 59, 1987, 256–262.
78 G. G. Berntson, J. T. Bigger, Jr, D. L. Eckberg, P. Grossman, P. G. Kaufmann, M.
    Malik, H. N. Nagaraja, S. W. Porges, J. P. Saul, P. H. Stone and M. W. van der
    Molen, 'Heart rate variability: origins, methods, and interpretive caveats', *Psy-
    chophysiology*, 34, 1997, 623–648.
79 B. H. Friedman, 'An autonomic flexibility-neurovisceral integration model of anxiety
    and cardiac vagal tone', *Biological Psychology*, 74, 2007, 185–199.
80 S. H. Boutcher, F. W. Nugent, P. F. McLaren and A. L. Weltman, 'Heart rate period
    variability of trained and untrained men at rest and during mental challenge', *Psy-
    chophysiology*, 35, 1998, 16–22.
81 A. Malliani, M. Pagani, F. Lombardi and S. Cerutti, 'Cardiovascular neural regula-
    tion explored in the frequency domain', *Circulation*, 84, 1991, 482–492; M. Pagani, F.
    Lombardi, S. Guzzetti, O. Rimoldi, P. Pizzinelli, G. Sandrone, G. Malfatto, S. Del-
    l'Orto and E. Piccaluga, 'Power spectral analysis of heart rate and arterial variabilities
    as a marker of sympathovagal interaction in man and conscious dog', *Circulation
    Research*, 59, 1991, 178–193.
82 Ibid.
83 P. Rainville, A. Bechara, N. Naqvi and A. R. Damasio, 'Basic emotions are associ-
    ated with distinct patterns of cardiorespiratory activity', *International Journal of Psy-
    chophysiology*, 61, 2006, 5–18.
84 R. McCraty, M. Atkinson, W. A. Tiller, G. Rein and A. D. Watkins, 'The effects of
    emotion on short-term power spectrum analysis of heart rate variability', *The Amer-
    ican Journal of Cardiology*, 76, 1995, 1089–1093.
85 J. A. Etzel, E. L. Johnsen, J. Dickerson, D. Trabel and R. Adolphs, 'Cardiovascular
    and respiratory responses during musical mood induction', *International Journal of Psy-
    chophysiology*, 61, 2006, 57–69.
86 D. T. Bishop, C. I. Karageorghis and G. Loizou, 'A grounded theory of young tennis
    players' use of music to manipulate emotional state', *Journal of Sport & Exercise Psy-
    chology*, 29, 2007, 584–607.
87 E. M. Sokhadze, 'Effects of music on the recovery of autonomic and electrocortical
    activity after stress induced by aversive stimuli', *Applied Psychophysiology and Biofeed-
    back*, 32, 2007, 31–50. It should be noted that this study had a major limitation, since
    one minute epochs of HRV were recorded suggesting that the LF component could
    not be assessed, given that at least two minute epochs are needed to assess LF
    (Berntson *et al.*, 1997). Further, for clinical studies of HRV, five minute epochs are
    recommended (Berntson *et al.*; Task Force, 1996).
00 The experimental conditions comprised of a music-only condition, a video with
    music condition, a video with music and primes condition, and a control condition.
89 Friedman, 'An autonomic flexibility–neurovisceral integration model of anxiety and
    cardiac vagal tone'.

90 Boutcher, Nugent, McLaren and Weltman, 'Heart rate period variability of trained and untrained men at rest and during mental challenge'.
91 McCraty, Atkinson, Tiller, Rein and Watkins, 'The effects of emotion on short-term power spectrum analysis of heart rate variability'.
92 Friedman, 'An autonomic flexibility-neurovisceral integration model of anxiety and cardiac vagal tone'; McCraty, Atkinson, Tiller, Rein and Watkins, 'The effects of emotion on short-term power spectrum analysis of heart rate variability'.
93 Sokhadze, 'Effects of music on the recovery of autonomic and electrocortical activity after stress induced by aversive stimuli'.
94 Karageorghis and Terry, 'The magic of music in movement'.
95 Ives, Straub and Shelley, 'Enhancing athletic performance using digital video in consulting'.
96 Task Force, 'Heart rate variability', *Circulation*, 93, 1996, 1043–1065.

3 Managing pre-competitive emotions with music

Daniel T. Bishop and Costas I. Karageorghis

In concluding *The Expression of the Emotions in Man and Animals*, Charles Darwin wrote that,

> the language of the emotions, as it has sometimes been called, is certainly of importance for the welfare of mankind. To understand, as far as is possible, the source or origin of the various expressions which may hourly be seen on the faces of the men around us, not to mention our domesticated animals, ought to possess much interest for us. From these several causes, we may conclude that the philosophy of our subject has well deserved the attention which it has already received from several excellent observers, and that it deserves still further attention, especially from any able physiologist.[1]

From the extraordinarily precocious writings of Darwin, through the equally influential accounts of William James and Walter Cannon, the subject of emotion has continued to captivate eminent researchers.[2] Music is a proven potent inducer of emotional responses, as revealed in phenomenological, behavioural and neurophysiological data.[3] Accordingly, people use music on a daily basis to alter their emotional state; and contemporary technological developments mean that individuals can control not only the availability of music in the home, car, gym and other everyday environments, but also various acoustical properties, such as tempo.[4]

Music has been used in sport and exercise to reduce perceptions of exertion, to enhance work output and strength performance, and to optimise psychological state for performance.[5] At the 2007 FINA Swimming World Championships in Melbourne, America's Michael Phelps achieved seven gold medals, five of which were in world record time. Before each race, Phelps listened to music on his *iPod*™ while making his entrance and when on poolside awaiting officials' instructions. Reportedly, it was rap music that moved him into his optimal emotional state, a purported favourite being Young Jeezy's 'Go Getta'. Media reports also suggest that music listening plays a key role in the pre-performance and training routines of elite tennis players such as Scotland's Andrew Murray, who has expressed a penchant for The Black Eyed Peas, amongst others.[6]

Despite such anecdotal reports, together with empirical evidence for the capacity of music to elicit strong emotions, and the prevalence of music listening for mood regulation in young people, music listening as a pre-performance strategy in sport has received limited attention in sport psychology research.[7] This may be a result of the inherent idiosyncrasies of individuals' musical preferences and responses to music, which renders empirical investigation problematic. However, the increasingly portable and versatile nature of contemporary music technology means that music listening is an emotion management strategy not only already accepted by athletes, but one that can easily be incorporated into training and competitive routines.[8]

Although we can fairly effortlessly identify a music track that makes us feel the emotion of *elation*, for example, and we may also be able to say, when asked, why the track makes us feel elated, no theoretically-driven guide hitherto exists for facilitating the process of selecting personally emotive music. To this end, we present an overview of our ongoing research, in which we examined the music listening habits of a group of young athletes and consequently developed a conceptual model for selecting personally emotive music in sport. We subsequently sought to test some elements of this model in relation to preparation for reactive performance in sport, and summarise our findings herein. In keeping with the applied focus of our work, this chapter culminates in a set of practical guidelines for optimising the selection of personally emotive music. First, this work will be briefly contextualised within emotion theory.

What are emotions and why do we need them?

Despite the ubiquity of the term *emotion* in everyday parlance, the question of what constitutes an emotion has remained a point of discussion for over a century; everyone knows what an emotion is until asked to explain it.[9] There is also some disagreement as to whether emotions possess functionality or instrumentality; this aspect has since been investigated in sport.[10] Regardless of their definition or perceived utility, widespread consensus exists that emotions are not only of evolutionary survival significance, existing in all cultures and in some higher animals, but also that they comprise different components, namely: neurophysiological, physiological, expressive, behavioural, cognitive and affective.[11] Thus, it is readily apparent as to why our ability to successfully regulate our emotions might enable us to function more effectively not only in competitive sport, but also in everyday life.[12]

Primary and secondary emotions

In their attempts to categorise emotions, a number of authors propose the concept of *primary* or *basic* emotions, although the precise make-up of this class of emotions has been the subject of much debate.[13] For example, Damasio postulated the existence of six primary emotions: *happiness*, *sadness*, *fear*, *anger*, *surprise* and *disgust*; while Izard had earlier suggested a more diverse array that included *contempt, distress, guilt, interest, joy* and *shame*.[14] However, a common underlying thread in all definitions is the implication of an innate or *hard-wired* set of adaptive responses to the environment. Emotions have the ability to strip away the layers of acculturation, sophistication and a lifetime of individualised learning, to produce the lowest common denominator of human response.[15]

Secondary or *social* emotions are relatively novel phenomena in evolutionary terms. They stem from greater involvement of frontal cortices (the reasoning part of the brain) during deliberation of an emotive situation or event; this is how we humans come to experience the debilitating and enduring effects of pre-performance anxiety, for example.[16] While Damasio asserted that secondary emotions are founded on primary emotions, travelling along similar neural pathways, others suggest that they are *blends* of primary emotions, or cognitive evaluations that occur together with a basic emotion.[17] The exact number of secondary emotions may only be constrained by our vocabulary, rather than the expressive behaviours which can betray primary emotions, such as facial expressions.[18] For example, *agitated, anxious, disconcerted, disturbed, nervous, perturbed* and *worried* all describe a watered-down and protracted version of the same underlying primary emotion: fear.

Emotions as motivational states

Appraisal theory has been propagated by a number of researchers, and it acknowledges the pivotal role of appraisal of a stimulus in eliciting an emotional response.[19] In their discussion of the role of appraisal processes in emotion, Oatley and Jenkins concluded the following:

> An emotion is usually caused by a person consciously or unconsciously evaluating an event as relevant to a concern (a goal) that is important; the emotion is felt as positive when a concern is advanced and negative when a concern is impeded.[20]

Frijda noted that appraisal does not lead directly to action. Instead, he suggested that appraisal is followed by the instigation of an *action tendency*, which is a state of readiness 'to achieve or maintain a given kind of relationship with the environment. [Action tendencies] ... can be conceived of as plans or programs to achieve such ends, which are put in a state of readiness'.[21] Regardless of type, action tendencies eventually lead to attempts to either change the world's objective state via overt action or by changing one's perception of the world via cognitive action. Thus, the experience of disgust in response to a stimulus may lead to the overt action of removing oneself from the stimulus, which can be described as an *avoidance action tendency*. Emotions with such approach or avoidance action tendencies are reasonably consistent predictors of the ability of emotions to facilitate performance across a range of individual sports.[22]

The integration of appraisal into models of emotion has been applied in the music domain also: Scherer noted that music may elicit both *utilitarian* and *aesthetic* emotions, defining the former as 'high intensity emergency reactions, often involving a synchronization of many organismic subsystems ... driven by the appraisals in the central nervous system'.[23] Utilitarian emotions appear to parallel primary emotions and their survival-oriented functionality. This is in stark contrast to the more common but weaker aesthetic emotions, which arguably mirror secondary emotions and come about as a result of appraisal of the music's artistic qualities.

Measuring the affective component of emotional states

Self-report measures have been the mainstay of the assessment of affective states.[24] They typically require that the respondent rates, on a Likert-type scale, the degree to which an emotion adjective represents their current or recent emotional state. Pivotal to such categorical approaches is the previously dis-cussed class of primary emotions, which collectively form the basis for all other emotional states. For example, one of the earliest measures of mood, Nowlis' Mood Adjective Check List, consists of 38 mood-related adjectives which sub-divide into 11 factors including *anxiety, depression, happiness and aggression; these resemble*, to varying degrees of departure, the primary emotions of fear, sadness, happiness and anger respectively.[25]

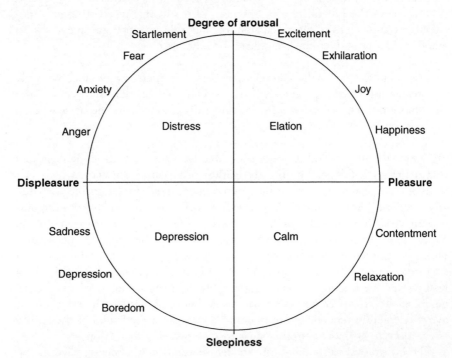

Figure 3.1 A variant of the circumplex model of affect.

A criticism that could be levelled at categorical approaches is their implicit acceptance that an individual's emotional experience is reducible to pre-specified categories of emotions, which ultimately precludes any description of emotions not described in the measure. Dimensional approaches, on the other hand, allow for idiosyncrasies in the subjectivity of affective experience, in that they seek to identify emotions based solely on a relatively small number of dimensions. One such example is the circumplex model of affect (Figure 3.1).[26] The model is demarcated by two perpendicular dimensions – *activation* (arousal) and *valence* (pleasantness) – to yield four quadrants; advocates contend that every conceivable emotion can be sited within these quadrants. Circumplex-based measures also provide a straightforward premise for the effects that emotions can have on behaviour: valence represents the evaluative outcome necessary to initiate an approach or withdrawal response, while arousal reflects the resource investment in the action tendency.[27]

Emotions in sport

Mood and emotions have been an area of considerable focus in sport.[28] Emotions exert diverse effects on performance, and athletes' emotional states fluctuate throughout the duration of athletic competition.[29] Despite a wide array of self-reported emotions, self-confidence and anxiety have remained the predominant affective phenomena of investigation in sport; this is the case in spite of the lack of a conceptually clear definition of either self-confidence or anxiety as an outright emotion.[30] However, differential emotions theory, for example, posits that anxiety is a complex emotion potentially encompassing both approach and avoidance action tendencies.[31]

Traditional approaches to assessment of pre-competitive emotion or mood typically require the respondent to indicate the extent to which they feel each emotion in a predetermined array, reflecting a categorical approach to emotion measurement. The Profile of Mood States (POMS) has been a major tool in this regard, and the characteristic *iceberg profile* has distinguished high-performing Italian national rifle shooters in World Cup competition and successful collegiate tennis players from less successful ones.[32] Stevens and Lane investigated mood-regulation among 107 athletes and found that athletes reported listening to music as a strategy for regulating each of the six dimensions of the POMS: *tension, depression, anger, vigour, fatigue* and *confusion*.[33] Further, music listening was the predominant strategy for regulation of anger (44.86 per cent of the sample) and tension (41.12 per cent).

Emotional responses to music

Sloboda and Juslin suggested that there are two broad sources of emotional response to music.[34] Intrinsic sources are structural characteristics of the music stimulus (e.g. tempo) which primarily mediate the intensity of emotions to promote action tendencies.[35] Extrinsic sources are psychological in nature and may be *iconic* (i.e. derived from resemblance between the overall musical structure and some other emotive agent) or *associative* – arbitrarily formed through associative learning, often via single-trial conditioning. Sloboda and Juslin proposed that extrinsic sources are stronger determinants of the content of musically-induced emotions; for example, whether they are positive or negative.

In the same opus, Scherer and Zentner identified three central routes by which emotions are induced via music listening.[36] The first of these is the *memory* route, wherein music acts as a powerful trigger to recollection of an emotive event (cf. associative sources). The *empathy* route necessitates the listener's ability to identify the emotions being expressed by the performer, which may be most viable when listening to a highly admired performer, or when the music is played in an emotional manner. The final route is *appraisal*, wherein the perceiver evaluates the personal significance of an event for his or her well-being, according to a number of criteria such as intrinsic pleasantness. Appraisal of pleasantness is a core feature of emotional responses and determines our orientation towards/away from environmental stimuli, including music.[37] Scherer and Zentner also noted two peripheral routes to musically-induced emotion: *proprioceptive feedback*, which they describe as a coupling of internal rhythms to external drivers; and *facilitating the expression of pre-existing emotions*, which refers to the loosening of emotional control typically exhibited in social contexts.[38]

Neural indices of musically-induced emotions

Any contemporary discussion of emotional responses to music should address the use of neuroimaging; hence the inclusion of this brief but important section. According to Koelsch, all available neuroimaging data point to the involvement of the neocortex (e.g. the orbitofrontal cortex, an evolutionarily recent brain structure) in addition to the classical emotion-processing limbic structures (e.g. the amygdala) in the emotional appraisal of music.[39] Koelsch argued that the more highly-developed neocortex enables us as music listeners to appreciate musical deviations from our expectancies; this can create tension and relaxation, which have been considered emotionally appealing features of music.[40] The potency of emotional responses to music has now been accepted to such an extent that music is being specifically employed in order to investigate emotion-processing structures; and these responses appear to evolve across the time course of a piece of music.[41]

The fact that musical emotions can act at the subcortical level by triggering the limbic system, an evolutionarily ancient brain structure, is also of primary importance. Under certain circumstances, music can access neural substrates that are associated with either primary reinforcers, such as food and sex, or with anticipation of danger, for example.[42] Thus, via limbic mediation, musical emotions resemble other stimuli with greater survival value. Whether music is unique in this respect remains to be seen; it may be one of a class of human constructs that elicits pleasure by co-opting ancient neural systems via inputs from the neocortex. Nonetheless, music serves as an excellent means by which we can explore the interactions between neocortically-mediated cognitive processes and subcortically-mediated emotional responses.

Measuring emotional responses to music

North and Hargreaves used a two-item measure based on Russell's circumplex model of affect to examine participants' perceptions of emotions expressed in music.[43] Participants' categorical descriptions of the emotions expressed in a musical excerpt were reliably predicted by the extent to which they liked the piece and the extent to which they were subjectively aroused by it. Arousal is a concept central to many theories and models of emotion, and arousal regulation strategies have been mooted as important moderators of emotional control in sport.[44] Liking for musical stimuli is related to the amount of pleasure derived when listening, and happiness – a key component of the feeling of pleasure – has attracted attention in contemporary sport emotion research.[45] Therefore, a circumplex-based measure such as the Affect Grid (Figure 3.2), which has been successfully used to assess sport-related affective states, represents an informative yet expedient tool for measuring emotional responses to music listening in sport.[46]

Schmidt and Trainor used EEG to examine 59 undergraduates' cortical responses to musical excerpts pre-selected for their collective representation of

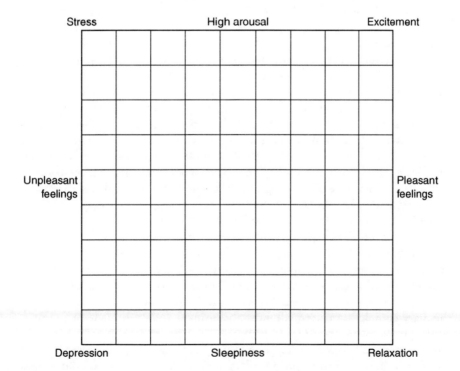

Figure 3.2 The Affect Grid.

different affective valences (i.e. positive and negative) and intensities (i.e. intense and calm) in keeping with circumplex models of emotion.[47] Overall frontal activity was more pronounced in the more intense emotions of *fear* and *joy*, when contrasted with *happy* and *sad*; these former emotions also have clearer approach or avoidance action tendencies associated with them.[48] There was significantly greater activation in the left frontal lobe in response to positively valenced music; the converse was true for negatively valenced music. Negative intense emotions also evoked greater frontal activity overall. It appears that the pattern of frontal lobe activity can differentiate emotional responses to music, based on the circumplex dimensions of valence and intensity. Because the frontal lobes are the location of motor cortex, the origin of all overt bodily movements, this finding may present implications for the role of emotional intensity in promoting performance-facilitating motor responses.

A working model for selecting effective pre-performance music

In the first stage of our research we investigated affective, behavioural and expressive components of young tennis players' emotional responses to music. Seven female and seven male full-time players (mean age = 18.4 years, $SD = 1.97$ years) with at least five or more years' competitive tennis experience (mean = 7.4 years, $SD = 2.6$ years) and representing four ethnicities (white UK/Irish, $n = 10$; white European, $n = 2$; Afro-Caribbean, $n = 1$; white US, $n = 1$) were invited to take part in an interview about their use of music in relation to their performance.

Prior to interview, each participant was given a music catalogue containing in excess of 2,000 tracks in order to aid their recall of otherwise elusive titles. To ensure that performance-related music was discussed at interview, the front sheet of the catalogue requested that participants list five emotional states they deemed crucial for success in tennis, and to specify music tracks which made them either feel or think about each state. All selected tracks were played during interview and each participant adjusted the volume of the music to one which they would typically use in order to engender the emotional states they had named. They were also requested to rate each track not only for liking and arousal potential, but also for familiarity – an important moderating variable in responses to emotive stimuli – and popularity with their peers.[49]

Six of the 14 participants completed and returned a two-week, page-a-day diary (Figure 3.3 depicts a diary page). Given that music may be an effective moderator of pre-performance mood, that athletes exhibit symptoms of competition-related emotional states up to one week prior to competing and that all participants were engaged in at least one competitive event during the diary completion period, all music listening episodes throughout the two-week period were considered relatable to pre-performance listening.[50] Participants were asked to log as many episodes as they could recall, and rated any music heard during diary completion for both liking and arousal potential.

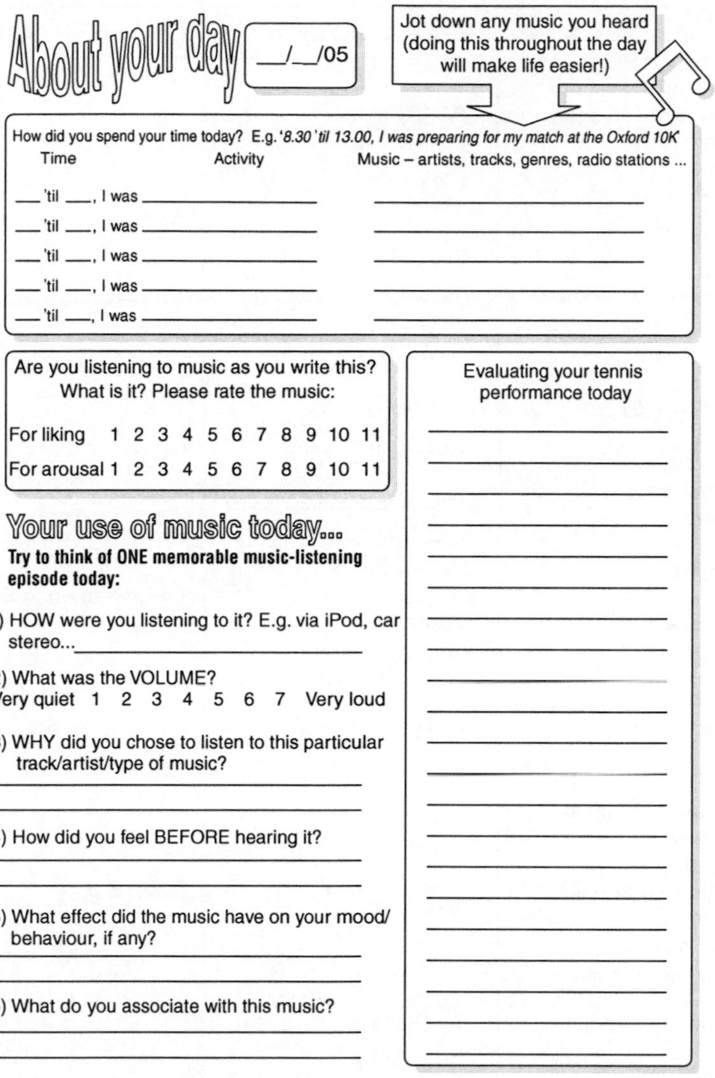

Aおロⅈⅈ your ⅆⅆⅈ ___/___/05

Jot down any music you heard
(doing this throughout the day
will make life easier!)

How did you spend your time today? E.g. '8.30 'til 13.00, I was preparing for my match at the Oxford 10K'

Time	Activity	Music – artists, tracks, genres, radio stations ...
___ 'til ___, I was _____		_____
___ 'til ___, I was _____		_____
___ 'til ___, I was _____		_____
___ 'til ___, I was _____		_____
___ 'til ___, I was _____		_____

Are you listening to music as you write this?
What is it? Please rate the music:

For liking   1 2 3 4 5 6 7 8 9 10 11

For arousal 1 2 3 4 5 6 7 8 9 10 11

Evaluating your tennis
performance today

Your use of music today...

Try to think of ONE memorable music-listening episode today:

1) HOW were you listening to it? E.g. via iPod, car stereo..._____

2) What was the VOLUME?
Very quiet 1 2 3 4 5 6 7 Very loud

3) WHY did you chose to listen to this particular track/artist/type of music? _____
_____

4) How did you feel BEFORE hearing it?
_____

5) What effect did the music have on your mood/ behaviour, if any?
_____

6) What do you associate with this music?
_____

Figure 3.3 Participants' music diary page.

Information obtained from interviews and diaries indicated that the athletes listened to music daily for two hours or more, on average, and they were predominantly travelling, preparing for competition or training, in their bedrooms or working out in the gym while doing so. Pivotal to the present data and the resultant model is that participants typically listened to music in order to attain five broad states: *appropriate mental focus, confident, positive emotional state, psyched-up,* and *relaxed* (see Table 3.1). While the latter three states undeniably represent three extremities of the circumplex model – highly fundamental

Table 3.1 Intended emotional outcomes of music listening

Raw data themes (k=42)	First order themes (k=18)	General dimensions (k=5)
Able to focus Accept bad shots and move on Concentration	Ability to focus	Appropriate mental focus
Clear mind Clear mind under pressure	Clear mind	
Clearly focused Focused Zoned in Keyed in	Focused	
Mentally in control Mentally prepared Prepared	Mentally prepared	
Belief and confidence	Self-belief	Confident
Confident Fearless, courageous	Confident	
Remembrance of previous good play	Past performance success	
Feeling fresh	Feeling fresh	Positive emotional state
General happiness	Feeling happy	
Positive Positive attitude Positive/happy	Positivity	
Tough (mentally)	Mentally tough	
Energised Excited/eager Fire it up	Energised	Psyched-up
Motivated Wanting the satisfaction of winning Determined Motivated (ready for anything) Never give up Prepared for a fight Willing to fight to the end Up for it	Driven to win	
Psyched-up	Psyched-up	
Pump-up Pumped	Pumped-up	
Calm Calm thinking Calmness	Calm	Relaxed
Loose 'no worries'	No worries	
Relaxed Relaxed/chilled/breathe	Relaxed	

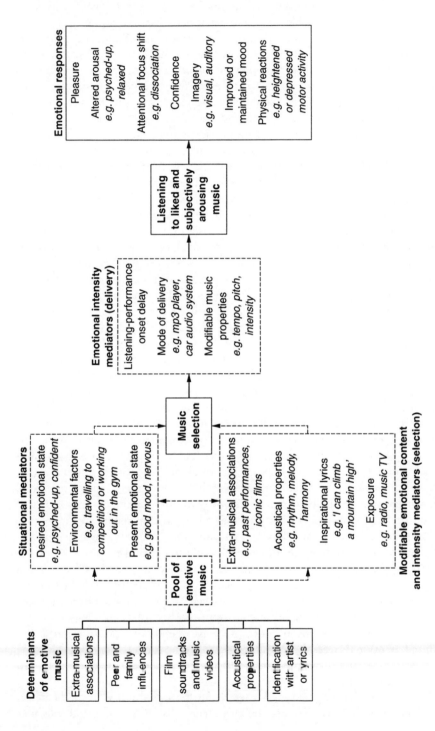

Determinants of emotive music

- Extra-musical associations
- Peer and family influences
- Film soundtracks and music videos
- Acoustical properties
- Identification with artist or lyrics

Situational mediators

Desired emotional state
e.g. psyched-up, confident

Environmental factors
e.g. travelling to competition or working out in the gym

Present emotional state
e.g. good mood, nervous

Pool of emotive music

Modifiable emotional content and intensity mediators (selection)

Extra-musical associations
e.g. past performances, iconic films

Acoustical properties
e.g. rhythm, melody, harmony

Inspirational lyrics
e.g. 'I can climb a mountain high'

Exposure
e.g. radio, music TV

Music selection

Emotional intensity mediators (delivery)

Listening-performance onset delay

Mode of delivery
e.g. mp3 player, car audio system

Modifiable music properties
e.g. tempo, pitch, intensity

Listening to liked and subjectively arousing music

Emotional responses

Pleasure

Altered arousal
e.g. psyched-up, relaxed

Attentional focus shift
e.g. dissociation

Confidence

Imagery
e.g. visual, auditory

Improved or maintained mood

Physical reactions
e.g. heightened or depressed motor activity

Figure 3.4 A working model for selecting effective pre-performance music.

components of all emotion states – the first two can arguably be described as secondary emotions, being blends of various primary/basic emotions.[51]

Figure 3.4 depicts the integration of all interview and diary data with existing music emotion theory. Upon entering the model at the left-hand side, we can see that there were five determinants of emotive music which were repeated themes throughout interview and diary data. Extra-musical associations with significant others, places and past events featured strongly in many of the participants' tracks. There were profound peer and family influences on many selections, and film soundtracks and music videos were widespread influences on participants' choices. All of these determinants suggest a role for Scherer and Zentner's memory route to emotion induction.[52] Participants also frequently made reference to the acoustical properties of the music as an influencing factor in their choices, which can be interpreted in terms of Scherer and Zentner's appraisal route; indeed, the fact that young babies orientate themselves away from disharmonious music suggests that this is an innate feature of our appraisal of all emotive stimuli.[53] Participants appeared to share some degree of identification with artist or lyrics, which corresponds to Scherer and Zentner's empathy route. All of these factors are potential considerations for athletes when developing a suitable pool of emotive music. However, it should be noted that they are predominantly extrinsic sources of emotion, with the exception of acoustical properties, which are intrinsic; this is consistent with Sloboda and Juslin's assertion that extrinsic sources are the stronger determinants of emotional content.[54]

From this pool, the athlete should make various considerations when selecting pre-performance music. One such consideration is *situational mediators* of the emotional response, such as the athlete's visual environment; emotive visual stimuli have been shown to interact powerfully with music to magnify emotional responses.[55] Participants declared various desired emotional states to attain, but all diary respondents used music on one or more occasions to maintain or up-regulate their emotional state (see Table 3.2) in terms of both emotional content (i.e. making it more positive) and emotional intensity (i.e. arousal), in accordance with previous research.[56] Interestingly, participants were not typically in a bad mood prior to listening to music, although all were tired on at least one occasion. Thus, the arousal potential of music may be more pertinent than its ability to ameliorate emotional state. This also suggests the athletes' use of music to facilitate the expression of pre-existing emotions.[57]

Modifiable emotional content and intensity mediators included acoustical properties such as tempo because evidence exists for their contribution to emotional responses to music from a very young age; this is supported in the present data.[58] Overexposure to stimuli can attenuate the emotional response, and inspirational lyrics have been continually associated with positive musically-induced emotional states, hence its inclusion in the model.[59] In acknowledging that extra-musical associations can modify emotional intensity, these were also included at this stage.[60]

Once a track has been selected, there is further opportunity for modification at the point of delivery. Because the participants listened to music throughout

Table 3.2 Participants' feelings before and after listening to music

	Text units	No. of respondents
Feelings before		
Tired	18	6
Good mood	18	6
Indifferent/okay	13	6
Bad mood	4	2
Depressed	3	2
Nervous	1	1
Bored	1	1
Feelings after		
Maintained/improved emotional state	22	6
Pumped/psyched-up	18	6
Calm/relaxed	8	5
No change	4	2
More focused	3	2
Don't remember	2	1
More motivated	1	1

the day, and the time course of emotional responses to music fluctuates, the impact on emotional state immediately prior to performance was consequently likely to vary as a function of the listening-performance onset delay.[61] In parallel with the fast rate at which music technology continues to develop, transducers for generating the sounds we hear are becoming increasingly sophisticated – such as contemporary earphones which dramatically reduce extraneous environmental noise. Therefore, mode of delivery was considered an important inclusion at this stage. Finally, and importantly to the next stage of the investigation, the aforesaid technological advances allow us to manipulate other music properties further at the point of delivery – tempo and intensity are two noteworthy examples to which we return shortly.

The consequent emotional responses at the final stage of the model are certainly not exhaustive, but were borne directly out of the present data. In addition to those already discussed, participants reported some form of *imagery* in response to hearing the music, which typically related to some memory from the past or an iconic representation of their achievement in tennis.[62] Participants also frequently became more animated and their facial expressions became more positive as a result of listening to many tracks; we exploited the potential utility of this action tendency in the second phase of our research.[63] Additional direction to our programme was provided by quantitative data obtained during interview (see Table 3.3) – on average, those tracks selected in order to psych-up or relax were played at higher and lower intensities (volumes), and exhibited faster and slower tempi, respectively (shaded cells). Tracks chosen for psyching-up were rated as possessing higher arousal potential on average. Less consistent is the fact that tracks selected in order to relax did not attract the lowest ratings for arousal potential. However, they were deemed most liked on average.

Table 3.3 Quantitative data for participants' personal music selections

Desired state	Selected intensity (dBA)	Tempo (bpm)	Liking[1]	Arousal potential[2]	Familiarity[3]	Popularity with peers[4]
Appropriate mental focus	93.8	101.3	10.2	8.7	9.5	7.7
Confident	98.8	113.0	9.6	9.0	9.2	7.1
Positive emotional state	93.1	114.0	10.3	9.7	9.3	5.3
Psyched-up	102.3	120.9	10.2	10.5	8.9	6.6
Relaxed	87.9	87.9	10.6	9.2	9.9	6.9

Notes
Mean values shown
1. 1 = −5 = not at all liked; 11 = +5 = highly liked.
2. 1 = −5 = not at all energizing; 11 = +5 = highly energizing.
3. 1 = −5 = not at all familiar; 11 = +5 = highly familiar.
4. 1 = −5 = not at all popular; 11 = +5 = highly popular.

Perhaps unsurprisingly, all selected tracks were very familiar to participants, and popularity with peers seemed to be of little importance when selecting music; this may reflect the fact that music affords young people the opportunity to develop a strong sense of their own unique identity.[64]

In summary

The content of personally emotive music in the present study was determined largely by extrinsic sources of emotion, although two intrinsic sources – intensity and tempo – appeared to be related to the arousal potential of music tracks, consistent with extant research.[65] There was evidence that each of Scherer and Zentner's central and peripheral routes to emotion induction via music listening were integral to the responses witnessed.[66] These responses encompassed an array of utilitarian (primary) and aesthetic (secondary) emotions, each of which was localisable somewhere on Russell's circumplex model of affect.[67]

Optimising pre-performance music via intensity and tempo manipulation

The principal aim at this phase was to intervene at the delivery stage of the newly-developed model; specifically, to examine the effects of manipulating tempo and intensity on the behavioural consequences of emotional responses to music.[68] In accordance with foregoing research and the present data, it was expected that suitably selected music played at a faster tempo and high intensity (volume) would promote a more positive and highly aroused state, culminating in an action tendency which incorporates an approach-type movement readiness and that this, in turn, would facilitate subsequent choice reaction time (CRT) performance.[69] A popular dance track was digitally recorded and its tempo manipulated using time-scaling technology to produce three 90-second excerpts with tempi of 99 bpm (slow), 129 bpm (normal), and 161 bpm (fast); all excerpts were otherwise qualitatively similar. Each of the three versions was modified further to yield moderate intensity (55 dBA) and high intensity (75 dBA) variants, thereby creating a total of six modified versions. Two 90-second excerpts of white noise (an anticipated approximation of undesirable background noise, for the purposes of the present study) were also created at each of the two intensities, as was a 90-second period of silence.

Thirty-three male and 21 female tennis players (mean age = 17.7 years, $SD = 2.1$ years; mean experience of competitive tennis = 84.8 months, $SD = 34.1$ months) representing 14 ethnicities (predominantly white UK) sat and listened to each of the nine auditory stimuli via earphones immediately prior to undertaking a CRT task. Participants logged their affective responses to the music using the Affect Grid and by circling as many from 28 affective descriptors (identical to those used by Russell) as they deemed apt.[70] Participants then stood to respond as quickly as possible to consecutive images of a tennis ball

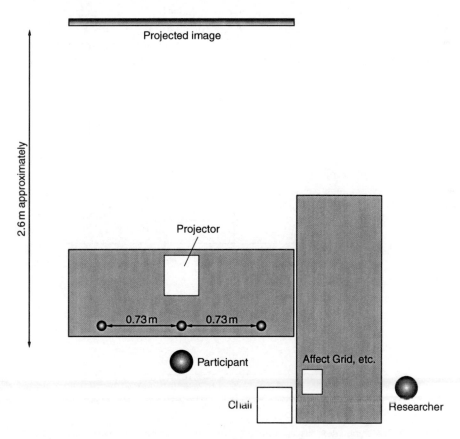

Figure 3.5 Experimental set-up.

appearing randomly in each of three locations on a tennis court backdrop, by striking one of three corresponding buttons; this was an approximation of the return-of-serve scenario in which the returning player is required to react as quickly and accurately as possible to the opponent's serve. Figure 3.5 displays the experimental setup.

In order to ascertain the validity of the Affect Grid as a measure of affective state, the affective descriptors selected by participants to describe their emotional state during each condition were located in two-dimensional space according to their corresponding mean Affect Grid ratings for each of the nine conditions.[71] It can be seen from visual inspection of Figure 3.6 that descriptors are arranged in a structure corresponding to that of Russell's original conceptualisation of the affective circumplex model, providing strong evidence that Affect Grid scores correspond very closely with more traditional categorical measures of affect.[72]

Figure 3.7 shows all Affect Grid scores and reaction times for each condition. Music per se was considered rated as significantly more pleasant (mean Affect Grid rating = 6.20, SD = 0.51) than both white noise conditions (mean = 3.22, SD = 0.43). A period of silence (mean = 2.94, SD = 1.92) was adjudged significantly less arousing than all of the remaining eight conditions (mean = 5.29, SD = 1.11). This latter finding suggests that any auditory stimulus is capable of increasing subjective arousal. However, the former validates the notion that

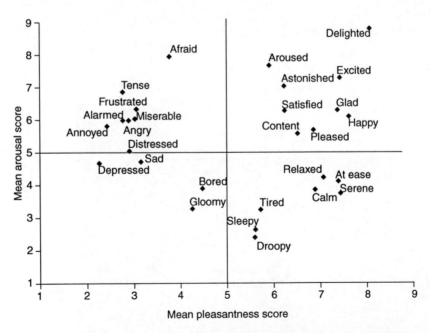

Figure 3.6 Affective descriptors arranged in two-dimensional space according to participants' mean Affect Grid ratings.

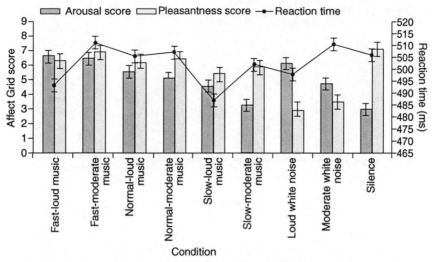

Figure 3.7 Mean arousal score, pleasantness score and RT for each condition.

music listening is an intrinsically rewarding activity, and therefore music listening is both acceptable and viable as a strategy for increasing arousal levels.[73]

When music conditions only were compared, it emerged that all music played at a fast tempo was perceived as more pleasant and arousing than music played at slower tempi, consistent with previous findings. Music played at loud intensity elicited higher subjective arousal and this, in turn, yielded significantly shorter (quicker) reaction times (see Figure 3.8 for a summary).[74] The fact that higher subjective arousal, irrespective of emotional valence, was related to superior CRT performance supports previous research implicating higher overall cortical activity as a predictor of subsequent CRT performance.

In summary

At this stage of our investigation we focused on two intrinsic sources of emotion: tempo and intensity. These acoustical properties are both easily manipulable for any consumer, thanks to contemporary technology. Data showed that listening to loud-intensity, fast-tempo music not only increases the intensity and valence of the emotional response to music, but that loud intensity pre-performance music also facilitated subsequent reactive performance by eliciting appropriate action tendencies.[75]

Conclusion and recommendations

We combined affective and behavioural data in our examination of emotional responses to music in young tennis players. The data presented herein have implications for emotion and arousal management prior to performance. Many

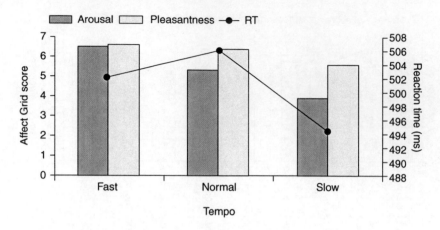

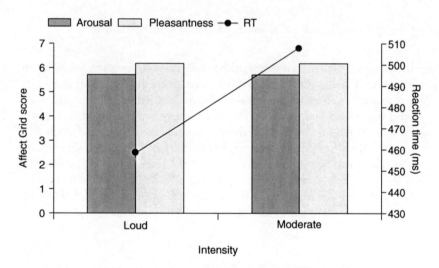

Figure 3.8 Mean Affect Grid and CRT scores by tempo and intensity.

sources of emotion contribute to the listener's pool of emotive music; but the strategy of listening to personally emotive music with a fast tempo, played at a loud intensity is likely to heighten subjective arousal, positive affect and choice reaction-time performance. Our model embraces the notion of idiosyncratic music use, offering a route map rather than an instruction, for practitioners and athletes alike to maximise their chances of selecting music appropriately.

Throughout this exposition, the temporality of emotional responses to music has been highlighted; this has enabled us to develop a clear position on the potential ergogenic benefits to be derived from the emotional response to music.[76] Our more recent research data only allow the identification of an approximately 30-second period from cessation of music listening, in which performance-facilitating emotional profiles may still remain; although this may be longer in actuality.[77] The principal contribution of our work here presented is to show that music variables may be carefully selected and/or manipulated to educe performance-facilitating emotional responses to music in competitive tennis players. The findings of the work laid out here are arguably therefore only generalisable to competitive tennis players; the wider implications are for the reader to judge.

Given the proven capacity of carefully selected music to rapidly and effortlessly elicit profound autonomic, affective, neurophysiological and behavioural responses, in combination with the flexibility offered by contemporary technological developments such as the *iPod*™, now is an ideal time for athletes to experiment with tracks from their pool of emotive music, to bring about a performance-facilitating idiosyncratic emotional profile, using this model as a guide.[78] Continuing the applied focus of the research outlined in this chapter, we present some generic guidelines for selecting personally emotive music, targeted primarily at athletes who wish to optimise their pre-performance emotions:

1 Be sensitive to the five determinants of emotive music detailed in the first stage of the model; these predominantly extrinsic sources of emotion will help you to establish a sliding scale of your personal emotional responses to music, which may perhaps range from 'relatively minor' to 'elicits chills'.[79]

2 Note down what you could conceivably describe as your typical responses to 20 or 30 of these tracks, which now constitute a finite pool of emotive music. Use the Affect Grid in Figure 3.2 to select tracks which collectively represent all four quadrants of the circumplex. Create a playlist on your mp3 player of these tracks, entitled 'pre-performance music'.

3 When seeking to moderate your emotional state, consider your present emotional state and desired emotional state, in terms of both valence and arousal: does your affective state need to become more or less positive; and does your state of arousal need to be increased or decreased? It may be the case that maintenance of one or both of these is required. Therefore, select tracks sited within a quadrant that is most likely to move you in the desired 'emotional direction'. For example, if you are presently feeling quite calm and placid, but being aroused and angry works best for you in your sport, selecting a track from the upper left quadrant of the circumplex may actually be a suitable stratagem.

4 Cursory examination of Figure 3.6 reveals that five adjectives are located within the region of the Affect Grid representing high arousal (scores 7 or greater): *afraid, aroused, astonished, excited* and *delighted*. Athletes wishing to heighten arousal may wish to engender one or more of these emotions

5 Bearing points 3 and 4 in mind, select a track from the pool whose extramusical associations are likely to bring about the desired emotional state; these seem to be important determinants of emotional content. The impact

of the track may be moderated further by the amount of exposure you have had to the track recently (e.g. overexposure can lead to a reduction in the emotional response); the acoustical qualities such as tempo (faster tempi will likely elicit happier responses); and inspirational, catchy lyrics which may enable you to sustain the emotional response as you sing to yourself.[80]

6   Stay attuned to your environment. Combinations of emotive music with equally emotive visual stimuli can lead to an enhanced response – which may or may not be desirable; this is for you to decide.[81]

7   Once a track has been selected, a decision needs to be made about the timing of the desired peak for the emotional response. Our more recent research suggests that 90 seconds of listening to music can elicit neural changes that continue to rise after cessation of the music, and the response during listening is greater after 30 seconds.[82]

8   The intensity of the emotional response is affected by the fidelity of the music delivery system, which also may affect the impact of background noise.[83] Higher quality systems and in-the-ear delivery are therefore likely to maximise emotional intensity – although this is yet to be empirically tested.

9   If some type of reactive performance will follow music listening, then listening at higher intensity (volume) and faster tempi will likely improve that performance; this may be due to a combination of emotion-mediated higher activation of visuo-motor decision-making pathways in the brain and priming of increased corticospinal excitability of motor pathways.[84] However, caution should be exercised when listening at loud volumes for prolonged periods.[85] Use time scaling features of either an mp3 player or a computer software program to increase or decrease the tempo.

10 Jot down your responses for future reference, together with all relevant performance outcomes.

Of course, these guidelines need not apply only to sportspeople: many of us are required to perform on a daily basis, be we educators, musicians or accountants; the list is long. Effective management of our emotional state is essential to successful execution of a host of skills, and music listening is a viable means to achieving that end.

Notes

1   C. Darwin, 'The Expression of the Emotions in Man and Animals', Chicago: University of Chicago Press, 1872 [1999], p. 360.
2   W. James, 'What is an emotion?' Mind, 9, 1884, 188–205; W. B. Cannon, 'The James-Lange theory of emotions: a critical examination and an alternative theory', American Journal of Psychology, 39, 1927, 106–124; A. Damasio, The Feeling of What Happens: Body, Emotion and the Making of Consciousness, London: Vintage, 2000; N. H. Frijda, The Emotions, New York: Cambridge University Press, 1986; R. S Lazarus, Emotion and Adaptation, New York: Oxford University Press, 1991; J. E. LeDoux, 'Emotion: clues from the brain', Annual Review of Psychology, 46, 1995, 209;

J. Panksepp, 'The basics of basic emotion', in P. Ekman and R. J. Davidson (eds), *The Nature of Emotion: Fundamental Questions*, New York: Oxford University Press, 1994, pp. 20–24; S. Schachter and J. Singer, 'Cognitive, social and physiological determinants of emotional state', *Psychological Review*, 69, 1962, 378–399; R. E. Thayer, *The Biopsychology of Mood and Arousal*, Oxford: Oxford University Press, 1989.

3 A. J. Blood, R. J. Zatorre, P. Bermudez and A. C. Evans, 'Emotional responses to pleasant and unpleasant music correlate with activity in paralimbic brain regions', *Nature Neuroscience*, 2, 1999, 382–387; V. Menon and D. J. Levitin, 'The rewards of music listening: response and physiological connectivity of the mesolimbic system', *NeuroImage*, 28, 2005, 175–184; J. A. Sloboda, 'Music structure and emotional response: some empirical findings', *Psychology of Music*, 19, 1991, 110–120; A. J. Blood and R. J. Zatorre, 'Intensely pleasurable responses to music correlate with activity in brain regions implicated in reward and emotion', *Proceedings of the National Academy of Sciences of the United States of America*, 98, 2001, 11818–11823; N. S. Rickard, 'Intense emotional responses to music: a test of the physiological arousal hypothesis', *Psychology of Music*, 32, 2004, 371–388; A. Gabrielsson, 'Emotions in strong experiences with music', in P. Juslin and J. A. Sloboda (eds), *Music and Emotion: Theory and Research*, Oxford: Oxford University Press, 2001, pp. 431–449.

4 R. E. Thayer, J. R. Newman and T. M. McClain, 'Self-regulation of mood: strategies for changing a bad mood, raising energy, and reducing tension', *Journal of Personality and Social Psychology*, 67, 1994, 910–925; S. Saarikallio and J. Erkkilä, 'The role of music in adolescents' mood regulation', *Psychology of Music*, 35, 2007, 88–109; A. C. North, D. J. Hargreaves and J. Hargreaves, 'Uses of music in everyday life', *Music Perception*, 22, 2004, 41–77.

5 J. A. Potteiger, J. A. Schroeder and K. L. Goff, 'Influence of music on ratings of perceived exertion during 20 minutes of moderate intensity exercise', *Perceptual and Motor Skills*, 91, 2000, 848–854; G. Atkinson, D. Wilson and M. Eubank, 'Effects of music on work-rate distribution during a cycling time trial', *International Journal of Sports Medicine*, 25, 2004, 611–615; C. I. Karageorghis, K. M. Drew and P. C. Terry, 'Effects of pretest stimulative and sedative music on grip strength', *Perceptual and Motor Skills*, 83, 1996, 1347–1352; J. Pates, C. I. Karageorghis, R. Fryer and I. Maynard, 'Effects of asynchronous music on flow states and shooting performance among netball players', *Journal of Sports Sciences*, 21, 2003, 357–358.

6 See Y. L. Hanin, 'Individual Zones of Optimal Functioning (IZOF) model: an idiographic approach to performance anxiety', in K. Henschen and W. Straub (eds), *Sport Psychology: An Analysis of Athlete Behavior*, Longmeadow, MA: Movement Publications, 1995, pp. 103–119; M. Blackley, 'Music boosts sport success by fifth', *The Scotsman*, 21 October 2005, 1–2.

7 Karageorghis, Drew and Terry, 'Effects of pretest stimulative and sedative music on grip strength'; Pates, Karageorghis, Fryer and Maynard, 'Effects of asynchronous music on flow states and shooting performance among netball players'.

8 D. T. Bishop, C. I. Karageorghis and G. Loizou, 'A grounded theory of young tennis players' use of music to manipulate emotional state', *Journal of Sport & Exercise Psychology*, 29, 2007, 584–607.

9 James, 'What is an emotion?'; C. J. Beedie, P. C. Terry and A. M. Lane, 'A comparison of academic and non-academic distinctions between emotion and mood.' (Abstract), *Journal of Sports Sciences*, 21, 2003, 340.

10 Frijda, *The Emotions*; D. Keltner and J. J. Gross, 'Functional accounts of emotions', *Cognition and Emotion*, 13, 1999, 467–480; E. Cerin, 'Anxiety versus fundamental emotions as predictors of perceived functionality of pre-competitive emotional states, threat, and challenge in individual sports', *Journal of Applied Sport Psychology*, 15, 2003, 223–238.

11 A. Sloman and M. Croucher, 'Why robots will have emotions', in *International Joint*

Conferences on Artificial Intelligence, Vancouver, 1981; J. A. Russell and M. Bullock, 'Multidimensional scaling of emotional facial expressions: similarity from preschoolers to adults', *Journal of Personality and Social Psychology*, 48, 1985, 1290–1298; P. Rainville, A. Bechara, N. Naqvi and A. R. Damasio, 'Basic emotions are associated with distinct patterns of cardiorespiratory activity', *International Journal of Psychophysiology*, 61, 2006, 5–18; T. Baumgartner, M. Willi and L. Jancke, 'Modulation of corticospinal activity by strong emotions evoked by pictures and classical music: a transcranial magnetic stimulation study', *Neuroreport: For Rapid Communication of Neuroscience Research*, 18, 2007, 261–265; A. Ortony and T. J. Turner, 'What's basic about basic emotions?', *Psychological Review*, 97, 1990, 315–331; P. Ekman and W. V. Friesen, 'A new pan-cultural facial expression of emotion', *Motivation and Emotion*, 10, 1986, 159–168; R. Plutchik, *Emotion: A Psychoevolutionary Synthesis*, New York: Harper & Row, 1980; M. M. Bradley and P. J. Lang, 'Measuring emotion: behavior, feeling, and physiology', in R. D. Lane and L. Nadel (eds), *Cognitive Neuroscience of Emotion*, New York: Oxford University Press, 2000, pp. 242–276; K. Erickson and J. Schulkin, 'Facial expressions of emotion: a cognitive neuroscience perspective', *Brain and Cognition*, 52, 2003, 52–60; C. E. Izard, 'Four systems for emotion activation: cognitive and noncognitive processes', *Psychological Review*, 100, 1993, 68–90; J. Panksepp, 'The neuro-evolutionary cusp between emotions and cognitions: implications for understanding consciousness and the emergence of a unified mind science', *Consciousness and Emotion*, 1, 2000, 15–54; R. E. Thayer, *The Origin of Everyday Moods: Managing Energy, Tension, and Stress*, New York: Oxford University Press, 1996; Damasio, *The Feeling of What Happens: Body, Emotion and the Making of Consciousness*.

12 D. Gould, R. C. Eklund and S. A. Jackson, 'Coping strategies used by U.S. Olympic wrestlers', *Research Quarterly for Exercise and Sport*, 64, 1993, 83–93; R. S. Lazarus, 'How emotions influence performance in competitive sports', *Sport Psychologist*, 14, 2000, 229; Lazarus, *Emotion and Adaptation*; R. S. Lazarus, 'From psychological stress to the emotions: a history of changing outlooks', *Annual Review of Psychology*, 44, 1993, 1; J. J. Gross, 'Sharpening the focus: emotion regulation, arousal, and social competence', *Psychological Inquiry*, 9, 1998, 287–290.

13 Panksepp, 'The basics of basic emotion'; Ortony and Turner, 'What's basic about basic emotions?'; C. E. Izard, F. Dougherty, B. M. Bloxom and N. E. Kotsch, 'The differential emotions scale: a method of measuring the subjective experience of discrete emotions', unpublished manuscript, 1974; T. J. Turner and A. Ortony, 'Basic emotions: can conflicting criteria converge?', *Psychological Review*, 99, 1992, 566–571; P. Ekman, 'Are there basic emotions?' *Psychological Review*, 99, 1992, 550–553; C. E. Izard, 'Basic emotions, relations among emotions, and emotion–cognition relations', *Psychological Review*, 99, 1992, 561–565; J. Panksepp, 'A critical role for "affective neuroscience" in resolving what is basic about basic emotions', *Psychological Review*, 99, 1992, 554–560; P. Ekman, 'Basic emotions' in T. Dalgleish and M. J. Power (eds), *Handbook of Cognition and Emotion*, Sussex: John Wiley & Sons Ltd, 1999, pp. 45–60.

14 Damasio, *The Feeling of What Happens*; C. E. Izard, *The Face of Emotion*, New York: Appleton-Century-Crofts, 1971.

15 R. W. Levenson, 'Human emotion: a functional view', in P. Ekman and R. J. Davidson (eds), *The Nature of Emotion: Fundamental Questions*, New York: Oxford University Press, 1994, pp. 123–126.

16 Gould, Eklund and Jackson, 'Coping strategies used by U.S. Olympic wrestlers'.

17 R. Plutchik, *The Psychology and Biology of Emotion*, New York: HarperCollins, 1994; K. Oatley, *Best Laid Schemes: The Psychology of Emotions*, Cambridge, MA: Harvard University Press, 1992.

18 P. Ekman, 'Facial expressions', in T. Dalgleish and M. J. Power (eds), *Handbook of Cognition and Emotion*, New York: John Wiley & Sons Ltd, 1999, pp. 301–320.

19 Frijda, *The Emotions*; Lazarus, *Emotion and Adaptation*; Izard, 'Four systems for

emotion activation'; K. Oatley and P. N. Johnson-Laird, 'Towards a cognitive theory of emotions', *Cognition and Emotion*, 1, 1987, 29–50; K. R. Scherer, 'Appraisal theory', in T. Dalgleish and M. J. Power (eds), *Handbook of Cognition and Emotion*, New York: John Wiley & Sons Ltd, 1999, pp. 637–663.
20 K. Oatley and J. M. Jenkins, *Understanding Emotions*, Blackwell Publishing, 1996, p. 96.
21 Frijda, *The Emotions*, p. 75.
22 Cerin, 'Anxiety versus fundamental emotions as predictors of perceived functionality of pre-competitive emotional states, threat, and challenge in individual sports'.
23 K. R. Scherer, 'Which emotions can be induced by music? What are the underlying mechanisms? And how can we measure them?', *Journal of New Music Research*, 33, 2004, 239–251.
24 M. Almagor and Y. S. Ben-Porath, 'The two-factor model of self-reported mood: a cross-cultural replication', *Journal of Personality Assessment*, 53, 1989, 10; L. Feldman Barrett, K. S. Quigley, E. Bliss-Moreau and K. R. Aronson, 'Interoceptive sensitivity and self-reports of emotional experience', *Journal of Personality and Social Psychology*, 87, 2004, 684–697; J. H. Kerr and S. Svebak, 'The acute effects of participation in sport on mood: the importance of level of antagonistic physical interaction', *Personality and Individual Differences*, 16, 1994, 159–166.
25 V. Nowlis, 'Research with the Mood Adjective Check List', in S. S. Tompkins and C. E. Izard (eds), *Affect, Cognition, and Personality: Empirical Studies*, New York: Springer, 1965, pp. 352–389.
26 J. A. Russell, 'A circumplex model of affect', *Journal of Personality and Social Psychology*, 39, 1980, 1161–1178.
27 R. J. Larsen and E. Diener, 'Promises and problems with the Circumplex Model of Emotion', in M. S. Clark (ed.), *Emotion*, Newbury Park, CA: Sage Publications, Inc, 1992, pp. 25–59; J. F. Thayer and M. Faith, 'A dynamical systems interpretation of a dimensional model of emotion', *Scandinavian Journal of Psychology*, 42, 2001, 121–133.
28 P. C. Terry, 'Mood and emotions in sport' in T. Morris and J. Summers (eds), *Sport Psychology: Theory, Applications and Issues*, Milton, Queensland: John Wiley & Sons Australia, 2004, pp. 48–73.
29 M. V. Jones and R. D. Mace, 'Relationship between emotional state and performance during international field hockey matches', *Perceptual and Motor Skills*, 90, 2000, 691; J. Butt, R. Weinberg and T. Horn, 'The intensity and directional interpretation of anxiety: fluctuations throughout competition and relationship to performance', *The Sport Psychologist*, 17, 2003, 35–54.
30 L. L. Craft, T. M. Magyar, B. J. Becker and D. L. Feltz, 'The relationship between the Competitive State Anxiety Inventory-2 and sport performance: a meta-analysis', *Journal of Sport & Exercise Psychology*, 25, 2003, 44–65; Beedie, Terry and Lane, 'A comparison of academic and non-academic distinctions between emotion and mood'; S. Hanton, S. D. Mellalieu and R. Hall, 'Self-confidence and anxiety interpretation: a qualitative investigation', *Psychology of Sport and Exercise*, 5, 2004, 477–495; S. D. Mellalieu, S. Hanton and G. Jones, 'Emotional labeling and competitive anxiety in preparation and competition', *The Sport Psychologist*, 17, 2003, 157–174.
31 C. E. Izard, *Human Emotions*, New York: Plenum Press, 1977.
32 D. M. McNair, M. Lorr and L. F. Droppleman, *Manual for the Profile of Mood States*, San Diego, CA: Educational and Industrial Testing Services, 1971; W. P. Morgan, 'Test of champions: the iceberg profile. Olympic athletes display a superior pattern of scores on tests of mental health', *Psychology Today*, 14, 1980, 92–99; A. Cei, U. Manili, F. Taddei and R. Buonamano, 'Mood profile and sport performance', *Movimento*, 10, 1994, 61–63; T. Covassin and S. Pero, 'The relationship between self-confidence, mood state, and anxiety among collegiate tennis players', *Journal of Sport Behavior*, 27, 2004, 230–242.

33 M. J. Stevens and A. M. Lane, 'Mood-regulating strategies used by athletes', *Athletic Insight: The Online Journal of Sport Psychology*, 3, 2001. Online, available at: www.ath-leticinsight.com/Vol3Iss3/MoodRegulation.htm.

34 J. A. Sloboda and P. N. Juslin, 'Psychological perspectives on music and emotion', in P. N. Juslin and J. A. Sloboda (eds), *Music and Emotion: Theory and Research*, New York: Oxford University Press, 2001, pp. 71–104.

35 Frijda, *The Emotions*.

36 K. R. Scherer and M. R. Zentner, 'Emotional effects of music: production rules', in P. N. Juslin and J. A. Sloboda (eds), *Music and Emotion: Theory and Research*, Oxford: Oxford University Press, 2001, pp. 361–392.

37 Lazarus, *Emotion and Adaptation*; M. R. Zentner and J. Kagan, 'Perception of music by infants', *Nature*, 383, 1996, 29.

38 P. Ekman, 'Universals and cultural differences in facial expressions of emotion', *Nebraska Symposium on Motivation*, Lincoln, Nebraska, 1972.

39 S. Koelsch, 'Investigating emotion with music: neuroscientific approaches', *Annals of the New York Academy of Sciences*, 1060, 2005, 412–418.

40 L. B. Meyer, *Emotion and Meaning in Music*, Chicago: University of Chicago Press, 1956.

41 S. Koelsch, T. Fritz, D. Y. von Cramon, K. Müller and A. D. Friederici, 'Investigating emotion with music: an fMRI study', *Human Brain Mapping*, 27, 2006, 239–250.

42 Menon and Levitin, 'The rewards of music listening'; N. Gosselin, I. Peretz, M. Noulhiane, D. Hasboun, C. Beckett, M. Baulac and S. Samson, 'Impaired recognition of scary music following unilateral temporal lobe excision', *Brain*, 128, 2005, 628–640.

43 A. C. North and D. J. Hargreaves, 'Liking, arousal potential, and the emotions expressed by music', *Scandinavian Journal of Psychology*, 38, 1997, 45–53; Russell, 'A circumplex model of affect'.

44 Thayer, *The Biopsychology of Mood and Arousal*; M. V. Jones, 'Controlling emotions in sport', *The Sport Psychologist*, 17, 2003, 471–486.

45 D. A. Ritossa and N. S. Rickard, 'The relative utility of "pleasantness" and "liking" dimensions in predicting the emotions expressed by music', *Psychology of Music*, 32, 2004, 5–22; M. V. Jones, A. M. Lane, S. R. Bray, M. Uphill and J. Catlin, 'Development and validation of the Sport Emotion Questionnaire', *Journal of Sport & Exercise Psychology*, 27, 2005, 407.

46 J. A. Russell, A. Weiss and G. A. Mendelsohn, 'Affect grid: a single-item scale of pleasure and arousal', *Journal of Personality and Social Psychology*, 57, 1989, 493–502; J. Hardy, C. Hall and M. R. Alexander, 'Exploring self-talk and affective states in sport', *Journal of Sports Sciences*, 19, 2001, 469–475; W. A. Edmonds, D. T. Y. Mann, G. Tenenbaum and C. M. Janelle, 'Analysis of affect-related performance zones: an idiographic method using physiological and introspective data', *The Sport Psychologist*, 20, 2006, 40–57.

47 L. A. Schmidt and L. J. Trainor, 'Frontal brain electrical activity (EEG) distinguishes *valence* and *intensity* of musical emotions', *Cognition and Emotion*, 15, 2001, 487–500.

48 N. H. Frijda, 'Emotion, cognitive structure, and action tendency', *Cognition and Emotion*, 1, 1987, 115–143.

49 North and Hargreaves, 'Liking, arousal potential, and the emotions expressed by music'; A. M. Colman, W. M. Best and A. J. Austen, 'Familiarity and liking: direct tests of the preference-feedback hypothesis', *Psychological Reports*, 58, 1986, 931–938.

50 P. D. Gluch, 'The use of music in preparing for sport performance', *Contemporary Thought*, 2, 1993, 33–53; S. Hanton, O. Thomas and I. Maynard, 'Competitive anxiety responses in the week leading up to competition: the role of intensity, direction and frequency dimensions', *Psychology of Sport and Exercise*, 5, 2004, 169–181.

51 Plutchik, *The Psychology and Biology of Emotion*.

52 Scherer and Zentner, 'Emotional effects of music'.

53 Zentner and Kagan, 'Perception of music by infants'.

54 Sloboda and Juslin, 'Psychological perspectives on music and emotion'.
55 Baumgartner, Willi and Jancke, 'Modulation of corticospinal activity by strong emotions evoked by pictures and classical music'.
56 Thayer, Newman and McClain, 'Self-regulation of mood'; Saarikallio and Erkkilä, 'The role of music in adolescents' mood regulation'.
57 Ekman, *Universals and Cultural Differences in Facial Expressions of Emotion*.
58 S. Dalla Bella, I. Peretz, L. Rousseau and N. Gosselin, 'A developmental study of the affective value of tempo and mode in music', *Cognition*, 80, 2001, B1–B10.
59 Karageorghis and Terry, Chapter 1, this volume.
60 Sloboda and Juslin, 'Psychological perspectives on music and emotion'.
61 Koelsch, Fritz, von Cramon, Müller and Friederici, 'Investigating emotion with music'.
62 See Sloboda and Juslin, 'Psychological perspectives on music and emotion'; Scherer and Zentner, 'Emotional effects of music'.
63 Frijda, 'Emotion, cognitive structure, and action tendency'.
64 R. Larson, 'Secrets in the bedroom: adolescents' private use of media', *Journal of Youth and Adolescence*, 24, 1995, 535–550.
65 E. Schubert, 'Modeling perceived emotion with continuous musical features', *Music Perception*, 21, 2004, 561–585.
66 Scherer and Zentner, 'Emotional effects of music'.
67 Russell, 'A circumplex model of affect'.
68 Bishop, Karageorghis and Loizou, 'A grounded theory of young tennis players' use of music to manipulate emotional state'.
69 Ibid; G. D. Webster and C. G. Weir, 'Emotional responses to music: interactive effects of mode, texture, and tempo', *Motivation and Emotion*, 29, 2005, 19–39; Frijda, 'Emotion, cognitive structure, and action tendency'.
70 Russell, 'A circumplex model of affect'; Russell, Weiss and Mendelsohn, 'Affect grid'.
71 Ibid.
72 Ibid.
73 Menon and Levitin, 'The rewards of music listening'.
74 Webster and Weir, 'Emotional responses to music'; Schubert, 'Modeling perceived emotion with continuous musical features'.
75 Frijda, *The Emotions*.
76 Bishop, Karageorghis and Loizou, 'A grounded theory of young tennis players' use of music to manipulate emotional state'.
77 D. T. Bishop, M. J. Wright and C. I. Karageorghis, 'Neurophysiological correlates of tennis players' emotional responses to pre-performance music', paper presented at European Federation of Sport Psychology Quadrennial Congress 2007, Halkidiki, Greece, 2007.
78 Gabrielsson, 'Emotions in strong experiences with music'; Menon and Levitin, 'The rewards of music listening'; Scherer, 'Which emotions can be induced by music? What are the underlying mechanisms? And how can we measure them?'
79 A. Goldstein, 'Thrill-producing effects of music', *Physiological Psychology*, 8, 1980, 126–129.
80 A. R. Halpern and R. J. Zatorre, 'When that tune runs through your head: A PET investigation of auditory imagery for familiar melodies', *Cerebral Cortex*, 9, 1999, 697–704.
81 See T. Baumgartner, K. Lutz, C. F. Schmidt and L. Jäncke, 'The emotional power of music: how music enhances the feeling of affective pictures', *Brain Research*, 1075, 2006, 151–164.
82 Bishop, Wright and Karageorghis, 'Neurophysiological correlates of tennis players' emotional responses to pre-performance music'; Koelsch, Fritz, von Cramon, Müller and Friederici, 'Investigating emotion with music'.
83 See F. Baumgart, T. Kaulisch, K. Tempelmann, B. Gaschler-Markefski, C. Tegeler,

F. Schindler, D. Stiller and H. Scheich, 'Electrodynamic headphones and woofers for application in magnetic resonance imaging scanners', *Medical Physics*, 25, 1998, 2068–2070.

84 Bishop, Wright and Karageorghis, 'Neurophysiological correlates of tennis players' emotional responses to pre-performance music'; D. T. Bishop, E. Z. Ross and C. I. Karageorghis, 'Corticospinal excitability and motor neuron recruitment as a function of pre-performance music listening', unpublished manuscript, 2008.

85 The Health and Safety Executive, *The Control of Noise at Work Regulations*, London: The Stationery Office Limited, 2005.

4 Music and figure skating

Glenn S. Harman, Sonia Bianchetti Garbato and David Forberg

Figure skating is one of the few competitive sports in which music currently forms a part of every phase of competition. In fact, among sports that are contested at the Olympic level, only rhythmic gymnastics and synchronised swimming share this distinction. Therefore, figure skating bridges the gap between sport and art in a relatively unique way.

This chapter will discuss the use of music and skaters' interpretation of music in figure skating. The history of the incorporation of music into skating will be traced from its first recorded use in the mid-nineteenth century to its gradual incorporation into competitive and exhibition skating. A historical overview of competitive skating will note the gradual shift from tracing figures on ice with no music to today's emphasis on free skating, which is judged not only for its technical merit, but also for its presentation and artistry, features that are dependent on the relationship of the skating moves to the music. A discussion of the evolution of the judging of artistry will include the various attempts to make this a more objective process. The appropriate selection of music and choreography for competition will be examined, including the factors used to pick music for a specific skater and the characteristics of music that should affect choreography. Examples of especially effective uses of music in competitive skating will be given, followed by an overview of the music selections used by world and Olympic champions and an analysis of the musical genres most frequently represented.

Although the use of music to accompany skating is a relatively recent development, skating on ice began in prehistoric times – the first skates were likely bones attached to the feet or to primitive shoes. The use of skates as a means of transportation in cold climates has long been quite important, leading to the development of more advanced and efficient combinations of blades and shoes or boots. The first published report of skating to music was in 1864. That year, Frank Swift and Marvin Clark published a book entitled *Skater's Text Book*, which mentioned waltzing to music as a single skater and the art of 'toe dancing' on ice.[1] By 1865, the *New York Times* had published accounts of the popularity of skating on ponds in New York, with music accompanying public skating.[2] However, it took the ingenuity and foresight of a very skilled and artistic man to bring skating to music into the public consciousness.

The American, Jackson Haines (1840–1875), became skating's first international figure. Although he developed many of his ideas and techniques in America, it was in Europe that his skating gained widespread acclaim and caught the imagination of the people. With his artistic style, Haines skated in exhibitions all over Europe. Advertisements exist from as early as 1865 that mention his use of music in his programmes. He founded the Viennese 'school of skating', the ancestor of current international styles, and clearly established himself as the person most responsible for launching the widespread use of music in skating, especially dance music.[3]

Speed skating competitions took place for hundreds of years before any figure skating competitions began. Races on canals in northern Europe were famous as far back as the Renaissance period. Figure skating competitions began in the second half of the nineteenth century. Initially, such competition was usually held as part of a speed skating competition. The competition involved tracing figures on ice without music and with none of the moves commonly used in competitive skating today. In more modern times, figures would become largely based on variations of the figure eight. But in the beginning, very ornate figures were required of competitors, with variations of the cursive letter 'Q' being especially popular. 'Special figures' became a popular feature of competition somewhat later. These were figures that were original to each competitor, allowing the competitors to show more creativity and difficulty in their tracings on the ice.[4]

Over the span of only a few decades, competitions in figures became much more popular, and national and international competitions began. The first European Championship occurred in 1891 and the International Skating Union (ISU) was formed a year later.[5] Although reorganised on numerous occasions, this ISU was the precursor of the international body that governs international competition in both speed skating and figure skating today. In 1896, the sport held its first World Championship[6] with only four male competitors. Beginning in 1897, competitions included both figures and free skating, but at first free skating scores contributed only a small percentage to the outcome. In 1902 the first woman, Madge Syers of Great Britain, entered the World Championship, but as there was only one competition, she was competing against men. In 1906, the first ladies' competition was held that was a form of 'world championship', but it was not given the same status as the men's competition. Only the winner of the men's competition was actually considered a 'world champion'.[7] In 1908, a pairs' event was added to international competition. Pairs' skating had grown out of two nineteenth-century concepts: 'combined figures', where two skaters would do figures together and 'hand-in-hand skating'. At that time, pairs' skating bore more resemblance to today's ice dancing than to today's pairs' competition.[8] Ice dancing as a separate discipline was only added to the World Championships in 1952. Figure skating first became an Olympic sport in 1908. In 1908 and again in 1920, figure skating was part of the Summer Olympics. A separate Winter Olympics began in 1924. Since that date, figure skating competition for men, ladies and pairs has been part of every Winter Olympics, with ice dancing added in 1976.

Competitive skating was slow to recognise the increased audience appeal of interpreting music while skating. Even when free skating became part of the competition, music was inconsistently used for several years. Also, for the first several decades of competition, when music was played during free skating, it was not chosen by the skater and the skater had no advance knowledge of which music would play while he or she skated. Therefore, the skater was neither required nor expected to interpret the music that was playing.

For much of the twentieth century, the skater's final score was determined 60 per cent from figures and 40 per cent from free skating. In 1967 the ISU changed the weighting to 50 per cent each.[9] The move to decrease the judging impact of traced figures was based on the realization that free skating with music was much more popular with audiences. Figures, in fact, had always been very difficult for a spectator to appreciate, because the judging process required close inspection of thin tracings on the ice. Also, as ice time for practice became more expensive and even harder to find, the hours required to practice figures at the competitive level became harder to justify.

The move to decrease the importance of figures in the judging process was largely spearheaded by Sonia Bianchetti Garbato, who was, at that time, chairman of the ISU's Figure Skating Technical Committee. In 1973, the importance of free skating was further increased with the addition of a 'technical programme' or 'short programme'.[10] This programme consisted of seven or eight required elements. While each competitor skated the same basic elements, it was each skater's responsibility to select music for this programme and choreograph those elements into a programme that also made artistic sense. So, for the first time, there were three phases of competition: figures; the short programme with required elements; and the longer free programme created by the skater. The free programme has always had certain expectations, restrictions and parameters, but it is largely the time where the skater is allowed to show his unique technical and artistic abilities.

After 1973, the importance of figures in competition continued to decline. The number of figures required in each competition gradually decreased, as did the percentage of the total score that was contributed by the figures score. Finally, in 1991, figures were completely omitted from international competitions and relatively few national championships around the world have included figures since that time.[11] Consequently, since 1991, all phases of competition at the international level have involved skating to music.

From the beginning of competitive figure skating, subjectivity always played a role in judging because of the difficulty of objectively quantifying the quality of any element of a skater's performance. For many years each phase of competition was judged by giving marks on a scale from 0.0 to 6.0. The short programme and the free programme were judged with two marks given by each judge. The first mark rewarded technical ability. The second mark, called 'artistic impression' or 'presentation', was the only mark influenced by the skater's use of music. The two marks were weighted equally in determining the total score given to each skater by a given judge. A complex system involving ordinal placements for each skater was used to obtain the final ranking of the skaters. Guidelines were in place to help the judges assign a value for the first and second marks. In judging the programme's artistry (the second mark), these guidelines were, perhaps necessarily, nebulous. This allowed for a wide range of interpretation of these guidelines and, therefore, it seemed quite easy to defend almost any artistic mark for a given skater. This practice often resulted in corruption, especially in international competitions where nationalism and collusion among judges became commonplace.

At the 2002 Winter Olympics in Salt Lake City, a huge judging scandal erupted when deals were made to fix the results of both the pairs' and ice dancing competitions. The ISU reacted to this crisis of credibility by developing a totally new way of assigning scores to skaters' performances. The goal was to make the system more objective and, therefore, less susceptible to manipulation by dishonest judges. However, there still remain numerous ways in which this system is subjective.

The technical merit of a programme is now judged element by element, with each jump, spin or footwork sequence assigned a base point value. Judges may add or subtract from the base value of each element by grading its quality (Grades of Execution). Judging of the artistry of a programme now falls under a concept called 'Programme Component Scores'. These, as a group, are meant to take the place of the former 'artistic impression' or 'presentation' scores. Each of the programme component scores has a range of possible values from 0 to 10. For all phases of competition in all four disciplines (except for the compulsory dance phase of ice dance), there are five programme component scores:[12]

1   Skating skills: this assesses the quality of execution of the very basics of skating, such as stroking, crossovers and basic turns.
2   Transitions/linking footwork/movements: this score assesses the quality of all parts of the programme that are not part of a technical element. The difficulty of these moves enters into the assessment of this mark.
3   Performance/execution: these are quite nebulous terms that, it would seem, could be included in the other programme component score categories, and even the technical scores. The manner in which the skater translates the intent of the music and choreography impacts on this mark.
4   Composition/choreography: this score is based on the quality of the programme from the standpoint of all the moves, both technical elements and otherwise, in regards to how well they fit with the music to form an artistic work.
5   Interpretation/timing: this score looks at the ability of the skater to express the meaning of the music in his or her skating. By evaluating 'timing', the judges are looking for the ability of the skater to fit the moves to the rhythm of the music.

Items three, four and five in the list are the three categories of scoring that are most affected by the skater's ability to use music to enhance the artistry and quality of a programme. Each judge enters a score for each of these five categories. Current judges and upcoming judges are being rigorously trained in what to look for in each of these categories. Nonetheless, there has already been significant reason to question whether the programme component scores represent any major improvement over the single score given for 'artistic impression' in the former '6.0' system. They remain almost totally subjective, and the vague nature of their terminology allows for a wide range of interpretation from the judges. Since this wide range of interpretation is so easy to defend, it allows the unscrupulous or inappropriately nationalistic judge to play with the marks to affect the outcome. However, to counter this possibility, the ISU now randomly selects by computer a subset of the presiding judges at an event whose scores will actually count. This is done so that no one knows which scores are determining the outcome. It remains to be seen whether this judging system will have the desired outcome of producing a more objectively reproducible result in a competition, and whether it will prevent collusion, nationalism and other forms of dishonest judging from affecting the outcome of competitions.

The only exception that eliminates creative interpretation to music from the five judging categories above occurs in ice dancing. The compulsory dance, the first of the three competitive phases of ice dancing, involves each couple performing the same dance steps to the same piece of music (or sometimes, to avoid audience boredom, to one of a few pieces of music with identical tempo and rhythm). Therefore, anything to do with choreography cannot be judged, and judges mark the following four programme component scores: skating skills, performance, interpretation and timing.[13]

Music, therefore, is a crucial part of all phases of competition. The interpretation of music through harmonious and elegant movements is crucial to the success of the programme. The choice of music must enhance the skater's personality, talent and technical ability. The music must allow originality and innovation. Keeping these factors in mind, the choice of music becomes one of the most important decisions in developing a programme. The music must fit the time limits, which vary by discipline, by level of competition and by phase of competition. The music selected may be one piece of music or different pieces that blend together. The latter concept is useful to allow changes of tempo and mood within the programme. In choosing the music, it is important for competitors to remember that the judges may represent different cultures, countries, ages and tastes. This fact makes it wise to avoid overly experimental music choices that might be unpleasant to some judges. Of note, at the present time, only ice dancing allows music with voices singing recognisable lyrics. All disciplines may use music where the voice is used as an instrument but not singing actual words.

After selecting the music, choreography of the programme is the next major undertaking. Each movement, gesture and position must be inspired by, and be compatible with, the music. Movements of the entire body should reflect the tempo and mood of the music. Technical elements should enhance rather than detract from the whole choreographic concept. They should be placed in parts of the musical selection that make musical sense. A good example of this would be placing a particularly big jump on a major climax in the music.

Many characteristics of a piece of music should be carefully considered when approaching the concept of skating choreography. Each of these, and especially changes in each of these, should bring about specific choreographic thoughts. All are crucial, and various ones may have relatively more importance in different music selections:

1   Tempo of the music is an obvious feature that determines much about the choreography. The steps, arm movements and changes in body position should all reflect the tempo of the music. An exciting programme often includes at least a couple of changes in tempo. For years, skaters commonly constructed a programme with three parts – a fast section, then a slow section, then another fast section. While many variations of this are now considered, this is still popular. It is also possible for a programme to be immensely successful with almost no changes in tempo. One special example is the free dance of Jayne Torvill and Christopher Dean for the 1983–1984 competitive season to the music of Maurice Ravel's *Bolero*. Since the tempo did not change, this outstanding programme is also a great example of the importance of paying attention to the other characteristics of the music.

2   In planning choreography, the skater and choreographer must also be very aware of the dynamics of the music and, especially, changes in dynamics. Some skaters define this as the 'energy' of the music, but musicians usually think of the differences in loudness as the 'dynamics'. There are many ways to interpret the dynamics with movements. Softer passages can be shown with smaller or more introspective moves. These should never be viewed as less important. Soft passages of many musical compositions are thrilling, and a good skating programme should be able to convey this. As dynamic levels grow louder, the movements should reflect this change by growing bigger and more demonstrative. Particularly big and climactic moments should get special attention with accented moves.

3   Changes in the pitch of the music should also be considered for choreographic importance. For example, dramatic upward or downward flourishes give the skater opportunities to add specific movements that reflect and enhance the feel of the music.

4   Within a piece of music with a certain tempo, the duration of the notes is an important feature that can change the feel of different musical passages. For example, a passage of quarter and half notes would have a totally different feel from a run of sixteenth notes at the same tempo. Change in the duration of notes is obviously a way that the piece can have the feel of speeding up or slowing down, while the actual tempo may be steady.

5   The key in which a piece of music is written, which can also have a huge impact on the feel of the music, is another feature that should be carefully considered in interpretation. The simplest concept to consider here is the

difference between major and minor keys. Major keys will often give the music a happy or upbeat feel, while minor keys often convey a sinister, sad or gloomy mood.

6   The final feature to consider is the complexity of tones or voices in the music. A piece of music may have only one melody or voice with sparse or no accompaniment. This would be far less complex than a piece with numerous countermelodies or obligato parts and a full, rich accompaniment. In that less complex situation, the skater would largely focus on the solo melody to determine the interpretation desired. In the more complex situation mentioned, there may be several things to consider before deciding on the choreography. One could again fit the moves and footwork to the main melody, or one could skate in a way to bring out a countermelody or even the rhythm of the accompaniment.

With the recent increase in complexity and difficulty of moves required to construct a competitive programme, the attention of skaters to choreographic detail has often been quite inadequate. Emphasis on speed and performance of technical elements has led many skaters to largely ignore the music that they themselves have selected. All too frequently, one has the feeling that the skaters would do the identical programme regardless of the music playing. Many people closely involved in the sport are bemoaning that fact and trying to find ways to improve the artistic side of skating.

To accomplish an artistic programme, the skater must first find the piece of music, keeping in mind the appropriateness of the piece for that skater, as discussed earlier. The best choice for one skater will change dramatically as the skater's age, maturity and ability changes. A ten-year-old may look fabulous skating to a children's song, while ten years later, the same skater might be best served with a dramatic, classical orchestral work. Often skaters choose music from a movie soundtrack that may be associated with a certain story or character. There may be costume or choreographic choices that are based on the character or story to be portrayed. Certainly, this often occurs with classical music as well. For example, the skater could portray a character from an opera or ballet. All too often, the competitive skater puts on the costume but does very little else to interpret the music.

Once this choice of music has been made, the skater, coach and choreographer must carefully listen to the music many times, being sure that the skater understands what the piece is about. The skater should be asked to demonstrate knowledge of the characteristics of the music that will be expressed in the choreography. The skater must be able to show where the tempo, duration of notes, pitch, dynamics, complexity and key of the music change. Then, when choreography is planned around these changes, the skater must be constantly aware of the music, and should be reminded as necessary to fit the mood and moves of the choreography to the music.

To best demonstrate successful use of choreography, some especially successful programmes from high levels of competition will be cited to illustrate all the various elements. In these examples, skaters were further along in their skating careers and at a point where they had truly mastered the artistic side of skating. But skaters of every level should carefully observe these and other successful programmes as often as possible to learn from them. Most of them are easily obtainable commercially in video recordings. Increasingly, they can be observed by links from various skating web sites. They are discussed here in chronological order.

In the late 1960s and early 1970s, one of the most artistic female skaters of all time thrilled worldwide audiences with her outstanding technical prowess and, especially, her ability to interpret every nuance of her music. Janet Lynn won several national championships in the United States, and also several world and Olympic medals, although none were gold. Her career was somewhat

Figure 4.1 Janet Lynn (photograph reproduced by courtesy of Janet Lynn).

hampered by her lesser ability in the tracing of compulsory figures, which lowered her overall scores. Perhaps her most memorable programme was her long programme from the 1973 competitive season to Claude Debussy's *Prélude à l'Après-midi d'un Faune*, choreographed by her coach, Slavka Kahout. Technical moves, especially jumps, flowed effortlessly out of connecting moves. What was even more memorable was her use of every subtle movement of her body, including facial expressions, to make the audience experience every beautiful and joyful moment of this music. She paid careful attention to the slightest tempo changes and made exquisite use of the sweeping upward and downward runs in this gorgeous melody.

Easily among the most artistic skaters of all time were the ice dancers Jayne Torvill and Christopher Dean of Great Britain. Christopher, with help from Jayne and their coach Betty Calloway, was responsible for almost all of their choreography. Their highly successful amateur career in the late 1970s and early 1980s culminated in four world titles and one Olympic title. Almost all of their competitive programmes could be used as examples of skating choreography at its best. But three of their programmes showed especially interesting choreographic concepts. In their free dance from the 1981–1982 season they skated to the overture from Jerry Herman's musical *Mack and Mabel*. The original overture was only shortened slightly to fit the required time of four minutes and nothing else was altered. With their artistic skills, this programme became a great example of interpreting virtually an entire musical composition that contained numerous changes of tempo and mood. In this case they were also portraying the two lead characters of this musical. Famous for making incredibly difficult dance footwork look effortless, Torvill and Dean were also known for innovative choreographic moves. One example was their interpretation of a train slowing down in this *Mack and Mabel* routine.

In the 1983–1984 competitive season, the original-set-pattern dance (that period's version of what is now the 'original dance') was the Paso Doble. Each couple devised their own Paso Doble to appropriate music of their own selection. The Paso Doble is a Spanish dance where the man is portraying a matador in a bullfight and the woman is portraying his cape. Torvill and Dean chose costumes that especially highlighted this concept, as Jayne looked very much like a cape when her arms were outstretched. As befits the Paso Doble, their choreography made the man the centre of attention. Highlights included a move where he appears to be dragging his cape (Jayne) and a move at the end where he flings his cape to the ice. They further heightened the mood by entering and leaving the ice with Jayne positioned behind Chris in such a way as to accent her appearance as his cape.

The third Torvill and Dean programme of special choreographic merit was the free dance to Maurice Ravel's *Bolero* mentioned earlier. This composition has no tempo changes at all, but the intensity and dynamic level grow steadily from beginning to end. From this much longer work, they used four minutes that accentuated the gradual growth in the dramatic quality of the music. Their choreography began with a romantic set of upper body dance moves done with

Figure 4.2 Jayne Torvill and Christopher Dean (© J. Barry Mittan).

them both on their knees. As the music came to its climax at the end, Chris did a series of rapid turns while flinging Jayne around him. He then released her as they both slid onto the ice in a final dramatic pose. This programme, and especially its final moves, produced what many consider the most unforgettable moments of their incredible career.

In 1988, Brian Boitano won the United States Championship for the fourth time, the World Championship for the second time, and the Olympic gold medal. For the 1987–1988 competitive season, he teamed with his coach, Linda Leaver, and choreographer Sandra Bezic to produce two of the best choreographic concepts in competitive skating history in his short and long programmes. But it was the short programme, skated to Giacomo Meyerbeer's composition *Les Patineurs* (*The Skaters*), which should be remembered as a true masterpiece. The choreography to this nineteenth-century waltz composition was intended to depict the skating of that period. Boitano was dressed in a formal-looking black outfit with a white ruffled shirt. From beginning to end, the programme contained poses inspired by what is known of Jackson Haines and other skaters of the period. At one point he removed the accumulated snow from his skate blade and flipped it over his shoulder. He also did a two-foot footwork sequence called the 'grapevine', which was popular with nineteenth-century skaters. This move involved intertwining the pattern his feet made on the ice to resemble a grapevine. Throughout even the technical elements of this programme, Boitano maintained the character that he presented initially with his opening pose.

Also in 1988, Katarina Witt of the German Democratic Republic ended the major phase of her competitive career with her fourth world title and second Olympic gold medal. Her short programme that season, choreographed by her coach Jutta Mueller, was skated to a medley of music from three Jerry Herman musicals: *Hello, Dolly, La Cage aux Folles* and *No No, Nanette*. Her costuming and personality in the character of a showgirl made this programme a success, but it was the ending footwork sequence that made this programme unforgettable. The music here was 'I Want to Be Happy' from *No No, Nanette* and included the sounds of tap-dancing. Her footwork was brilliantly choreographed to fit every beat of the music and there were moments where she appeared to be tap-dancing on the ice. Unlike the construction of most short programmes, this footwork was the final element of the programme, culminating at one end of the ice with a flourish into the final pose. This surprising ending added to the appeal of this captivating programme.

A male skater who showed a wonderful feel for music throughout his career was Alexei Yagudin of Russia. His competitive success included four World Championships and the Olympic gold medal in 2002. His programmes of the 2002 season are great examples of what made him successful. His short programme was to *Winter* by Bond, and his long programme was to the soundtrack of the movie *The Man in the Iron Mask*. Both programmes were choreographed by Tatiana Tarasova and Nikolai Morozov. Yagudin was a master at drawing the audience into his programmes. He clearly felt the emotion of every beat and nuance of his music, and maximum energy was put into not only the technical elements but also each slight choreographic move. This was always most evident in his incredibly fast footwork sequences. The outgoing personality that was so much on display in his skating made him a major favourite of fans worldwide.

One of the most memorable moments in skating history was the long programme of Xue Shen and Hongbo Zhao of China at the 2003 World Championships in Washington, DC. They had missed most of the competitive season due to an injury that Xue Shen had suffered. Even during those World Championships, it was questionable up to the moment of skating each programme whether she could continue. Since they had competed so infrequently that season, very few skating fans or judges had seen their programmes. Their long programme was set to Vanessa-Mae's *Fantasy for Violin and Orchestra* on themes from Giacomo Puccini's opera *Turandot*, and it was masterfully choreographed by Lea Ann Miller. The arena had a feeling of great anticipation as these reigning world champions took the ice. Perhaps never have any skaters seized a big moment as they did. The programme exuded phenomenal energy and emotion from the opening move. As they continued to execute each technical element to perfection, the energy and emotion from them and the audience continued to escalate. Despite incredibly difficult elements, every moment of the programme enhanced the grace, beauty and drama of Puccini's great music. This programme was a true work of art. The way everything came together to create this atmosphere made this truly one of the best examples of the excitement that

Figure 4.3 Xue Shen and Hongbo Zhao (© J. Barry Mittan).

the competitive sport and art of figure skating can create. Nearly everyone in the arena was standing and cheering well before the final pose. There are many serious skating fans who have gone so far as to call this 'skating's greatest moment'.

Compared to the skaters mentioned above, Stephanie Rosenthal of the United States is less well-known. However, her short programme for the United States National Championships in 2006 was a choreographic masterpiece, choreographed by the skater herself and her coach Stephanee Groscup to 'Rockit' by Herbie Hancock. Off the ice, she was a big fan of hip-hop music. She took her love and knowledge of this music and dance form to the ice. This dance form uses rather rapid, angular and somewhat jerky movements and is very rhythmic. Rosenthal's programme became one of the best examples of picking a style of choreography and sticking to it completely for every second of the programme. Notably, her commitment to this style carried through all of the technical elements as well. The spiral sequence, spins, footwork and even jump landings all included the body positions, movements and facial expressions typical of this dance genre. This programme also demonstrated that, given the required understanding of the music and the dance, a very modern musical composition and style can be quite successfully used to create a competitive programme.

While the best piece of music for competition is totally dependent on the individual skater and factors discussed above, it is interesting to consider which musical styles have led to successful competitive programmes. Table 4.1 shows a breakdown by musical genres of the programmes of world and Olympic champions from 1988 through 2007. The short and long programme music is included for single skaters and pairs. Only the free dance music for ice dancers is included because both the compulsory and original dance segments are prescribed selections. If a programme of mixed music has one clearly predominant genre, the programme is classified under that predominant genre. Only those that are such a mix that there is no predominance are listed as 'mixed'. Obviously, a wide variety of music has been successfully used. Among the opera selections, Puccini operas, especially *Turandot*, and Bizet's *Carmen* have been most frequently used. The other classical programmes have included a wide range of compositions and composers. However, Rachmaninoff's Piano Concerti no. 2 and no. 3 and his *Rhapsody on a Theme of Paganini* have been used quite often. The competitors in men's single skating have clearly used the most movie soundtracks, usually from action movies. Men have also most frequently used popular or modern music.[14]

This chapter has intentionally dealt mostly with the competitive field of figure skating. However, exhibition and show skating continue to be types of skating very familiar to a wide range of audiences. During exhibitions, skaters

Table 4.1 Musical selections used in world and Olympic gold medal programmes (1988–2007)

	Ladies	Men	Pairs	Dance	Total
Popular/Modern	7	13	10	3	33
Classical (Total)					
Opera	5	5	7	3	20
Ballet	2	1	5	0	8
Other	189	10	20	7	56
Musical Theatre	3	0	1	2	6
Movie soundtracks	6	18	3	6	33
Dance/ethnic	4	2	4	4	14
Mixed (none dominant)	0	1	2	0	3
Unavailable	6	2	2	1	11
Total	52	52	54*	26	214

Note
*Higher total for pairs due to duplicate gold medals at 2002 Olympics.

are not being judged and therefore have far fewer restrictions on music choices and choreography. Technical elements are not required in any specific number, so the programmes can consist mostly of moves chosen for the sense they make in interpreting the music. Moves and vocal music that are illegal in competition can also be incorporated to enhance the creative programme. The best artists in the sport have created some of their true masterpieces in this environment. Some skaters with relatively unsuccessful competitive careers can become quite popular through this more artistic side of the sport. On the other hand, skaters who have little musical sense as competitive skaters are often much less successful as exhibition or show skaters. Many musical concepts have been successfully used in exhibitions and shows. This has included exhibitions of well-known skaters each doing a number completely of his or her own choosing, or each doing a number to fit into a theme for the entire show. Also, musical theatre productions, ballets and circus acts have been transferred to the ice very successfully.

Watching figure skating can be a very exciting experience, not just due to the difficulty of the elements executed, but also for the fascinating, captivating and appealing art form that it can be. Many competitors can execute good and well-choreographed programmes, highlighted by difficult and spectacular elements, but only a few are able to transform the programme into a piece of art that we would like to watch over and over. For great skaters, the jumps, spins, lifts, footwork and choreographic moves become the instrument through which they express the music. The truly great skater will not be remembered for the number of jumps executed in their programme, but rather for their personality, their originality, the way they move on the ice, the emotion they are able to transmit to the audience and for having set a path in the sport that others will want to follow. These are concepts that make this sport unique and magical.

Notes

1 James R. Hines, *Figure Skating: A History*, Urbana and Chicago, IL: University of Illinois Press, 2006, pp. 45–46.
2 Ibid., p. 47.
3 Ibid., pp. 51–53.
4 Ibid., pp. 70–71.
5 Lynn Copley-Graves, *Figure Skating History: The Evolution of Dance on Ice*, Columbus, OH: Platoro Press, 1992, p. 12.
6 Michael Boo, *The Story of Figure Skating*, New York: William Morrow and Company, 1998, p. 22.
7 Hines, *Figure Skating*, pp. 87–88.
8 Copley-Graves, *Figure Skating History*, p. 22.
9 Hines, *Figure Skating*, p. 197.
10 Ibid., p. 207.
11 Ibid., p. 234.
12 International Skating Union, 'ISU new judging system-program components overview'. Online, available at www.isu.org/vsite/vfile/page/fileurl/0,11040,4844-152077-169293-64120-0-file,00.pdf.
13 Ibid.
14 Skate Music List. Online, available at www.skatemusiclist.com.

5   The energy of festivity

Atmosphere, intonation and self-orchestration in Danish popular sports

Henning Eichberg

Popular sports in Denmark have been referred to by a Swedish sociologist as follows:

> In Denmark, they have a type of sport that they call *folkelig* ('popular'). It is difficult to understand what it is, and I myself never really understood it. But if you hear people starting with a song, this must be *folkelig* sport.[1]

The sociologist made an important point. You can 'hear' Danish popular sport – and maybe, folk sport more generally is an audible phenomenon.

When analytically approaching the field of sport, singing and intonation, one may get help from another quotation from the field of Danish popular sport: 'Folk der mødes skaber energi' ('Folk in meeting create energy'). This is what 20,000 people were singing continuously at the national festival of Danish gymnastics and sports in 2002, the so-called *landsstævne* that was arranged on the Baltic island of Bornholm. The tune was the refrain of the official festival song, launched by DGI, the organisation of Danish *folkelig* (i.e. popular) sports and Sport for All. After several days, the tune became familiar to the participants: 'Folk in meeting create energy....'

The keyword 'energy' may help us towards a cultural analysis of festivity and festival in sports. For this analysis, five researchers from the University of Southern Denmark joined the sports festival in 2002. The *landsstævne* is regarded as a central expression of Danish *folkelig* sports, originating from rifle tournaments and, later, mass gymnastics, nearly 150 years ago, and is arranged every fourth year at different places in the country. An in-depth analysis of the *landsstævne* was attempted: its time and space, its social relations and 'products' and its organisational and ideological superstructure.[2] Among these dimensions, there was, however, a sort of empty space – and this is what participants through decades described as the particular atmosphere of this festival, its 'energy'. It is this that is the focus of the following observations and reflections.

The word 'energy' in the festival song seems at first sight (or first hearing) to be the usual pop-poetical metaphor for expressing simply something positive, effective and impressive. 'Energy' also has ideological and rhetorical signification of something 'magic'. This refrain refers to landscape and light as sources towards which to turn for inter-human relations:

> Meeting, sun and water
> Create together
> Magic light, which is only on Bornholm.
> Golden glowing fire.
> The sea is hitting against the rocks.
> People who meet create energy.[3]

The song records in short sketches different people being 'pulled into the stream and becoming part of something larger'. Further nuances of this 'energy' are expressed in the 'movement song' (Bevægelsessangen) that is often sung by people of DGI sports and of Danish people's academies or 'folk high schools' (folkehøjskoler):

> There is a power in the soul
> An eternal energy
> Which grows in the web of thinking
> In the enchantment of love
> It turns up and down what you believe you know and want
> And shows you your face in a magic play of masks.[4]

In this song 'energy' is implied in a more bodily sense. It is something with soul and power – with rhythm and swing, desire and love, with the living word connecting human beings. It points towards body cultural techniques like dance, play and game, singing and festivity.

If one takes the bodily contents of 'energy' seriously, the word touches a dimension that tends to escape analytical attention, attention that normally focuses on the body in space and time. Space and time is what we measure in sports, not energy. Social science goes in the same direction when analysing human movement or other cultural phenomena in space and time – and again there is something important missing. Thus, festivity can be described as an assembly of human beings in space and time, following certain purposes and organised in certain social relations. And yet, what is its atmosphere? There is something missing even if we keep to the purely physical level. It is this missing dimension that the concept of 'energy' both inside and outside physics tries to catch.

In general, the concept of energy refers to 'the potential for causing changes'. In physics, energy is the ability to do work and has many different forms (potential, kinetic, electromagnetic, etc.) No matter what its form, physical energy has the same units as work; a force applied through a distance. Furthermore,

> energy is a fundamental quantity that every physical system possesses; it allows us to predict how much work the system could be made to do, or

how much heat it can produce or absorb. Basically, if something changes, some sort of energy was involved in that change.[5]

Besides the world of physics, where energy was established as basic term after 1800, 'energy' has also become a concept in psychology: what is the human potential of change and what makes people work or behave? So there is good reason not to take the 'energy' of the festival song only as rhetorical metaphor, but to listen to the psychological and bodily history it is telling us: about a special atmosphere or mood, something that 'streams' through the participants and at the same time causes a certain 'swing' for the individual. There is also a connection with what in popular sports is called 'soul on fire' (ildsjæl) which means active people with strong motivations inhabiting the milieu of popular sports and 'burning for something'. 'Stream', 'swing', 'fire' and 'burning (for)' – all these are connected with each other by picturing the world of 'energy'.

More than a rhetorical metaphor: bodily qualities of energy

'Energy' describes, then, an individual as well as an inter-individual intensity. It is especially this quality of inter-being (mellemværende) that makes the concept difficult to understand and to handle in cultural and social analysis. Energy withdraws from the handling 'hand' and from the 'grip' of our space–time terminology. The concept of energy is a searching term that goes beyond narrow space–time rationality.

In the analysis of body culture, the term 'energy' has been applied in various theoretical explorations of movement practice. 'Energy' can be found in the dance theory of Rudolf von Laban, the expressionistic instructor and theorist of movement in the 1920s. Laban introduced the concept of energy into the description of bodily movement. In his theory, 'force' and 'flow' were further phenomena besides – or inside – space and time. 'Dynamic energy' and 'concentrated energy clusters', as he called them, had their effects in the structure of movement.[6]

In the world of theatre, Eugenio Barba and the 'theatre anthropology' of Odin Teatret used the concept of energy. What Barba called 'the energy of the actor' was characterised as a physical quality, unfolding on an elementary level preceding its explicit expression. Energy in this understanding is 'pre-expressive', being developed in connection with vibration and rhythm, with techniques of balance working against gravity and deforming the normality of everyday movements with energy-concentrated breaks and with the actor's 'presence' on the scene. The understanding of energy in theatre anthropology was inspired by East Asian body techniques such as Chinese kung fu and Japanese No theatre.[7]

Indeed, East Asian practices have, through the centuries, used body cultural concepts of energy. In the Tibetan tradition, Xi is the origin of the world that is revealed by energy. In Chinese tai chi, chi gong and other systems of movement and traditional medicine, the force of chi or ki is worked upon by poetical body exercises. The concept of chi refers at the same time to life energy, to the breathing of the human being and to wind and air. The body is thought of as a system of energy channels, meridians whose streams of energy can be influenced by movement practices.[8]

Eastern inspirations entered also into the school of psychoanalysis during its 'bodily turn'. In contrast to Sigmund Freud – who used the terms 'psychic energy' and 'mental energy' in a non-bodily way, later followed by C. G. Jung – Wilhelm Reich developed a theory and therapeutic practice which was directed towards 'body armour', breathing, orgasm and sexual energy. Later, Reich also reflected about what he called 'orgon energy'.[9]

With body-oriented psychoanalysis, feelings and emotions enter the picture. Inside the sociology of emotions, terms like 'flow' and 'stress' have attracted attention. Flow describes a holistic feeling where the human being, without conscious intervention, nevertheless feels control over a situation or action. Flow wipes out the limits between self and environment.[10] Flow is discussed in connection with intensity, self-transgression and high-sensation seeking with an experience of wholeness, focus and universe while the contrasting experience of stress is characterised by emotive struggle, boiling over and blocking up. All this has energetic undertones.[11]

The analysis of emotions is always in danger of derailing into directions that conceal the diversity of the emotional world. A typical temptation is to apply some sort of dualistic pattern, for instance understanding flow as a good feeling versus stress that is seen as bad. Another variant consists of some sort of system construction, typically built as an axial field between four poles. Both intellectual strategies are characteristic of Western thinking. The world of emotions is, however, much more complex, as recent philosophical studies of emotions and virtues have shown.[12]

Nevertheless, in the context of body culture, the concepts of feelings and emotions are not without problems. The use of 'emotion' with its 'individual' undertones does not always hit what more social concepts like energy and atmosphere express. The discourse of 'feeling' tends to narrow analysis towards an individualistic understanding of the single human being and its subjectivity. It is the individual that feels, thinks, expresses or acts according to certain emotions. The concept of feeling as related to the individual has, therefore, difficulties in grasping the inter-individual. This requires a deeper analysis, which takes the inter-personal and in this respect the trans-personal dimensions of energy seriously.[13] This is what has been touched on by some studies of shamanism, ecstasy and possession states.[14] Research has even tried to use electroencephalographic technologies (EEG) to register 'unusual states of conscience' in connection with electric currents in the brain.[15]

The neuro-physiology of phenomena like musicogenic epilepsy has also included the energetic dimension. Music can have effects on individuals who may break down in spasms, lose conciousness, experience daydreams and move in violent convulsions.[16] There do exist strong empirical relations between music, bodily movement and bodily sensitivity, which are, however, theoretically far from being resolved.

Studies in the effects of drumming have affirmed this connection, bridging the 'sick' reactions of individuals and 'normal' collective cultural techniques. Laboratory experiments show that drumming has effects on the central nervous system, with electrical activities in the brain, unusual sensual experiences and muscular spasms as consequences.[17] The bodily effects of drumming do not follow, however, in a mechanical way, but they depend of certain cultural dispositions and attitudes in relation to the drum and to 'possession'.

Thus energy describes physical and physiological phenomena which have seriously troubled Western rationality. It challenges the usual reduction of the physical world to 'space, time, materiality and causality'[18] (which dominated the criticism of Immanuel Kant[19] and the narrow materialism of Lenin[20]), a reduction that excluded the observation of energy.[21] Energy is not only inside the individual, but also between human beings. Energy constitutes, thus, a social–psychological 'aura'.[22] It is in this field between the physical and the psychical that music has its place, too.

There is – as already named – a further related term which describes the energy of a festivity, and which may lead us nearer to the bodily substratum of this concept. It is 'atmosphere'.[23] The Danish word for atmosphere is *stemning* (mood, humour, spirit), which is like the corresponding German term *Stimmung* derived from *stemme* (voice, or *Stimme* in German) and *at stemme* (to tune). These words are related to *stum* (silent, voiceless) and *at stamme* (to stammer). All this is related to a physical–psychical complex of intonation, where the bodily vocal expression plays together with emotional movement and social togetherness.[24]

Folkelig song in the sports festival

Aspects of atmosphere and intonation, the musical elements of the Danish sports festival, deserve closer examination: joint singing as a *folkelig* tradition, the music of gymnastics, the recent invasion of the rock concert and the significance of clapping.

Danish popular sport can be characterised as a singing movement. Joint singing is found in many collective situations, especially at the gymnastic *stævne*. The federation of Danish popular sport, DGI, has a songbook of its own.[25] The songbook is one of the few elements which unite the diverse activities in *folkelig* sports. It contains a broad range of genres: songs about seasons and times of the day, psalms, patriotic songs, songs about human life and love, historical tunes, folk ballads, children's songs, pop and rock songs and songs about community. It also includes English and international songs, from Nigerian folk and African-American spirituals to The Beatles. Songs from this book are used when official meetings of the organisation are opened by joint song – which is a customary procedure.

The national festival of popular sport in Denmark, *Landsstævne*, also has its own songbook.[26] Joint singing of the thousands of participants is a characteristic feature of this type of mass meeting. A specific festival song for each festival is composed by pop artists and serves as a mediated leitmotiv of the event. This 'hit' is also used as a joint song of the masses.

In the everyday life of local sport associations, there are many opportunities of singing together. This tradition has, however, decreased to some degree in recent years in which singing has been reduced to the more festive occasions. The annual club meetings often include joint singing and sometimes a revue, which uses satirical song and play to comment on the course of the year. Also, in the local associations of 'sport of the elderly' (ældreidræt) which have flourished in recent years, weekly meetings are often opened by a joint song, and people sing together during intervals in activities.[27]

The links between song and sports are permanently renewed through the influence of the people's academies or 'folk high schools' (folkehøjskole) which have close connections with popular sports.[28] It is here that singing has an educational dimension. Consequently, there is an audible difference between mainstream sport and popular sport in Denmark. The 'normal' type of sport, whether competitive or health-oriented, lacks singing. The other, the folkelig sport, sings. However, there is no clear line separating the one from the other.

When Danish folkelig sport appeared in the 1880s as a people's movement of gymnastics – being a part of the democratic farmers' movement – song culture was from the very beginning a characteristic feature. Popular gymnastics was originally linked to the institution of the people's academy and from that time on 'popular education' was marked by a triad, which consisted of joint song, lecture and gymnastics. Højskole education can, indeed, be characterised as a sort of singing education. The day's routines at a højskole usually begin with a morning assembly which includes singing and it is customary to open every lecture with: 'Let us sing number X.' The songbook of the people's academies (Folkehøjskolens sangbog) can be regarded as the foundation of the Danish people's academies.[29] Generally, the people's academies lack any codified written texts. This type of school is based on oral and practical traditions, not on 'the book'. The only exception is 'the blue book', the højskole songbook, which all people's academies, as different as they may be, have in common. Even the 'spirit of the founder', N. F. S. Grundtvig, is present – not so much through his theoretical writings, as by quotations from his songs which are passed on in Danish culture as a sort of humming poetry.[30]

Singing popular movements, singing democracy

The practice of singing together has roots in the culture of democracy. In the course of modern history, choral singing has often been linked with democratic movements, the French Revolution giving birth to the Marseillaise. Subsequently, this revolutionary song engendered a long series of national patriotic anthems on one hand and of democratic and revolutionary tunes on the other.[31] In Denmark, too, the early popular movements, whether religious or political, were singing movements. It has been suggested that the patriotic singing from nineteenth-century Denmark has 'defined the nation in song'.[32] This National

Romantic tradition is the source from which the *folkehøjskole* drew its 'singing craze': singing the nation – singing democracy.

What is special for the atmosphere and intonation of Danish democratic culture is that it had important roots in religious revivals. The Pietist farmers' movement from the early nineteenth century, which spread as an oppositional movement against the state church and against the Absolutist monarchy, let Christian psalms from the Protestant tradition enter into the song tradition of the national and cultural movements. This explains the strong position which Grundtvig's psalms have in *folkelig* songbooks. Later, the workers' movement developed a socialist song culture of a similar type. The workers created their own choirs, festivities and speaking choruses.[33] Some of this 'red' material was integrated into the repertoire of *højskole* songs in the 1970s and 1980s.

Another source of joint singing is the revue as it developed between the First and Second World War and after. Songs from revues and cabarets transported not only the critical contents of intellectual Cultural Radicalism, but also added new undertones of an ironic and light-hearted style. Since then, and under this influence, singing became more than the serious expression of psalms and national patriotic songs: it obtained elements of play and game, of improvisation and joking.

During the Second World War, serious elements emerged again when Danes met in large song rallies, starting in July 1940 after the Nazi occupation of the country (*alsang* or 'all-singing'). In a subversive but peaceful way, the singing Danes demonstrated against the occupant. It is estimated that at the largest all-singing rallies of 1 September 1940, more than 700,000 Danes joined to express their oppositional Danishness.[34] Danish *alsang* reminds us of what happened around 1990 in the Baltic countries, when huge song rallies contributed to the collapse of Soviet rule.[35]

Another wave of revitalisation came with rock songs from the Danish counterculture of the 1960s and 1970s. The ironic element was enforced again when song composers and poets like Benny Andersen, Piet Hein and Halfdan Rasmussen renewed *folkelig* songs. Jazz tones entered with Poul Dissing, rock rhythms with Kim Larsen and the anarcho-folk group Shu-bi-dua. The individual singers did not only translate new experiences into new song material, presenting this in a professional way 'onto the scene', but their songs are sung by ordinary people in schools, academies and associations as *fællessang*, as joint singing.[36] An important role was played by the people's movement against the European Community (later European Union), which rose in connection with the referendum of 1972. The broad opposition to this occurence gave important impulses to song culture.

In the light of these developments, choral singing appears as something like a bodily correlative to people's democracy.[37] By their voices, people establish bodily togetherness. They sing identity: 'We are the people!' They do not only allow others to sing for them, such as professionals on the scene, they sing themselves and together. The self-intonation of the people creates group cohesion and mobilisation.

At the same time, singing people express differences and inner contradictions. There is difference between what one sings and what one does not sing. Singing is not an automatic or 'organic' process, but a dialectical practice. Singing is an expression of cultural contradictions and diversity.

Gymnastic music, rock concert and clapping – rhythmic self-hypnosis

Let us return to the festival, the Danish *landsstævne*. Besides joint singing, the music of gymnastics plays an important role. The music of gymnastics started in the field of female gymnastics at the women's academy in Snoghøj during the 1930s. The gymnastic music, which at that time had accompaniment by piano, became, however, highly controversial. Up to the 1950s, the topic of gymnastic music was debated and sometimes used to set up gender stereotypes. Critics confronted 'pure' gymnastics without any music as 'truly male', with musically accompanied gymnastics being 'feminine', 'un-male', 'jazz-like' and even 'un-Danish'. These polemics could not hinder the way of gymnastic music: at the *landsstævne* in Odense in 1954, all female teams performed with music; in Vejle in 1961, 18 male teams used music; and in Esbjerg in 1976, all teams, male and female, performed to music. Meanwhile, the piano was replaced by mechanical, electronic music.

The next step was the invasion of new body techniques connected to 'ethnic' music. Stomp, tramp and clapping became popular during the 1990s and influenced the intonation of the 2002 *landsstævne* in Bornholm. They counterbalanced the tendency to separate music from gymnastic movement, which had meanwhile been effected by the electronic reproduction of music. Now, new types of 'living body music' were created.

Another development of the traditional gymnastic festival was the introduction of rock concerts. Rock festivals spread with alternative youth culture, headed since the 1960s by the Roskilde Festival – 'the Danish Woodstock'. This festival culture has strongly influenced the *landsstævne* of *folkelig* sports. In 2002, the largest crowd of the festival was attracted when the pop-rock group Shu-bi-dua entered the scene. Shu-bi-dua cultivate a highly ironical nationalism, which was taken over across the generations. Also, the performance of the percussion group Safri Duo was a great hit, and its tunes are used by many gymnastic teams all over the country. They are therefore well-known to many participants who joined in humming the tunes during and after the concert. Furthermore, rock bands played night after night in the tents in the centre of the festival tent town. Dance also contributed in high degree to the atmosphere of the event.

This musical and audible atmosphere, which was created by gymnastic rhythmic music, stomp, rock concerts and pop dance is in some way following the traditions of the *stævne*, and yet it is very different from the 'auditory *gesamtkunstwerk*' of earlier festivals. In the mid-nineteenth century, the rifle and gymnastic festivals, which were forerunners of today's *landsstævne*, included marches accompanied by military music through the town. These marches had already disappeared by the later nineteenth century, while the German *Turnfest*, which can be compared to the Danish *landsstævne*, has kept the march as a central feature of the festival. From marching music to rock festival, this is both tradition and a shift of atmosphere.

Last but not least, clapping is a ritual feature that goes through the whole event of the gymnastic festival. Whether the spectators sit on the grassed dikes around the oval main field of the stadium or attend gymnastics on minor stages in the towns around, they join again and again in the process of performance by rhythmic clapping. By clapping for the performers, the people of the audience also clap for themselves. By bodily communicative action they affirm: 'This is us!'

What is going on in the festival by these audible and rhythmic techniques is, thus, a form of rhythmic autohypnosis. Self-orchestration by means of music, song and bodily rhythm contributes in a conspicuous way to popular identity building: 'We are the people!'

What sort of energy?

Song and music are, therefore, more than simply 'near neighbours' among the fine arts which comprehensively are called *musisch* (in German) or *musisk* (in Danish). As movement practice, sport also has an inner relation to sound and rhythm. This is expressed in fighting arts (among others) from all over the world. The Indonesian martial art *pencak silat* is traditionally accompanied by drums or the gongs of *gamelan*. Drums give rhythm to traditional forms of Arab wrestling. The Turkish oil wrestling *yagli gures* is opened by the music of Janissary bands. Iranian *zurkhaneh* combines drum, bell and chanting with club exercises, whirling and wrestling. And the Afro-Brazilian *capoeira* is a fight and dance at the same time, moving the body to the sound of the singer, the chorus, the drum and the string instrument *berimbau*.

Deeper inside sportive activity itself, movement and sound are connected by bodily resonance. Sports are activities of breathing and shouting, of rhythm and energy. You can 'hear' them. Attacking, the kendo fighter screams 'kiyai'. There is inner music and inner rhythm in body movement. It is this field that we try to describe by the term 'energy'. The energy of movement has hypnotic and autohypnotic dimensions.

The concrete connection between sound and movement, however, varies from activity to activity, from country to country, and from (sub)culture to (sub)culture. The Danish festival of popular gymnastics presents just one special model, and 'energy' is a way of describing this particular relation. However, the different forms of music and song are not the only contributions to the energy of the festival. Energy is a broader concept. For example, other elements come from the culture of laughter, from popular carnivalism. In various situations of the Danish *landsstævne*, people invent grotesque bodily display and thereby contribute to the *folkelig* atmosphere of sport festivity, sometimes deliberately contrasting it with the seriousness of national-patriotic intentions.[38]

This shows that the question is not – or not only – about atmosphere or not, about good *stemning* or bad *stemning*. The festival reminds us about the multiplicity and diversity of atmospheres in plurality, about different energetic states of mind and body. Festivities of sport differ by their particular mixtures and contradictions of energies – energies of fight, match and tension, energies of high performance, energies of joint singing, energies of drumming, energies of trance, ecstasy and intoxication, energies of carnival and laughter, energies of national euphoria, energies of arousal and revival, energies of indignation, protest and revolt.

The body between the people

The awareness of energy and its socio-cultural differentiation has practical political significance. Among other things it illustrates the contradictions between the show of achievement sport in its Olympic form, on the one hand, and the atmospheres of popular sport and Sport For All on the other.[39] It makes us reflect about the differences between the energy of the market event and the popular energies inside civil society.

The attention to the energy of bodily practice also has philosophical significance. The phenomenon of atmosphere and collective mood (German *Stimmung*) as it is produced by literary and musical techniques, or just as a certain 'climate' of feeling and thinking, has come to our awareness in modern philosophical thinking. *Stemning* has played an important role in the work of Søren Kierkegaard. Later, Ernst Bloch's philosophy of hope underscored the social revolutionary dimension of *Stimmung*, making it enter into modern socialist utopian thinking.[40] And, as *stemthed*, the concept of atmosphere was developed in the philosophy of life of the influential Danish thinker K. E. Løgstrup.

These and other philosophical approaches were significant, but could also include some problems of focus. The concepts of *stemning* and *stemthed* – just like 'energy' – could, in philosophical and cultural studies, be treated as ambiguous and obscure metaphors which described anything between sensual activity and non-distanced feeling, human meeting, presence and opening to the world, experience of nature or music, dispositions and emotions, experience of the here-and-now, intensity and timing, situations of being 'seized' and affected by something, feelings of being devoted to something, of moving or being moved.[41] But this array of metaphors does not diminish the fundamental significance of *stemning* and 'atmosphere', for cultural analysis: 'Without dreams and visions there is no life. The human being is a being of atmosphere (*et stemningsvæsen*)....'[42] as Hal Koch, the Danish theorist of democratic culture, expressed it.

This has an important social–philosophical point. Energy is not only somewhere 'in the body', it is between bodies. Energetic atmosphere is an inter-being, a relation – but not just a relation in itself, but a bodily, material and physical quality related to social relations. Energy is something like the body between the people. Through 'the body between the people', the study of the energy of festivity points towards a broader understanding of the materialistic study of body culture.

Acknowledgement

This chapter is dedicated to Eugenio Barba on the occasion of his seventieth birthday.

Notes

1 Bo Schelin, sociologist at the University of Lund, speaking in 1996.
2 Henning Eichberg and Bo Vestergård Madsen, *Idræt som Fest. Bogen om Landsstævnet*, Århus: Klim, 2006.
3 Ricco Kjær and Martin Rauff-Nielsen, *Stævnehåndbog*, 2002, p. 118.
4 Jens Sejer Andersen, *Gerlev Idrætshøjskoles Årsskrift*, 1988, p. 13; *DGI sangbog*, 2000, no. 274.
5 Definitions from Wikipedia. Online, available at http://en.wikipedia.org/wiki/Energy. In Danish see *Ordbog*, 1922, 401.
6 Rudolf von Laban, *A Vision of Dynamic Space*, London and Philadelphia: Falmer, 1984.
7 Eugenio Barba et al., *L'énergie de L'acteur. Anthropologie Théatrale.* (Bouffonieries. 15/16), Lectoure/Frankrig u.å, 1994, pp. 63–96.
8 Michael Page, *The Power of Chi. an Introduction to Chinese Mysticism and Philosophy*, Wellingborough: Aquarian Page, 1988.
9 Wilhelm Reich, *Charakteranalyse*, Frankfurt/Main: Suhrkamp, 1933. In the 1920s, the early Reich wrote about psychical energy in 'Trieb- und libidobegriffe von forel bis jung' (1922) and 'Zur triebenergetik' (1923), both in *Zeitschrift für Sexualwissenschaft*. These writings are re-edited in Wilhelm Reich, *Frühe Schriften I. Aus den Jahren 1920 bis 1925*, Frankfurt/Main: Fischer, 1983. He uses the concept of energy, however, without deepening the problem, in contrast to the concept of *Trieb* ('instinct', 'driving force') on which he focuses.
10 Mihaly Csikszentmihalyi, *Beyond Boredom and Anxiety: the Experience of Play in Work and Games*, San Francisco: Jossey-Bass, 1975; Victor Turner, *From Ritual to Theatre*. New York: PAJ, 1996, p. 55.
11 Charlotte Bloch, *Flow og Stress. Stemninger og følelseskultur i hverdagslivet*, Frederiksberg: Samfundslitteratur, 2001.
12 A philosophical approach to emotions like hubris, humility and humilation, to *Schadenfreude* and to pain in sport was developed in studies by Mike McNamee. See his 'Hubris, humility, and humilation: vice and virtue in sporting communities', *Journal of the Philosophy of Sport*, 29, 1, 2000, 38–53; 'Schadenfreude in sport: envy, justice and self-esteem', *Journal of the Philosophy of Sport*, 30, 1, 2003, 1–16; 'Suffering in and for sport: some philosophical remarks on a painful emotion', in Sigmund Loland, Berit Skirstad and Ivan Waddington (eds), *Pain and Injury in Sport. Social and Ethical Analysis*, New York and London: Routledge, 2006, pp. 229–245. McNamee's philosophy of emotions, by placing human feelings in the broader framework of virtues and ethics, keeps distance from both dualistic constructions and attempts at creating systematic order in this field. Attempts at system building can be found in contributions about the emotional response to music. For instance, by the use of the categories of the pleasant and the unpleasant on one axis, arousal and sleepiness on the other (see Chapter 3, this volume).
13 Important emotions in sport such as the contradictory complex of hubris versus humility and the phenomenon of *Schadenfreude* are obviously and basically relational

and cannot be thought strictly individual. See McNamee, 'Schadenfreude in sport' and 'Suffering in and for sport'. But also pain, which is normally treated as an individual feeling, can in an alternative way be understood as expression of a relationship. See Kirsten Kaya Roessler, 'Sport and the psychology of pain', in Sigmund Loland, Berit Skirstad and Ivan Waddington (eds), *Pain and Injury in Sport. Social and Ethical Analysis*, New York and London: Routledge, 2006, pp. 34–48.

14 I. M. Lewis, *Ecstatic Religion. A Study in Shamanism and Spirit Possession*, London and New York: Routledge, 1989 (1971); Thomas Hauschild, *Magie und Macht in Italien. Über Frauenzauber, Kirche und Politik*, Gifkendorf: Merlin, 2002.

15 Raymond Prince, 'Can the EEG be used in the study of possession states?', in Raymond Prince (ed.), *Trance and Possession States*, Montreal: R. M. Bucke Memorial Society, 1968, p. 121; see also E. I. Bányai, 'On the technique of hypnosis and ecstasy: an exceptional psychophysiological approach', in Mihály Hoppál (ed.), *Shamanism in Eurasia*, Göttingen: Herodot, 1984, pp. 174–183.

16 Macdonald Critchley, 'Musicogenic epilepsy', *Brain*, 60, 1937, 13–27.

17 Andrew Neher, 'A physiological explanation of unusual behaviour in ceremonies involving drums', *Human Biology*, 34, 1962, 151–160; see also the more detailed work of Henning Eichberg, 'Dansens energi. Kulturens sving i kroppens felt', *Centring*, 8, 1987, 172–222.

18 Stephen Kern, *The Culture of Time and Space*, London: Weidenfeld and Nicolson, 1983, p. 2. But what is said here also includes some self-criticism. The author's own earlier analysis of configurations also ignored energy as a fundamental category for the description of cultural behaviour: see Henning Eichberg, *Leistung, Spannung, Geschwindigkeit. Sport und Tanz im gesellschaftlichen Wandel des 18/19. Jahrhunderts*, Stuttgart: Klett-Cotta, 1978.

19 Kant characterised space and time as fundamental transcendental a priori categories of the pure reason of the human being, i.e. he placed the spatial and the temporal, not the energetic in the centre.

20 In his philosophical main work, *Materialism and Empiriocriticism* (1908), which was polemically directed against the physician and philosopher Ernst Mach, Lenin failed to understand the challenge which energy constituted for the traditional materialistic philosophy of matter, space and time. In spite of the Leninist limitations, research in human energy, animal electromagnetism and aura flourished in the later Soviet Union: see Aleksandr Samuilovich Presman, *Electromagnetic Fields and Life*, New York: Pleum, 1970 [1968] and Wanda Belezkaja, 'Biofelder: mythos oder wirklichkeit?', *Sowjetunion heute*, 2, 1988, 26–28. On the 'energetic materialism' in late Soviet medicine see Vilhelm Schjelderup, *Lægekunsten På Nye Veje*, Copenhagen: Hans Reitzel, 1975 [1974] and Vilhelm Schjelderup, *Elektromagnetismen og Livet. En Konfrontasjon Mellom to Supermakters Vitenskap*, Oslo: Dreyer, 1987.

21 See the critical remarks of Schjelderup, ibid.

22 Ibid.

23 An attempt to describe the atmosphere of the mass theatre of Max Reinhardt (1903–1922) as a start for new mass games in the twentieth century – Olympic Games' ritual, socialist workers' mass games, Nazi *Thingspiel*, American Zionist pageants – was undertaken by Erika Fischer-Lichte in *Theatre, Sacrifice, Ritual. Exploring Forms of Political Theatre*, London: Routledge, pp. 52–68. Atmosphere as an aesthetical term, in contrast to the Kantian aesthetics of judgement, was rediscovered by Gernot Böhme, *Atmosphäre. Essays zur neuen Ästhetik*, Frankfurt/Main: Suhrkamp, 1995.

24 *Stimmung* played an important role in creating the atmosphere and the genres of modern literature around 1800. See Johannes Burkhardt, 'Vom handlungstheater zum modernen stimmungsprinzip', in August Nitschke (ed.), *Verhaltenswandel in der Industriellen Revolution*, Stuttgart: Kohlhammer, 1975, pp. 49–56 and Henning Eichberg, 'Stimmung über der heide. Vom romantischen blick zur kolonisierung des

raumes', in Götz Grossklaus and Ernst Oldemeyer (eds), *Natur als Gegenwelt. Beiträge zur Kulturgeschichte der Natur*, Karlsruhe: Loeper, 1983, pp. 197–233. It was not by accident that the term 'energy' appeared in physics at the same time, parallel with 'energetic' pictures in poetry: August Nitschke, 'Energieübertragung, Ströme, Felder und Wellen. Beobachtungen zur Lyrik von Goethe, Novalis und Eichendorff', in Helmut Kreuzer (ed.), *Gestaltungsgeschichte und Gesellschaftsgeschichte*, Stuttgart: Metzler, 1969, pp. 201–223. And again, it seems not to be accidental that the genesis of 'singing democracy' in the age of the 'great revolution' between 1789 and 1848 was synchronic with this process.

25 *DGI sangbog*, 2000.
26 Kjær and Rauff-Nielsen, *Stævnehåndbog*, 2002, pp. 117–131.
27 Bjarne Ibsen, 'Vi har det så godt sammen, men hvorfor skal det være en forening?', in Bent Hansen (ed.), *Ældre i Bevægelse – København*, Copenhagen: DGI Copenhagen Sund By, 1999, pp. 37–49.
28 On other historical and actual links between sport and people's academies in Denmark see Henning Eichberg, 'The physical culture academy: people's education through sport in Denmark', in *Grundtvig-Studier, an International Journal for the Study of Nicolai Frederik Severin Grundtvig*, Copenhagen: Grundtvig-Selskabet, 2006, pp. 188–209.
29 *Folkehøjskolens sangbog*, 1995.
30 On Grundtvig's life history in songs see Ebbe Kløvedal Reich, *Solskin og Lyn. Grundtvig og Hans Sang til Livet*, Copenhagen: Vartov, 2000.
31 On detailed research about song, music and festivity in democratic revolution see Jean Ehrard and Paul Viallaneix (eds), *Les Fêtes de la Révolution. Colloque de Clermont Ferrand*, Paris: Société des Études Robbespierristes, 1977.
32 Hans Kuhn, *Defining a Nation in Song. Danish Patriotic Songs in Songbooks of the Period 1832–1870*, Copenhagen: Reitzels, 1990.
33 *Arbejdersangbogen*, 1987.
34 The 'resistance' of *alsang* has, however, received ambivalent evaluations. Sometimes *alsang* and armed political resistance were polemically confronted with each other: see Ole Feldbæk (ed.), *Dansk Identitetshistorie. 1940–1990*, Vol. 4, Copenhagen: Reitzel, 1992, p. 13 and Per Warming, *Folkelig Sang der Swinger. Fra Grundtvig til Kim Larsen*, Egtved: Edition Egtved, 1988. The contradiction between singing resistance on one hand and shooting resistance on the other existed, indeed. The psychological relation between cultural 'awakening' and active resistance was, however, more complex.
35 Harri Kiisk, *Körsången i Estland*, Stockholm: Estniska Nationalfonden, 1967 and Ingrid Rüütel, 'The singing revolution: living traditional cultures and folklore movement in Estonia today', *European Network of Traditional Music and Dance – Newsletter*, 1, 2003.
36 Warming, *Folkelig Sang der Swinger*; Per Warming, *Store ører. Verden Ifølge Sangskriverne*, Egtved: Edition Egtved, 1992; for Sweden see, Krister Malm, *Fyra Musikkulturer. Tanzania, Tunisien, Sverige och Trinidad*, Stockholm: Almqvist & Wiksell, 1981.
37 Henning Eichberg, *The People of Democracy. Understanding Self-Determination on the Basis of Body and Movement*, Århus: Klim, 2004; Ron Eyerman and Andrew Jamison, *Music and Social Movements. Mobilizing Traditions in the 20th Century*, Cambridge: Cambridge University Press, 1998.
38 On the complex relation between sport and laughter see Henning Eichberg, 'Laughing in sports and popular games. Towards a phenomenology of laughter', in *Le Rire Européen*. Perpignan: Presses Universitaires, 2008.
39 Henning Eichberg, Jerzy Kosiewicz and Kazimierz Obodyńsky (eds), *Sport for All as a Form of Education*, Rzeszów: University of Rzeszów, 2007, pp. 184–209.
40 Ernst Bloch placed *Stimmung* in the context of dream, driving forces (*Trieb*), feelings

(*Triebgefühle*) and daydream. Critically turned against Heidegger, Bloch underscored the historical and sociological place of *Stimmung* as social energy and as a hope, which confronts human alienation under capitalism. See Ernst Bloch, *Das Prinzip Hoffnung*, Frankfurt/Main: Suhrkamp, 1998, p. 86f.

41 This problem is visible in Kirsten Fink-Jensen, *Stemthed – en Basis for Æstetisk Læring. Det Musiske i et Livsfilosofisk Lys*, Danmarks Lærerhøjskole: Udviklingsprogrammer Fink-Jensen, 1998.

42 *Ungdom & Idræt*, 1951 (quoted in Vestergård Madsen, *Oplysning i Bevægelse. Kultur, Krop og Demokrati i den Folkelige Gymnastik*, Aarhus: Klim, 2003, p. 5.)

6 Music as sport history

The special case of Pietro Metastasio's *L'Olimpiade* and the story of the Olympic Games

Jeffrey O. Segrave

Sport and music have a deep and abiding relationship, as other chapters in this volume clearly illustrate. But there is a further dimension to the sport/music dyad that I would like to explore: namely, the idea that music serves as a repository for history, that music, as Alan Merriam puts it, contributes to the continuity of culture, that it serves as 'a vehicle of history, myth, and legend'.[1] As Theodor Adorno has argued, music is linked to cognitive habits, modes of consciousness and cultural meaning, and therefore operates not only as a powerful force in the construction of personal and cultural life, but also in the transmission of cultural memory, even historical consciousness.[2] The postmodernist transformation in the study of music in particular has led to a concerted attempt to uncover its socio-historical meanings and effects,[3] to unravel what Abraham Lincoln once poetically called 'the mystic chords of memory'.[4] In other words, music has historical salience. It is not devoid of social representation and historical information; it is not, to use Susan McClary's phrase, 'an innocent accompaniment'.[5] Rather, it is a discursive social practice that works in the manipulation of affect, the validation of ideology, the rationalisation of cultural practice and the perception of history.

Consequently, I want to argue that music serves *as* sport history, or to be more precise, that opera serves *as* Olympic Games history. More specifically, I would like to suggest that Pietro Metastasio's (1698–1782) popular eighteenth-century libretto, *L'Olimpiade*,[6] publicised, celebrated and transmitted a particular ideological and historicised conception of the Olympic Games that would ultimately contribute to the rationalisation and legitimisation of Pierre de Coubertin's own idiosyncratic Olympic ideology – what he called Olympism. Just as historians have increasingly employed anthropological questions to interrogate the organisation of gender and sexuality, notions of subjectivity, and how discourses operate to structure, reproduce and transform social reality,[7] so I would like to interrogate Metastasio's *L'Olimpiade* and Coubertin's formulation of Olympism and argue that the hegemony of the contemporary Olympic Games movement is grounded in part on the appropriation of the ancient games as transmitted in Metastasio's beloved work.[8]

The Olympic Games serve as a particularly striking and salient example of sport because the games exemplify a tradition of sport that harks back to the ancient Hellenic era and whose legacy has precipitated what Michel Foucault beautifully describes as 'echoes' throughout history.[9] References to the ancient Olympics appear in the professional records of historians, travellers, educational theorists and philosophers, archeologists, cartographers and palaeographists, as well as in the performing arts and literature.[10] In both practice and ideology, the Olympics offer an identifiable tradition that stretches back across the millennia and that connotes a humanitarian ideology whose roots can at least in rhetoric be traced back to the practices and culture of ancient Greece. Metastasio's *L'Olimpiade* is only one 'echo' of Olympic history, but one that sustained the Olympic tradition during the eighteenth and early nineteenth centuries in Europe.

Theoretically, this chapter will borrow from musicological readings of opera, socio-linguistic conceptions of meaning and, ultimately, postmodern social perspectives on material culture. My argument that opera can serve as Olympic history is grounded in part in the premise that the semiotic force of musical works can be decoded and that semiotic analysis can reveal how music works in social life and how musical pieces can imply, enable and transmit certain modes of conduct, ways of thinking, frames of reference and historical traditions.[11] But opera is more than just music: it is constituted of music, text and stage – the celebrated trilogy of melody, recitative and mimetic and mechanical show. As both texted and dramatic music, as well as a consciously visual spectacle, opera can serve as what Tia DeNora calls 'a container for the temporal structure of past circumstances'.[12] It is my contention that Metastasio's *L'Olimpiade*, in both narrative, music and production, sustained a particular image of the games, an image that nourished Coubertin's own ideological formulation at the same time as it paved the way for further musical representations of the games that to this day lend authority to the hegemony of the Olympics by appealing to a musically transmitted mythologised and Hellenised past.

In order to make my case, I first offer my theoretical orientation, follow with a brief characterisation of Metastasio's *L'Olimpiade*, continue with an analysis of *L'Olimpiade* as a historical locus for history, pointing out in particular the opera's prescience with regard to Coubertin's creation, and end with a discussion of the role of music in the modern Olympic era.

Theoretical orientation

Not long ago, the cognition of music languished in what Adorno called 'inane isolation', severed from the social macrocosm, and musicology was simply 'accounting for the biographical circumstances of composer and work'.[13] Musicologists, as Paul Henry Lang put it, had restricted themselves to 'chronology, paleology, morphology, typology and general *Fachlehre*'.[14]

Rejecting the idea of music as a set of icons, as simply the creativity of individual composers, and therefore devoid of social, historical, or political agency, Adorno insists on treating music as a medium through which important cultural contradictions and tensions are enacted and relevant cultural messages communicated. Historical human dilemmas, rather than transcendent truth, are salient to Adorno's understanding of music and, within his perspective, even non-representational instrumental music serves as one of the most delicate and sensitive social barometers in culture; or, as Christopher Ballantine puts it, 'the musical microcosm replicates the social macrocosm'.[15] Music then is not merely a personally meaningful or simply communicative medium: at the level of everyday life, music has power and it is implicated in every dimension of social agency. Music does not just reflect social and personal issues, it is often constitutive of them: music influences how we compose our bodies, how we conduct ourselves, how we feel about ourselves, about others, about situations, about how we experience the passage of time and how we develop our sense of history.[16]

Within the postmodern formulation, music operates as a social discursive practice. Far from finding the pleasurable aspects of the arts as trivial, without socio-historical and socio-political salience, Foucault maintains that pleasure becomes political and one of the principal means by which hegemonic culture maintains its power and influence and imposes its own particular version of reality on culture. Music is central in the political and historical machinations of culture and hence salient to issues of personal agency, including feeling, perception, cognition, consciousness, identity, energy, perceived situation and scene and embodied conduct and comportment.[17]

If music can affect the shape of social agency, then the control of music in social settings becomes the source of enormous power: it provides the opportunity to structure the parameters of action, it becomes 'a device for collective ordering', as DeNora puts it, a means of 'organizing potentially disparate individuals such that their actions may appear to be intersubjective, mutually oriented, coordinated, entrained and aligned'.[18] Not only does social ordering at collective and collaborative levels occur across time and inform cultural memory, but it endows music with significant manipulative properties that operate at the personal, social and political levels. Within this theoretical framework, music works in the manipulation of affect, social formation and ideology, in the construction of identity and consciousness, and in the development of our sense of history.

Stage and text also contribute to the construction of our sense of history. Even though sets are artifice, ingenuity and mechanical construction, they nonetheless present us with a visual, and often enduring, impression of history. Catherine Clément argues that stage landscapes are signs, 'the words of a complex language', and that characters are symbolic figures, 'tiny actors in a history'.[19] Text offers an especially salient mechanism for recapitulating and transmitting history, and in concert with music, consummates the dialectics of conscious and unconscious, information and impression, memory and reality. In short, opera can serve not only as a powerful ingredient in the construction of our daily reality, but as an important source of our perception of history.

Pietro Metastasio's *L'Olimpiade*

L'Olimpiade was written during the first decennium of Metastasio's residence as Caesarian court poet in Vienna,[20] and is one of 27 *dramma per musica* (music dramas) written by the famed librettist. The premiere of *L'Olimpiade*, with music by Antonio Caldara, and likely overseen by Metastasio himself, was held by order of Emperor Charles IV in Venice in the garden of the Imperial Favorata on 28 August 1733 to celebrate the birthday of Empress Elisabeth Christine. Over the next century, more than 50 settings of Metastasio's libretto were produced throughout Europe.[21] Forty-seven composers, including Vivaldi, Pergolesi, Traetta, Hasse and Leo, are known to have produced complete settings of Metastasio's text,[22] and some of the most striking set pieces attracted the attention of prominent composers such as Gluck, Johann Sebastian Bach, Mozart and Beethoven. Exceeded in popularity only by *Artaserse* and *Alessandro nell'Indie*, and as highly acclaimed as *Demofoonte* and *Didone Abbandonata*, *L'Olimpiade* is still considered one of Metastasio's best works. According to the eminent poet, Giosue Carducci, 'all of the eighteenth century joined in acclaiming the divine *L'Olimpiade*, in which the lyricism and the Italian songfulness joined in an unequalled and unattainable perfection'.[23] Translated as *Der Wettkampf zu Olympia oder die Freunde*, *L'Olimpiade* was last known to have been set to music prior to the twentieth century by the German composer Johann Nepomuk Poissl. This opera was performed at the Munich Court Opera on 21 April 1815.

The story itself is set in the country of Elis, close to the city of Olympia, on the banks of the Alpheus. The greater part of Act I, Scene I is given to a descriptive evocation of the Olympic atmosphere, the religious rituals and obsequies, the mass excitement, the sports, the rules and the prizes. Act III specifically opens at the ruins of the ancient hippodrome, and Act III, Scene VI is held before the majestic Temple of Jove. Metastasio's text – clearly based on Herodotus's *Trial of the Suitors*[24] – is a quintessential example of eighteenth-century *opera seria*[25] and the plot features a wide variety of disguises, ruses, mistaken identities and last minute revelations before it arrives at the predictable *lieto fine* (happy ending).

L'Olimpiade, in fact, is more a melodrama about the courtly conflict between honour and friendship than it is a story about athletics or athletes. The Olympic site simply provides a fittingly heroic setting for a drama that embodies the tensions and aspirations of a *Settecento* audience raised on *dramma musicale* (musical drama) that took their inspiration from the classical world and were convinced from the very beginning of the Renaissance that they were the direct and legitimate heirs of Rome and the only rightful arbiters of the classic.[26] Although *L'Olimpiade* is less than historically precise in its characterisation and description of the Olympic festival, it nonetheless served as a powerful repository for Olympic Games history throughout the eighteenth and nineteenth centuries.[27] Hence it exerted a powerful influence on the environment that nurtured Coubertin's own idiosyncratic Olympic project, and likely played a significant, although hard to define, role in facilitating the rise of the Olympics to the place of dominance they occupy in the contemporary world of competitive sport.

Opera as sport history

Regarding the extent to which it was prescient of Coubertin's particular brand of Olympism, *L'Olimpiade* nourished Olympic Games history in several important respects. First and perhaps most obviously, Metastasio's famed *dramma per musica* both sustained and popularised the name and fame of the Olympic Games: after all, Hasse's 1796 Dresden rendition was entitled *Das Olympische Spiele* and Fiorillo's 1745 version was revised in 1749 and presented as *Die Olympischen Spiele*. *Opera seria* was the major operatic form of the eighteenth century and, as Metastasio himself commented to Saviero Mattei, *L'Olimpiade* was successfully 'performed and repeated in all theatres of Europe',[28] from London to Prague, from Moscow to Lisbon,[29] and it drew encomia throughout its stage life. Numerous *pasticci* also kept the name of the games in front of a widespread European audience. In London, nearly 40 *pasticci* featuring *L'Olimpiade* arias graced the stage of Kings Theatre between 1770 and 1780, including works by Piccini, Sarti, Traetta, Bertoni, Gluck and Paisiello.[30] Furthermore, the world of opera was also deeply connected to the worlds of the other arts, each in its own way publicising the reputation and heritage of the ancient Olympic Games. In dance, numerous eighteenth-century ballets and opera-ballets featured the Olympic idea, including *Les Jeux Olympiques*, *Les Fêtes grecques et romaines*, and Jean-Georges Noverre's heroic ballet, *La Mort d'Hercule*, which specifically choreographed wrestlers competing for the Olympic wreath. In literature, Pindar and Pausanias served as inspiration to a wide variety of poets who embraced the Olympic allusion, including Milton and Keats in England, Ronsard and Du Bellay in France, Kochanowski and Szymonowic in Poland and Hölderlin and Goethe in Germany.

But *L'Olimpiade* did more than just keep the name of the games alive in the consciousness of Europe: it ennobled the games because opera was born of courtier patronage; opera was the inspiration of aristocratic *camerata* and *literati*, conceived for them and reflective of their spirit in both music and text.[31] *Opera seria*, in which heroes from mythology and classical history were represented in stereotyped conflicts between love and honour, reflected themes near and dear to the hearts and culture of the privileged classes. Unlike *opera buffa*, whose characters and texts primarily reflected the tastes of the petite-bourgeoisie and working classes (and in fact often ridiculed and parodied the nobility) and was local and open to all, *opera seria* was a courtly spectacle, invariably attended by invitation only, and international in scope and appeal.[32] As Henri Prunières puts it, the 'spectacle of princes with its voluptuous melodies, amorous intrigues, scenery and ballet, could not fail to seduce an elite whose sensuality, no less than its intellectual refinement had reached its highest point of development.'[33] *L'Olimpiade* was a common fixture on the calendars of Europe's royalty and was performed for Philip V, Catherine II, Queen Mariana Vittoria, Charles III, the Emperor Joseph II and the Empress Elisabeth. Also, because of the enormous success and appeal of the work, not to mention the aristocratic privilege it enjoyed, *L'Olimpiade* showcased the most prestigious virtuosi of the day, including Luigi Marchesi, Faustina Hasse, Maria Marchetti, Teresa Colonna, Belardi d'Ancona, Felice Salimbeni and Gaetano Guadagni. Huge choirs, massive orchestras, emphatic ensembles, the brilliance of counterpoint and ornate and grandiose stage settings, constituted the 'display of splendor'[34] which served as one of the principal social functions of music in the patrician courts of the day. As McClary reminds us, even when the modes and goals of culture changed in post-aristocratic Europe and an emergent nineteenth- century bourgeoisie demanded new venues, new forms, new themes and new operas, the 'ornate temples' which presented opera revealed 'a deep-seated desire on the part of the bourgeoisie to emulate the nobility, to traipse about in pseudo-aristocratic drag'.[35]

Like *L'Olimpiade*, Coubertin's Olympics too were awash in blue blood, and while Coubertin may well have advocated that no aspect of culture, especially sport, should be denied the working class, he was much too politic, pragmatic and ambitious not to recognise that the realisation of his specifically Olympic dream lay not in promoting the lower classes but in patronising the upper classes. And so, he utilised his own patrician connections and influence to assemble and animate the first International Olympic Committee which, although international in scope and ambition, was initially distinctly elitist in style and make-up, comprised of the upper classes and primarily European in complexion. If, as Neville argues, Metastasio's texts collectively contained ideals and precepts that greatly enhanced the image of the Hapsburg monarchy through association and identity, and played a critical role in the 'image of majesty' essential to the welfare of the monarch itself,[36] then *L'Olimpiade* played a similar role in enhancing the image of majesty that increasingly came to dignify the Olympic Games, an image that appealed to, and in fact helped rationalise and legitimise, Coubertin's idealised, romanticised and initially elitist Olympic Movement.

But the image of majesty that accrued to the Olympics was more than a matter of social class: it was also a matter of pedigree. *L'Olimpiade* transmitted a Hellenised and distinctly hallowed image of the games, one that celebrated Olympia as a sacred festival and consecrated the games as powerful religious obsequies. The opera is set at various sites in or near Olympia: in the hills around the sacred grove, near a bridge over the river Alpheus, at the ruins of the ancient hippodrome and in front of the great Temple of the Olympic Jove. Many of the characters, particularly Cleisthenes and Megacles, are taken from Herodotus' history, an account that specifically sought to celebrate the 'great and marvelous deeds' performed by the Greeks. Based on the work of Pausanais, Metastasio also incorporates a variety of ancient Olympic customs into his narrative: athletes competing for the sacred olive wreath and swearing to compete honourably at the altar of Jove, ritual sacrifices and the exclusion of women from the athletic arena. Megacles is immortalised in heroic, deified fashion: 'He has Athena's arts of war, the wings of Love, Apollo's handsomeness, the strength and daring of a Hercules.'[37] And choruses of priests intone: 'Great father of the gods, hold back your thunderbolts, the cause of fright and awe in mortal men. Pray, lay them down, of god of earthly kings!'[38] Even the music of *L'Olimpiade*, in the hands of composers as diverse as Caldara and Vivaldi, Pergolesi and Mysliveček, Paisiello and Hasse, appeal to noble passions and higher ideals through scores that feature wind, strings, timpani and voice in the production of martial processionals, heroic fanfares, stately anthems, grandiose choruses and exhilarating and touching arias.

Recapitulating Metastasio's classic representation of the games, Coubertin, too, embraced and iterated a noble and transcendent sporting cosmology. Coubertin's Olympic lexicon is littered with religious terminology. A self-proclaimed philhellene, he rejoiced in the opportunity to place his 'Gospel of Sport' under the auspices of 'that civilizing force whose past merits every honor and whose future deserves every confidence – Hellenism'.[39] Articulating his own conception of the Olympics within a late nineteenth-century *zeitgeist*, Coubertin reinterpreted Hellenism as a cult of humanity, a secular religion, and he characterised modern athletics, like the athletics of antiquity, as 'a religion, a belief, a passionate movement of the spirit that can range from "games to heroism"'.[40] In order to identify and legitimise, even sanctify and elevate, his particular brand of international sport and his particular athletic moral cosmology – what he variously referred to as Olympism or *la pédagogie sportive* – Coubertin appropriated a wide variety of quasi-religious rituals, symbols and pageantry from the cult of ancient Olympia. As a result, Coubertin's Olympics emerged as the most powerful expression of modern sport, an intoxicating and compelling amalgam of sport, ideology and mythology, and throughout the course of the twentieth and twenty-first centuries the games increasingly assumed a hegemonic position in the pantheon of competitive sport.

Encoded in the *lieto fine* of the Metastasian *Olympiade* resides another ideal embraced by Coubertin: the notion of the cumulative advancement of humanity. To Metastasio and many of his contemporaries, the *lieto fine* represented a rationalistic morality more civilised and evolutionary than the devastating catastrophes of classical drama. As Planelli wrote at the time, the 'evolution of the Drama from sad ends to the happy end is a certain proof of the progress of civilisation and the development of human attitudes, whatever our misanthropes may say'.[41] Coubertin, too, subscribed to an ideology of unilinear progress, to a view that history was a process in the progressive revelation and self-realisation of the human spirit. He believed, like so many other Victorian modernists, in the infinite development of knowledge and the infinite advance towards social and moral betterment. In Metastasio's *dramma per musica*, the triumph of human virtues bore a striking resemblance to the agonetic philosophy of the Age of Enlightenment. Metastasian virtues were habitually required to prove themselves through a contorted series of intricate inner conflicts and intimidating external trials before attaining final vindication. Likewise, in Coubertin's formulation, the promise of sport reflected the agonetic ideology of an incipient capitalism: human betterment through athletic struggle. Ultimately, both Metastasio's and Coubertin's oeuvres evinced an optimistic faith in the rational perfectibility of the sovereign individual:[42] 'O Sport', wrote Coubertin in his pseudonymous 'Ode to Sport', 'You are Fecundity, you tend by straight and noble paths toward a more perfect race.... O Sport, You are Progress.'[43]

The essential message of humanism was also encoded in the various musical interpretations of *L'Olimpiade* that graced the Enlightenment stage. As Deryck Cooke argues, western tonal music bears the ideological stamp of modern humanism and the language of tonal music expresses the values of the great social current precipitated by the Renaissance and the Enlightenment, 'the individual's right to progress towards personal material happiness'.[44] McClary makes a similar argument with regard to the social values embedded in Bach's music: 'Belief in progress, in expansion, in the ability to attain ultimate goals through rational striving, in the ingenuity of the individual strategist operating both within and in defiance of the norm.'[45] If, as Harris and Sandresky claim, 'music plays a remarkable role in communicating a notion of the "character" or style of emotional expression of a particular people, nationalities, and historical periods',[46] then Metastasio's *L'Olimpiade* served as a powerful and salient semiological transmitter of humanism that helped Coubertin devise, popularise and rationalise his own particular idiosyncratic brand of Olympic humanism, an ideology derived from an admixture of classical, renaissance, romantic and Enlightenment traditions.[47]

But while humanism may well be the 'philosophical champion of human freedom and dignity', it can also rationalise 'the marginalisation and oppression of the multitudes of human beings in whose name it pretends to speak'[48] – specifically in the case of *L'Olimpiade* and the *fin de siècle* Olympic games, women. Consequently, as noble and progressive as Metastasio's sentiments may have been, or as tender and magnanimous his characters, *L'Olympiade* not only acknowledged the ancient Olympic games as the sacred preserve of men but, as a forerunner to Coubertin's conservative ideology, it specifically reaffirmed the marginal, occasional and indeed demeaning role of women within the Olympic rite. Metastasio, in fact, takes advantage of the gendered culture of the games to enervate his drama with even greater intensity. First, in offering the hand of his daughter as the Olympic prize, Cleisthenes not only serves as the prime mover of the entire plot of *L'Olimpiade*, but his gesture instantiates the patriarchal orthodoxy that governed Metastasio's languid and voluptuous eighteenth-century society. Metastasio's ploy is in fact disingenuous, contrary to the historical record, even in Pausanias' work, for while fathers may well have brought their daughters to Olympia with the intention of securing a suitable wedding match – perhaps even with an Olympic champion – women were most certainly not offered as prizes in the games. Second, Aristea and Argene are excluded from the athletic venue and forced to await news of the games outside the stadium: 'No, beautiful Argene', Aristea exclaims, 'the regulations forbidding us women from being spectators are unnecessarily harsh', and in a prelude to the patronising, and indeed inferiorising attitudes that were to govern Coubertin's games, in which women were celebrated more as spectatorial accessories to cheer on men rather than as athletes themselves, Argene notes that: 'Nevertheless, it would perhaps be a severer punishment to see one's love in such great danger, and, without being able to help him.'[49] In keeping with Metastasio's patriarchal values, and writing more than a century later, Coubertin described the Olympics as 'the solemn and periodic exaltation of male athleticism, based on internationalism, by means of fairness, in an artistic setting, with the applause of women as a reward'.[50]

Metastasio's libretto is, of course, the classic representation of the traditional Western patriarchal narrative, in which, as de Lauretis writes: 'The hero must be male, regardless of the gender of the text-image, because the obstacle, whatever its personification is morphologically female.'[51] In *L'Olimpiade*, narrative closure is predicated on the subjugation of the female, of both Argene and Aristea, of the 'weaker sex', as Cleisthenes calls them,[52] or at least in the resumption of their rightful place within society. In a narrative schema that is played out routinely and extensively in opera, the women in *L'Olimpiade* are often portrayed as dissonant Others, who, in McClary's words, are 'necessary for the motivation and sustaining of the plot'.[53] Ultimately, as Clément argues, 'the triumphant ones are the fathers, kings, the uncles, and the lovers'[54] – in the case of *L'Olimpiade*, Cleisthenes, Megacles and Lycidas.

Metastasio actually imbued his characters with consistent traits, what he called 'ruling passions', which he drew in the dialogue, soliloquies and set pieces, and which in the case of *L'Olimpiade* clearly validate a traditional image of femininity and masculinity. For example, Aristea's 'character portrait' is constructed as 'beautiful, loving, afflicted, suffering grieving' (dialogue, Act I, Scene I), 'anguished, longing, despairing, entreating' (aria, *Tu di Saper*, Act I, Scene VI), 'demonstrative lover, believes her love pure, womanish (swoons)' (dialogue, Act II, Scene IX) and 'sympathetic, tender, loving' (aria, Act III, Scene II). Megacles, on the other hand, is characterised as 'grateful, unquestioningly loyal' (dialogue, Act I, Scene II), 'proud, confident, loyal in friendship' (aria, *Superbo*, Act I, Scene II), 'upholds virtue, though it cause extreme suffering and demand extreme fortitude, which he imputes to himself' (dialogue, Act II, Scene IX) and 'selflessly courageous, loyal' (aria, *Lo Seguitai Felici*, Act III, Scene III). In the famous duet, *Nei Giorni* (Act I, Scene I), Aristea is described as 'confused, grieving' and Megacles as 'grieving but resolved in his duty'.

Characterisations are also reinforced in music. On the basis of the theoretical proposition that dominant forms of music reflect male hegemony,[55] McClary argues that in Western societies tonal music encodes patriarchal values and routinely creates a 'musical semiotics of gender'.[56] Even more specifically, McClary posits the semiotic relationship between chromaticism and femininity. While chromaticism as an octaval convention is not a prevailing feature of most versions of *L'Olimpiade*, chromaticism, in the sense of a colourful application to the coloratura soprano or the related soubrette voice, does apply to female singing roles in some renditions of Metastasio's libretto, most especially Vivaldi's. In other words, while *L'Olympiade* bore witness to the triumph of human virtues, it would also have conjured up in both text and music, both consciously and unconsciously, another conception of the games, one which will have well served not only Coubertin who was besotted with the ancient

Hellenic model, but other commentators and ideologues who during the course of the late nineteenth century proselytised sport as a worthy institution in which to feature Anglo-Saxon, amateur, male – and distinctly not female – athletic accomplishments.

But despite overt elitism and sexism, in its conceits and affectations, *L'Olimpiade* instantiates a positive and progressive moral cosmology, one that would ultimately pave the way for Coubertin's Olympic ruminations. After all, *L'Olimpiade* is a chivalric story in which noble values and ideals are validated and extolled. Megacles, like numerous other Metastasian heroes, offers his human emotions as a holocaust to individual virtue and communal harmony: 'Brave young man, standing humbly amid so much glory, allow me to kiss your honored brow and to press you to my heart.'[57] In keeping with the lofty ideals and noble principles of *opera seria*, *L'Olimpiade* ends in the universal acclaim of honourable behaviour and communal stability: 'Everyone here has displayed courage', the king declares, 'must I be the only exemplar of weakness? The world shall not hear about me. Priests, stir up the fire on the altar.'[58]

Coubertin's Olympism was likewise grounded in exalted ambitions and noble intentions. In *L'Olimpiade*'s ultimate victory of virtue and the re-establishment of communal harmony, the ground is laid for Coubertin's later progressive rationalistic morality in which the individual hero, in Coubertin's case the individual athlete, was to instantiate the 'sentiment of honor' and embody heroic qualities which spoke to the 'physical, moral, and social'[59] role of sport in the service of individual and societal equilibrium. Both Metastasio and Coubertin validated 'the efficacy of virtue producing stupendous results'.[60] Just as Metastasio's eighteenth-century *dramma musicale* affirmed a moral code rooted in the values of honour, loyalty, devotion and chivalry, so Coubertin's *fin de siècle* Olympism preached the virtues of 'initiative, daring, decisiveness, the habit of self-reliance, and of taking responsibility for one's own failure'.[61] Coubertin's athlete is no less chivalric or heroic than Metastasio's Megacles, and no less ascetic, or Hellenic, just more modern.

Like Metastasio, Coubertin too was a doctrinaire moralist, an idealistic didact striving through an altruistic disposition to enhance the quality of human life. The role of sport in the service of moral education and social good resonates throughout Coubertin's entire oeuvre: sport becomes an 'instrument of moral training',[62] a source of 'moral hygiene',[63] a 'school of moral nobility and purity',[64] a moral enterprise dedicated to 'progressive work done with judicious boldness, an ever-vigilant concern for ideals and selflessness, and finally, daily adaptation to the common good, to the service of all'.[65] No doubt, like Metastasio, for whom the power of achievement would have been marred if the antagonists in his dramas were not brought, along with the audience, to moral truth, so too would Coubertin have been chagrined if in the end his ideation of Olympism as a moral crusade did not induce in athlete and spectator alike a vision of social peace, international magnanimity and cosmopolitan harmony.

Ultimately, Metastasio's descriptions and depictions of Olympic practices and protocol were more the function of poetic licence than historical accuracy, more a response to the dictates of the Arcadian reform, the conventions of *opera seria*, and the dictates of a *Settecento* European audience than an effort to provide accurate details about the ancient games. Consequently, the significance of Metastasio's *L'Olimpiade* resides less in the work's historical precision than in its underlying moral philosophy, a metaphysics grounded firmly in the principle of *utile et dulce* and shaped by a Cartesian rationalism that impacted Jesuit teachings and helped frame Coubertin's own moral cosmology as well as his own particular Olympic philosophical formulation, Olympism.

Music and the modern Olympic Games

Unlike all other sporting events, music has been an identifiable feature of Olympics history from the very beginning. Although ancient Olympic organisers never admitted musical contests, singers were often honoured for their Olympic hymns, which may have accompanied the opening procession, the great sacrifice to Zeus and the prize-giving ceremony.[66] Athletes were summoned to compete in the ancient games by the 'hot, competitive, and piercing' echo of the Olympic trumpet,[67] and flautists played during the jumping events in the pentathlon.[68] Dr William Penny Brookes' nineteenth-century *Much Wenlock Olympic Games* featured parades and processions led by the Wenlock marching band, and at the conclusion of the tilting competition young girls cast flowers before the tilting champion while the band played 'See the Conquering Hero'.[69] During the 1896 Athens games, music served as a crucial, central component of the ritualisation of the games, a key performative, dramatic element in the opening festival and an ongoing feature of the celebratory and ideologically charged atmosphere that characterised both the formal and informal components of the Olympic spectacle.[70]

Consequently, music has been more than an incidental component of the Olympics, a simple matter of entertainment: from the very beginning of the modern games, classical music has served to canonise the games, set them apart from what Coubertin called 'plain sporting championships',[71] and endow them with an aura of mythological, even theological, and certainly special, significance. In 1927, in his celebratory speech on behalf of the new Panathenean Games, Coubertin proposed a musical festival in the theatre Herod Atticus, featuring what he called a 'Gluck Cycle', and as late as 1935, he thrilled at the planned inclusion of the finale of Beethoven's ninth Symphony as part of the opening ceremonies for the Berlin Olympiad. Perhaps, most obviously, Coubertin engineered the Pentathlon of the Muses, the arts festival held for the first time in 1912 at Stockholm that, along with painting, sculpture, architecture and literature, featured music competitions in orchestra and choirs, repertoire, rhythms and alternation and fanfares. Among the classical composers featured in Olympic ceremonies throughout the course of twentieth and twenty-first centuries were Elgar, Brahms, Dvořák and Gershwin. A worldwide audience has also been captivated by the signature work of John Williams, especially with his well-known pieces, 'Fanfare Olympique' (1984, Los Angeles), 'Olympic Spirit'

(1988, Seoul) and 'Summon the Heroes' (1996, Atlanta). Recapitulating the mystique of the Olympics, Williams remarks that 'the inspiration for me ... comes from the mythological idea that we all seem to feel. It's all about deities and heroes that lived up in the mountain somewhere that could do something we couldn't do.'[72]

Not all modern Olympics music speaks to a mythologised, Hellenic past. Increasingly throughout the unfolding of the modern games, and particularly during those moments left to the discretion of the organising committee, a wide variety of popular music – ranging from rock to country, gospel to blues and folk to rap – has served to enliven the Olympic arena and attract a global audience. But the music officially and traditionally linked to the games, the music that defines and connotes the modern games, the music that elevates the games and accrues to them a hegemonic position of global superiority, remains the classical hymns, marches, fanfares and processionals that stir the imagination and speak to the sacred, historical heritage of the games. If, as Richard Middleton proposes, certain musical styles accumulate long-standing, widely accepted connotations,[73] then the classical music of the Olympics has, since the debut performance of Metastasio's *L'Olimpiade*, evoked a powerful and compelling tradition that harkens back to the ancient games and in the process facilitated the enormous political and commercial success of the games, and endows them with a public, global persona as the pre-eminent expression of modern sport.

Conclusion

Music is not just a meaningful or communicative activity; it is a constitutive social discursive practice. *L'Olimpiade* was not just an entertainment spectacle; it was the creator and transmitter of historical memory. It was constitutive of history itself, of Olympic history, and hence a powerful ingredient in the Olympic story, particularly as the story unfolded during the late nineteenth century in the form of Coubertin's idiosyncratic renovation as well as throughout the twentieth and twenty-first centuries as the Olympics have assumed a position of unprecedented and unparalleled supremacy in the panoply of international sport. Background music designer, Howard Martin, once remarked that

> People will start to look at music the way they used to look at dope. They will see music for its specific psychological effects. Music has the power to change moods and attitudes. Using music with these applications makes more sense now with the time crunch everyone's in.[74]

The most important issue here, as DeNora has identified,[75] is that if music is a medium for the construction of historical and social reality, then control over the production, distribution and application of the music in and through which we are constructed as social beings will become an increasingly politicised process through which nothing less than the matter of consciousness and social order is at stake. Olympic music from this point of view is neither innocent nor neutral. Acting in consort with a variety of other Hellenised and romanticised symbols and messages, the Olympics encourage our acceptance of the status quo, affirm the hegemony of the Olympic Movement in contemporary sport and facilitate our escape into fantasies, imaginary utopias about world peace and global brotherhood, utopias which may well obliterate our social and political consciousness of the insidious and rampant commercialism that now defines the Olympic Movement.

Acknowledgements

I would like to thank those colleagues who read and commented on earlier versions of this chapter, namely, Anthony Bateman, David Castonuovo, Lewis Rosengarten, Denise Smith and Marc-Andre Wiesman.

Notes

1 Alan Merriam, *The Anthropology of Music*, Chicago: Northwestern University Press, 1964, p. 225.
2 Theodor Adorno, *Prisms*, trans. S. and S. Weber, London: Neville Spearman, 1967; Theodor Adorno, *Philosophy of Modern Music*, trans. A. G. Mitchell and W. Blomster, New York: Seabury, 1973; Theodor Adorno, *Introduction to the Sociology of Music*, trans. E. A. Ashby, New York: Seabury, 1976.
3 Jacque Attali, *Noise: The Political Economy of Music*, trans. Brian Massumi, Manchester: Manchester University Press, 1985; Catherine Clément, *Opera, or the Undoing of Women*, trans. Betsy Wing, Minneapolis: University of Minnesota Press, 1988; Susan McClary, *Feminine Endings: Music, Gender and Sexuality*, Minneapolis: University of Minnesota Press, 1991.
4 Quoted in William Guegold, *100 Years of Olympic Music: Music and Musicians of the Modern Olympic Games 1896–1996*, Mantua, OH: Golden Clef, 1996, p. xiv.
5 McClary, 'Foreword', in Clément, *Opera, or the Undoing of Women*, trans. Betsy Wing, Minneapolis: University of Minnesota Press, 1988, p. xiv.
6 The best modern translation of *L'Olimpiade* is provided in *Three Melodramas by Pietro Metastasio*, trans. J. G. Fucilla, Lexington: University Press of Kentucky, 1981, pp. 113–155. Let me also note that I have chosen to use the Italian spelling of *L'Olimpiade* throughout this chapter, i.e. *L'Olimpiade* with an 'i', not with a 'y', as is commonly employed.
7 McClary, *Feminine Endings*, p. 29.
8 See also Jeffrey O. Segrave, 'Pietro Metastasio's *L'Olimpiade* and the survival of the Olympic idea in 18th century Europe', *Olympika: The International Journal of Olympic Studies*, 2005, 14, 1–28.
9 M. Foucault, *The History of Sexuality*, New York: Vintage Books, 1980, p. 149.
10 In particular, see Karl Lennartz, *Kenntnisse und Vorstellungen von Olympia und den Olympischen Spiele in der Ziet von 393–1896*, Schorndorf: Verlag Karl Hofmann, 1974.
11 T. DeNora, *Music in Everyday Life*, Cambridge: Cambridge University Press, 2000, pp. 21–22.
12 Ibid., p. 67.
13 Adorno, *Introduction to the Sociology of Music*, p. 62.
14 Paul Henry Lang, 'Musicology and related disciplines', in Barry Brook, Edward Downes and Sherman van Solkema (eds), *Perspectives in Musicology*, New York: Norton, 1972, p. 186.

15 C. Ballantine, *Music and its Social Meanings*, New York: Gordon and Breach Science Publishers, 1984, p. 5.
16 DeNora, *Music in Everyday Life*, p. 17.
17 Ibid., p. 20.
18 Ibid., p. 109.
19 Clément, *Opera, or the Undoing of Women*, p. 20.
20 Metastasio served as Caesarian court poet from 1730 to his death in 1782.
21 For a full list of the premiere productions of Metastasio's *L'Olympiade* see Don Neville, 'Pietro Metastasio', in S. Sadie (ed.), *The New Grove Dictionary of the Opera*, New York: Macmillan Press, 1992, p. 356.
22 Scores by only 23 composers are known to survive in manuscript or printed form. See J. K. Wilson, 'L'Olympiade: Selected Eighteenth-Century Settings of Metastasio's Libretto', PhD dissertation, Harvard University, 1982, pp. 21–22.
23 Giosue Carducci, 'Pietro Metatstasio', in *Prose di Giosue Carducci MDCCCLIX–MCMIII*, Bologna: Nicola Zanichelli, 1907, pp. 903–904.
24 Herodotus, *The History*, VI, 125–131, trans. David Grene, Chicago: University of Chicago Press, 1987, pp. 458–461.
25 For a concise analysis of *opera seria* see Marita McClymonds and Daniel Heartz, 'Opera seria', in S. Sadie, *The New Grove Dictionary of the Opera*, New York: Macmillan Press, 1992, pp. 698–709.
26 Nathaniel Burt, 'Opera in Arcadia', *The Musical Quarterly*, 1955, 41, 145–170.
27 Jeffrey O. Segrave, 'Pietro Metastasio's *L'Olimpiade*: a textual exegesis and an analysis of the role of *L'Olimpiade* in Olympic Games history', in Nigel Crowther, Robert Barney and Michael Heinne (eds), *Cultural Imperialism in Action: Critiques in the Global Olympic Trust*, London, ON: International Centre for Olympic Studies, 2006, pp. 41–64.
28 Quoted in Brian Pritchard, 'L'Olimpiade', in Sadie, *The New Grove Dictionary of the Opera*, p. 662.
29 *L'Olimpiade* was also performed in Venice, Milan, Naples, Turin, Rome, Copenhagen, Parma, Dresden, Vienna, Stuttgart, Munich, Salzburg, Berlin, Warsaw and Paris.
30 Ibid., pp. 105–250.
31 For a history of opera, see Donald Jay Grout, *A Short History of the Opera*, New York: Columbia University Press, 1965; David Littlejohn, *The Ultimate Art: Essays Around and About Opera*, Berkeley, CA: University of California Press, 1992; Ethan Mordden, *The Splendid Art of Opera: A Concise History*, New York: Methuen, 1980; Michael Robinson, *Opera Before Mozart*, London: University Library, 1966; Michael Robinson, *Naples and Neapolitan Opera*, Oxford: Clarendon Press, 1972.
32 Theodor Adorno, 'Bürgerliche Oper', *Klangfiguren, Musikalische Schrifeten, I*, Berlin-Frankfurt/Main: Suhrkamp, 1959, pp. 32–54; Manfred Bukafzer, *Music in the Baroque Era*, New York: Norton, 1947, pp. 395–399.
33 Henri Prunières, *L'Opéra Italien en France Avant Lulli*, Paris: Champion, 1913, p. 3.
34 Bukafzer, *Music in the Baroque Era*, p. 394.
35 McClary, 'Foreword', p. xii.
36 Don Neville, 'Metastasio and the image of majesty in the Austrio-Italian baroque', in Shearer West (ed.), *Italian Culture in Northern Europe in the Eighteenth Century*, Cambridge: Cambridge University Press, 1999, pp. 140–158.
37 Fucilla, *Three Melodramas by Pietro Metastasio*, p. 132.
38 Ibid., p. 149.
39 Ibid., p. 269.
40 Pierre de Coubertin, *Olympism: Selected Writings*, Lausanne, Switzerland: International Olympic Committee, p. 576.
41 Antonio Planelli, *Dell' Opera in Musica*, Naples: D. Campo, 1771, p. 72ff.
42 Carl Becker, *The Heavenly City of the 18th Century Philosophers*, Yale University Press: New Haven, 1932, especially pp. 31, 49, 128–129, *passim*.

43 Pierre de Coubertin, *The Olympic Idea: Discourse and Essays*, Stuttgart: Carl-Diem-Institut, 1967, p. 40.
44 Deryck Cooke, *The Language of Music*, Oxford: Oxford University Press, 1959, p. 54.
45 Susan McClary, 'The blasphemy of talking politics in Bach's year', in Richard Leppert and Susan McClary (eds), *Music and Society: The Politics of Composition, Performance, and Reception*, Cambridge: Cambridge University Press, 1987, p. 22.
46 Catherine Harris and Clemens Sandarsky, 'Love and death in classical music: methodological problems in analysing human meanings in music', *Symbolic Interaction*, 1985, 8, 291–310.
47 Ben Carrington, 'Cosmopolitan Olympism, humanism and the spectacle of "race"', in John Bale and Mette Krogh Chrtistensen (eds), *Post-Olympism? Questioning Sport in the Twenty-First Century*, Oxford: Berg, 2004, pp. 81–98.
48 Tony Davies, *Humanism*, London: Routledge, 1997, p. 5. See also Kate Soper, *Humanism and Anti-Humanism*, London: Hutchinson, 1986.
49 Ibid., p. 128.
50 Coubertin, *Olympism*, p. 713.
51 T. de Lauretis, *Alice Doesn't: Feminism, Semiotics, Cinema*, Bloomington: Indiana University Press, 1984, p. 118.
52 Fucilla, *Three Melodramas by Pietro Metastasio*, p. 152.
53 McClary, *Feminine Endings*, p. 57.
54 Clément, *Opera, or the Undoing of Women*, p. 22.
55 John Shepard, *Music as Social Text*, Cambridge: Polity, 1991.
56 McClary, *Feminine Endings*, p. 7.
57 Fucilla, *Three Melodramas by Pietro Metastasio*, p. 132.
58 Ibid., p. 155.
59 P. de Coubertin, 'L'éducation anglaise', *La Réforme Sociale*, 1887, 13, 642.
60 Metastasio's letter to Hasse' in Charles Burney, *Memoires of the Life and Writing of the Abate Metastasio*, Vol. 1, London: G. C. and J. Robinson, 1796, p. 351.
61 Coubertin, *Olympism*, p. 115.
62 Coubertin, *The Olympic Idea*, p. 8.
63 P. de Coubertin, *Une Campagne de 21 Ans*, Paris: Librairie de L'Éducation Physique, 1908, p. 6.
64 Coubertin, *Olympism*, p. 560.
65 Ibid., p. 122.
66 Thomas Scanlon, *Eros and Greek Athletics*, Oxford: Oxford University Press, 2002, pp. 55–56.
67 William Blake Tyrrell, *The Smell of Sweat: Greek Athletics, Olympics, and Culture*, Wauconda, IL: Bolchazy-Carducci, 2004, p. 200.
68 V. Pausanias, *Description of Greece*, Vol. 5, trans. W. H. S. Jones, Cambridge: Harvard University Press, 1965, pp. 162–163.
69 David Young, *The Modern Olympics: A Struggle for Survival*, Baltimore: Johns Hopkins University Press, 1996, p. 11.
70 John MacAloon, *This Great Symbol: Pierre de Coubertin and the Origins of the Modern Olympic Games*, Chicago: Chicago University Press, 1881, pp. 195–275.
71 Ibid., p. 614.
72 Quoted in Guegold, *100 Years of Olympic Music*, p. xiv.
73 Richard Middleton, *Studying Popular Music*, Milton Keynes: Open University Press, 1990.
74 Quoted in Joseph Lanza, *Elevator Music: A Surreal History of Muzak, Easy-Listening and Other Moodsong*, London: Quarter Books, 1994, p. 231.
75 DeNora, *Music in Everyday Life*, pp. 162–163.

7 'Anyone for tennis?'

Notes on the genre 'tennis composition'[1]

*Heinrich W. Schwab**

I

'Anyone for tennis ...?' – such is the invitation extended by English rock and blues musician Eric Clapton in the title of a recording made in 1968 for the soundtrack to the film *Savage Seven*.[2] The full quote of the chorus of this winsome ditty, with its quirky images and lyrics by Martin Sharp, is: 'Anyone for tennis, wouldn't that be nice?', a recurring line which acts throughout the song as a jovial and unexpected punchline. When looked at within the context of the centuries-old history of the game of tennis, to say nothing of the sport's social significance as a cultural idiosyncrasy, the title might best be passed on with a nod and a wink to the historian as an exhortation to scrutinise more closely this 'royal game' and its manifold variations.[3]

There is certainly no shortage of topics as far as the study of folklore or general cultural history are concerned, though sport seen and interpreted as a cultural historical phenomenon is, in Germany at least, only now beginning to be intensely investigated and portrayed. Sports studies, the discipline covering this field, has now found its way into numerous universities or has established its own research institutions. Yet, unlike musicology at university level, which undertook to constitute itself as a primarily historical discipline well over 100 years ago, sports studies seems to have preferred to give its allegiance to the scientific field. Thus, as far as the cultural history of tennis is concerned, the standard work in the German language is the study published in 1990 by Heiner Gillmeister, not a scholar of sports studies but a philologist working at the English Department of the University of Bonn. As its title indicates, this monograph sees itself as 'a cultural history of tennis'.[4]

At the same time, the aforementioned book synthesises individual investigations which Gillmeister has been publishing in a variety of international journals since 1977. Some were devoted to the Gotland game of *pärkspel*,[5] others to tennis as an Olympic discipline;[6] others still were to do with the origins of European ball games[7] or with tennis's bewildering way of scoring.[8] In a remarkably varied way, and often fascinating in its choices, Gillmeister's monograph provides the reader with facts about the game of tennis which partly go back to medieval epics or Shakespearian dramas, partly to emblem books or the rare 'textbooks' of tennis, and not least to the statutes and individual histories of the first tennis clubs. Specific chapters deal with 'the language of the game of tennis', or with 'tennis in literature'. Occasionally, medieval carols are referred to in which tennis is sung about, and in which one already finds complaints voiced as to the mercenary nature of the game:[9]

> Money, money, now hay goode day!
> Money, where haste thow be? ...
> At tables, tennes, and other games
> Money hath euer the floure.

The connection between tennis and music is very old. Already the first pictures reproduced by Gillmeister indicate that under the heading of 'leisure' ('otium') medieval illustrators would revealingly place the ball game next to music, and tennis players next to those making music.[10] Artistic 'tennis pictures' – such as those by Max Liebermann or John Lavery – are not only used by Gillmeister as richly colourful illustrations; as often as not our eye is drawn to significant sporting or culturo-historical details.

Anyone who has undertaken to paint a culturo-historical portrait of tennis can, in the light of what Gillmeister has accomplished, do little more than contribute ancillary information or point out peripheral details. A musicologist, however, who is interested in the history of both culture and sport and who perforce regards the general subject from the perspective of his or her own subject, can nevertheless draw attention to something which Gillmeister does not touch on in the context of traditional cultural history: not only to the fact that it was specifically in England that the first public concert halls arose through the conversion of 'ballrooms' or 'tennis halls', but also to the existence of the particular musical genre of tennis composition.

II

The term 'tennis composition' is intended to cover each and every piece of music which makes any reference to the multifaceted event known as tennis. Generally this is already evident from the title of the music in question. Representative examples include:

- 'The Lawn-Tennis Quadrille' from 1881 by the American George W. Allen.
- 'The Tennis Polka' by John C. Wild, the score of which was printed in Boston in 1887 but which is also available in a version for banjo and guitar.
- The piano piece 'Le Tennis' (21 April 1914) by Erik Satie, which has become perhaps the best known specimen of the genre (see Figure 8.1 and discussion further into this chapter).
- Movement no. IV 'The Tennis Players', composed by Edmund Severn and incorporated in a suite for strings printed in 1926 by the publisher C. Fischer in New York.

- 'Playing Tennis' (1949), an unpublished piece for wind quintet, written by Norman P. Dearborn and submitted as part of his examination work for Northwestern University in Chicago.
- 'It's Tennis', the penultimate piece in an anthology with the title *The Sports Program*, compiled in 1964 by the Adjutant General, Dept. of the Army in Washington, DC ('not for sale or other commercial use').
- 'Tennis? Tennis?', a children's song suitable for 'games with music', composed by Kay Lande, included in the collection *Busy Bodies*, published in 1981.
- 'Tennis Club', published in 1988 by L. Oddo in Maywood NJ, composed by Rocael Hurtado for marimba ensemble with five players.
- 'The Tennis Song', composed by Cy Coleman, included as an arrangement for voice and piano in the collection *Hey, Look Me Over: Cy Coleman's Broadway Showstoppers*, published in 1993 by Warner Bros, Secaucus, NJ.
- 'Tennis Racket, Unstrung', a piano piece by Elissa Brill, included in his *Divertimento for Piano*, published by Arsis Press in 1994.

The genre also includes a piano piece by H. E. Darewski (Junior) with the title 'Amour et Tennis', 'Morceau de salon, d'où a été Tirée la Chanson Populaire du Même Titre', published in 1908 in London and later in Paris,[11] as well as a 'Tennis-Sko-Trot' (1923), in which Albert Theilgaard – otherwise a Master of Engineering candidate and director of the rubber factories in the Danish town of Køge – composed a fashionable foxtrot for the purposes of advertising the tennis shoes he manufactured.[12]

At first glance one would hardly expect to find any timeless examples of this genre. Often it is more a matter of the composers in question, whose names are not always to be found in the standard musical works of reference, indulging in 'musical jokes' or sound-curiosities that highlight amusing connections. This applies, for example, to Gwyneth V. Walker, in whose orchestral work *Match Point* (1985) the percussion section is enhanced by the inclusion of 'tennis balls for special effects' and in which the conductor is instructed to use a tennis racket. Sometimes, however, works have survived amongst the panoply of tennis compositions which are of interest both from a cultural and from a sports history point of view and which, in a highly original way, seek to capture and to reflect the phenomenon of tennis and its distinctive ambience through sound and tone. Thus vocal and instrumental pieces reflect changing musical fashions, the existence and dominance of social norms, an elitist consciousness of class as well as the critique thereof. The lyrics of tennis songs assert prevalent opinions and prejudices, serve the purposes of the cult worship of individuals or of publicity and mutually reinforce an increasing trend towards the commercialisation of both music and sport. These are phenomena which are altogether familiar in general cultural and social history and have long since been the subject of scrutiny in other contexts.

Erik Satie described his album *Sports et Divertissements* – written in 1914 just before the outbreak of the First World War[13] as 'musique contemporaine'. As such it serves as a faithful mirror of contemporary fashion and the hedonism to be found in the sophisticated, opulent society of cosmopolitan Paris, which endeavoured to dispel its proverbial boredom ('*l'ennui*') to a large extent through sporting events. As with 'Le Yachting' or 'Le Golf' (see Chapter 8, this volume), Satie relished parodying 'Le Tennis' in this collection. These pieces are not only meant to be listened to: for the individual pieces and themes Charles Martin had given the composer a series of drawings upon which the publisher had commissioned musical commentaries. Along the lines of an 'Œuvre de fantaisie', which according to the composer's wording in the foreword he wished to be played with a 'doigt aimable & sourirant', these short *pièces*, notated without barlines (see Figure 7.1), convey the effect of being improvisations accompanying silent movie sequences. Thus, one may regard the notes and commentaries written into the music as explanatory subtitles.

'Le Tennis' initially depicts the ceremony that surrounds the opening of play. The players having warmed up and the question having been posed whether they are ready to start play, the *staccato* piano bass appears to imitate the ball being bounced on the spot. A figure characterised by a descending third presumably then represents the service, for which 'le bon serveur' receives due praise. (One CD production of these pieces has Satie's text markings spoken over the music by trained actors, to suitable effect.[14]) That it was not only to witness sporting prowess that spectators watched tennis matches but also – depending on their own particular erotic sensitivities – in order to revel in the players'

Figure 7.1 Erik Satie, 'Le Tennis' from *Sports et Divertissements* (Édition Salabert).

'belles jambes' or 'beau nez' was an observation Satie was no less keen to capture. Satie's tennis composition does nonetheless end with a sporting detail: the musical rendition of a slice serve which finally brings about match point. Unlike the previous service, this 'service coupé', in which the descending third A–F# is woven into a scale-like passage, now begins *forte*, going – to remain within the language of tennis – right down the line, and no longer able to be returned: 'Game!' If the musical notation is anything to go by there is actually no need to spell out the result. Nevertheless the annotation does make it all the clearer that the match point has not yet been played. Thus Satie's 'Le Tennis' devotes itself to no more than a momentary snippet taken from the course of an entire game.

Jean Sibelius offers a different species of tennis composition than Satie, namely the tennis song which examines the sport through words and music. Here though, the final notes of the Finnish composer's piano-accompanied song have a ring to them which – thanks to the chosen text – is anything but droll. Composed in 1899 after a poem by the Swede Gustav Fröding,[15] the song first appeared in print in 1901 in Helsinki under the title 'Bollspelet vid Trianon', having been performed there in concert. Published by the Leipzig publishers Breitkopf & Härtel as early as 1904, the song was incorporated into the composer's opus 36 in a bilingual edition featuring both the original Swedish text and a singing translation in German.[16] Nowadays the song can be sung – in accordance with those editions available on the music market – in either Finnish, English or French. The fact that 'Ballspiel in Trianon' is to do with a

Figure 7.2 Jean Sibelius, 'Tennis at Trianon'.

game of tennis may be deduced from the wording of individual lines from the poem,[17] as well as, with a little imagination, from the music itself: if for example one regards a two-bar figure established in the opening bars which recurs a number of times in the piano-part as being a possible reference to the lunging movement which takes place when serving (Figure 7.2).

The song, in A major, describes untroubled outdoor delights. 'Distinguished demoiselles' and noble gentlemen have gathered for a tennis party in the Parisian park, decked out as shepherds and shepherdesses. However, the dance-like flow of the game comes to an abrupt standstill. The initial idyll has been disturbed at that moment when, at the end of a descending chromatic line – no doubt depicting the trajectory of a ball – the rally goes out of court and the players discover an inquisitive voyeur. The piano accompaniment falls silent only for the voice to have recourse to a declamatory outburst.

Figure 7.3 Jean Sibelius, 'Tennis at Trianon'.

Figure 7.3 continued

Admittedly it is not difficult to make out the ball's renewed bouncing back and forth in the motivic dialogue between bars 36 and 63 once the initial momentum (*Tempo I*) has been resumed. Later, the service motif from the opening even makes a return appearance. However, by the end it is the disquiet caused by the infiltrating plebeian son 'Jourdan Coupe tête' which dominates. The song closes with an unaccompanied *parlando* (as if spoken) and the final cadence even goes into the darker key of A minor. Sibelius's setting of the end leaves no doubt as to the composer's pointed criticism of this exclusive society, indulging in a ball game which it is apparently at pains to keep to itself.

Tennis is generally regarded as an individual sport. Like other sports it may have been organised in associations, though it was especially doubles – and more specifically mixed doubles – which the upper classes used to fulfil a decidedly social function. Since the 1870s tennis clubs have also been founded in towns and cities within Germany.[18] For associations in the German Empire, Austria-Hungary and Switzerland, Baron von Fichard elucidated the rules of the game through almanacs and frequently reprinted manuals, as well as setting out in more detail its code of conduct.[19] Association songbooks, such as those found for other sports (football, cycling, etc.)[20] do not appear to have existed for tennis associations. As one would expect of the elitist spirit prevalent in the tennis clubs of the time, it seems not to have been deemed necessary that they rally themselves by joining together in a vocal celebration of the association's name or of its colours or emblems, nor that they should foster a specific club mentality through the singing of songs.

Tennis composition is a genre which can hardly be said to exist in abundance. Nevertheless in the following section the focus will be on a further selection of examples in order to make the case for a systematic investigation.[21]

III

The oldest musical work which can be seen as belonging to this defined subject matter is the pastoral of 'Robin et Marion', attributed to Adam de la Halle. It can be dated to the second half of the thirteenth century.[22] Here the young shepherd Robin and a knight are rivals for the favour of the maiden Marion. The difference in social rank between the two adversaries finds expression in the different sports they pursue. The shepherd returns from a game of football, the knight from a tournament,[23] which he is eager to emphasise in song at the outset: 'Je me repairoie du tournoiement.'[24] Significantly, the chivalric tournament is the forerunner of the duelling that forms the basis of tennis; indeed, the Old French term for tennis – 'tenes/tenez' ('hold!') – comes from the language of medieval tournaments.[25]

Tennis compositions in the wider sense of the term also include documents such as those found in prestigious reference books without anyone having been hitherto successful in categorically identifying their origins. This applies to the copper engraving of an operatic scene from the early eighteenth century, reproduced in Clerici's history of tennis. This visual representation is unique in being accompanied by the following explanatory text (translated here from the original German): 'Two players with rackets emerge from each side, hit the ball with their rackets during the dance as is the wont of the game, the aria being played three or four times.'[26] The engraving also reproduces the 8 + 4 + 8 bars of the aria's melody to which the scene is to be danced.

If tennis compositions render homage, then as a rule it is to the great stars of the game, the intention being to honour them equally in sound. The legendary Suzanne Lenglen, who became a worldwide celebrity in the 1920s thanks to her successes at the Olympic Games,[27] was as late as 1989 posthumously commemorated in Avignon by the choreographer Rachel Salik in a ballet composition called *La Diva du Tennis*.[28] Already in 1924, the year of the eighth modern Olympic Games, no other person than Suzanne Lenglen was meant when the Ballets Russes performed the ballet *Le Train Bleu* in Paris, which included 'une Championne de tennis' as one of its four principal roles. The title of this 'opérette dansée' is a reference to the luxury train which transported irrepressible post-war Parisian society to the Côte d'Azur. The libretto was written by

Jean Cocteau with music by Darius Milhaud.[29] The choreography originated
from Bronislava Nijinska, who also created the part of the tennis player.[30]

This 20-minute ballet does not have much plot to speak of. It is much more
concerned with portraying the main figures (the beautiful Perlouse, the gigolo
Beau-Gosse, the tennis champion and a golfer) as individual characters and
showing the relationships between them, as well as with illustrating them in
characteristic poses. For this purpose Nijinska had specifically studied photos
and film cuttings of the Wimbledon champion Lenglen. The suspended scene in
which the tennis champion enters the stage for the first time, 'standing on one
leg, mouth open, arm ready to strike, emphatically artificial',[31] was also intended
to create an effect similar to that of a picture from the illustrated magazines of
the time. The music which Darius Milhaud composed for this ballet is in
keeping with the catchy style then common in the music halls. However, the
composition *Duo Sportif* which actually brings the tennis champion together
with Beau-Gosse makes absolutely no reference to the game itself. The *Entrée*
no. 6 becomes a tennis composition merely by virtue of allowing a 'Championne de tennis' to present herself on the stage to this music.

IV

The list of composers who have written tennis compositions includes a number
who are of international renown: aside from the Frenchmen Erik Satie and
Darius Milhaud, their compatriot Claude Debussy also needs to be mentioned,
as does the American Virgil Thomson,[32] the Argentinian Mauricio Kagel who
in recent years has been mostly active in Germany, not forgetting the Finn Jean
Sibelius, the Swede Wilhelm Peterson-Berger and the Norwegian Ragnar
Söderlind.[33] As for Arnold Schoenberg, even if his enthusiasm for the sport of
tennis was not directly reflected in a particular composition, he did nonetheless,
and with characteristic fastidiousness, invent a symbolic script intended to
minutely record the course of a match (for instance, 'player rushes to the net').
His 'Symbols for Recording of Tennis Games' concern not only the type of
points which can be won ('service ace') but also the causes of the errors committed ('foot fault', 'too short'). In 1948 the composer even added a 'Copyright
by Arnold Schoenberg' to his inventory.[34]

Wilhelm Peterson-Berger made significant contributions to the sport of
tennis, at the time being introduced and cultivated in Sweden. His piano piece,
printed in 1896 and bearing the title 'Lawn Tennis', is, it would seem, the
oldest European composition to be dedicated specifically to this form of the
game. It refers to the modern form of tennis which emanated from England only
in the late nineteenth century, usurping the *jeu de paume* which had been
developed and cultivated in France and then consigned to oblivion.[35] The piece
(Figure 7.4), included as no. 3 in the 'bouquet' entitled *Frösöblomster* op. 16[36]
starts *allegro con eleganza* and is cast in conventional song form of A |: B A':|.
Anyone not knowing the title of this composition will be hard pressed to make
any connection to the world of tennis, even if listeners may claim to have

Lawn tennis.

Figure 7.4 Wilhelm Peterson-Berger, 'Lawn Tennis', 1896.

detected an exchange of strokes in the opening bars – the conversing between right and left hands showing a kinship to the third movement of Beethoven's Tempest sonata – or the depiction of a winning stroke at the culminating moment, prepared and realised in terms of gesture and tonality by bars 24–30. Peterson-Berger's 'Lawn Tennis' – framed between 'Summer Song' (no. 2) and 'Roses' (no. 4) – is more of a song of praise to outdoor sports, and a far cry from an action piece of the sort staged by the likes of Mauricio Kagel in the following century.

In Kagel's *Match für 3 Spieler*, first performed in 1965 by the broadcasting station Sender Freies Berlin and filmed one year later by Kagel himself for transmission in 1967,[37] two cellists are preparing for a duel. The third person is a percussionist who effectively acts as 'umpire'. He has a large battery of instruments at his disposal, including loud whistles. Sounds of this nature are certainly 'not tennis' – except if one recalls the pervasive behaviour of fanatical spectators at many a Davis Cup match spurring on their respective national teams. Admittedly, anyone who can make out the 'noises imitating a game of table tennis' in the opening passages of Kagel's *Match* will attribute the piece to a different sport, but what is nevertheless beyond dispute is the combative constellation which is specific to tennis and which determines the piece. Moreover, what the two cellists are each required to produce on their instruments in terms of virtuosity during this composition (lasting just 20 minutes or so) really does qualify them as musical athletes. 'Athletic' is also the term often applied to describe the 'players' gesticulations' called for by the composer in performance: 'in *Match* gestures and tonal results are treated as independent elements of the composition', whereby Kagel's wish is 'not to create unity' or 'achieve integration'; he is far more interested in 'the tensions which are created in the course of the composition through the piecing together of heterogeneous elements'.[38]

One of the most recent tennis compositions, penned in 1998 between symphonic and operatic projects, originates from the composer Ragnar Söderlind, resident in Oslo and teacher at the local music academy (Figure 7.5). Its title, *Matchball*, draws our attention to that event with which a game of tennis ends and which always means victory or defeat, this being a sport which may permit the state of deuce (or *égalité*) but does not allow for a draw.

Söderlind's *Matchball* is a concert duel 'for two hands' in which the right hand represents player A and the left hand represents player B. Player A accordingly begins by serving (a_1). An ensuing single-line melody approximately resembles the trajectory of a ball being thrust into the air, to be struck at its apex before hurtling into the opponent's side of the court. On hitting the ground (bar 4/1), it is 'returned' by the other player with a rising, then falling line (a_2), as if faultlessly playing it back over the net. This rally lasts for altogether eight strokes (a_1–a_8) before the point is finally won in bars 25/26 (c). Nor is it as if at the moment of service (bar 1) the opposing player just stands idly around; after a moment's hesitation he seems to take up position for his return (b_1). This routine then repeats itself for whichever player is next to prepare a return (A: with b_2; B: with b_3; A: with b_4, etc.).

Single-line melodies predominate in this 'tennis improvisation'. For those brief moments where the ball is served, or where return balls are subsequently hit, the composer employs chords. Just as the players A and B seek to distinguish themselves through rhythmically differentiated melodic lines (to start with only player B has triplets), so it would appear that both are to be discriminated by chords which are consistently related to one another by the interval of a tritone (cf. bar 1: player A = C major in the treble versus player B = F# major in the bass; bar 23: player A = A flat major in the treble versus player B = D major in the bass). From this constellation one may fairly safely conclude that the composer intended to use such means in order to portray different styles and techniques of playing, or contrasting personalities on the part of the players.

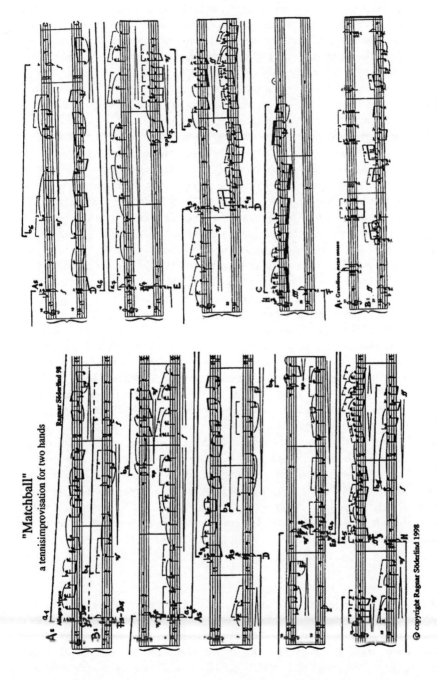

Figure 7.5 Ragnar Söderlind, *Matchball. A Tennis Improvisation for Two Hands* (reproduced by kind permission of the composer).

Söderlind's piece for piano lasts less than one minute. Making logical sense as it does, it proves to be an amusing *moment musical* in the manner of a French *pièce descriptive*. As its title would suggest, it is constructed in such a way as to make a musical event of the all-important moment of the 'matchball': a smash hit delivered in bars 25/26 at top speed (*allegro vivace* semiquavers) with the greatest possible dynamic impact (fff) and careering through a range of two octaves (from d''' to d') leaves player B powerless to make any further return. The game is over. The piece culminates in this 'winner' and in the subsequent general pause with fermata – a half-bar which should be fittingly celebrated. Thereafter begins the victory celebration, *grandioso, meno mosso* (bar 27). This, at any rate, goes for player A who has used his service to win the match. He is allowed to bathe in triumphant triplet chords reminiscent of the hero at the end of the Grieg Piano Concerto. Nor has the composer failed to think of an intelligible way of musically conveying the mood of the loser, whose part, logically, remains in the bass; the open fifth (bar 27) is infiltrated by a minor third and flattened fifth acting as blues notes. And nothing more pointedly captures the players' respective sensitivities after the 'matchball' than the final chord. Since a tennis match cannot end in a draw, there must always be a winner and a loser: the key of A major in the final bar represents here the winner, the bare fifth A–E the loser. The left hand is denied a C sharp – it would seem as if the runner-up cannot share in his opponent's victory, thus casting a shadow over the conclusion though refraining from adding any extra dissonance.

There is a further, not inconsequential detail which is not to be missed in these 'improvisations for two hands'. Although an uninterrupted rally dominates the action after the service and, musically speaking, the sections a_1–a_8 follow on from one another in various registers without interruption until the winning point (c) is reached, no ball within this musical combat ever returns by exactly the same curve – just like in any real game of tennis. Sometimes the first or last note is higher or lower, sometimes the rhythmic profile is varied, sometimes the intervals within the melodic lines are altered and sometimes the placing of chords is varied between treble and bass. In other words, the piece is not a two-part invention based on the imitation of voices but rather a suspended improvisation which – in the full flow of play – never produces an exact reprise. Ragnar Söderlind would appear to know Debussy's three-person ballet *Jeux* extremely well – a work which may even have inspired him to write his piano piece.

V

According to our definition, Debussy's *Jeux* is undoubtedly a 'tennis composition'. Perhaps it is even the most contrived example of the genre that one is likely to meet. The reason can be seen above all in the fact that Debussy in this composition took it upon himself to, in the view of Claudia Jeschke, 'metaphorically thematise and reflect on feelings and their communication as a "game", as "sport"', a trend prevalent amongst artists at that time.[39] *Jeux* was written for Sergei Diaghilev's *Ballets Russes* and was first performed in Paris in 1913. According to Vaslav Nijinsky, the dancer 'found inspiration for the choreography in the game of tennis which was [then] becoming fashionable'.[40] The ballet exists in no fewer than three versions. The content of the tennis-based version was described by Nijinsky in the following words:

> In a park at twilight a tennis ball has been lost; a young man and later two young girls are searching for it. The artificial illumination of the great electric candelabras surrounds them with a fantastic light and sets them off playing like children; they look for each other and lose each other, chase each other, fight with one another and sulk at each other for no particular reason; it is a balmy night, the sky is bathed in soft light, they kiss one another. But the magic is broken by another tennis ball cast by some malicious hand. Surprised and frightened, the young man and the two young girls disappear into the depths of the nocturnal park.[41]

With regard to the scene in which the tennis ball is first thrown, the annotated piano score includes the following comment: 'Une balle de tennis tombe sur la scène' (see score, bar 70), 'un jeune homme, en costume de tennis, la raquette haute, traverse la scène en bondissant' (bar 74). Later it goes on to say: 'Une balle de tennis tombe à leurs pieds' (bar 689). According to exponents of 'Neue Musik' such as Herbert Eimert[42] and Karlheinz Stockhausen,[43] it is not only in these bars that the composition display 'wavy lines' which, according to them, reflect in microcosm the structure of the entire composition. Searching throughout the 1950s for 'new laws of form' (*neue Formgesetze*),[44] both these composers thought they had discovered a new latent and/or ornamental waveform in *Jeux*. Regarding this kind of waveform it would be obvious to make a connection between this new feature and the bouncing tennis balls which spectacularly determine the beginning and end of the scene. Even if under closer analytical scrutiny it is not possible to confirm the purported waveform,[45] it should nevertheless be stressed that Debussy has very consciously eschewed any

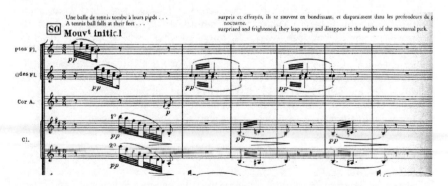

Figure 7.6 Claude Debussy, *Jeux*, Paris 1913: 'Une balle de tennis tombe sur la scène.'

kind of reprise here as traditional form would dictate. In 1972 Pierre Boulez referred again to the notable fact that this composition was, with a certain rigorousness, 'no longer constructed architecturally'.[46] This in turn accords – as already elucidated in the case of Söderlind – with the non-repeatability of individual scenes of the game. Thus Jeux reveals a compositional intention which correlates with the nature of the game, even if the latter is played out according to fixed rules.

It was largely on account of this modernistic form, which even for someone with an understanding of music is not easy to perceive, that Debussy's Jeux found little favour with audiences.[47] It was not until the end of the 1950s that Herbert Eimert drew attention to this feature. Debussy was subsequently seen in a different light, that of inventor of new formal concepts, which is why Jeux rose into the echelons of the most advanced musica nova compositions of the twentieth century. The fact that this is a 'tennis composition', ultimately seeking to musically render the identical flow of a game being played, elevates the entire genre onto a higher pedestal. The genre of 'tennis composition' does indeed include a unique masterpiece.

Notes

* This chapter was translated from the German original by Graham Welsh.
1 The original German version of this text appeared as Heinrich W. Schwab, 'Anyone for tennis. Anmerkungen zum Genre Tenniskomposition', in Marianne Sammer (ed.), Leitmotive. Kulturgeschichtliche Studien zur Traditionsbildung (= Festschrift für Dietz-Rüdiger Moser), Kallmünz: Verlag Michael Lassleben, 1999, pp. 457–483.
2 Cf. here the CD The Very Best of Cream (c.1995 PolyGram International Music B. V., 523 752–2). The song is printed in the Eric Clapton edition: Crossroads, Vol. 1, Milwaukee, WI, 1989, no. 2.
3 The number of documents and studies to be found in the wide-reaching international literature on the subject is anything but small, but the following publications deserve to be singled out: Robert Frh. von Fichard, Handbuch des Lawn-Tennis Spieles, Baden-Baden: Emil Sommermeyer, 1887; E. de Nanteuil, Georges de Saint-Clair and C. Delahaye, La paume et le Lawn-Tennis, Paris: Librarie Hachette, 1898; George Whiteside Hillyard, Forty Years of First-Class Lawn Tennis, London: Williams & Norgate, 1924; John Arlott (ed.), The Oxford Companion to Sport & Games, Oxford: Oxford University Press, 1975; Ulrich Kaiser (ed.), 100 Jahre Tennis in Bad Homburg. 1876–1976, unpublished document, Frankfurt/Main, 1976; Gianni Clerici, 500 Jahre Tennis. Vom Spiel der Könige zum Milliarden-Dollargeschäft, trans. Ulrich Kaiser, Berlin: Ullstein, 1987; Angela Lumpkin, Woman's Tennis. A Historical Documentary of the Players and Their Game, New York: The Whitson Publishing Company, 1981; Juliet R. V. Barker, The Tournament in England 1100–1400, Woodbridge: Boydell & Breer, 1986; in addition works by Heiner Gillmeister listed individually in the following notes.
4 Heiner Gillmeister, Kulturgeschichte des Tennis, Munich: Wilhelm Fink Verlag, 1990.
5 Heiner Gillmeister, 'Den skriftliga utmanigen i de gotländska bollspelen. Dess kulturella och historiska innebörd', in Idrott Historia och Samhälle. Svenska idrottshistoriska föreningens årsskrift, Helsingborg: Schmidts Bogtryckeri, 1988, pp. 21–41.
6 Heiner Gillmeister, 'Tennis bei Olympischen Spielen (1896–1924)', Stadion, 11, 1985, 193–262.
7 Heiner Gillmeister, 'The origin of european ball games: a re-evaluation and linguistic analysis', Stadion, 7, 1981, 19–51.

8 Heiner Gillmeister, 'Über Tennis und Tennispunkte. Ein Beitrag der Sprachwissenschaft zur Sportgeschichte', Stadion, 3, 1977, 187–229.

9 Gillmeister, Kulturgeschichte des Tennis, p. 160.

10 Ibid., pp. 16–17.

11 I am sincerely indebted to Dr Dan Fog (Copenhagen) for having presented me with a copy of this print.

12 See Anne Ørbæk Jensen (ed.), Musik og Reklame. En Udstilling om Brugen af Musik I Trykte Réklamer Katalog, Copenhagen: Musikhistorisk Museum, 1992, p. 6.

13 Erik Satie, Sports et Divertissements, Paris: Salabert, 1964.

14 Erik Satie, 'Compositeur de Musique', Eversongs, 2001.

15 See Fabian Dahlström, The Work of Jean Sibelius, Turku: The Sibelius Society 1987, p. 112; Fabian Dahlström, Jean Sibelius. Thematisch-Bibliographisches Verzeichnis seiner Werke, Wiebaden: Breitkopf & Härtel, 2003, p. 160.

16 See Jean Sibelius, Sånger Lieder, Leipzig: Breitkopf & Härtel, 1904. Song no. 3 here has the German title 'Ballspiel in Triano'.

17 In the original the lines describing the game and the players read as follows:

> Det smattrar prat och slår boll och skrattar.
> och monseigneur slog förbi sin boll,
> och bollen flyger fran par till par.
>
> (Hitting went well
> and the gentleman swiped past his ball
> and the ball flies from couple to couple).

18 Gillmeister, Kulturgeschichte des Tennis, pp. 277–280.

19 See Robert Frh. von Fichard, 'Deutsche Lawn-Tennis-Ausdrücke', in Zeitschrift des Allgemeinen Deutschen Sprachvereins 1212 (1897), Col. 1–7; von Fichard, Handbuch des Lawn-Tennis Spieles; Robert Frh. von Fichard, (ed.), Illustriertes Lawn-Tennis-Jahrbuch für das Deutsche Reich, Österrich-Ungarn und die Schweiz auf das Jahr 1903, Baden-Baden: Emil Sommermeyer, 1903.

20 See Heinrich W. Schwab, 'Das Lied der Berufsvereine. Ihr Beitrag zur "Volkskunst" im 19. Jahrhundert', in Zeitschrift für Volkskunde, 63, 1967, 1–16.

21 This search has recently been facilitated by information from the internet. For the acquisition of sources I am greatly indebted to Øyvind Norheim, Director of the Norsk musikksamling in the University Library Oslo for his kind assistance.

22 See Ernest Langlois, Adam le Bossu, Trouvère du XIIIe siècle. Le Jeu de la Feuillée et Le Jeu de Robin et Marion, Paris: de Boccard, 1923, pp. 93–106.

23 See Heiner Gillmeister, 'The Flemish ancestry of early English ball games: the cumulative evidence', in Norbert Muller and Joachim K. Rühl (eds), Olympic Scientific Congress 1984. Sport History. Official Report, Niederhausen: Schors-Verlag, 1985, p. 61.

24 The extract is taken from the edition by Friedrich Gennrich (ed.), Adam de la Halle. Le Jeu de Robin et de Marion li roudel Adam, Langen: n.p, 1962, p. 9 (Musikwissenschaftliche Studienbibliothek 20).

25 See Gillmeister, Kulturgeschichte des Tennis, pp. 133–137, 400.

26 Clerici, 500 Jahre Tennis, p. 26, figure 3.

27 Ibid., p. 142.

28 See the note by Gabriele Brandstetter in Carl Dahlhaus et al. (eds), Pipers Enzyklopädie des Musiktheaters, Vol. 4, Munich and Zurich: R. Piper, 1991, p. 441.

29 Le Train Bleu. Opérette dansée de Jean Cocteau. Choréographie de La Nijinska. Musique de Darius Milhaud, Paris: Heugel, 1924.

30 See Gabriele Brandstetter, 'Nijinska, Le train bleu (1924)', in Dahlhaus et al. (eds), Pipers Enzyklopädie des Musiktheaters, Vol. 4, Munich and Zurich: R. Piper, 1991, pp. 439–441.

31 Ibid., p. 440.
32 See Virgil Thomson, 'Tennis. A portrait of Henry McBride', in *32 Portraits for piano solo (1929–45)*, album 4, New York: Carl Fischer, 1948.
33 See Harald Herresthal, *Norwegische Musik von den Anfängen bis zur Gegenwart*, Oslo: Norsk Musikforlag, 1987, p. 97; Nils Grinde, *Norsk Musikkhistorie. Hovedlinjer i norsk musikliv gjennom 1000 år*, Oslo-Bergen-Tromsø: Universitetsforlaget, 1971, p. 395; Knud Ketting, 'Ragnar Söderlind', *Nordic Sounds*, 4, 1992, 17; Harald Herresthal, 'Söderlind', in Ludwig Finscher (ed.), *Die Musik in Geschichte und Gegenwart*, Kassel: Bärenreiter, 2006, pp. 992–994.
34 Reproduced in Christopher Hailey (ed.), *Arnold Schoenberg 1874–1951. Ein Interaktive Multimediale Ausstellung*, Venice: Marsilio Editioni, 1996, p. 53.
35 Gillmeister, *Kulturgeschichte des Tennis*, p. 336.
36 Til Lars Tirén, *Frösöblomster. 8 Melodier för Piano av Wilhelm Peterson-Berger*, op. 16, Stockholm: Abr. Lundquist Musikförlag, 1896.
37 Mauricio Kagel, *Match für Drei Spieler*, Vienna: Universal Edition no. 15197 (facsimile of the autograph score).
38 Christian Martin Schmidt and Rainer Franke, 'Kagel, Match (1965)', in Dahlhaus *et al.* (eds), *Pipers Enzyklopädie des Musiktheaters*, Vol. 4, Munich and Zurich: R. Piper, 1991, pp. 231–233.
39 Claudia Jeschke, 'Nijinski, Jeux (1913)', in Dahlhaus *et al.* (eds), *Pipers Enzyklopädie des Musiktheaters*, Vol. 4, Munich and Zurich: R. Piper, 1991, p. 451.
40 Ibid., p. 450.
41 Léon Vallas, *Achille Claude Debussy*, trans. Kurt Lamerdin, Potsdam: Athenaion, 1944, p. 132.
42 See Herbert Eimert, 'Debussy Jeux', *Die Reihe*, 5, 1959, 5–22.
43 See Karlheinz Stockhausen, 'Von Webern zu Debussy. Bemerkungen zur statistischen form', in Dieter Schnebel (ed.), *Texte zur Elektronischen und Instrumentalen Musik. Aufsätze zur Theorie des Komponierens 1952–1962*, Vol. 1, Cologne: DuMont Schauberg, 1963, pp. 75–85.
44 Ibid., p. 75; see also Claudia Maurer Zenck, 'Form- und farbenspiele: Debussy Jeux', *Archiv für Musikwissenschaft*, 33, 1976, 29.
45 See Erwin Hardeck, 'Debussy's Jeux. Struktur-stellung im gesamtwerk', in Carl Dahlhaus and Hans Heinrich Eggerbrecht (eds), *Bericht über den Internationalen Musikwissenschaftlichen Kongreß Bonn 1970*, Kassel-Basel: Bärenreiter, 1971, pp. 424–426.
46 See Pierre Boulez, 'Nahsicht und Fernsicht', in Pierre Boulez (ed.), *Werkstatt-Texte*, trans. J. Häusler, Frankfurt/Main: Ullstein, 1972, p. 73.
47 See Emile Vuillermoz, 'Jeux de Debussy au Théâtre des Champs-Elysées', *La Revue Musicale*, 1 (2 December 1920, numéro spécial), 203.

8 Ludus Tonalis
Sport and musical modernisms 1910–1938

Anthony Bateman

> I love all kinds of spontaneous cheerful gatherings, and my profoundly lowbrow
> devotion to soccer knows no bounds.
>
> Dmitri Shostakovich[1]

The writings of the neo-Marxist philosopher, sociologist and music critic,
Theodor Adorno, were both a rigorously dialectical analysis of, and a contribution to, the increasing polarity between 'high culture' and the 'popular' that
became a defining feature of the twentieth-century cultural field. In his music
criticism Adorno championed the atonalism and serialist techniques of Arnold
Schoenberg with his 'negation of illusion and play' and thus identified modernist compositional procedures that in their sheer esotericism could resist the
alienating forces of commodification and the 'culture industry'.[2] At the same
time he argued that these forces found one of their most perfidious expressions
in the field of organised spectator sport. Although modern sports 'seek to restore
to the body some of the functions of which the machine has deprived it ... they
do so only to train men all the more inexorably to serve the machine'.[3] For
Adorno musical modernism and sport occupied, or at least ought to occupy,
diametrically opposite poles of the cultural field.

Adorno's attitudes to both music and sport also highlight another significant
dimension of early twentieth-century culture: namely, the dynamic tension
between tradition and modernity, a tension that infiltrated all the arts of the
period. As has been well documented, the first decades of the century witnessed
a series of extraordinary and unprecedented developments in the visual, literary,
dramatic and musical arts: in their different ways Walter Gropius and Henri Le
Corbusier in architecture, Pablo Picasso and Wassily Kandinsky in painting and
Ezra Pound, T. S. Eliot and James Joyce in literature, all radically engaged with
the modern world by pushing to the limits and going beyond what had hitherto
seemed aesthetically legitimate.[4] Music too paralleled these developments. In
1913 the premiere of Igor Stravinsky's *Rite of Spring*, a brazen affirmation of the
value of raw sound in which the traditional elemental hierarchy of music was
radically overturned in an outrageous privileging of motor rhythms and harmonic dissonance, literally caused a riot. As Pierre Boulez has commented, the

unleashing of the work upon a scandalised Parisian public was an 'exemplary moment of modernity'.[5]

Although Stravinsky's masterpiece was set deep in the pagan past, much modernist culture sought to comprehend and cope with the ephemera of modern life, with what Paul de Man has called the 'unprecedented now',[6] including newly emerging forms of popular culture. Again this development was manifest in all art forms and often went hand-in-hand with formal innovation. While the musical genre of jazz was the most obvious element of popular culture to have been assimilated into early twentieth-century music (including that of Stravinsky), this chapter shows that composers also absorbed novel extra-musical influences, including sport, as they attempted to engage with the new clamour and dissonance of modern life. To do so the chapter examines three European case studies. The first discusses a number of sport-related works composed and/or performed in the highly experimental artistic milieu of early twentieth-century Paris. Then, in the light of the shifting relationship between high and popular culture outlined above, the second section considers some critical responses to those and other sports compositions in the more culturally conservative context of inter-war England where, despite the presence of influential modernist innovators such as Eliot and Wyndham Lewis, modernism was generally moderate and slow to take hold. The final section explores the music/sport relationship in former Czechoslovakia. Here the analysis suggests how modernist musical engagement with organised body cultural practices articulated with broader patterns of cultural nationalism.

Sport and music in Paris, 1910–1930

Although, as other chapters of this volume show, sport-related music had been written before the twentieth century, it was not until that decisive break with the cultural past known as modernism – a moment contemporaneous with the codification, organisation and international dissemination of sport – that composers engaged with body cultural practices in any meaningful way. As musicians instinctively foresaw Pound's dictum to '[M]ake it new',[7] sport provided them with a suitably contemporary and impertinently anti-Romantic subject matter. The remarkable American composer, Charles Ives, was the earliest exponent of serious sports music: his *Yale–Princeton Football Match* of 1898 includes highly abstract sonic representations of the crowd, the referee's whistle and various aspects of the game itself such as kick-off and the quarterback signalling to the rest of his team. As Timothy A. Johnson has shown, in several of Ives' other works the composer evoked the equally American sport of baseball as he sought to forge a distinctively national and unimpeachably masculine idiom of musical modernism.[8] But Ives worked in a musical vacuum and these astonishingly innovative compositions were not performed until considerably later. It was in the experimental environment of early twentieth-century Paris where sport and music formed a more instantly recognised, if short-lived, relationship.

In May 1913 the Paris-based Russian Ballet of Sergei Diaghilev premiered both Stravinsky's *Rite of Spring* and Claude Debussy's *Jeux*, both of which became seminal to the development of twentieth-century music. Although almost totally eclipsed by the unruly reception of Stravinsky's masterpiece, *Jeux* was nevertheless a remarkably audacious work, exhibiting as it did an unprecedented structural and harmonic freedom. Concerned with the volatile emotions and restless movements of three young people at a tennis party, *Jeux* is the first major work of twentieth-century music concerned, albeit it loosely, with sport. The choreography for the ballet was provided by Vaslav Nijinsky and, according to Marie Rambert, was based on a series of stylised sports movements. The production also involved Nijinski and the two female dancers wearing tennis flannels.[9] Debussy struggled with the surreal excesses of the original scenario, which at one point included an aeroplane crashing onto the tennis court (a topical symbol of the turbulence of the newly emerging technological world), but eventually Debussy and Nijinsky agreed on the following narrative:

> In a park at twilight, a tennis ball has got lost; a young man and then two girls come looking for it. The artificial light from the lamp-posts, which spread a fantastic radiance around them, puts ideas of childish games into their heads; they play hide and seek, chase each other, quarrel and sulk for no reason; the night is warm; the sky bathed in a gentle night, they kiss. But the charm is broken by another tennis ball thrown by who knows what malicious hand. Surprised and alarmed, the young man and the girls disappear into the depths of the park at night.[10]

Evidently this scenario has little to do with serious competitive tennis and more with an idea of unregulated play. Nijinsky clearly desired a plot that could provide a metaphorical transgression of bourgeois sexual norms (the suggestion of a *ménage a trois* is clearly implicit). On the other hand, the idea of play offered Debussy images of movement, that like in his earlier 'jeux de vagues' ('play of the waves') from his tone poem *La Mer*, were both constantly different and constantly the same.[11] Debussy's musical treatment of bodily movement is, according to his usual compositional practice, impressionistic: the use of whole tone scales, novel orchestrations and constant thematic development (or musical 're-creation') form indistinct musical images that are even more ambiguous than in Debussy's earlier, more programmatic impressionistic works. For Adorno this indistinct quality not only cost *Jeux* its popularity (for him a good thing), it radically precluded closure: 'There is no "end": the composition ceases as does the picture, upon which the viewer turns his back.'[12] By pointing to the work's apparent 'formlessness', Adorno thus circumvented what was for him the problematic issue of art music's illegitimate relationship with the body.

Jeux registered a shift in Debussy's creative development from impressionism into abstraction, with the idea of 'play' rendered in musical terms as a radical formalism that largely eschewed the idea of the extra-musical referent. It is ironic, therefore, that in so doing Debussy had legitimised the musical depiction of sport. In the same year as the premiere of *Jeux*, the Parisian music publishers, Salabert, approached Stravinsky with the idea of him composing music on the topical subject of sport and leisure. Never a composer to knowingly undersell himself, Stravinsky demanded an extortionate fee and Salabert turned instead to the remarkable musical eccentric, Erik Satie. Satie, who had clearly heard of their approach to Stravinsky, protested that their offer was too generous and only agreed to write the work for half the suggested amount. An influential figure in the Parisian modernist scene, Satie and his group of young followers (known as *Les Six*) were closely associated with avant-garde artists and writers, and particularly the experimental poet, Jean Cocteau. Eschewing Romantic notions of inspiration and sublimity, Satie and *Les Six* attempted to make a decisive break with nineteenth-century musical aesthetics, particularly Wagner and Debussy, by creating a new French art music based on popular sources such as cabaret, circus and music hall.[13] Satie's *Sports et Divertissements* is a multi-media experiment in irreverent musical Dadaism, a series of short piano pieces illustrating middle-class leisure pursuits such as tennis, golf and sailing, accompanied by Charles Martin's drawings. Satie also included his own droll verbal commentary but forbade 'anyone to read the text aloud during the performance'. His preface to the collection was typically flippant and anti-Romantic:

> This publication embodies two arts, drawing and music. The drawing part consists of lines, witty lines; the musical part of plain black dots. These two parts put together make an album. I suggest you turn its pages with a tolerant thumb and with a smile, for this is a work of pure whimsy.
>   Let no one look for more.[14]

Sports et Divertissements is a fine example of what Adorno described as 'Satie's pert and puerile piano pieces'[15] and we should not earnestly listen for serious sporting content in the collection which also depicts such diversions as picnics and even flirting. The sheer brevity and playful informality of these facetious vignettes (Satie dispenses with bar lines, time and key signatures throughout) suggests a deliberately frivolous and typically ironic attitude to the representation of sport and leisure on the part of the composer. Indeed, some of the pieces aurally resemble popular newspaper caricatures in their jocularity and use of sporting stereotypes. In 'Le Golf', for example, the whole issue of impassioned involvement in leisure pursuits is gently mocked. The colonel, 'wearing bright green Scotch tweeds', strolls out to the green 'with enthusiasm', his caddy walking behind. Against a surreal golfing landscape ('The clouds are amazed', 'The holes are all a-tremble') the colonel 'measures his shot'. Finally, in a frenzy of rising semiquavers, 'His club bursts into splinters!' Any punning resemblances between the opening and the popular song 'Tea for Two', which was not composed until 1924, are purely coincidental.

Whereas Satie took sporting and leisure pursuits as the stimulus for an aesthetic of almost total inconsequentiality, in the context of a strong post-war reaction to the old musical orthodoxies, a younger generation of Paris-based

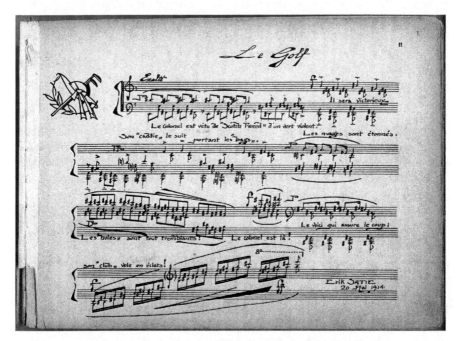

Figure 8.1 Erik Satie, 'Le Golf' from *Sports et Divertissements* (Édition Salabert).

composers found modern spectator sport, with its associations of democratic modernity, an exciting and serious source of inspiration.[16] The transformation of sport and leisure activity had been part of a more general modernisation of France during the *belle époque* period and, by the 1920s, sport was becoming an integral element of French popular culture.[17] Particular interest was shown in the 1924 Paris Olympic games when, amidst the glare of the international media, 44 countries fielded over 5,000 athletes in the newly built Colombes Stadium and in other new state-funded facilities.[18] The contemporary popularity of sport was reflected in a number of musical compositions such as Louis Beydt's *Fanfares* and in Jean Cocteau's ballet score, *Le Train Bleu*, which includes two sporting scenes set to the music of *Les Six* member, Darius Milhaud (see Chapter 7, this volume). Another composer with a particular interest in the sporting context was the young Czech, Bohuslav Martinů. Shortly after arriving in Paris in the early 1920s Martinů shared a flat with a compatriot, the journalist Ondřej Sekora, who was then a sports correspondent for the Brno-based *Lidové Noviny* newspaper and who soon afterwards introduced the sport of rugby union to their native country. Before he came to Paris, Martinů had composed a ballet score called *Who is the Most Powerful in the World?* In a foreword to the 1927 edition of the ballet, the surrealist writer, Vítěslav Nezval, laid out a manifesto for young artists such as himself and Martinů. Nezval's words are a reminder that in modernism the relationship between art and its others, including popular body cultural practices, took on a new significance:[19]

> We are going to study the possibility of new ballet on the street, in the ring and the dance hall, everywhere movement is naturally manifested. We are going to look for immediate expressions of it at football and boxing matches....[20]

Despite the somatic radicalism of Nezval's statement, nothing could be further from Adorno's notion of 'non-conforming music': that which 'preserves its social truth through the isolation resulting from its antithesis to society'.[21]

Nevertheless, as one of Stravinsky's 'facile followers',[22] Martinů, to again quote Adorno, willingly 'acquiesced to the collective tendency of the times'.[23] He often went to sports events with Sekora and, in 1924, signalled his conversion to Stravinskian modernism with an orchestral rondo called *Half-time*, a work inspired by football. Martinů owned a score of *Jeux*, suggesting that he had studied Debussy's masterpiece in detail; however, while the subject matter has superficial similarities, gone is Debussy's post-impressionistic idiom, hitherto an enormous influence on Martinů. In *Half-time* Martinů attempted to convey a sense of the movement and noise of a football crowd in music of a predominantly rhythmic character. The brisk tempo, which only dissipates for a few bars in the middle of the work, also conveys this context. In terms of its orchestration, the predominance of winds, brass and percussion and the use of an obligato piano part lend the work a suitably aggressive, even masculine, vigour and vitality. Structurally the entire work is based upon a short rhythmic motif (the referee's whistle?) which appropriately opens the piece and is then subjected to a process of continuous development. It also recurs to separate the seven different variations or 'phases of the game':

Figure 8.2 The opening of Bohuslav Martinů's *Half-time*.

Like a game of football, the work has a remarkable rhythmic freedom within a relatively rigid formal structure: harsh ostinati, motoric rhythms and aggressive stabbing chords create a palpable sense of dramatic tension. In this sense the work demonstrates Martinů's stylistic debt to two of Stravinsky's great early ballet scores: *Petroushka* (with its bustling evocations of the fairground so detested by Adorno for their populism) and, equally appropriately given that sport itself is a quasi-religious social ritual, *Rite of Spring* (with what Adorno described as its 'anti-humanistic sacrifice to the collective'[24]). At the same time,

Figure 8.3 Half-time. Cartoon by Bohuslav Martinů (source: M. Šafránek, *Martinů. Život A Dílo,* Prague: Státni Hudebni Vydavatelství, 1961).

though *Half-time* relates to professional competitive sport, a more child-like sense of play, with its violent rough-and-tumble, permeates the work, a tendency reflected in a number of charmingly naive drawings the composer sketched during the work's composition.

Half-time was first performed in Prague by Václav Talich and the Czech Philharmonic on 4 December 1924 with the audience in the Smetana Hall divided in loyalties like a football crowd, one section loudly enthusiastic and another vociferously hostile to the obvious influence of Stravinsky. Nevertheless, the work heralded Martinů as an important new musical voice, and in 1926 he composed a companion piece to *Half-time*, *La Bagarre* (*The Tumult*). By the time of its first performance in 1928 Martinů had cleverly dedicated the work to Charles Lindbergh in the light of his solo non-stop flight across the Atlantic the previous year (also the subject of an opera by Berthold Brecht and Kurt Weill,

The Lindbergh Flight). While the composition's aviation links were clearly an opportunistic afterthought, as with *Half-time*, *La Bagarre* is fundamentally a musical expression of the crowd. According to the composer:

> In *Half-time* ... I have portrayed the tension of spectators at a football match. *La Bagarre* is, properly speaking, an analogous subject, but multiplied, transported to the street. It's a boulevard, a stadium, a mass, a quantity which is delirium, clothed as a single body. It's a chaos ruled by all the sentiments of enthusiasm, struggle, joy, sadness, wonder. It's a chaos governed by a common feeling, an invisible bond, which pushes everything forward ... a new form of powerful, unconquerable human mass.[25]

In this resolutely anti-Adornian statement, Martinů gave eloquent expression to the modernist preoccupation with the crowd with no fear of mass culture resulting in an Adornian 'liquidation of the individual';[26] rather, the movements, sounds and passions of the crowd betoken sport's democratic immediacy. Sport is therefore regarded as a suitable subject matter for a new form of radical art music.

Although Martinů evoked the reception of organised sport, the Franco-Swiss composer, Arthur Honegger, focused more on its embodied performance in his 1928 *Mouvement Symphonique no 2 (Rugby)*. Like Martinů, Honegger had been drawn to the vibrant artistic atmosphere of post-war Paris where he became a somewhat semi-detached member of Satie's *Les Six*. Earlier he was associated with Martinů and the Russian émigré, Alexander Tcherepnin, in a musical grouping known as *École de Paris*. Sport music seems to have been firmly on the school's agenda. In 1922 Tcherepnin had composed 'For Boxing Training', one of his *Three Pieces for Chamber Orchestra*, a highly contrapuntal and suitably punchy work first performed in Riga in 1926. Honegger, an enthusiastic Bugatti driver, first musically indulged his love of sport in 1922 with a ballet score called *Skating Rink* based on a scenario by the avant-garde poet, Ricciotto Canudo. This highly effective work reflected the contemporary craze for roller-skating in the French capital and recalled the Futurist fascination with all forms of mechanical movement. The influence of the latter was also evident in his *Mouvement Symphonique no 1 (Pacific 231)* of 1923, a musical evocation of a steam locomotive. He followed this Futuristic celebration of the mechanical with *Rugby*, a work akin to Martinů's *Half-time* in that it is a non-graphic representation of a sporting contest. Like *Half-time* it attempts to rejuvenate the traditional rondo form (in which a recurring theme is interspersed with contrasting episodes). Also like *Half-time* it is profoundly influenced by Stravinsky and is primarily rhythmic in nature, only dissipating during a short slower episode suggesting the release of dramatic tension during the half-time changeover. After a bustling opening section that reflects the excitement in the stadium as the players enter the field, there is a chorale-like theme in the brass that returns on a number of occasions. As much as the work relies heavily on motoric rhythms and strenuous harmonic dissonance to portray the physical exertion and violence of a rugby match – Neville Cardus suggested that 'the match seems never to break away from the scrum'[27] – a broad and harmonically tonal string melody provides contrast and suggests the more elegant, flowing qualities of the game. Finally, the chorale theme returns victoriously, although we do not know which team has won.

Although increasingly impatient with listeners and critics who overstated the pictorial elements of the work, Honegger later explained his title:

> I very much like the game of football, but I prefer rugby. I find it more spontaneous, more direct and closer to nature than football which is a more scientific game. I am aware of a carefully controlled rhythm in football and for me the savage, brusque, untidy and desperate rhythm of rugby is more attractive. It would be wrong to consider my piece as programme music. All it does is to try and express in my own musician's language, the attacks and ripostes of the game, and the rhythm and colour of a match at the Colombes Stadium; I honestly feel it is only right to name my sources. That is the reason why this short composition bears the title of *Rugby*.[28]

Honegger's words uneasily veer between acknowledgement and disavowal of any extra-musical referent, but he seems to suggest that the rhythmical nature of particular sports might lend themselves to different forms of musical representation. As the Honegger scholar, Geoffrey Spratt, has argued: 'To express the incredible dynamism of a game which combines sheer force with vibrancy and even lyricism of rhythmical activity, is no easy task, yet it is ideally suited to Honegger's technique.'[29] At the same time, while we can search for direct musical references to sport in works such as *Half-time* and *Rugby*, both Martinů and Honegger doubted that the abstract language of music was capable of representation in any mimetic sense. Martinů explicitly denied that *La Bagarre* was 'descriptive music'.[30] Instead, these works use musical language to create *abstract expressions* of the *essence* of the sporting experience and thus have visual parallels in abstract art works of the 1920s such as Willi Baumeister's *The Footballer* and John Heartfield's *Football*.[31] In counterpoint to Adorno's and other neo-Marxist critiques of sport, the apparent mechanisation of the human body entailed by sport, and the mass collectivity of the sporting crowd, became the subject of aesthetic celebration rather than of ideological censure.

English critical reception ('not suitable subject matter for the concert hall')

Much as Honegger increasingly denied *Rugby*'s pictorial function and became impatient with critics who claimed to hear the referee's whistle or the roar of the crowd in his music, his choice of title inevitably begged this kind of interpretation. When the work was performed in London in January 1930, *The Times* responded with the following droll notice:

After the interval came Honegger's 'Rugby'. In this we might have imagined hearing the forward fiddles engaging in a scrummage around the conductor, the half-back wood-wind passing the ball to the brass, and the basses tackling the trombones low – were it not that we were warned against reading into this work any 'programme.' We were to regard it as a symphonic movement, the latter word being employed in its literal sense of something which moves. But movement implies some sense of direction, and it must be confessed that, for all its bustle and energy, Honegger's music seems to stay all the time in one place – within the oblong of a football field, perhaps – and never scores a try. We, at least, remain unconverted.[32]

According to this critic, Honegger's greatest fault was in failing to portray bodily movement convincingly in music. In so doing the writer provided a non-Marxist counterpart to Adorno's attitude to Stravinskian 'motility' as later expressed in his *Philosophy of Modern Music*:

The school rooted in Stravinsky has been called motoric. The concentration of music upon accents and time relationships produces an illusion of bodily movement. This movement, however, consists of the varied recurrence of the same: of the same melodic forms, of the same harmonies, indeed of the very same rhythmic patterns. Motility ... is actually incapable of any kind of forward motion.[33]

If Adorno was correct, then the sports compositions of Stravinskians such as Martinů and Honegger were fundamentally flawed. Their privileging of motoric rhythm, although an endeavour to musically render the body, only served to prove the impossibility of such representation. Yet for Adorno the attempted intrusion of the body into the elevated and abstract realm of art music was transgression enough.

The politically conservative gatekeepers of the English musical scene were equally hostile to the fashion for sports music, seeing this development as symptomatic of a broader process of cultural decline in which the boundary between art and popular culture was becoming dangerously blurred. A blend of cultural snobbery and political angst often informed English critical attitudes to sport in music. For one writer 'the unpleasantness of Honegger's piece comes of its subject, or of his faithful realisation of the spirit of that subject'; hence he 'puts together something that is as revolting to a delicate spirit as are the faces and cries of the average [sporting] audience'.[34] Such an attitude to mass culture in music already had precedents: when Ralph Vaughan Williams expurgated references to football in his 1909 musical setting of A. E. Housman's *A Shropshire Lad* on the grounds that it was 'not suitable subject matter for the concert hall', he not only wilfully conflated what was clearly an informal rural leisure practice with organised sport, but also revealed the elitism underlying his avowedly democratic, folk-inspired modernism[35]

(Housman was furious at Vaughan Williams' act of bowdlerisation, writing, 'I wonder how he would like me to cut two bars out of his music'[36]). In the early 1920s Vaughan Williams composed a nationalistic ballad opera, *Hugh the Drover*, in which a prize-fight functions as a pivotal scene. However, this was a rambunctious dramatisation of virile bare-knuckle pugilism set during the Napoleonic Wars, a musical representation of a resolutely pre-industrial, rural sporting practice and thus apparently legitimate subject matter for the leading light of the English musical renaissance.

Vaughan Williams's rebellious pupil, Constant Lambert, was both a composer and an influential writer whose musical and literary output reflected some of the ambiguities of modernism's relationship with popular culture. Revered by the American jazz composer, Duke Ellington, Lambert himself wittily assimilated jazz idioms into works such as *The Rio Grande* (1929). In Paris such fusions of musical styles had become relatively commonplace as works such as Stravinsky's *Ragtime*, Martinů's *La Revue de Cuisine* and Milhaud's *La Création du Monde* testify. In Britain, however, Lambert's use of jazz was a radical aesthetic statement. In the words of the author and composer, Anthony Burgess, Lambert 'was a fearless reconciler of what the academies and Tin Pan Alley alike presumed to be eternally opposed'.[37] In his struggle against what he saw as the narrow parochialism of Vaughan Williams and the other English pastoralist composers, Lambert had even written a sport-inspired work called *Prize-fight* in 1924, a pointedly modern and internationalist counterpart to Vaughan Williams' historical depiction of pugilism. In this homage to Satie and Cocteau, Lambert utilised novel instrumentations redolent of the music hall and employed the simple but effective technique of labelling the two boxers with contrasting musical leitmotifs. However, by the time he wrote his influential survey of contemporary music, *Music Ho! A Study of Music in Decline* in the early 1930s, he had seen the error of his populist ways, particularly with regards to sport. The very title of the book, taken from Shakespeare's *Antony and Cleopatra* ('The Music, ho! Let it alone, let's to billiards ...'[38]) very deliberately evokes an evaluative binary opposition between music and games. Lambert had been educated at an English public school where he had disliked all sports except boxing, and in *Music Ho!* he consistently projected his anti-sport sentiments onto his bleak analysis of the contemporary musical scene.[39] For Lambert, Debussy's vaporous impressionism successfully distanced *Jeux* from any taint of hearty masculinity, or what he termed the 'slap-you-on-the-back, hiking spirit' of 'sportsman composers' such as Honegger. Like Adorno, he could forgive *Jeux* on the grounds of its indistinct, non-corporeal qualities and because 'the dim tennis players who flit inconsequently through the garden are no more genuinely *sportifs* than croquet players in a fan by Conder'. Thus 'Debussy harps back to Baudelaire, not forward to [Jean] Borotra' (the celebrated French tennis player of the 1920s).[40] But for Lambert, Honegger and Martinů's choice of sporting subject matter betrayed a debased 'obsession with topicality'. Works such as *Half-time*, *Rugby* and *Pacific 231* had merely replaced 'Romantic pictorialism' with an equally questionable and 'naively realistic ... mechanical picturesque'.[41] Lambert saw the trend in gendered terms, as a hollow and pretentious quest for artistic virility:

> The glamour of the 'pale and interesting' musician is now supplanted by the glamour of the suntanned and boring athlete, and plus-fours are a more potent symbol than the black hat …. If we see a begoggled leather-coated and plus-foured figure, starting off with a *démarrage formidable* in a rakish racing model, we may be sure that the driver is really more at home in La Rue de la Boëtie than at Brooklands.[42]

The '*sportif*' works of Honegger and Martinů riled Lambert for their pictorialism, but such 'mechanical romanticism' only affected 'the façade of music as we know it'.[43] Far worse was what Lambert perceived as an insidious sportification or mechanisation of the process of musical composition itself. The prolific German modernist, Paul Hindemith – whose music was equally censored by Adorno for his apparent submission to the 'collective tendency of the times'[44] – was seemingly particularly culpable:

> It will be observed that Cleopatra emphatically preferred billiards to music. This attitude, though somewhat philistine perhaps, is to be praised in that it recognizes that music and billiards represent two different sides of life. Cleopatra neither confused the functions of the two diversions nor suggested that they were better combined. Today, however, she would either have wireless turned on continually in the billiard room, or else she would have to listen to composers like Hindemith, who reduce music to the spiritual level of billiards, pingpong and clock golf.[45]

Hindemith's anti-Romantic, craftsman-like approach to composition, and particularly his notion of *Gebrauchsmusik* (utility music), was for Lambert representative of a socially and politically dangerous form of musical constructivism. Again, sport metaphors are used to convey the 'mechanical' quality of Hindemith's music:

> Listening to his firmly wrought works we seem to see ourselves in a block of hygienic and efficient workman's flats built in the best modernismus manner, from which emerge troops of healthy uniformed children on their way to the communal gymnasium. Hindemith's technique is indeed a gymnastic technique, and his attitude towards 'expressive' music is reminiscent of an instructor in physical jerks pooh-poohing the poses and affectations of ballet …. A display of gymnastics, though admirable from many points of view, is boring to watch, and a display of musical gymnastics is not only boring to listen to but hopelessly sterile in aim.[46]

Not only do such dystopian images of mass physical education reveal fears of the contemporary militarisation of Nazi Germany, Lambert's notion of sportified approaches to musical composition formed part of a broader discourse in which perceptions of the mechanisation and standardisation of cultural processes figured in the regulation and standardisation of social and personal life more generally.[47] In England particularly, music's relationship with sport in its various guises was a loaded cultural, and indeed political, issue. By way of contrast, the final section of this chapter explores the reception and institutionalisation of sports music in newly independent Czechoslovakia.

Sport and musical modernism in Czechoslovakia

The years leading up to, and immediately following, the formation of post-imperial Czechoslovakia in 1918 were culturally fraught as politicians and cultural figures grappled with the problem of how best to represent the new nation. Here the tension between tradition and modernity had a distinctively national dimension. On the one hand the Czech National Revival, which had flourished since the mid-nineteenth century during a relatively liberal period of Austro-Hungarian governance, had promoted, rediscovered and reinvented Czech culture in its broadest sense – its language, literature, folklore and mythology. But while this strong sense of the past informed the symbolic formation of modern Czechoslovakia, a younger generation of artists, influenced by the international modernist developments discussed above, sought to break away from the fusty confines of history – indeed, Martinů's gravitation to Paris can be understood in this context.[48] For example, in 1913 a Futurist manifesto written by the poet, Stanislav Kotstka Neumann, appeared in *Lidové Noviny*: 'Long live: Machinism, sports fields, Frištenský [a famous Czech boxer] ... Laurin and Klement [the first Czech car makers], the crematorium, the future cinema, the Circus Henry ... the World Exhibition, railway stations, artistic advertisements, steel and concrete!'[49] As with Parisian Futurism, sport is here seen as a dynamic element of the 'here and now', something that along with other demotic entertainments and the newly emerging technologies, represents the replacement of the old guard by the indisputably new. Yet post-imperial Czechoslovakian sport continued to have a strong historical and nation-building aspect in the form of the Sokol Gymnastic Association. The Sokol (or 'Falcon') movement was formed in 1862 in order to promote Czech cultural and social life and to cultivate the physical and intellectual development of its members. Although gymnastics was the organisation's primary means of developing a national ideal in which the strong and healthy human body and the body politic were symbolically conflated, it also sought to nurture moral, educational and cultural principles. From 1882 Sokol held mass festivals (or 'slety') in Prague, large-scale patriotic jamborees featuring vast collective gymnastic displays as well as theatrical, literary and musical events.[50] Musical accompaniment to gymnastics was introduced at the second slet in 1891 and, at the 1895 slet, a large contingent of Moravian Sokols performed an exercise routine with Indian clubs to the music of a lifelong Sokol member, Leoš Janáček.[51] The composer's *Music for Gymnastic Exercises* was suitably imbued with Moravian folk melos and dance rhythms, with each short piece consisting of a brief fanfare followed by a gymnastic set.[52]

Music had played an integral part in the ceremonial and social aspects of Sokol culture since its earliest days. In the early 1860s the great Czech composer, Antonín Dvořák, amended the title of a short musical fragment to 'Sokol March', although the sketch was never completed.[53] Later, the talented composer of band music, František Kmoch (1848–1912), received a regular salary from Sokol to provide marches for its ceremonial occasions and music for callisthenics, such as a brass band arrangement of Janáček's *Music for Gymnastic Exercises*. Shortly after the foundation of independent Czechoslovakia in 1918 Martinů's teacher, Josef Suk, wrote a suitably patriotic and uplifting march, *Towards a New Life*, for the 1920 slet. The work later received a silver medal in the music competition at the 1932 Los Angeles Olympics. In addition, the movement's pan-Slavic ambitions meant that Sokol branches were formed in other Eastern European nations. In the Soviet Union, for example, Serge Prokofiev wrote music for Sokol and for the Soviet alternative to the Olympics, the Spartakiad. But the most well-known composition with Sokol connections is undoubtedly Janáček's *Sinfonietta*, a work first performed during the Prague slet in June 1926. Janáček was a committed nationalist and was particularly drawn to Sokol's nation-building and patriotic elements. By 1926 he had forged a distinctively modernist idiom of national music based closely on the rhythms and inflections of the Czech language ('nápěvky' or 'speech melody'). The 'meaning' of the *Sinfonietta* is a particularly slippery matter, especially given the sporting context of its first performance and some of Janáček's own reflections

Figure 8.4 Leoš Janáček, *Sinfonietta* (first movement, bars 47–52) (© 1979 Ernst Eulenberg Ltd, London. Reproduced by kind permission).

upon it: not only did the composer favour the subtitle 'Military' over 'Sokol' but he also gave each movement a further subtitle, each evoking a feature of his native city of Brno in the new post-imperial context ('The Castle', 'The Monastery', 'The Street' and 'The Town Hall'). Nevertheless, in the *Sinfonietta's* majestic opening 'Fanfare', perhaps we can hear the emphatic syllables of the word 'Sokol' in the timpani part over which, in the long phrases of the trumpets, a newly liberated falcon soars. Here, as in much of the *Sinfonietta*, the music evinces a honed muscularity (see Figure 8.4).

Janáček's disclaimers notwithstanding, his and other Czech composers' connections with the Sokol movement underline the broader social and cultural role of the organisation within newly independent Czechoslovakia. The same is true in relation to his compatriot, the composer of *Half-time*, Martinů. Martinů's father was an active member of the Sokol in their hometown of Polička and his son was thus involved with the society from his early childhood. The Polička Sokol provided moral and financial support for the composer's studies in Prague and also gave the young musician performing opportunities. For example, in spring 1920 Martinů played the piano in two musical events organised by Sokol, the first of which formed part of the celebrations marking President Tomáš Masaryk's eightieth birthday. Later, in 1933, the Sokol in Mělník expressed an interest in performing his ballet, *Who is the Most Powerful in the World?* suggesting the extent to which Sokol was a cultural, as well as a sporting, organisation. On his summer trips back to Czechoslovakia during the 1920s and 1930s Martinů made a point of attending the Sokol festivals in Prague. As his letters suggest, Sokol gymnastic displays provided this deracinated figure with a sense of national belonging. In 1931 Martinů entered a Sokol competition for an orchestral work due to be performed at the slet of the following year. He received second prize (no first prize being awarded) for his *Festive Overture*. The judges included Josef Suk and the conductor of the first performance, František Stupka and Martinů received a prize of 3,000 Czech crowns. When the work was later performed at the 1938 slet a critique of the performance in *Radiojournal* highlighted the contemporary interface of sport and music in the most positive way:

> The relation of today's music to sport is all the stronger in so far as the new generation of composers draws inspiration from sport .... Bohuslav Martinů wrote in Paris the football-inspired *Half-time* and today gives us his *Festive Overture*. However, we have a lot of other composers who have found a strong stimulus for their creation in the Sokol exercises. The model is, of course, Suk's immortal march whose introductory fanfare has already created a school.[54]

In recognising a canon of Czech sports music (to which could be added Pavel Bořkovec's orchestral scherzo, *Start*), the writer reveals a critical attitude to contemporary music and body cultural practices, and a relaxed attitude to tradition and modernity that is clearly at odds with that of Adorno and the English critics. As Tia DeNora has written: 'The matter of [music's] social significance is not pregiven, but is rather the result of how that music is apprehended within specific circumstances.'[55] In the context of the new Czechoslovakia, modernist sports music, as institutionalised and mediated by Sokol, was an accepted and integral manifestation of the nation's social, cultural and political aspirations.

Coda

However much the various compositions discussed here differ in terms of their contexts of production and consumption, they all testify to the increasing popularity and institutional significance of sport in the early twentieth century. Furthermore, they demonstrate the willingness of many musical modernists to radically engage with popular culture and the body as they sought to break away from what they saw as the worn-out musical languages, conventions and subject matters of the past. As Alex Ross has noted, in writing works such as *Half-time* and *Rugby* the works' composers 'weren't simply engaging in artificial games; they were asking mighty questions about what art meant and how it related to society'.[56] But even if such compositions ultimately failed to convey musically the sporting experience, if we return to the words of the modernist artist and author, Wyndham Lewis quoted in the introduction to this volume, it is arguable that the ability of music to engage the body made it the art form most suited to the representation of body cultural practices:

> The coldest musician ... cannot help interfering with your body .... As you listen to music you find yourself dashing, gliding or perambulating about: you are hurried hither and thither, however rhythmically; your legs, your larynx, your heart are interfered with as much as is the membrane of the ear.[57]

Nevertheless, the intrusion of the body into music and into the reified category of the aesthetic more generally has long been a vexed issue.[58] With the exception of Debussy's *Jeux* and Janáček's *Sinfonietta* – now successfully shorn of its gymnastic associations in all countries save the Czech and Slovak Republics – this loose constellation of works presently occupies only a marginal status in the modernist canon. The music of Hindemith, with its 'gymnastic techniques', is also distinctly out of fashion, not least because of the role of critical discourse, including the influential writings of Adorno and Lambert, in this evaluative process. Ironically, in the context of the recent populist 'musicalisation' of sport,[59] a concert of sports works from the 1920s and 1930s would now seem hopelessly 'highbrow'; yet these compositions remain fascinating reminders of the radicalism, complexity and multifaceted character of musical modernism, they show that many composers resisted Adorno's call to seek refuge from the popular in the arcane recesses of extreme formalism and they suggest how postmodern patterns of cultural crossover and hybridity were already implicit within aspects of the modernist project.

Acknowledgement

I would like to thank Jeffrey O. Segrave and John Bale for their helpful comments on earlier versions of this chapter.

Notes

1 Solomon Volkov (ed.), *Testimony: The Memoirs of Dmitri Shostakovich*, trans. A. W. Bouis, London: Faber & Faber, 1979, p. 237. Space does not allow for a full discussion of Shostakovich's interest in, and musical/journalistic engagement with, Soviet football or of his propagandist football ballet, *The Golden Age* (1929). Written during a short-lived era of artistic freedom and experimentation in Soviet culture, the ballet is concerned with a Soviet football team who triumphantly visit corrupt and decadent western Europe to play an exhibition match. From a purely musical aspect its pivotal football match scene resembles the sports works of Martinů and Honegger discussed in this chapter and likewise represents a significant breaking down of cultural hierarchies, albeit in a very different ideological context.
2 Theodor Adorno, *Philosophy of Modern Music*, trans. A. G. Mitchell and W. Blomster, New York: Seabury, 1973, p. 41.
3 Theodor Adorno, *Prisms*, trans. S. and S. Weber, Cambridge, MA: Harvard University Press, 1981, p. 81.
4 Steven Connor, *Postmodernist Culture: An Introduction to Theories of the Contemporary*, Oxford: Blackwell, 1989.
5 Quoted in Jean-Jacques Soleil and Guy Lelong, *Musical Masterpieces*, London: Chambers, 1991, p. 15.
6 Paul de Man, *Blindness and Insight: Essays in the Rhetoric of Contemporary Criticism*, New York: Oxford University Press, 1971, p. 153.
7 Quoted in Connor, *Postmodernist Culture*, p. 104.
8 Timothy A. Johnson, *Baseball and the Music of Charles Ives*, Lanham, MD: Scarecrow Press, 2004.
9 Marie Rambert, *Quicksilver: The Autobiography of Marie Rambert*, London: Macmillan, 1973, p. 68.
10 Quoted in Gerald Larner, programme note for Claude Debussy, *Jeux*, Hallé Concert Society, 2005.
11 Paul Griffiths, *A Concise History of Modern Music from Debussy to Boulez*, London: Thames and Hudson, 1978, p. 48.
12 Adorno, *Philosophy of Modern Music*, p. 188.
13 Nancy Perloff, *Art and the Everyday: Popular Entertainment and the Circle of Erik Satie*, Oxford: Clarendon Press, 1991, p. 2.
14 Erik Satie, 'Preface', in *Piano Music, Volume 3: Sports et Divertissements*, Paris: Salabert, 1987, p. 1.
15 Theodor Adorno, *Minima Moralia: Reflections from Damaged Life*, trans. E. F. N. Jephcott, London: Verso, 1978, p. 151.
16 While the Parisian modernists chose sporting subjects in their quest for topicality, the rapidly expanding field of sport needed music at its local, national and international levels. For example, in 1928 the Danish modernist, Carl Nielsen, was commissioned to write a cantata for the opening of a new municipal swimming pool in Copenhagen (he also composed an educational song on the theme of boxing). At the international level the writings of the founder of the modern Olympic Movement, Pierre de Coubertin, stressed the importance of music to the ceremonial, competitive and even spiritual aspects of Olympic culture. Given Coubertin's adoration of Wagner it is not surprising that Olympic music culture tended to hark back to the language and forms of nineteenth-century Romanticism (Richard Strauss's *Olympic*

Hymn, first performed at the 1936 Berlin Games, being an example). On the other hand, the Danish composer, Rudolph Hermann Simonson's *Hellas Symphony*, which won an Olympic bronze medal in 1928, is distinctly Nielsenian in its musical language.

17 Richard Holt, *Sport and Society in Modern France*, London: Macmillan, 1981, p. 213.
18 Ibid., p. 196.
19 Georgina Born and David Hesmondhalgh (eds), *Western Music and its Others: Difference, Representation and Appropriation in Music*, London: University of California Press, 2000, p. 12.
20 Vítěslav Nezval, 'Modern ballet', foreword to Bohuslav Martinů, *Who is the Most Powerful in the World?*, Prague: B.M. Klika, 1927.
21 Adorno, *Philosophy of Modern Music*, p. 21.
22 Ibid., p. 7.
23 Ibid., p. 4.
24 Ibid., p. 145.
25 Quoted in Miloš Šafránek, *Bohuslav Martinů: His Life and Works*, trans. R. Finlayson-Sambourová, London: Allan Wingate, 1961, pp. 108–109.
26 Adorno, *Philosophy of Modern Music*, p. 190.
27 Neville Cardus, '"Unfamiliar" Works', *Manchester Guardian*, 16 January 1931.
28 Quoted in Geoffrey K. Spratt, *The Music of Arthur Honegger*, Cork: Cork University Press, 1987, p. 149. Honegger later composed the score for the 1943 film, *La Boxe En France (Boxing in France)*.
29 Ibid., p. 150.
30 Šafránek, *Bohuslav Martinů*, p. 109.
31 Pierre Lanfranchi, Christiane Eisenberg, Tony Mason and Alfred Wahl, *100 Years of Football: The Fifa Centennial Book*, London: Weidenfeld and Nicolson, 2004, pp. 204–208.
32 *The Times*, 1 February 1930. I am grateful to Tony Collins for drawing my attention to this notice.
33 Adorno, *Philosophy of Modern Music*, p. 178.
34 'Football in Music – Honegger's *Rugby*', *British Musician and Musical News*, February 1931, 39–40.
35 Merion Hughes and Robert Stradling, *The English Musical Renaissance 1840–1940: Constructing a National Music*, Manchester: Manchester University Press, 1993, p. 186. During the first half of the twentieth century it became almost *de rigeur* for English pastoralist composers to set Housman's deeply elegiac, bitter-sweet verse to music and, as settings by George Butterworth, John Ireland and Ivor Gurney testify, they largely respected the text's formal and thematic integrity, including its evocation of the sports of football, cricket and athletics.
36 Archie Burnett (ed.), *The Letters of A.E. Housman vol. 1*, Oxford: Clarendon Press, 2007, p. 458.
37 Anthony Burgess, *Little Wilson and Big God: Being the First Part of the Confessions of Anthony Burgess*, London: Vintage, 2002, p. 110.
38 Constant Lambert, *Music Ho! A Study of Music in Decline*, London: Faber and Faber, 1937.
39 An observer of the 1930s Bloomsbury scene, the Trinidadian writer, C. L. R. James, described Lambert as resembling a prize-fighter. C. L. R. James, *Letters from London*, Oxford: Signal Books, 2003, p. 27.
40 Lambert, *Music Ho!*, p. 57.
41 Jaromil Burghauser, *Antonín Dvořák Themeatic Catalogue*, Prague: Bärenreiter Supraphon, 1996, item 806.
42 Lambert, *Music Ho!*, p. 208.
43 Ibid., p. 211.
44 Adorno, *Philosophy of Modern Music*, p. 4.

45 Lambert, *Music Ho!*, p. 217.
46 Ibid., p. 212.
47 Francis Mulhern, *The Moment of Scrutiny*, London: New Left Books, 1979.
48 Derek Sayer, *The Coasts of Bohemia: A Czech Cultural History*, Princeton: Princeton University Press, 1998, pp. 154–163.
49 Quoted in ibid., p. 158.
50 Ibid., pp. 105–106.
51 Claire E. Nolte, *The Sokol in the Czech Lands to 1914: Training for the Nation*, Basingstoke: Palgrave, 2002, pp. 121–130.
52 Because of their gymnastic origins, the Czech author, Milan Kundera, afforded these pieces a marginal status in the Janáček canon: 'O composers, control yourselves when pretty ladies from a gym come to ask a little favour! Your good turn will outlive you – as a laughing-stock!' Milan Kundera, *Testaments Betrayed*, trans. Linda Asher, London: Faber & Faber, 1995, p. 190. While watching callisthenic performances at Sokol slety Janáček decided the discipline deserved a richer musical component and intended to write a treatise on musical accompaniment for mass callisthenics. It was a project he never realised.
53 Jaroslav Mihule, *Martinů: Osud Skladatele*, Prague: Charles University Press, 2002, p. 278. I am grateful to Hilda Hearne for assistance in translating passages from this book from the original Czech.
54 Quoted in ibid., p. 278. Martinů later continued this tradition by writing a 32-bar fanfare entitled 'Greetings to Sokols and the Sokol Festival' for the 1948 event. The piece was never performed and was smuggled into exile by Marie Provazníková, a Sokol official. It was subsequently arranged for nine wind instruments from the original piano version by Jan Hanus and published in 1976 in the Swiss journal, *Konfrontace*. The 1948 Sokol festival was the last before the organisation was banned by the communist regime. I am indebted to the staff of the Martinů Institute in Prague, and particularly Lucie Berná and Aleš Březina, for their guidance and help in researching this most underrated composer's relationship to sport and the Sokol movement.
55 Tia DeNora, *Music in Everyday Life*, Cambridge: Cambridge University Press, 2000, p. 23.
56 Alex Ross, *The Rest is Noise: Listening to the Twentieth Century*, London: Fourth Estate, 2008, p. 110.
57 Wyndham Lewis, 'The Credentials of the Painter', in Paul Edwards (ed.), *Creatures of Habit and Creatures of Change: Essays on Art, Literature and Society 1914–1956*, Santa Rosa: Black Sparrow Press, 1989, p. 70.
58 Terry Eagleton, *The Ideology of the Aesthetic*, Oxford: Blackwell, 1990.
59 Steve Redhead, *Post-Fandom and the Millennial Blues: The Transformation of Soccer Culture*, London: Routledge, 1997, pp. 70–79.

9   War, remembrance and sport

'Abide With Me' and the FA Cup Final in the 1920s

Jeffrey Hill

Sounds have long been a cherished feature in the collective memory of the English Cup Final: the cheering of the crowd, the stirring music of military bands before the kick-off and at half-time, and the singing, both of the spectators and, in more recent years, of celebrated singers brought in to perform well-known songs as a climax to the pre-match entertainments. Thus it was that in 2007, at the first Cup Final to be played in the 'new' Wembley,[1] the divas Sarah Brightman and Lesley Garrett gave, with the benefit of microphones, a powerful rendition of the old Victorian hymn 'Abide With Me'.[2] As the television cameras panned the faces of massed spectators, however, the music might have seemed to be evoking a less-than-cherished response. Some people, to be sure, were seen to be singing along. But many were not. They possibly felt (as had the organisers of a supporters' lobby the previous year) that songs, if they were to be sung at all, should be performed by the assembled crowds themselves, and not by professional musical stars.[3] Most, however, looked simply bemused by the whole ceremony; perhaps they were questioning what this song, with its strange words, had to do with a football match.[4] Some spectators would no doubt have been aware that 'Abide With Me' was part of a Wembley tradition that was being carried forward from the old stadium to the new one. But how many would have known that the song's inclusion in the programme had originally been because of its popularity as a funeral hymn? Had they know this, its presence in 2007 would no doubt have seemed even stranger.[5]

I

The English FA Cup Final became a national institution, with profound meanings for English (if not British) life, in the 1920s. The competition of which the Cup Final was the climax had started in the early 1870s, and by the end of the century it had acquired a large following. Until the 1920s, however, it had remained essentially a 'football' event, an opportunity for supporters to follow their team and enjoy a day out in London.[6] The staging of the Cup Final at the popular leisure arena of Crystal Palace in south London underlined the idea of the event as a 'holiday'. In the early 1920s, however, the leisurely spontaneity of

Cup Final day changed. What transformed an informal occasion of popular culture into a more 'official' ritual of national life was the moving of the Cup Final to Wembley in 1923. There, in a new stadium built as part of an extensive site for the British Empire Exhibition (1924–1925), the Cup Final acquired characteristics more usually associated with state ceremony than with sport. The presence of the monarch, and the presentation to him of the teams, was the principal feature of the Cup Final's new status. To this was added, in 1927, the broadcasting of the match by the BBC, which quickly gave the event a prime place in its annual calendar, a 'must' as Asa Briggs has described it in his history of broadcasting.[7] During the course of the first few Cup Finals at the new venue a programme of music developed which served as a prelude to the matches. It included the playing of stirring traditional tunes by the military bands of elite regiments and, from 1927, 'community' singing by the crowd as it assembled and waited for the kick-off (wartime songs such as 'Tipperary' and 'Pack Up Your Troubles' were especially popular).[8] The music concluded, after the presentation of the football players to the king, with the singing of the national anthem. By the late 1920s this ceremony had acquired a character and pattern that was to change little during the next three decades. One moment in particular of these musical rituals always had a deep impact on the crowds. It came before the national anthem and was associated with the singing of the hymn 'Abide With Me', which had been introduced into the programme as part of the community singing in 1927.

The musical programme of the Cup Final drew upon precedents for its form and content. The cultural historian Dave Russell has shown how the singing of 'Abide With Me' was one aspect of a mid-1920s enthusiasm for the singing in public places of well-known songs and hymns by large groups of usually untrained people under the direction of a conductor.[9] The fashion seems to have been relatively short-lived at this time, possibly fading in its appeal by the late 1920s; but it derived from earlier movements of singing together, notably in northern chapels in the mid-nineteenth century, by British music-hall audiences in the later nineteenth century and by troops during the First World War. The mid-1920s revival of these older forms of popular musical entertainment came about, as much for commercial reasons as anything else, largely through the prompting of the *Daily Express*. Under the direction of its owner, Max Aitken (later Lord Beaverbrook), the newspaper was seeking to establish a place in the fierce circulation wars being waged by the leading titles of the national press.[10] Community singing at this time took place in many different locations, league football grounds being one such, and the success of football singing in the 1926 and 1927 seasons seems to have been the cause of its incorporation in the Cup Final programme.[11] Sponsorship was forthcoming from the *Daily Express*, which saw the opportunity of advertising itself through the distribution of thousands of *Daily Express* song sheets printed with the lyrics of the songs to be performed. There has been much discussion about who was responsible for choosing the particular hymn 'Abide With Me' for the Cup Final of 1927. Evidence is inconclusive and contradictory, and we may never know the answer; it seems most probable that an FA representative proposed it at a committee meeting. However, it is important to note that a popular belief developed in the late 1920s that the hymn had been included at the suggestion of the Royal Family. 'Abide With Me' was said to be Queen Mary's favourite, and this legend gave weight to the 'public' status of the singing.[12] Though it is clear that there was no conscious attempt to make 'Abide With Me' a formal ritual of remembrance – its appearance in the programme had more to do with its popularity as a hymn than with any desire to honour the dead – its inclusion in a programme that had already acquired the characteristics of state ceremony bestowed upon the hymn a very particular significance at this time.[13]

'Abide With Me' begins:

> Abide with me; fast falls the eventide;
> The darkness deepens; LORD, with me abide;
> When other helpers fail, and comforts flee,
> Help of the helpless, O abide with me.[14]

There are seven more verses in this vein. The words are rather stilted to twenty-first-century ears, but when accompanied by the tune 'Eventide', written by the prolific Victorian hymn composer W. H. Monk, the combination of words and music is capable still of arousing powerful emotions. The words were written in 1847 by the Anglican clergyman H. F. Lyte, curate of Brixham, Devon, well before football in its modern form was invented.[15] They deal not with sport but with death. The 'me' of the verse is preparing to die and to meet his or her Maker. The hymn celebrates this anticipation, as the frailties of mortal life are about to be transcended by life eternal:

> I fear no foe with Thee at hand to bless;
> Ills have no weight, and tears no bitterness;
> Where is death's sting? Where, Grave, thy victory?
> I triumph still, if Thou abide with me.

In spite of its subject matter the hymn is far from morbid and looks forward to a new and more glorious existence in heaven. By the late Victorian period the hymn, to the tune 'Eventide', had become a standard item in religious services and was well known to all those brought up in the tradition of sacred music performed in church or chapel. In the post-war years its historical longevity no doubt provided comforting memories of a time remembered as more stable. Though a Protestant hymn, 'Abide With Me' spoke of personal religious solace in a form that eschewed the more rampant expressions of Christianity to be found in certain other hymns (notably 'Onward Christian Soldiers'). Its sentiments enabled it to be adapted to many denominations, and as may be imagined 'Abide With Me' was much in demand at funerals in all parts of the English-speaking world. It was popular for many years in the United States, for example, where it was sung at memorial ceremonies for leading politicians.[16]

If, as historians, we attempt to understand the effects of the singing of the hymn in Wembley Stadium on Saturday, 23 April 1927 we are more than ever confronted by the problem of sources: how we might use them and how we can interpret the possible meanings they mediate. The event was reported in the daily press, though most of the accounts dwell on the football match rather than the ceremonies preceding it. Very few press reports go into any detail about the singing. Even had they done so, what cannot adequately be captured is the *atmosphere* of occasion. Sporting sounds are transient and therefore elusive phenomena when studied historically. Nonetheless, there seems no doubt that, at this time, experience of singing 'Abide With Me' was (as one historian of the Cup Final has put it) 'a moment of deep emotion that moved the great crowds'.[17] Another writer has noted how this song taps into 'basic human sensibilities'.[18] What is more, the context of the singing wrought its own particular influences, creating a form of reception that was particular to the singers themselves. In 1927 the match was played between The Arsenal and Cardiff City. The former club was making its first appearance in a Cup Final, though Cardiff City had appeared at Wembley two years earlier when they lost to Sheffield United. The presence of the Welsh team and their supporters, numbering some 30,000, conspicuous in sight and sound, enabled commentators to endow the proceedings with a *British* flavour.[19] It also ensured that thousands of fans, many doubtless from a rich chapel culture, might bring a distinctive choral accent to the community singing. Three years earlier at an international rugby match at Cardiff Arms Park there had been an impressive display of crowd singing *in harmony* when the bandmaster had led the crowd in 'Cwm Rhondda'.[20] At Wembley in 1927 'Land of My Fathers' was sung in acknowledgement of the Welsh presence and *The Times* noted the 'unmistakeable quality of Welsh voices' that made the singing so memorable.[21] The *Daily Express* anticipated that 'the melodious Welsh voice will make itself heard at Wembley'.[22] 'When the call came for the hymn "Abide With Me"', reported the *Daily Dispatch*, 'every man [sic] in the packed stadium stood with bared head and joined with fervour in the music.'[23] The slow cadences of the tune 'Eventide' were well suited to singing by a vast and unrehearsed crowd. The Master of Ceremonies, Mr Ratcliffe, was a former physical-training instructor, 'and it was his knowledge of the well-swung arm' (claimed *The Times*) 'quite as much as his sense of beat and time, that lured on the crowd to unheard-of vocal triumphs'.[24] A sound recording exists of the singing of 'Abide With Me' and conveys well the atmosphere of the occasion.[25] In the moment or two before the singing there is an odd shout or whistle from somewhere in the crowd of some 91,000 souls, but otherwise a marked silence prevails. The band then introduces the hymn with a few opening bars and the crowd sings the first verse as a practice. Mr Ratcliffe then calls for verse one again, followed 'straight on' by the next two verses. They are sung mostly in unison, with some harmonising by the tenors on certain lines, notably 'When other helpers *fail*' and 'Change and decay in all around I see'. In support of the claims made by *The Times*, a Welsh intonation is clearly discernable.

The performance was unquestionably disciplined and sincere. The king was reported as having told Mr Ratcliffe that the singing of 'Abide With Me' was 'a most impressive experience'.[26] The journalist Hannen Swaffer, writing in the *Daily Express*, doubtless summed up the feelings of many when he said:

> I wish I could find words in which to recapture the magic of that scene …. To my dying day I shall remember Saturday's football match, not because of the game but because, for the first time in my life I realised that, deep in the souls of all of us, is a love of song and singing.[27]

However, remembering that it was his newspaper that had sponsored the occasion and given its Saturday edition the banner headline 'SINGING CUP FINAL',[28] Swaffer did not fail to exploit an advertising opportunity. While acknowledging that the singing had brought tears to the eyes of many he concluded that the love of singing, which had been 'lying latent all through the years', had been brought to life through the 'touchspring' of the *Daily Express*.[29]

II

This particular rendition of 'Abide with Me' had a meaning that extended well beyond sport; and, it might be argued, well beyond the love of song noted by Hannen Swaffer. It formed an essential part of a major feature of contemporary British culture. Taking place only a few years after the end of the First World War, it stands as a major invocation in the litany of collective grief that had developed during the war itself and afterwards.[30] 'Remembrance' was a widespread, indeed universal, feature of post-war Britain that took on varied aspects. The idea of remembering the loss of life in the war was one that presented many ambiguities, and acts of remembrance had to carefully balance them. Some succeeded more than others. It was essentially a matter of combining a national with a local presence in manifestations of both public and private grief. This is neatly illustrated in the ceremonies held in 1919 to celebrate both the signing of the Armistice and the coming of peace. A conscious attempt appears to have been made to avoid suggestions of triumphalism and to bestow on the proceedings a sense of a 'people's peace'. Though the official ceremonies were orchestrated at a government level, there had from the very inception of such rituals been a concern to articulate public ceremony with popular culture. In the organisation of the first Armistice Day and the two minutes silence in 1919, entrusted to a Cabinet committee chaired by Lord Curzon, there had been a deliberate intention to minimise the role of establishment figures and give prominence to the wives and mothers of fallen soldiers. In the burial of the Unknown Soldier at Westminster Abbey, which with the unveiling of the Cenotaph made up the principal part of the entire memorialising events of 1920, prominence was given in the seating arrangements in the abbey for the mothers and widows of fallen soldiers.[31] Strict measures had been devised to preserve the anonymity of the entombed soldier so that he could be thought of as universal, anyones's son, brother, husband or father – as well as the son, brother, husband or father of everyone: 'one who stands for all our Glorious Dead'.[32] Such sentiments were also evident in the construction of war memorials, which in Britain mostly eschewed militaristic representations of war,[33] and in particular in the memorial of the nation itself: the Cenotaph. Sir Edwin Lutyens's design, originally erected as a temporary structure in Whitehall for the Peace Day parade of 1919, evoked such an emotional popular response that plans to re-locate the memorial were abandoned, and a permanent structure replaced the temporary one on what had become the nation's foremost site of mourning.[34] The memories associated with the site 'could not be uprooted', as *The Times* graphically noted in approving the decision not to relocate it.[35]

This broad social and cultural commitment to remembrance remained strong throughout the 1920s and into the 1930s, in spite of a growing realisation by then that 'war to end war' was an unachievable aim.[36] By the second half of the 1920s remembrance was in full swing: this was the high peak of monuments in material and spiritual form, expressed in literature, visual arts, buildings, film and music.[37] The singing of 'Abide With Me' was, to be sure, one aspect of this commitment. In it, and in other forms of remembrance, there was frequently inscribed a powerful conservative ideology. It was clearly illustrated in the press reportage of remembrance ceremonies in the 1920s, which sought to represent a fundamental unity of people and nation. It also found expression in the building of war memorials. Whatever else these structures might have symbolised about the dead, they exercised, as Bob Bushaway has observed, a form of moral sanction over the living. Acting as an ever-present source of guilt to the survivors, they might serve to de-politicise the war, and at the same time inhibit a critique of its purpose. The war memorial might thus work to dishonour present-day political struggles as being, in some sense, disrespectful to the dead.[38] This mentality chimed with the post-war cultural 'language' – the architectural styles, verse, visual imagery and literature – adopted by artists to create memorials. It frequently reached back into the past, eschewing modern (modernist) forms as being inappropriate for mourning.[39] Wembley itself, the stadium and the exhibition site devoted to re-affirming the imperial idea, was conceived in essentially traditional terms, drawing upon a neo-classical artistic vocabulary. It contained a series of heavy buildings with colonnades and pediments whose leaden style was further emphasised by the universal and generally unimaginative use of the new material of reinforced concrete.[40] Though the stadium was among the more innovative designs in the assemblage of exhibition buildings, it could not be considered as part of the modern movement in architecture, drawing as it did upon Roman influences in its rounded arches and low towers.[41]

Violent death in great numbers, never without its traumatic effects upon the survivors in any era, presented a specific historical problem for people of this time. The numbers had been so great and so extensive, and this explains the extent and intensity of mourning and grief.[42] At the same time, however, the means of coping with this psychological trauma converged with other problems. To an extent, in fact, the post-war emphasis on remembrance might be seen as an attempt to divert attention from a series of serious contemporary economic and political problems that had arisen during the war itself and which had both domestic and international causes.[43] In short, the immediate post-war years were a time of grave public unrest in Britain, exacerbated on occasions by signs of disloyalty in the armed services and industrial action on the part of the police. Historians have traditionally conceived of this in terms of the challenge of organised labour to the status quo in politics and industrial relations, some-times regarded as part of a wider European 'crisis' related to the emergence of the Bolshevik party in Russia and manifested in the rise of mass communist parties in Germany, Italy and France. Hence the terms 'challenge of labour' and 'crisis of the British state' have been coined to describe the tensions of these years, which culminated in the General Strike of 1926.[44] The strike was, of course, essentially a coalminers' affair, and probably not the revolutionary moment some had anticipated. But it did rekindle fears of Bolshevism that had been smouldering since 1917, and provoked an image of the divided nation.[45] The aftermath of the strike saw a contradictory approach adopted towards organised labour: on the one hand victimisation of miners in the coalfields; and on the other, the creation nationally of corporatist mechanisms for seeking con-ciliation in industrial relations. This latter strategy offered an image of the nation re-unified, and was an important intervention in the general process of stabilisation in British economy and society.[46]

More recent historical research, however, has thrown a fresh light on the developments of these years. In place of an emphasis on institutions and organ-ised movements, attention to the more spontaneous politics of the street and neighbourhood has revealed a groundswell of popular concern in the immediate aftermath of the war over the treatment of demobilised servicemen and the poor. Such sentiments were evident most dramatically in demonstrations that were organised in many parts of the British Isles to coincide with the Peace Day celebrations on 19 July 1919.[47] In a number of British towns and cities the demonstrations erupted into violence.[48] When seen alongside the bitter con-flicts in industry that saw troops stationed on the streets of Glasgow and a warship moored off Birkenhead[49] these developments produced one of the gravest crises of public order seen in Britain for many years, the combined effect of which was, as Jon Lawrence's research has shown, to fuel anxieties over the supposed 'brutalising' effects of the war.[50] This was seen not only as a mentality that the war had visited on society in general, but also as a legacy bequeathed by the war to government itself, most clearly evident (it was claimed) in colo-nial policy, notably in Ireland and India. A recurring motif in the discourse of 'brutalisation' was the countervailing idea that the British were an innately peaceable people: '[T]hroughout the interwar period the British reassured them-selves that they were a peaceable people, not given to extremism and the excesses of Continental-style political violence.'[51]

III

Where, and how, might sport fit into this ideological battleground? We have already seen that the singing of 'Abide With me' at the Cup Final might be linked to notions of death and loss. We have seen, as far as the evidence allows, that the programme of events in post-war Cup Finals does not seem to have been designed with any conscious thought of commemorating the war dead. Though the subject has been relatively under-investigated by historians, it seems that organised sport's role in the cult of remembrance was minimal.[52] This is not to say, however, that sentiments that had spread widely through the nation since the end of the war were absent from sporting events. Having attempted to 'deconstruct' the singing it is worth pausing to consider the actual venue for the performance of the hymn: to shift our gaze from 'text' to 'place'.

The associations that had already developed around the place of Wembley by 1927 contributed profoundly to a sense of nation. The setting was, at that time, a *new* sports ground, the Empire Stadium, opened in April 1923 for the FA Cup Final between Bolton Wanderers and West Ham United, and at that point in time the first part of the British Empire Exhibition site to be completed and brought into use. The occasion of this football match became, again by accident rather than design, the source of a powerful myth. The match was remembered for years afterwards as the 'white horse Final'. As the simple expedient of making the match 'all-ticket' had not been considered by the organisers (such an arrangement had never been applied in previous Cup Finals), many more spectators arrived than the stadium was capable of holding. The number of people congregating in the ground and its immediate vicinity was probably double the maximum capacity.[53] The consequences were chaotic, with traffic in north London brought to a standstill and spectators swarming everywhere, attempting to gain entry to the ground by various means, legitimate or otherwise. In spite of everything the match started, some 45 minutes later than the designated kick-off time. This was possible due to the clearing of the pitch by mounted policemen employing the method of pushing back a front line of spectators with linked arms in ever increasing circles. The procedure has become the main image in the folk memory of Wembley 1923, symbolised in the figure of the policeman on the white horse. At the time the white horse was also associated in the public mind with another image, that of King George V. It was claimed that the presence of the king had a calming influence over the crowd. A Metropolitan Police report made shortly after the events observed that when the king made his appearance in the arena at 2.59 pm, the stadium was 'completely thronged with people'.[54] But when the Guards' band struck up the national anthem everyone broke into song, a response which underlined the police claim that the crowd was in 'good temper and good humour'.[55] Writing some ten years after the events the Secretary of the FA, Sir Frederick Wall, claimed that George V had not been pleased with the scene that met him on his arrival, and especially at the suggestion that the match might have to be abandoned. Such thoughts were dispelled, according to Wall, largely by the fact that the king himself became an attraction in his own right. His presence in the Royal Box started a counter-surge by spectators anxious to cast eyes on their monarch. 'Tens of thousands', in Wall's words, filed past him thence to be directed through a tunnel out of the arena.[56] In this way space was cleared in the ground. The match, which then proceeded, was won 2–0 by Bolton Wanderers. It was, claimed West Ham United's local paper the *Stratford Express*, a 'fiasco'.[57]

But what is interesting about the whole episode is the way in which notions of the crowd were articulated. The idea of the crowd as 'threat' was transformed into a re-assuring image of the virtues of the nation. In the constructing of stories that tell of the people and their habits what is remembered is not always exactly what happened. A day which, if not 'ugly' (as described by *The Times* newspaper[58]), was at the very least extremely disorganised, came to be embedded in popular memory as a source of pride in a nation where people knew how to behave and remained calm in difficult situations. Constable Scorey – the policeman on the white horse – later admitted that on arriving at Wembley from his base in Rochester Road he thought the situation hopeless and didn't know what to do; but, he said, 'the crowd was good-natured and seemed to respect the horse'.[59] *The Times* moderated its judgement of the 'ugly' situation in two respects – the spirit of people and police working together, and the absolute loyalty of the 'mixed congregation' to the king.[60] For years afterwards millions of English football followers were inducted into the game's culture through a literature of books, magazines and pictures in which the image of the white horse took a prominent place. And since English football culture was always informed by a sense of the nation's place in the wider world, a notion of 'the Other' was latent in it. Thus the *Daily News* commented on the essentially moderate nature of both crowd and police, with the latter conspicuously preferring to spend time in patient crowd control rather than attempting a quick dispersal by violent methods, 'as the police in more excitable lands might do'.[61] In stark contrast to the portrayal of the riotous and violent behaviour of crowds at foreign football grounds, with their moats, fences and armed police, the Wembley Cup Final of 1923 worked as an icon representing English fans to themselves as self-disciplined, peaceable, essentially co-operative, needing only the firm coaxing of a single policeman and his horse to bring them to order. Moreover, this image influenced to a large extent later assumptions about crowd control measures at big sporting events. It was a recurring theme in the report of the events at the match, commissioned by W. C. Bridgeman at the Home Office in 1923;[62] it sustained the belief that crowds could manage themselves, and thus delayed for many years the use of statutory regulations to ensure safety.

In this respect the 1923 Cup Final represents one of those moments in the creation of the mythology of a nation, to which the singing of 'Abide With Me', first in 1927 and then on each occasion thereafter until the later part of the century, provided ideological reinforcement. In the particular historical circumstances of the turbulent years immediately following the First World War, when, as Lawrence has noted, political conflicts appeared to threaten the very moral fabric of the nation, bringing into question the long-held idea of the 'peaceable' community, what happened at Wembley provided an ideological symbol of class and national unity that no doubt helped some people to convince themselves that stability was possible. It was an aspect of national life in which people could find 'reassurance that they were a uniquely peaceable people'.[63]

IV

But times change, and what seemed an honourable and deeply-moving cere-mony to the people of the 1920s carried less relevance to their grandchildren; at best it seemed maudlin, at worst irrelevant. Change, however, was slow in coming. While the enthusiasm for community singing quickly faded in the late 1920s, 'Abide With Me' remained a firm favourite with Wembley crowds until well beyond the end of the Second World War. Attachment to it was possibly even strengthened by the televising of the Cup Final each year from 1953. The hymn acquired a new relevance in 1958 when sung at the Cup Final between Bolton Wanderers and Manchester United, the club that had lost several of its leading players in an air crash just a few months previously.[64] When, therefore, in 1959 it was proposed that the hymn be omitted in favour of a gymnastic display by the women of the Coventry Keep Fit Association there was an outcry, and 'Abide With Me' was restored by popular demand.[65] In the 1960s the tradition of the hymn remained, as reflected in sportspeople's autobio-graphies where it was often portrayed as an iconic moment, as much one of per-sonal solace as of public memory.[66] In his centenary history of the FA Cup, Tony Pawson could still claim a pride of place for the hymn in the ceremonials of the early 1970s. But, equally, during these years, football culture was begin-ning to change, with a gradual rejection of the legacies in finance, labour rela-tions and playing styles that had survived since the Victorian era. Perhaps the most dramatic of these changes was in the behaviour of spectators, with the appearance of new and more spontaneous forms of expression. It was difficult, in this new climate, to imagine that some 40 years previously football crowds had readily responded to community singing. The old songs were now challenged and in many cases displaced by home-grown chants from terrace choirs who were more inclined to impose their own ditties on the proceedings than to accept what was offered by a man on a rostrum who asked them to wave their song sheets. The emergence of this more independent and often aggressive spec-tator voice replaced the deferential and 'disciplined' crowd that had been por-trayed in the pages of the Shortt Report almost half a century earlier. With all this the attempt to persuade the Wembley crowd to sing 'Abide With Me' became a more difficult one, even for seasoned professional performers such as Frankie Vaughan and Gerry Marsden who were drafted in to enliven the pro-ceedings in the 1980s. *The Guardian* reported in 1989 that when Marsden attempted to lead the crowd in 'Abide With Me' 'neither he nor they knew the words and when he faltered there was nothing'.[67] Renditions of the song in the past 30 years have exhibited none of the discipline and fervour witnessed in 1927, and we go back to the assumption with which we began, drawn from the Cup Final of 2007: that for contemporary crowds the singing of 'Abide With Me', even as an example of 'retro' culture, is a fairly meaningless exercise. The sportswriter Frank Keating, writing in *The Guardian* in 2002 after learning that television viewing figures for the Cup Final were lower than those for a contemporaneous snooker tournament, expressed the new mood thus:

> [S]ome seismic rumblings are undermining hitherto accepted habits and perceptions in the world of sports broadcasting ... the nation seemed to be saying, these days we can take it or leave it, that once great 'national bonding' occasion which is the FA Cup final. Abide with me? Not any more mate.[68]

It was, therefore, both interesting and surprising to encounter the supporters' petition to the Football Association in 2006 not to engage professional singers at the Cup Final and for 'the crowd [to] sing "Abide With Me" and "God Save the Queen" on the cue of the band. We as football supporters feel that this would be a return to the best traditions of this remarkable competition'.[69] There is after all, perhaps, a sense of history among some football fans.

V

In this chapter I have sought to turn attention to a well-known sporting ritual that deserves at least the brief analysis offered here. In itself the singing of 'Abide With Me' might appear to have little significance. Historians have certainly paid scant attention to it, in spite of the growing interest in recent years in the study of symbolic cultural representations, which has sustained much of what is now called the 'cultural turn'. This is in part explained, perhaps, by the problems of analysing the 'sensuous', that is to say those aspects of history relating to experiences of the senses – sights, sounds, smells, touch – that do not lend themselves to conventional historical method. The work of the French cultural historian Alain Corbin[70] provides a marker here, but it has not been much followed in Britain. This is one area where historians have been content to leave such issues to the creative writer.[71] If, however, we recognise that the rituals of the Cup Final had, by the 1920s, come to play an emblematic role in the formation of an English national identity, then we can begin to explore a number of interconnecting threads. Remembrance of the dead is honoured in 'Abide With Me', which in turn has a place in the community singing movement that, as Russell argues, acted as a 'social emollient' in a society 'unusually ill at ease with itself'.[72] Linked with all these is a memory of the pre-war era, an age that the prism of the war itself rendered to all those viewing from the perspective of the 1920s as better and more stable. When considered in this light, then, the place of 'Abide With Me' at the Cup Final, though still a marginal cultural activity, nonetheless says something about the mentalities of a country trying to come to terms with a profound trauma.

Notes

1 The original Wembley stadium was closed in 2001 for re-building. It was re-opened in 2007.
2 It was followed shortly afterwards by the singing of the national anthem by the divo Russell Watson.
3 *2006 FA Cup Final Abide With Me Petition* (www.PetitionOnline.com/19272006/petition.html).
4 As did Mr Martin Knapp, who wrote to *The Times* newspaper in 1983 to make this very point:

> [c]an there be anything more incongruous than the singing of 'Abide with me' before a Cup Final? There must be many for whom the words of this splendid hymn bring a very special message of comfort and strengthened faith. They must find it blasphemous that what is part of their religious experience immediately precedes the bawling of a football crowd.
>
> (*The Times*, 28 May 1983, 9)

5 Until, perhaps, the match itself started, when the pace at which the contest between Chelsea and Manchester United was played might have made 'Abide With Me' seem entirely appropriate.
6 Looking back on this time in football, William Pickford, a long-serving member of the FA Council, noted that '[T]hose who remember the series of Finals [at Crystal Palace] always speak of them happily ... the Crystal Palace era was more than a venue of a football match; it took on the character of a pic-nic.' W. Pickford, *A Few Recollections of Sport*, Bournemouth: n.p., n.d., p. 65.
7 See Jeffrey Hill, 'Cocks, cats, caps and cups: a semiotic approach to sport and national identity', *Culture, Sport, Society*, 2, 2, 1999, 1–21; Jeffrey Hill, 'Rite of spring: Cup Finals and community in the North of England' in Jeffrey Hill and Jack Williams (eds), *Sport and Identity in the North of England*, Keele: Keele University Press, 1996, pp. 85–112.
8 In 1927 there were two: the Irish and the Grenadier Guards. *The Times*, 25 April 1927, 6.
9 Dave Russell, 'Abiding memories: the community singing movement and English social life in the 1920s', *Popular Music*, 27, 1, 2008, 117–133.
10 The Manchester-based *Daily Dispatch* sponsored a similar programme of singing at northern sporting grounds in 1927. See *Daily Disptach*, 22, 23, 29 April 1927.
11 Russell, 'Abiding memories'.
12 Tony Pawson, *100 Years of the FA Cup: The Centenary History*, London: William Heinemann, 1972 repeats this story (p. 215), though in 1927 Hannen Swaffer in the *Daily Express* claimed that the hymn had been included at the suggestion of the king. See *Daily Express* 25 April 1927, 2.
13 Football Association (FA), Finance Committee Minutes, 23 February, 30 March 1925; 8 March 1926.
14 *Hymns Ancient and Modern: for use in the Services of the Church*, standard edition, London: William Clowes and Sons Ltd, 1916, p. 21.
15 See Henry James Garland, *Henry Francis Lyte and the Story of 'Abide With Me'*, Manchester: Torch Publishing Company, 1957, especially chapters VII and XIII. Lyte was himself ill at the time of writing his hymn, and shortly afterwards died while convalescing in the South of France. He is buried in the Anglican churchyard in Nice.

16 See Ian Bradley, *Abide With Me: The World of Victorian Hymns*, London: SCM Press Ltd, 1997, pp. 197, 200, 225; J. R. Watson, *The English Hymn: A Critical and Historical Study*, Oxford: Oxford University Press, 1997. In the USA the hymn was sung at the funerals of Herbert Hoover and Adlai Stevenson, who both died in the mid-1960s.

17 Pawson, *100 Years of the FA Cup*, p. 215.

18 Garland, *Henry Francis Lyte and the Story of 'Abide With Me'*, pp. 126–127.

19 This was summed up in an interview with David Lloyd George, not a notable football fan (he was attending his first 'cup tie', as he described it): both teams, he observed, had fought the context with 'British pluck'. See *Athletic News*, 25 April 1927, 1. The newspapers delighted in including pictures of Cardiff fans wearing leeks in their hats. See *Daily Express*, 23 April 1927, 1; *Daily Herald*, 23 April 1927, 9.

20 Dai Smith and Gareth Williams, *Fields of Praise: The Official History of the Welsh Rugby Union 1881–1981*, Cardiff: University of Wales Press, 1981, pp. 285–286. '[T]he sound of the ascending bass line … [rose] majestically from thousands of Welsh throats to hold wayfarers spellbound in the streets and eddy outwards to the suburbs of the city' (p. 286).

21 *The Times*, 25 April 1927.

22 *Daily Express*, 23 April 1927, 2.

23 *Daily Dispatch*, 25 April 1927, 2.

24 *The Times*, 25 April 1927.

25 Recording made by BBC Wales, probably from an original recording made of the community singing at the 1927 Cup Final by the Columbia Gramophone Company (FA Finance Committee Minutes, 16 January 1928). I am indebted to Professor Gareth Williams of the University of Glamorgan for providing me with a copy of the recording.

26 *Daily Express*, 25 April 1927, 1.

27 Ibid., 2.

28 With the standfirst: 'Community Songs for the King [...] 92,000 People To take Part in the Great Concert', ibid., 1.

29 Ibid.

30 Katherine Kennedy, *The Crucifix: An Outline Sketch of its History*, with a supplementary chapter by the Rev. E. Hermitage Day, London: AR Mowbray and Co., 1917, pp. 77–84.

31 *The Times*, 1 November 1920, 12.

32 *Daily Express*, 12 November 1920, 1.

33 See Jay Winter, *Sites of Memory, Sites of Mourning: The Great War in European Cultural History*, Cambridge: Cambridge University Press, 1995; Alex King, *Memorials of the Great War in Britain: The Symbolism and Politics of Remembrance*, Oxford: Berg, 1998. For France: Antoine Prost, 'Monuments to the dead' in P. Nora (ed.), (L. Kritzman (ed.) English language edition), *Realms of Memory: The Construction of the French Past, Volume 2 – Traditions*, trans. Arthur Goldhammer, New York: Columbia University Press, 1997, chapter IX.

34 *The Times*, 21, 31 July 1919. See also Eric Homburger, 'The story of the Cenotaph', *Times Literary Supplement*, 21 November 1976, 1429–1430; Allan Greenberg, 'Lutyens's Cenotaph', *Journal of the Society of Architectural Historians*, 48, 1, 1989, 5–23.

35 *The Times*, 31 July 1919, 12. Many of these issues are dealt with in Mark Whittacker's very sensitive programme 'The Roots of Remembrance' for BBC Radio 4, 12 November 2006.

36 Adrian Gregory, *The Silence of Memory: Armistice Day 1919–1946*, Oxford: Berg, 1994.

37 Not to be forgotten alongside the well-known writings of R. C. Sheriff, Richard Aldington, Ford Madox Ford, Siegfried Sasson, Robert Graves, Edmund Blunden and

Frederic Manning – which all appeared between 1928 and 1930 – was the construction by the mid-1920s of 970 architect-designed war cemeteries in France and Belgium alone; these and other memorial structures constituted 'one of the largest schemes of public works ever undertaken'. Gavin Stamp, *The Memorial to the Missing of the Somme*, London: Profile Books, 2006, p. 99.

38 Bob Bushaway, 'Name upon name: the Great War and remembrance', in R. Porter (ed.), *Myths of the English*, Cambridge: Polity Press, 1992, pp. 136–167.

39 Winter, *Sites of Memory, Sites of Mourning*, especially chapter 6.

40 J. Hill and F. Varrasi, 'Creating Wembley: the construction of a national monument', *The Sports Historian*, 17, 2, 1997, 28–43.

41 See Stamp, *Memorial to the Missing of the Somme*, who argues that the war did in part stimulate the rise of modernism, but also generated a 'late but vital' (p. 13) flowering of the European classical tradition in architecture, of which Lutyens's memorial at Thiepval is a part.

42 Gregory, *Silence of Memory*, pp. 19–23.

43 Greenberg, 'Lutyens's Cenotaph'.

44 See for example, Keith Burgess, *The Challenge of Labour: Shaping British Society*, London: Croom Helm, 1980; James Hinton, *The First Shop Stewards Movement*, London: Allen and Unwin, 1973.

45 This idea was starkly expressed in a famous cartoon published in the magazine *Punch* entitled 'Under which flag?', which showed a solid John Bull figure sporting the Union Jack confronting an equally defiant striker sporting the banner 'General Strike'. The image is used on the front cover of Burgess's book, *The Challenge of Labour: Shaping British Society*.

46 See Peter Clarke, *Hope and Glory: Britain 1900–1990*, London: Penguin Books, 1996, chapter 3. For Europe: Charles S. Maier, *Recasting Bourgeois Europe: Stabilization in France, Germany, and Italy in the Decade After World War One*, Princeton, NJ: Princeton University Press, 1974.

47 Designed to mark the signing of the peace treaty that brought the war to an end (the Armistice of 11 November 1918 having been only a ceasefire).

48 London, Liverpool, Cardiff, Glasgow, Wolverhampton, Bilston, Coventry, Luton, Swindon and Doncaster were the main ones. In Luton, rioters burned down the town hall (see note 37).

49 See, for example, Robert Keith Middlemas, *The Clydesiders: A Left-Wing Struggle for Parliamentary Power*, London: Hutchinson, 1965.

50 See the important article by Jon Lawrence, 'Forging a peaceable kingdom: war, violence, and fear of brutalization in post-First World War Britain', *Journal of Modern History*, 75, 2003, 557–589.

51 Lawrence, 'Forging a peaceable kingdom', 562.

52 The exception was rugby union, where the English Rugby Football Union appears to have been far more vigorous in promoting the idea of its contribution to the war effort and the sacrifices made by its players than either association football, rugby league (Northern Union rugby) or cricket, where memorialising of the war was low-key. See Tony Collins, 'English Rugby Union and the First World War', *Historical Journal*, 45, 4, 2002, 797–817.

53 Estimates varied. The capacity at that time was 126,000, and most accounts put those attempting to gain entry to the stadium at 200,000 at least. See Jeffrey Hill, '"The day was an ugly one": Wembley, 28th April 1923', *Soccer and Society*, 5, 2, 2004, 152–168.

54 National Archives (NA), HO45/11627/445340/12 (Commissioner of Police, 2 May 1923).

55 Ibid.

56 Sir Frederick Wall, *Fifty Years of Football*, London: Cassell, 1935, p. 164.

57 Quoted in Charles P. Korr, 'A different kind of success: West Ham United and the

creation of tradition and community', in R. Holt (ed.), *Sport and the Working Class in Modern Britain*, Manchester: Manchester University Press, 1990, p. 145.

58 *The Times*, 30 April 1923, 6.
59 Alan Brown, 'Didn't we have a lovely time the day we went to Wembley', *Guardian*, 1 April 1995, 22.
60 *The Times*, 30 April 1923, 9.
61 *Daily News*, 30 April 1923, 10.
62 Crowds Committee, *Report of the Departmental Committee on Crowds*, London: HMSO, 1924, Cmd. 2088. The report was made in March 1924, and is usually known as the Shortt Report after its chairman, Edward Shortt. For a fuller discussion of the report see Hill, '"The day was an ugly one"', 160–166.
63 Lawrence, 'Forging a peaceable kingdom', 588.
64 See Gavin Mellor, 'The genesis of Manchester United as a national and international "Super-Club", 1958–68', *Soccer and Society*, 1, 2, 2004, 151–166.
65 Pawson, *100 Years of the FA Cup*, p. 215.
66 For example, the Manchester United player Noel Cantwell recounts in his life story how his team-mate Pat Crerand overcame pre-match nerves by listening to the crowd sing 'Abide With Me', saying 'It's done me a world of good.' Noel Cantwell, *United We Stand*, London: Stanley Paul, 1965, p. 55.
67 *Guardian*, 22 May 1989, 18.
68 Ibid., 13 May 2002, 26.
69 www.petitiononline.com/19272006/petition.html.
70 See Alain Corbin, *Time, Desire and Horror: Towards a History of the Senses*, trans. Jean Birrell, Oxford: Polity Press, 1995; *Village Bells: The Culture of the Senses in the Nineteenth-Century French Countryside*, trans. Martin Thom, New York: Columbia University Press, 1998; and *The Foul and the Fragrant: Odor and the French Social Imagination*, trans. Miriam L. Kochan, Cambridge, MA: Harvard University Press, 1998. One area in which 'emotion' is being explored is in sport museums: see Christian Wacker, 'The German Sport and Olympia Museum', unpublished paper for the AHRC-funded seminar series 'Sport, history, and heritage: studies in the public representation of sport', Lord's Cricket Ground, London, 14 November 2007.
71 I have attempted to explore some of this sensory terrain in Jeffrey Hill, *Sport and the Literary Imagination*, Peter Lang: Oxford, 2006, especially in the discussion of David Storey's *This Sporting Life* (chapter 2) and Nick Hornby's *Fever Pitch* (chapter 6).
72 Russell, 'Abiding memories', 29.

10 'Friday Night and the Gates are Low'[1]

Popular music and its relationship(s) to sport

Mike McGuinness

> To say soccer fans cheer is like saying moles dig or Kennedys drink. They cheer.
> They chant. They sing. First at the games. Then in the pubs. Then in the jails.
>
> Rick Reilly[2]

There has been a growing interest and a developing literature in relation to sports fans and the notion of fandom. However, amongst the plethora of studies from, inter alia, Desmond Morris in 1981 to John Williams in 2007,[3] there are minimal references to music and sport. On the other hand, fans are increasingly being studied in relation to late modern sports fandom in the context of commodification and patterns of consumption in sport[4] and music has a place in these studies. The beginning of the 1980s witnessed an increase in the study of popular music[5] and in this context both Steve Redhead and John Bale have identified a musicalisation of football developing from the mid-1980s.[6]

But the relationship between sport and music has been traced further back. Han-Dieter Krebs had suggested that from earliest times sport and music, which are highly individual and autonomous partners, have formed a 'fragile and at times intense sporadic union'.[7] Garry Crawford supports this view by suggesting that there is a substantial interconnection between sport and music[8] and Philip Scowcroft suggests that sport and music are both forms of entertainment and it is therefore natural that they interact with one another.[9] It has been further suggested by Erhard Höhne that there is a possibility and necessity of achieving a genuine synthesis of art and sport and that music is capable of enhancing physical culture and sport.[10] Some sports rely very heavily on the input of music in the execution of their activities, including the interpretation of the music in their points or marking schemes. Most of these are Olympic sports, some relatively recent additions to the programme, and include dressage, synchronised swimming, rhythmic gymnastics, women's floor exercises, skating and freestyle skiing. Most of the music accompanying these activities is of a more 'classical' nature or from the show repertoire. The advantage is that the length of time they play allows for a fuller programme.

Although there has been a growing interest in the relationship sport has with popular culture, its relationship to music has been relatively neglected.

This is all the more surprising because, as David Rowe states, sport and rock music are two of the most significant forms of popular culture.[11] One problem could be that music, and particularly popular music, has been little studied within the social sciences.[12] Likewise, within the humanities, musicology – or the scientific study of music – developed in nineteenth-century Europe to study Western or European classical music and this remains its touchstone with a concomitant devaluing or marginalisation of popular music within that discipline.[13] Defining what is meant by 'popular music' is another difficulty. Confusion can develop when 'popular' is confused with 'pop', with the latter being an abbreviation of the former.[14] Popular music can be a whole range of styles covering a broad period of history, whereas 'pop' music can be described as a whole complex of musical styles mostly contained within the framework of popular music from the 1960s[15] (or one might even cite the mid-1950s for the advent of modern pop[16]). Popular music can also be seen as music which is accessible to a wide audience or any genre of music having wide appeal, or even 'music of the people'. Forms of popular music have existed since the development of organised musical production, but they have had to compete with other forms of music which have been regarded as superior and of greater value. This has been particularly so since the nineteenth century. What one might consider its starting point for the purposes of this discussion is open to conjecture. Ian Whitcomb talks about the dawn of the twentieth century as seeing the emergence of popular music, with the publication of *How to Write a Popular Song* by Chas K. Harris.[17] Thus it may be, as Ken McLeod suggests, that though popular music forms an important nexus of cultural production, it is little understood.[18]

Music and sport are both enormously popular and, as McLeod states, their confluence is an increasingly prevalent feature of cultural production.[19] Within this cultural context Krebs has identified four characteristics shared by sport and music: both follow set rules in play and movement, rules which can nevertheless be varied almost inexhaustibly; both involve continuous mental and physical training for discipline and excellence and the constant testing of skills against others; both involve a performance pyramid from amateur to elite performers; and both cultural spheres constitute 'universal forms of expression'.[20] Music, like sport, has a capacity for emotional stimulation and the ability to evoke a tangible sense of time and place.[21] More than this, both music and sport involve performance and narrative.[22] McLeod even suggests that music and sport allow individuals to assert their excellence as soloists while remaining part of a cohesive group.[23] At the same time, from another perspective, rock or popular music could also be regarded as the antithesis of sport, where the promotion of the notion of healthy minds, healthy bodies and self-imposed discipline is at the core.[24] However, even if one accepts the latter view, the increasing convergence of music and sport, and especially of popular music and sport, can be partly explained, according to Rowe, because of both the decline of the generational ideology of 'rock culture' and a shift in the cultural and economic location of sport.[25]

There are many forms of popular musical representation through which sport manifests itself. The main areas under discussion here are:

- the sport record as represented by the football record
- sportsmen and women and the music industry
- the popular music industry and representations of sport
- anthems and their association through popular music
- music adopted by sport
- sports and their association with popular music, e.g. surfing.

Football records

These tend to fall into two types: the team or event record and attempts by football people to enter the world of show business. Football records are generally ephemeral and are usually associated with a particular event such as the FA Cup Final or World Cup qualification. In most cases they are regarded with some contempt, although there are the odd exceptions to this rule. It is worth quoting the comment made by Peter J. Seddon to get a flavour of the style and conditions involved:

> Making a football record is rather like having eight pints of Old Thumper, followed by a fiery curry, the night before a big day at work – at the time it seems like a great idea but in the cold light of day it's a clear case of 'never again'.[26]

Equally as damning is the comment by Redhead that such songs are leaden singalongs by 'lumpen' footballers in blazers,[27] or that of Peter Hooton who said that football songs are almost always rubbish.[28] Certainly the success in the commercial charts for many of them (but by no means all) is often short-lived and it is generally agreed that they are of questionable quality and of dubious musical value. In this sense it could be concluded that they are exploitative of the fans and of the record-buying public and are simply products of the growing commercialisation of sport. However, could it be that there is more to them, that they may be seen by the open minded as 'treasure troves of eccentricity'[29] or afforded a positive value as idiosyncratic and ephemeral in nature?[30]

The first real football/sporting record to commemorate or celebrate an event was in relation to the 1966 World Cup in England. This event also produced the first World Cup mascot in 'World Cup Willie', an English lion emblazoned with the Union Jack rather than the ubiquitous Cross of St George of more modern times.[31] The merchandising and marketing of the World Cup produced the song called 'World Cup Willie', sung by the Scottish 'King of Skiffle' Lonnie Donegan, although it failed to appear in the charts. Despite this, Paul Lewis considers this to be the only song that has the 'power to evoke memories of real jubilation' as it is associated with England's only major trophy win.[32]

At the same time some sportspeople, mainly footballers, have felt the need to enter the world of entertainment and to produce 'pop' records. This has not always been a successful process. It has been claimed that the first footballer to release a record was the Leeds United and Juventus legend John Charles in 1958. He made a number of records including 'Sixteen Tons' which made it to number 1 in the Italian charts. Perhaps the most famous examples have been 'Diamond Lights' by Glenn Hoddle and Chris Waddle,[33] 'Head Over Heels In Love' by Kevin Keegan, 'Fog On The Tyne' by Lindisfarne with Paul Gascoigne ('Gazza'), 'Wooly Bully' by Vinnie Jones and, particularly forgettable, 'Side By Side' by Peter Shilton and Ray Clemence. This form of representation is not confined to the United Kingdom as is illustrated by such records as 'Het Is Fijn In Itallie Te Zijn' by Marco van Basten and Frank Rijkaard when they were at AC Milan in 1990, 'Moleque Danado', written and sung by Pele (1979) and 'Oei Oei Oei (Das Was Me Weer Een Loei)' by Johan Cruyff (1969).[34] Although some of these became popular hits and appeared in the hit parade listings (Hoddle and Waddle at number 12 in 1987), they have also featured in listings of the 100 worst pop records. A recent Channel 4 listing had 'Diamond Lights' at number 33 and Gazza at number 43.[35]

Alongside these records are those produced by teams to commemorate events such as getting to the FA Cup Final, gaining promotion and national squads qualifying for international tournaments such as the World Cup in football. Some significant, even classic, records have appeared, including 'Back Home' by the England 1970 World Cup squad (number 1 in the popular music charts), 'Ossie's Dream' by the Tottenham Hotspur 1981 FA Cup winning side (number 5 in the charts), 'Anfield Rap' by the Liverpool 1988 FA Cup squad (number 3 in the charts), 'Blue Is The Colour' by the Chelsea FA Cup Final squad in 1972 (number 5 in the charts)[36] and 'I'm Forever Blowing Bubbles' by the West Ham United 1975 FA Cup squad (number 31). A rare European example is 'Red Devil Rock' by the Belgian national squad in 1980 for the European Football Championships.[37] 'Ossie's Dream' raises a number of questions. There is no doubt that this was/is a popular addition to the catalogue of records but it, like many others, has dubious elements. In national team records there is a very strong nationalistic element which may also disparage other nations as in, for example, 'Ally's Army' which has the immortal line 'England cannae dae it as they didnae qualify'. They are equally full of extreme optimism. 'Ossie's Dream' refers to the desire of Osvaldo Ardiles to achieve his ambition of playing at Wembley and winning the FA Cup. Unfortunately, the university-educated and World Cup winning player for Argentina in 1978 is presented as a simple person in awe of the occasion: 'Ossie's going to Wembley, His knees have gone all trembly ....' He is also presented as communicating in an amusing and demeaning way as he utters the phrase that he is 'Playing for Tottingham ...'.

Allied to these are those records produced by other people, usually celebrity fans of the team, with contributions by the sportspeople involved. Significant examples of this type include 'Nice One Cyril' by the Cockerel Chorus in honour of the 1973 Tottenham Hotspur FA Cup squad (which got to number 14 in the charts), 'Ally's Tartan Army' by Andy Cameron supporting the Scotland World Cup squad in Argentina in 1978 (which reached number 6 in the charts), a version of 'I'm Forever Blowing Bubbles' by West Ham United fans, the Cockney Rejects, celebrating their team's FA Cup Final appearance in 1980 (which reached number 35 in the charts),[38] 'All Together Now' by The Farm for England at the 2004 European Championships,[39] 'World In Motion' by New Order for England at the 1990 World Cup (which reached number 1 in the charts)[40] and 'Three Lions (Football's Coming Home)' by comedians David Baddiel and Frank Skinner with the Lightning Seeds (which reached number 1 in the charts and even made number 30 in the German charts!). 'Three Lions' is an interesting example of this type of record as it was designed as an anthem as much as a celebratory record, with the expectation that it would be taken up by the fans. The basic theme of the song is to connect English football to its finest moment in winning the World Cup in 1966, its only major championship trophy, and to bemoan the 'thirty years of hurt'. Writers like Ben Carrington have offered a critique of the song as being overly nationalistic and ethnocentric.[41] It was re-released in 1998 for the World Cup in France as 'Three Lions '98' despite there being an official World Cup song called '(How Does It Feel To Be) On Top Of The World' by England United. The former reached number 1 in the charts and the latter peaked at number 9. Interestingly, an alternative anthem for 1998 emerged in the guise of a release by the group Fat Les, created by Keith Allen, a comedian, with Alex James from Blur, Guy Pratt from Pink Floyd, the comedian Roland Riveron and the artist Damian Hirst. The song, called 'Vindaloo', reached number 2 in the charts.

Supporters' anthems

Popular songs often become anthems taken up, mainly spontaneously, by the fans and become associated with a team or a sport. McLeod sees these as the most prominent manifestations of the convergence of music and sport.[42] Further, Joseph Bradley, referring to football supporters, stated that their songs are an important part of their 'diet of communication'.[43] According to its dictionary definition, an anthem is both a song of loyalty, often to a country, and a piece of 'sacred music',[44] definitions that are both applicable in sporting contexts. Again, this genre is dominated, although not exclusively, by football and has produced a number of examples where popular songs become synonymous with the club and are enthusiastically adopted by the fans. More than this they are often spontaneous expressions of loyalty and identity and, according to Desmond Morris, have 'reached the level of something approaching a local art form'.[45] A strong element of the appeal of such sports songs is that they feature 'memorable and easily sung choruses in which fans can participate'.[46] This is a vital part of the team's performance as it makes the fans' presence more tangible.[47] This form of popular culture can be said to display pleasure and emotional excess in contrast to the dominant culture which tends to maintain 'respectable aesthetic distance and control'.[48] The source or sources of this form of activity is open to conjecture but Morris suggests that it has been subject to three major influences. One is the Victorian tradition of community hymn-singing before sporting events, something that has remained at the FA Cup Final and the Rugby League Cup Final with the singing of 'Abide With Me,' (see Chapter 9 in this volume). More recent was the influence of Mediterranean and South American football fans, caused by the increase in air travel and the exposure of British football fans to 'different fan customs', especially drumming and clapping, galvanised by experiences at the 1962 and 1966 World Cups. Third was the influence of Liverpool fans as they took the songs of the Mersey Beat and Beatlemania onto the terraces as a way of expressing the superiority of their pop culture and adapting them to the 'mood of the moment'.[49] Although it is clear that basic singing skills are often missing and the songs can be flat and tuneless, Howard believes that it is heartening that it exists as an exuberant form of support for their teams and it would be 'inappropriate to do anything to dampen this'.[50]

It is possible to associate this communal singing with the concept of the imagined community as propounded by Benedict Anderson. Massed singing at a sporting event involves thousands of people working together in a highly structured manner, without any conductor, no starting note being given but with the words and music known by heart.[51] In Anderson's terms it involves a large group of people congregated together, not knowing each other yet sharing a common communion.[52] H. F. Moorhouse reinforces this by stating that imagined communities need celebrations, events and incidents to feed their imaginations and sport provides this.[53] It is not difficult to find examples of anthems or popular songs associated with sport. rugby union at the national level is represented by the long-established songs linked to Wales and England. Welsh supporters sing a mixture of hymns such as 'Bread Of Heaven' and 'Calon Lân' and popular songs such as Tom Jones's hit single 'Delilah' (also popular amongst football supporters generally) and Max Boyce's 'Hymns And Arias'. In the case of England the African-American spiritual song/hymn 'Swing Low, Sweet Chariot' was appropriated during the 1988 season and has been sung regularly ever since.[54] Fans and supporters of the England football team have favoured the aforementioned 'Three Lions' and 'Vindaloo', although in more recent times the theme tune to the film The Great Escape, led by a supporters' band, has roused the crowd.

At club level in football there is a very rich vein of offerings having both relevant and irrelevant relationships and meanings to the club. There are many examples available, but a limited number will be used for illustration and discussion here. From the 1990s the song 'Always Look On The Bright Side of Life', originally sung by Eric Idle in the Monty Python film The Life of Brian, was appropriated by football supporters generally and was re-released because of its popularity as an anthem.[55] Liverpool FC supporters have appropriated the song 'You'll Never Walk Alone', which was originally in the stage and film musical Carousel written by Rogers and Hammerstein II. Its association with Liverpool comes through the popular local singer Gerry Marsden who, as a member of Gerry and the Pacemakers, was part of the Mersey Beat of the 1960s. He recorded the song in 1963 and it remained number 1 in the charts for four weeks.[56] Through its links with the Kop end of Liverpool's ground at Anfield, where the most dedicated supporters of the club stood, this has become the most famous of football anthems. The themes of the song, according to John Williams, of struggle, pride, community and 'hope in your heart' seemed ideal for the 'trials and emotions' of football fans.[57] The song's lyrics have also been incorporated into the Shankly Gates, which commemorate an iconic manager of the club who was particularly associated with the rebirth of the club in the 1960s and the establishment of its style and reputation, Bill Shankly. The song is also associated with Glasgow Celtic, a club which had strong associations with Liverpool. Raymond Boyle claims that Celtic's adoption of the song developed because of the mutual respect and friendship between Shankly and the Celtic manager, Jock Stein, and was reinforced during communal singing at a match held in the wake of the Hillsborough stadium disaster.[58] A further link between Glasgow Celtic and Liverpool is the song 'Fields Of Athenry', a modern folk song/ballad written by Pete St John in the 1970s, about the Great Irish Famine of 1845–1849. Both clubs have strong Irish connections because of the migration caused by the famine. There was an attempt in 1994 to have Celtic fans cease singing the song, but it was defended and defeated on the basis that the club had been founded by Irish immigrants who had lived through the famine.[59] 'You'll Never Walk Alone' has also gained some popularity with the fans of other clubs across the world, including Rapid Vienna, Feyenoord, Schalke 04, FC Tokyo and Royal Antwerp.

At Everton, the other club in Liverpool, the 'Z Cars Theme' has been used for a number of years to fanfare the teams onto the pitch. This is the theme tune to a television drama of the 1960s concerning a Liverpool-based motorised police unit. The theme itself is based upon an old Merseyside folk song called 'Johnny Todd' which had been arranged for television by Fritz Spiegl and reached number 6 in the charts in 1962. Its entrenchment within supporters' minds was demonstrated when there was an attempt to drop it by the Everton Board of Directors during the 1994–1995 football season. This was met with extreme resistance by the fans, with the support of the then manager, Joe Royle, and forced a reversal of the decision by the Board of Directors. It is still being played at the start of every Everton home game. West Ham United, a club in the East End of London, has a long association with the music hall song 'I'm Forever Blowing Bubbles', written in 1918 and introduced to the club in the 1920s by a former manager, Charlie Paynter. It is so associated with the club that it has official anthem status and is played before the teams come onto the field of play in order to develop enthusiasm within the crowd. This could be seen as a case of the club using the identity of the crowd to generate support for the team. This approach does not always work as was found by Jimmy Hill when he was manager of Coventry City in the early 1960s. Hill introduced 'The Sky Blue Song' sung to the tune of the 'Eton Boating Song' with lines such as 'While we sing together we will never lose'. It was not a great success.

As can be seen, a number of supporters' anthems come under the category of popular songs as opposed to 'pop' songs which often have a shorter life span.

Newcastle United is closely associated with the Victorian music hall song 'Blaydon Races' which originated at Balmbara's Music Hall in the city. However, the club and fans have also adopted a more modern anthem in 'Local Hero', written and performed by locally born Newcastle fan and member of Dire Straits, Mark Knopfler. The associations and meanings of the tune are clear to see. Another music hall song, 'Keep Right On To The End Of The Road', was adopted by Birmingham City. This was written by the music hall star, Sir Harry Lauder, in the aftermath of his son's death during the First World War in 1916 and seems an inappropriate anthem. However, it was taken up by Birmingham fans during the FA Cup campaign of 1955–1956 where each round, including the final, was an away tie. In this context the theme of perseverance on the long way home seems appropriate. Such is the entrenchment of the song within the Birmingham fan-base that a fanzine was named after a line in the song – 'Tired and weary'.

Music adopted by sport

There has been increasing development in this area, with a major interest in music's association with exercise (e.g. aerobics, kick boxing, circuit training, Pilates) and dance with the 'explosion of health consciousness'.[60] It is not the intention of this chapter to look at this specific area but to interrogate the use of music to create an atmosphere or set a mood in the form of the introduction of players or teams, covering breaks in the action, presaging events in the performance or being representational. According to Ken McLeod music associated with most sports is 'sonically, rhythmically and vocally aggressive'[61] and there can be an analogy between the dynamics of a sport and the dynamics of music.[62] Although not specifically written for sport, many popular songs can be appropriate to the mood or ambience, or incorporated to create such a mood. Darts, recently officially recognised as a sport, has used music as a means of modernising and selling its product with popular music identifiers or signature theme tunes for the players and the use of music to stimulate and encourage crowd involvement. In cricket the introduction of the Twenty20 format has been developed, incorporating popular music to make the game entertaining and promoting the game to a wider and younger audience. It is also there to identify various points in the action. Purists certainly find this an unwelcome addition to the sport. McLeod suggests that sports organisations such as NASCAR (National Association for Stock Car Auto Racing) and the NBA (National Basketball Association) in the United States of America have associated themselves with various types of musical styles in order, amongst other things, to forge a wider fan base.[63]

Some popular music lends itself easily and directly to use in sport. Obvious examples are 'We Are The Champions' released by Queen in 1977. This song has been used at tournament presentations including the Premier League Trophy in football. Tina Turner's rendition of 'The Best', often called 'Simply The Best' due to the words in the chorus, is a particularly well-known example.

Originally released by Bonnie Tyler, it was recorded by Tina Turner in 1989 and has continued to be associated with sport since the 1990s. It was used by the boxer Chris Eubank and has become the representative song of rugby league. An equally recognisable piece of music is 'Eye Of The Tiger' written and released by a band called Survivor in 1982 for the film *Rocky III*, starring Sylvester Stallone as the fictional boxer, Rocky Balboa. The theme of the song is one of aggressiveness and the killer instinct – it has been used by boxers and boxing promoters because of the 'Rocky' connection. The wrestler Hulk Hogan (sometimes known as Hollywood Hogan) had also used it as his ring-entrance music. The Baha Men's song 'Who Let The Dogs Out?' was originally broadcast at baseball games and gained it's popularity from this rather than being adopted by the sport or a particular club.[64] From a different perspective, the German electronic band Kraftwerk was commissioned to write a piece for the centenary of the Tour de France in 2003. This came out as 'Tour de France Soundtracks', with a small extract being used as promotional film advertising the race on Eurosport.

Popular musical references to sport

Alongside the above forms of popular music there have been a number of artists who have produced material with a sporting theme not to celebrate an event or to be used as part of the action of sport. Despite David Rowe's comments that sport and rock music are significant forms of popular culture there is not as much of this music as might be expected. Indeed, Ken McLeod suggests that sport is rarely the subject of popular music.[65] Attempts have been made by some researchers to compile lists of such music, but they invariably end up with a limited number of examples and rarely any mainstream artists. In Redhead's 'Playlist on "Soccer into Pop"', for example, there were some examples with rather tenuous links to the sport, some of which appear to have been produced in an exploitative manner.[66]

One major exception to this is the Mersey group (all Tranmere Rovers supporters), Half Man Half Biscuit who have produced a number of direct references to a wide variety of sports in their songs. Inevitably football dominates, as indicated by the title song 'Friday Night And The Gates Are Low', which refers to Abba's 'Dancing Queen' and the fact that Tranmere Rovers once played their games on a Friday evening in order to avoid clashes with the more successful Merseyside teams, Liverpool and Everton. Further songs are, amongst others, 'All I Want For Christmas Is A Dukla Prague Away Kit', 'I Was A Teenage Armchair Honved Fan', 'Dead Men Don't Need Season Tickets', '1966 And All That' (an obvious reference to England's win in the World Cup in that year), 'The Referee's Alphabet' and 'Bob Wilson – Anchorman' (a reference to the former Arsenal and Scotland goalkeeper who developed a successful media career, especially in television). Other sports covered are cricket, with songs about the former Yorkshire and England player, Hedley Verity ('Hedley Veri-tyesque') and former Middlesex and England player, Fred Titmus, celebrated in 'Fuckin' 'Ell, It's Fred Titmus'. Tennis is covered by 'Outbreak Of Vitas

Gerulaitis' (the successful American Australian Open winner), and snooker, with a reference to the snooker referee Len Ganley in 'Len Ganley Stance' as well as the psychological inability to hit the ball in 'Yipps (My Baby Got The)'. An interesting offering from the band was 'Dickie Davies Eyes' which has a number of contemporary references. Dickie Davies was the very popular presenter of a Saturday afternoon sports programme on Independent Television (ITV) called *World of Sport* which ran between 1965 and 1985. It has a strong cross-cultural element and contains the line 'Brian Moore's Head Looks Uncannily Like The London Planetarium' which became the title of a football fanzine at Gillingham FC where the football commentator was once a Director of the club.

Other artists have also used sport as a theme and two interesting ones which use boxing are 'Foreman vs Frazier, Round Two' by Big Youth (1973) which is in a ska-dub style, and 'Hurricane' by Bob Dylan (1975). The latter has a strong political dimension, concerned as it is with the case of Rubin 'Hurricane' Carter, a former middle-weight championship contender who spent 19 years in jail for a murder he claims he did not commit. Dylan became interested in the case after Carter sent him his autobiography, causing Dylan to visit him in gaol and then write the song to support the campaign to get him released. Mike Marqusee suggests that it was a return to protest for Dylan and that the song stressed the endurance of racism in America.[67] It was also a track on the Dylan album *Desire* (1976) and the singer headed a benefit concert for the boxer called 'Night of the Hurricane' at Madison Square Garden.[68] This was not the first boxing related song Dylan had penned. He also wrote 'Who Killed Davey Moore?' questioning the death from brain damage of the boxer Davey Moore during a fight with Sugar Ramos in 1963.[69] Carter was also the subject of a film called *Hurricane*, starring Denzil Washington. Idolatry came in the form of Don Fardon's 'Belfast Boy', commemorating George Best, the Manchester United and Northern Ireland footballer who died in 2005. The heavy metal band Iron Maiden produced a track called 'The Loneliness Of The Long Distance Runner' from the *Somewhere in Time* album (1986) referring to the short story (and later a film) of the same name by Alan Sillitoe. It also refers to the 'Tough of the Track', a comic book athlete by the name of Alf Tupper.

Alternative and lifestyle sports and sub-culture

According to Robert Rinehart alternative sports are activities that 'either ideologically or practically' provide alternatives to mainstream sports and mainstream values.[70] They have been broadly associated with, and originate from, the countercultural social movements of the 1960s and early 1970s in opposition to dominant sporting cultures[71] In these sports there is a tendency to develop different lifestyles and competitive approaches, and music is an essential element in their identity and formulation. In this context the most studied sports have been surfing, skateboarding and snowboarding and the X-Games where the identification of sub-cultural aspects is essential to an understanding of the sports. These are found in a coordinated and internalised world composed of clothes, music, stickers, board design, language and 'other forms of communication'.[72] It is also a world which may face prejudice because they wear different clothes and hairstyles, speak a different language and listen to different music.[73] A recurring theme here is music, and all three of the above are closely associated with it as a means of expressing the culture of the sports. A competitor in a skateboarding contest interviewed by David Browne made the claim that 'music and skating [skateboarding] have always gone together',[74] and the anarchic aspects of both the sport and the music associated with it were a piece of youth culture.[75] The types of music referred to across the spectrum of extreme and alternative sports encompass punk, alternative hip-hop, ska, hardcore rap, cut and paste DJ, scratching, etc. It could hardly be described as 'middle of the road'. Browne identifies a survey on the music of alternative sports conducted in 2002 by a journal called *Transworld BMX* which identified hard rock/heavy metal (67.6 per cent), punk (50.8 per cent) and rap/hip-hop (45.2 per cent) as the dominant musical tastes. Interestingly, country music comes in with a 6.4 per cent rating.[76] However, since snowboarding has become an Olympic event and skateboarding has been considered for future Olympics it will be interesting to see how 'alternative' or 'sub-cultural' they can remain.

Surfing has been most heavily identified with a form or style of music said to represent the lifestyle and culture of the sport. The most well-known connection is with the group, the Beach Boys, who have continued to be associated with the sport and its attendant way of life. The group's strong connections with surfing culture is manifest in songs such as 'Surfin' Safari', 'Surfer Girl', 'Catch A Wave' and 'South Bay Surfer' and are reinforced by images of the sport on their album covers. Other 'surfing bands' include The Surfaris (with songs such as 'Wipe Out', 'Walkin' On Water', 'Hot Surf Sunday') and Jan and Dean ('Surf City', 'Linda'). More recently, Jack Johnson, a former champion surfer turned singer-songwriter, has pursued a successful music career exploiting the surfer lifestyle and imagery. This has included directing and providing the soundtrack for the surf film *Thicker than Water*. Jan and Dean (Jan Berry and Dean Torrance) have further connections with alternative and lifestyle sports and they are credited with the first successful song written about extreme sports. They took the melody from the Beach Boys' hit song 'Catch A Wave', and produced 'Sidewalk Surfin'' which did well in the charts in the USA, reaching number 25 in 1964.[77] Snowboarding has been represented by the German rock band Guano Apes with a successful record in 1998 called 'Lords Of The Board', with the line 'I've got the snowboard under my feet I can fly so high, I can fall so deep.'

Concluding thoughts

Despite the earlier claims that sport and music have a significant relationship, the level of academic interest in these associations has been somewhat limited. This is particularly the case when it comes to looking at sport's relationship with popular music or, more appropriately, the music of the fans. Classical and 'high' culture music have been discussed with composers such as Erik Satie (*Sports et Divertissments*), Dimitri Shostakovich (the ballet *The Golden Age* being about football), Claude Debussy (the ballet *Jeux* which takes place on a tennis court), Michael Nyman (*After Extra Time* on football) and many others being prepared to produce work with a sporting theme.[78] Yet it is the importance of music and singing, along with chanting, that can identify the fans, their sport, their team, their locality and their history. With the redevelopment and reconstruction of stadiums, especially following the Taylor Report (1989–1990) and particularly in England, it has been felt that the atmosphere once created in stadiums has been muted. The lack of fluidity and the opportunity to freely associate with other fans caused in seated stadiums, with seat allocation and increased supervision and control, does not allow for fans to form groups as they did in the past. There is a general consensus that the quality of popular music associated with sport has not always been of the highest quality. However, it is a genre which is extremely popular and engages sports fans on a short-term and a long-term basis.[79]

Notes

1 The title refers to a song by the Merseyside indie band, Half Man Half Biscuit.
2 R. Reilly, 'The Sweet Songs of Soccer', *Sports Illustrated*, 104, 24, 2006.
3 Desmond Morris, *The Soccer Tribe*, London: Jonathan Cape, 1981; John Williams, 'Rethinking sports fandom: the case of European soccer', *Leisure Studies*, 26, 2, 2007, 127–146.
4 Ibid., 127–131.
5 J. N. de Surmont, 'From oral tradition to commercial history: the misunderstood path of popular song', *Georgian Electronic Scientific Journal: Musicology and Cultural Science*, 1, 2, 2006, 3. Online, available at: www.osgf.ge/~internetacademy/gesj/gesj_articles/1206.pdf.
6 Steve Redhead, *Post-Fandom and the Millennial Blues: The Transformation of Soccer Culture*, London: Routledge, 1997, p. 80; J. Bale, *Sport, Space and the City*, London: Routledge, 1993.
7 H. D. Krebs, 'Sport and music: an uncommon partnership', *Olympic Review*, 37, 2001, 41–44.
8 G. Crawford, *Consuming Sport: Fans, Sport and Culture*, London: Routledge, 2004, p. 131.
9 Philip Scowcroft, 'The interface between sport and music', *Classical Music on the Web*. Online, available at: www.musicweb-international.com/classrev/2001/Jan01/Sport_and_Music.htm (accessed 9 January 2008).
10 E. Höhne, 'Music and sport', *Olympic Review*, 141–142, 1979, 437–439.
11 David Rowe, *Popular Cultures: Rock Music, Sport and the Politics of Pleasure*, London: Sage, 1995, p. 9.
12 Dave Russell, 'Music and northern identity 1890–c.1965', in N. Kirk (ed.), *Northern Identities: Historical Interpretations of 'The North' and 'Northernness'*, Aldershot: Ashgate, 2000, p. 23.
13 Brian Longhurst, *Popular Music and Society*, Cambridge: Polity Press, 1995, pp. 158–159.
14 G. Melly, *Revolt into Style. The Pop Arts in Britain*, Harmondsworth: Penguin, 1970, p. 3.

15 De Surmont, 'From oral tradition to commercial industry', p. 7.
16 N. Cohn, *Awopbopaloobop Alopbamboom*, London: Paladin, 1969.
17 I. Whitcomb, *After the Ball*, Harmondsworth: Penguin, 1972, p. 3.
18 K. McLeod, '"We are the Champions": masculinities, sports and popular music', *Popular Music and Society*, 29, 2006, 531–547.
19 Ibid., p. 544.
20 Krebs, 'Sport and music', 41.
21 Russell, 'Music and northern identity 1890–c.1965', p. 23.
22 Simon Frith, 'Music and identity', in S. Hall and P. du Gay (eds), *Questions of Cultural Identity*, London: Sage, 1996, p. 109.
23 McLeod, '"We are the Champions"', 532.
24 Quoted in Rowe, *Popular Cultures*, p. 10.
25 Ibid.
26 P. J. Seddon, *A Football Compendium. An Expert Guide to the Books, Films and the Music of Association Football*, Boston Spa, Wetherby: The British Library, 1999, p. 645.
27 Redhead, *Post-Fandom and the Millennial Blues*, p. 81.
28 P. Hooton, 'England expects', *Observer*, 23 May 2004.
29 F. Plowright, 'Record attempts', in 'Football memorabilia special', *When Saturday Comes*, 227, 2006, 5.
30 Seddon, *A Football Compendium*, p. 646.
31 Liz Crolley and David Hand, *Football, Europe and the Press*, London: Frank Cass, 2002, p. 28.
32 P. Lewis, 'That time … they got it oh so wrong', *Guardian*, 6 March 2006, 3.
33 Chris Waddle also made a record with Basil Boli during his time at Olympique de Marseilles called 'We've Got a Feeling' in 1991.
34 M. van Hoof, 'Euro visions', *When Saturday Comes*, 110, 1996, 28–29.
35 Channel 4 home page. Online, available at: http://.channel4.com/entertainment/tv/microsites/G/greatest/pop_records/results (accessed 13 November 2007).
36 This is still being played and sung at Stamford Bridge today.
37 van Hoof 'Euro visions', 29.
38 R. Newson, 'Music to your ears?', *When Saturday Comes*, 110, 1996, 25.
39 This song was originally produced in 1990 for their LP, *Spartacus*, and remade for the 2004 tournament. In 2006 Atomic Kitten remade it as the official song for the 2006 FIFA World Cup. It was also used by Everton for their appearance in the 1995 FA Cup Final. Its lyrics refer to the First World War truce in December 1914 when British and German troops met in 'No Man's Land' and played football.
40 The record included six members of the England squad: John Barnes, Peter Beardsley, Paul Gascoigne, Steve McMahon, Chris Waddle and Des Walker. Keith Allen of 'Vindaloo' fame was also involved.
41 B. Carrington, '"Football's Coming Home" but whose home? And do we want it? Nation, football and the politics of exclusion', in Adam Brown (ed.), *Fanatics! Power, Identity and Fandom in Football*, London: Routledge, 1998, pp. 110–113.
42 McLeod, '"We are the Champions"', 541.
43 J. Bradley, '"We Shall Not be Moved!" mere sport, mere songs?', in Adam Brown (ed.), *Fanatics! Power, Identity and Fandom in Football*, London: Routledge, 1998, p. 203.
44 *Collins Compact Dictionary*, London: Collins, 1989.
45 Morris, *The Soccer Tribe*, p. 304.
46 McLeod, '"We are the Champions"', 541.
47 D. Howard, 'Measuring the tuning accuracy of thousands singing in unison: an English Premier Football League table of fans' singing tunefulness', *Logopedics Phoniatrics Vocology*, 29, 2004, 77–83.
48 Quoted in de Surmont, 'From oral tradition to commercial history', 5.

49 Morris, *The Soccer Tribe*, pp. 304–305.
50 Howard, 'Measuring the tuning accuracy of thousands singing in unison', 82–83.
51 Ibid., 77.
52 Benedict Anderson, *Imagined Communities: Reflections on the Origin and Spread of Nationalism*, London: Verso, 1983, p. 6.
53 H. F. Moorhouse, 'One state, several countries: soccer and nationality in a "United" Kingdom', in J. A. Mangan (ed.), *Tribal Identities: Nationalism, Europe, Sport*, London: Frank Cass, 2002, p. 71.
54 C. Jones and S. Fleming, '"I'd rather wear a turban than a rose": a case study of the ethics of chanting', in *Race Ethnicity and Education*, 10, 4, 2007, 401–414.
55 Steve Redhead, 'Always look on the bright side of life', in Redhead (ed.), *The Passion and the Fashion. Football Fandom in the New Europe*, Aldershot: Averbury, 1993, p. 7.
56 Gerry Marsden also wrote and recorded 'Ferry Across the Mersey' which has strong associations with Liverpool.
57 John Williams, 'Kopites, "scallies" and Liverpool fan cultures: tales of triumph and disasters', in John Williams, Stephen Hopkins and Cathy Long (eds), *Passing Rhythms: Liverpool FC and the Transformation of Football*, Oxford: Berg, 2001, p. 103.
58 R. Boyle, 'Football and religion: Merseyside and Glasgow', in John Williams, Stephen Hopkins and Cathy Long (eds), *Passing Rhythms: Liverpool FC and the Transformation of Football*, Oxford: Berg, 2001, p. 47.
59 Bradley, '"We Shall Not be Moved!" mere sport, mere songs?', p. 209.
60 McLeod, '"We are the Champions"', 545.
61 Ibid., 536.
62 Redhead, *Post Fandom and the Millennial Blues*, p. 70.
63 McLeod, '"We are the Champions"', 540.
64 Ibid., 531.
65 Ibid., 533.
66 Redhead, *Post Fandom and the Millennial Blues*, pp. 83–86.
67 Mike Marqusee, *Redemption Song: Muhammad Ali and the Spirit of the Sixties*, London: Verso, 1999, p. 160.
68 J. Hirsch, *'Hurricane'. The Life of Rubin Carter, Fighter*, London: Fourth Estate, 2000, pp. 120–124.
69 Marqusee, *Redemption Song*, p. 290.
70 R. Rinehart, 'Emerging/arriving sport: alternatives to formal sports', in Jay Coakley and Eric Dunning (eds), *Handbook of Sports Studies*, London: Sage, 2002, p. 506.
71 B. Wheaton '"New lads"? Masculinities and the "new sport" participant', *Men and Masculinities*, 2, 4, 2000, 435.
72 I. Borden, *Skateboarding, Space and the City: Architecture and the Body*, Oxford: Berg, 2001, p. 152.
73 D. Humphreys, 'Snowboarders: bodies out of control and in conflict', *Sporting Traditions*, 13, 5, 1996, 3.
74 D. Browne, *Amped. How Big Air, Big Dollars and a New Generation took Sports to the Extreme*, New York and London: Bloomsbury, 2005, p. 154.
75 Ibid., p. 161.
76 Ibid., pp. 160–161.
77 Ibid., pp. 157–158.
78 See Krebs, 'Sport and music' for a broader discussion.
79 For a representation of the songs of the fans see J. Bremner, *Shit Ground No Fans. It's by Far the Greatest Football Songbook the World has Ever Seen*, London: Bantam Press, 2004.

11 Supporter rock in Sweden

Locality, resistance and irony at play[1]

Dan Porsfelt

Over the last few decades, Swedish football supporter culture has developed and continually changed. This chapter focuses on one particular dimension of that culture: namely, rock music. More precisely, this chapter is a study of rock bands or artists that are in symbiosis with Swedish football clubs and their supporters. The chapter begins with a short account of three perspectives on the theme of support. This is followed by a description of three analytical perspectives and three different bands/artists with close connections to different Stockholm-based football clubs: Djurgårdens IF, Hammarby IF and AIK.[2]

Support

Identity construction, globalisation and glocalisation

There are many ways to look at the theme of support. Identity and identity construction is one.[3] There is no doubt that the emotional, time-consuming and expressive connection with a football club may be a manifestation of a class, social or geographical position in which the identification with a certain club is, so to speak, taken in with the mother's milk. Born in East London? Well, then you *are* 'West Ham' (or, less likely, 'Leyton Orient'). Grew up in inner-city Torino? Well, then you *are* 'FC Torino' and not 'Juve' (those 'rednecks from the countryside and southern Italy'). The examples are many. As a sports geographer, John Bale observed in 1988: 'There can be little doubt that it is through sport that current manifestations of localism (and regionalism and nationalism) are most visible.'[4] There is some scientific support for stating that among dedicated supporters in particular, there are strong senses of local pride and identification within particular cities and locations, and that the local football team becomes an important catalyst for, and a manifestation of, these identifications.[5]

On the other hand, many claim that postmodern society and media globalisation has led to a decline in local identification and that an increase in distant identifications with, for example, Real Madrid's 'Galacticos' or Manchester United, can be more important than local connections. As Giulianotti and Robertson confirm, there are 'self-invented virtual diasporas' within a more general process of globalisation.[6] However, the opposite tendency coexists within patterns of globalisation and can be best theorised through the concept of *glocalisation*, a term originally coined in Japanese business life. In short, glocalisation is a concept that 'helps to explain how the symbiosis of the local and the global differs according to particular cultural circumstances'.[7] It is my contention that among Swedish, Nordic and European football spectators alike, both dimensions of glocalisation, i.e. globalisation and locality, are evident. Glocalisation is manifest in the form of local reconstructions of globally dispersed aspects of football and supporter culture; in the form of local resistance against 'others' and in the glorification of the personal sphere.

Commercialisation and commodification – a part of the experience economy?

An alternative approach to understanding or problematising support is that of commercialisation. Entrepreneurial literature, following Pine and Gilmore's influential book *The Experience Economy*, overflows with thoughts and pointers regarding how sport is part of an 'experience industry' (just like music or tourism).[8] In the last 10–15 years in Sweden, this has been most prominent in ice hockey. The process was perhaps initiated in 1989 with the construction of the Globe Arena in Stockholm, and was definitely accentuated via the construction of new 'experience arenas' in cities around Sweden. It is most clearly manifest in Americanised names for hockey clubs in the manner of the NHL: Malmö IF becomes 'MIF Redhawks' and Västra Frölunda becomes 'Frölunda Indians'. Most clubs in today's top hockey league have been exposed to this, the aim being to attract the affluent, experience-seeking middle-class family to ice hockey where they can buy popcorn as well as American-style souvenirs. Within these new consumption patterns supporters become 'customers' who need to be 'communicated' with in order to ensure a constant flow of money from their wallets to 'the sports industry'.[9] However, the commodification, commercialised merchandising and obsession with branding in ice hockey in Stockholm has clearly alienated traditional supporters of the AIK, Djurgården and Hammarby hockey clubs. The combined attendance at regular matches for all three clubs has now declined to approximately 7,000. The Globe Arena alone seats 14,000 spectators. Instead, spectators have flocked to their respective club's football team, which today collectively attract around 50,000 spectators per match. Fifteen years ago, the combined number of spectators at ice hockey was higher than the combined number of spectators in the football stadiums of the three clubs. I would not dream of suggesting that commercialisation has not affected football in Sweden or in Stockholm. However, as yet, the three major clubs in the city have not sacrificed their souls on the altar of commercialisation to such a degree as in ice hockey.

Hooliganism, casuals and violence

Hooliganism is undoubtedly another important aspect of supporter culture.[10] As illustrated by Swedish football historian, Torbjörn Andersson, this is not a new phenomenon in Sweden.[11] Historically speaking, violence in connection with sports is not unusual. However, if we define hooliganism as acts of violence committed within organised contexts in which violence is a central part of an 'organisation's' culture as a basis for identification, then this is a fairly recent phenomenon in Sweden, originating in late 1970s Stockholm.[12] Here, modelled on British supporter culture, the fans of the city's three main clubs formed their own 'cheering sections'[13] and supporter clubs: 'Black Army' (AIK), 'Blue Saints' (Djurgårdens IF) and 'Bajen Fans' (Hammarby IF). Of course, the increased violence that had erupted at and around British football stadiums since the late 1960s was also a source of inspiration. In the late 1970s and the first half of the 1980s there were numerous confrontations between these groups and supporters from other parts of Sweden.[14] At the Stockholm Derbies violence between supporters was almost always present. Nevertheless, a kind of naiveté on the part of the authorities, such as placing Blue Saints and Black Army on the same terrace at *Råsunda Stadion* was still obvious in those days. This inevitably led to violence between the groups. Years went by and obvious cultural boundaries between the three cheering sections were established, albeit within a more general supporter culture. Events became stories and various myths were created. Different artefacts such as songs and rhymes (about the enemy), symbols (often related to the enemy or hostility) and practices such as the establishment of various territories to visit in connection with matches or parties also arose. In particular, certain pubs were confirmed over time as being AIK, Djurgården or Hammarby haunts. Following Giulianotti and Armstrong, location and personal 'territory' are important ingredients in general supporter culture as well as hooligan culture; although for the latter this is more plastic and flexible.[15] To briefly reconnect with the theme of globalisation mentioned above, we may conclude that 'de-territorialisation' in the form of a detachment of the more commercial, transnational 'company clubs' or 'brands' from their local origins (when, for instance, home games can be played in other cities, countries or continents to market merchandise and widen the fan base) is already a reality.[16] However, I will argue that in the case of these Stockholm clubs the process described above is an example of territorialisation or localisation of previously relatively 'un-territorialised' clubs and supporters. I will return to this later.

Returning to hooliganism as an angle of approach, by the late 1990s and early 2000s all these teams' supporters had well-established 'firms'. Hammarby's firm, *Kompisgänget Bajen* was, perhaps, initially somewhat less organised than AIK's *Firman Boys*, Djurgården's *Baby Firman/Järngänget* (the Iron Gang) and *Djurgården Fina Grabbar* (Djurgården Fine Lads). Based on British 'casual' role models, they developed through personal relations with foreign fans and contacts with established firms abroad. Media, in the form of newspaper articles, books, music, and later numerous internet sites and a few films dedicated to hooliganism or casual culture, were nevertheless equally important factors in the spread of this phenomenon, both in general and in this particular case.

Supporters and music

There are undoubtedly more angles to the analysis and understanding of support and supporter culture than the three briefly described above. An aspect less focused on in Sweden is supporters and music, although internationally there have been a couple of attempts to do so.[17] Bands or artists that fully or substantially base their repertoire, stage performances, image, social and commercial existence on their identification with a football club and its supporters have not received much attention though. I will devote the rest of this chapter to this aspect, against the background of what I have discussed so far. I would like to stress that I am aware of the fact that there have been songs in honour of, and for, sportsmen and sports clubs for a very long time. I am also aware of the fact that the twentieth century has provided us with numerous songs that have been composed and performed or recorded by artists who try to make an effort for 'their club' or perhaps their national team. The artists I will discuss later, however, have gone beyond this.

Since the 1970s there have been a number of examples of bands or artists who have expressly identified with certain clubs. Early on was the oi-band, The Cockney Rejects, formed in London's East End in 1979 and active until 1985. Their West Ham United sympathies were hardly concealed by their choice of songs ('I'm Forever Blowing Bubbles', the club's anthem) or lyrics for their own songs (for example, 'War on the Terraces').[18] It was obvious to everyone with the least insight into British football and supporter culture that these lads 'were' West Ham and were proud of it. The few gigs the band did outside of London resulted in riots when local football supporters tried to start fights with the group and their fans. These incidents were thus football and supporter related due to the strong ties between band, music and West Ham.[19] The German punk band, Die Toten Hosen, has, in its long career, expressed both in its choice of songs and use of artefacts such as team shirts at their gigs, sympathy for, and identification with, the German football club Fortuna Düsseldorf. The band has over the years reached success and hence reaped the economic fruits of this. The football club, on the other hand, has declined in recent years but was promoted to the German third league once more in 2005. Die Toten Hosen is one of the club's main sponsors (the band logo appears on the team shirt) and has also financed the acquisition of several players for the team in recent years.[20] Other artists worth mentioning in this respect are, for example, Half Man Half Biscuit (Tranmere Rovers) and The Farm (Liverpool FC).[21]

In Sweden this form of symbiosis has, until recently, been less apparent. Certainly, more or less well-known artists have shown their support for particular clubs and have contributed individual songs for various albums released by the clubs or supporter clubs over the years. Since the mid-1990s, however, we have seen a number of bands or artists that are more overtly linked to different football clubs and their supporters. Of course this is not a uniquely Swedish phenomenon. One of the more obvious examples in a non-Swedish context is Glasgow band, Charlie and the Bhoys (Celtic FC), who play before and after

Saturday home games in The Brazen Head pub near to Celtic's home ground of Parkhead.[22] It is this highly engaged type of supporter rock which I will focus on henceforth.

Three clubs – three bands – three themes

Djurgårdens IF – Coca Carola – locality and the construction of identity

The punk band Coca Carola was formed in Åkersberga, a suburb northeast of Stockholm, in 1986 and became one of the more prominent bands in the Swedish punk scene.[23] It was not until 1998–1999, though, that a more distinct link with the club and its supporters became publicly visible. Without doubt some of the band members had a history as Djurgården supporters on the terraces for a number of years. However, the commitment of other members was somewhat more ambiguous and rumour has it that one is a closet AIK supporter! The band was, according to themselves,[24] asked by the club to record some songs for a Djurgården album. The album was released in time for the 1999 football season and eight of the 12 songs are performed by Coca Carola. The album cover shows the band drinking the supporter club's own lager brand, Järnkaminernas Guld, in the supporter hangout, *Östra Station* (East Station) pub, with one of the members wearing a Djurgården shirt. The band has since played for Djurgården supporters on many occasions, has written more Djurgården songs and released several live CDs recorded at concerts for Djurgården supporters before away games in Kalmar, Borås and Sundsvall. The band has played for supporters numerous times in Stockholm but also at the club's official *Allsvenskan* gold party in 2003. Coca Carola's CDs are regularly played at supporter club events in Sweden and abroad, often accompanied by the community singing of travelling supporters. Coca Carola's Djurgården songs are played at the club's home ground, the Stockholm Stadium, at home fixtures (and in some cases even at away games!). In 2004 the band officially split.[25]

Examples of Coca Carola's Djurgården songs are (our translations):

- 'We Are Djurgår'n'
- 'Järnkaminerna'
- 'My Shirt'
- 'We Love You'
- 'Stadium's Boiling'
- 'Adrenaline'
- 'Our City Our Team'
- 'Stockholm's Pride'
- 'Promenade'.

In general, the songs (top to bottom) are about love for the club, club symbols, team, supporter solidarity, drinking beer with your mates before matches, disappointment and occasional euphoric joy, shedding blood for the club on the terraces as well as in streets and squares and drowning one's sorrows after a game. In short, there are two main themes: the club and the supporter lifestyle.

However, there is also an apparent third theme in Coca Carola's Djurgården songs: the significance of *locales*.[26] All of this stands in clear contrast to the thoughts of de-territorialisation and dislocation from the local discussed earlier. Instead, the texts bring into mind the concept of *topophilia*,[27] the love of a location. Let us take a look at the last song mentioned in the list above, 'Promenade':

> I went out walking on a Sunday afternoon
> In local areas where I'd played as a boy
> I saw people laughing and people sharing hugs
> I saw guys playing football and girls who'd had enough.
>
> I came to the Red Castle from nineteenhundredtwelve
> With grass as green as polished marble floors
> I bought myself a ticket to Lidingö and sat
> Felt the joy bubbling and threw off my hat.
>
> Is it wrong to be happy?
> Although we know it wasn't supposed to be
> Is it wrong to dance and be glad?
> I just want to cry out that we won today.
>
> After the game we went and had some beer
> Danced and sang at pub Östra and cheer'd
> Toasted our victory and strolled all over town
> Made fun of the losers ha ha ha.
>
> I came home as a hero fell asleep right away
> Dreamed of victory dreamed of hooray
> Woke up smiling knowing that we had won
> We will win once again and wear the crown.
>   (Lyrics: C. Sandgren; music: Coca Carola, DIF AB
>   1999; our translation)

The emphasis and glorification of the local in the form of national romance, the accent on a long local history embodied in the home arena and the veneration of the local Djurgården pub, *Östra Station* typify the *topophilia* of this rock genre. The lyrics conclude with a walk home through Stockholm city, in which the city 'is ours'. There is no doubt that this is the home base for Djurgården as regards the strong emotions of pride and joy that it induces. For a variety of reasons, compared to the other two main Stockholm clubs, Djurgårdens IF has, over its 126 years, been least permanently rooted in one stadium or part of the city. The strong emphasis on topophilia in Coca Carolas' lyrics is a means of dealing with this by constructing locales and thus territorialising the club and its supporter culture in Stockholm city, perhaps in answer to processes of, and attempts at, de-territorialisation. It can be seen as an attempt at constructing *homotopia*:[28] a place with more or less a singular meaning.

Hammarby IF – Bajen Death Cult – resistance to commercialisation, commodification and control

Established in 1998, Bajen Death Cult[29] is a self-professed 'voodoo metal' band. Sometimes it cheerfully describes itself as a 'hooligan metal' band (á la the 'hooligan house' of The Streets and Audio Bullys). One of the members is otherwise known for playing in the Stockholm metal band, Grand Magus, and two of the others play in death-metal band, Necrophobic. In 2004 the band released a four-track CD. In 2005 they released a full CD to coincide with a large rally of Bajen Fans at Söder (the south part of the inner-city) in Stockholm.

The band has its own homepage and guestbook,[30] and portrays itself as one of the various supporter factions existing outside the larger supporters' club, Bajen Fans. The band members have named themselves according to the dark metal scene's customs and are officially known as Draugadrottin, Lodbrok, Mjölner and Nidhögg. We may assume that these are not their birth names. An air of mysticism, occultism, voodoo, Norse mythology and fairytales is blended with masculinity, Hammarby scarves and fanaticism. The band's trademark combines these elements with traditional metal craftsmanship. A strange admixture, some might think, but popular among Hammarby supporters. Musically, the band present a blend of rough heavy metal fortified with power and thrash metal. The band, like Coca Carola, has played several times at different supporter events and away games. Unlike Coca Carola, all Bajen Death Cult songs are supporter related. The band would not exist without Hammarby IF or its supporters. Some of the titles of the band's songs released are (our translation):

- 'We Who Glow'
- 'Jabbing Song'
- 'El Corazón (The Heart)'
- 'Everyone Loves a Bajare'
- 'Bajen Death Cult'
- 'Wooden Shoes Diesel and Dialect'
- 'Welcome to the South'.

The lyrics cover many of the same themes as those of Coca Carola. If anything, masculinity has been given more emphasis and the theme of *tifo* (spectacular choreographies performed by supporters on the terraces) are more prominent in the lyrics. In 'Nidvisa' the rivals AIK and Djurgården are ridiculed and degraded forcefully, a theme less openly visible in Coca Carola's songs. But like Coca Carola, the band also makes fun of 'peasants'. The tension between city and countryside is an old theme in supporter rock in Sweden as well as elsewhere.[31]

There is another theme more evident than in Coca Carola: namely, resistance towards commercialism and commodification in modern football and supporter contexts, in which football magnates and club magnates (lacking 'real heart') act in ways that damage the club and sell out its 'soul'. The band also detests the possibility that the freedom of fans ('the twelfth player' or 'number twelve' as quoted below) to fully support the club is hindered by club representatives or the Football Association's increasing attempts to regulate and limit supporters' rights to express themselves in the stands. The authorities have acted by forbidding symbols (for example, skulls) on flags and banners, by trying to control the language used in the stands, by forbidding parts of the *tifo* such as lighting Bengali fires and smoke torches, by using heavy-handed security guards who threaten, hit and throw people out, or by banning supporters from attending the stadium. Reactions to these restrictions are present in all three clubs' supporter groups, but in the last few years have been most evident among Hammarby supporters. In the lyrics of Bajen Death Cult, we find much glorification of this 'forbidden part' of everyday life as supporters. For example, here is a section of the song 'El Corazón (The Heart)':

> 'cause on the South Stadium we crush
> And number twelve makes a damn fuss
> This is where I'll always be
> 'cause I've sold my soul to Hammarby
> Forza Bajen! Forza Bajen! In with the ball hey hey!
> Bengali fires, pyrotechnic, exploding tifos, unlike any other, emergency
>   firework, green smoke, fireworks
> Our hearts burn for Hammarby!
>   (Lyrics and music: Bajen Death Cult 2005; our translation)

Below follows a quote 'Welcome to my South' from Bajen Death Cult's second album, which I interpret as reflecting resistance towards commercialisation and the regulation of Hammerby supporter culture (and also, for that matter, the supporter cultures of the other two clubs):

> Welcome to my South
> Here the flag is green and white
> An' if you don't support Bajen
> You ain't worth shit.
>
> Welcome to my pubs
> Here we have our beer and grub
> Here we take life day-by-day
> For life is an eternal play.
>
> O let them support us
> O let them befriend us

But if you try to tame us
We will stand up an' fight
– Let's reclaim the South, reclaim all that's ours
And out with the newly rich snobs, let's play rough.
(Lyrics and music: Bajen Death Cult 2005;
our translation)

Certainly, one may interpret the lyrics as saying that the opposition supporters are not welcome in the 'Hammarby territory' (the South); but the band itself claims that the lyrics are mostly directed towards the invasion of the newly rich, a development that threatens 'the soul of the South'.[32] Here is topophilia once again. However, I claim that the last two sentences also capture and convey resistance towards the football association and the club management, and particularly their attempts to commercialise and 'clean up' the football stands in recent years. These unwanted participants are attributed a value that is worth less 'than shit' and placed at the bottom of the hierarchy, even lower than the opposition supporters. As a counter image to these suited-up businessmen or politicians, the band endorses 'the Bajen supporter who takes life day-by-day', the impoverished bohemian who is nevertheless a potent figure in the club's mythology.

To further illustrate some of the attitudes of Hammarby (and other Stockholm clubs) supporter groups to the forces of authority and commodification, we may read an extract (our translation) from a homepage maintained by the supporter group, Ultra Boys. I interpret Bajen Death Cult's 'threat' that the band is ready to use violence if someone tries to tame it as a formulation of the same thoughts and mentality:

> **'Fight for the rights of the supporters'**
> Sweden is not an easy country to live in for ultras. The repression and oppression of ultras in Southern Europe that is spoken of is nothing compared to what we experience in Sweden. Up here, many of the natural rights of supporters are very limited. We want other supporters to realise the problems we are faced with. Ultra Boys always strive to use verbal methods as a first option to resolve things when problems arise. When this does not work or bureaucracy takes too long, immediate action is required. We do not consider it morally wrong to violate any laws or directives; we only look to what is best for Hammarby and Ultra Boys.[33]

In short, the band manifests a resistance towards attempts to turn the club into a product, into nothing more than a facet of Pine and Gilmore's 'experience economy'.[34] This form of resistance is widespread in Stockholm supporter culture in general.

AIK, the AIK Troubadour and the self-ironical staging of the hooligan

An artist who claims to represent the 'royal black yellow entertainment'[35] is *AIK-trubaduren* (the AIK Troubadour), the final example of supporter rock discussed here. On his former homepage he described his own music as 'hooligan music' (our translation):

> When 'Derbykungar' (*Derby Kings*) was released in December, 2000, some record stores sold the album. The person responsible for purchasing at Mix Records in Farsta is an old Gnagare[36] and he put the album at the front of the store, and 'Derbykungar' reached higher than Britney Spears, as well as Absolute Music 178 in the charts, and came in a flattering 3rd place. Moral of the story? More hooligan music to the people![37]

The AIK Troubadour (Mats Hellberg) started playing in 1994 and has ever since, just like the previously mentioned groups, played in front of AIK supporters in clubs and at away and home fixtures. Similar to Coca Carola, the artist has played at his favourite club's gold party, in this case in 1998. On his personal homepage his output of approximately ten albums are on sale. In 2004 he released a compilation CD entitled *AIK-trubadurens Bästa 1994–2004* (*Best of the AIK Troubadour 1994–2004*). Apart from sales via the supporter club at games and events, the CDs are also sold via a small network of supporters in various Stockholm suburbs or towns in other parts of the country.[38] Furthermore, the CDs were sold via the personal homepage's web shop and in certain highstreet record stores. A documentary about the AIK Troubadour was televised in 2006.

The titles of the songs – commented on below by the artist himself – on his latest AIK CD are entitled (our translation):

'I Hate Djurgår'n'	'Already available in a raw mix version on the band's homepage'
'All Rodents to Götet'	'Rock'n'roll about the annual invasion'
'Råsunda Belongs to Us!'	'No comments required'
'Get Out of Our Arena!'	'See above'
'Make Way for Baxter's Boys'	'About four black ghost riders who guard Råsunda castle'
'Away Game'	'About beer and away games (impossible to separate)'
'I Like it Best on the North Terrace'	'A celebration of our home on earth and the team in our hearts'
'No One Could be More Sick'	'Show-down with the ref who hates Gnaget'
'We are Black Army'	'A story about the positive sides to being notorious'
'Black Yellow AIK'	'Beer vs. pot'.[39]

The songs 'Råsunda Belongs to Us!' and 'Get Out of Our Arena!' are about the fact that Djurgården played their home games at Råsunda Stadium in the season of 2004. The AIK Troubadour's songs are covers of well-known songs, with supporter or club-related lyrics.

The themes most apparent in the AIK Troubadour's lyrics are familiar to the reader by now: love of the club and its symbols, topophilia in the form of love of Råsunda Stadium and the city, supporter life and beer drinking, away games and conflicts with the police, etc. The AIK Troubadour, however, devotes more time than those artists previously mentioned to the degrading of others. Primarily the 'others' are Djurgården and its supporters who are portrayed as being sissies, unmanly (they cannot drink or fight), blabbering baboons and upper-class trash. Hammarby supporters are also strongly degraded and portrayed as begging social welfare cases with heavy drug problems, living in dirty, smelly suburbs. Furthermore, Hammarby supporters are particularly unmanly and people living in Gothenburg in particular are 'peasants' and generally degraded by AIK Troubador.

Compared to Coca Carola and Bajen Death Cult, the AIK Troubadour concentrates more on violence, police brutality, hooliganism and feelings of omnipotence when different locations or the opposition stands are 'conquered' by the 'mighty' AIK supporters. We may in conclusion call this a *hooligan theme*.

'Crazy Hooligans'
We left three-hundred lads from our elongated land
With trains, buses and car-caravans
An' wherever we came everyone screamed: 'They're crazy those hooligans!'

In the city of Copenhagen we are known
We're awaited by militant vegans
It was beautiful to see all of them running frantically
From crazy hooligans.

On the ferry they sold beer and cheap booze
A trip taken by millions
But we're not sure if it has ever been worse
Than the one trip with the BA's battalions.[40]

Rödby set the stage for the trip's next phase
With unhealthy drinking and consumption
The German coast guard got a Mayday from the town
'Please save us from those hooligans!'

Hello!

An' we drank an' we drank an' we fought an' we drank
A sea battle without any guns

But this trip, my friend, will go down in history
As will the BA's battalions.

At the pier in Puttgarden the cops were waiting
An' two military divisions
Imagine three-hundred men jumping overboard
Those were the BA battalions.

When we'd come out and were drier the ferry was on fire
We waved our black and yellow flags
A message was sent to an entire continent
Here are crazy hooligans!

We left three-hundred lads from our elongated land
With trains, buses and caravans
An' wherever we came everyone screamed: 'They're crazy those hooligans!'
        (Lyrics: the AIK Troubadour; music: traditional Irish; our translation)

Here the listener and reader meet the self-proclaimed hooligans, the 'feared Black Army' and its credo 'May they hate us as long as they fear us!'[41]

The travel narrative quoted above is, appropriately enough, a cover version of 'Irish Rover', previously recorded by The Pogues and The Dubliners. And yes, there is a strong smell of liquor about the AIK Troubadour's travelogue. In that respect, the lyrics give a highly accurate description of the phenomenon of the away game. What we find is a narrative of *carnival*. Not only can we discern the more organised carnival (in the form of the match and the arrangements surrounding it) but we are given an insight into the spontaneous, disorganised and 'dangerous' side of the phenomenon. The carnival is constructed, in the true spirit of Mikhail Bakhtin, as an entry into an almost utopian kingdom of freedom and equality in which everyday rules, structures and power struggles are inverted or pushed aside and become something 'frank and free, permitting no distance between those who come in contact with each other and liberating them from the norms of etiquette and decency imposed at other times'.[42] A third space inbetween (social) order and (revolutionary) chaos is constructed in carnival situations. The third space may be seen as liminal:[43] a space in between[44] that enables other actions, expressions or ideas than those permitted in everyday life. In Michel Foucault's terminology, we can speak of a form of *heterotopia*.[45] A heterotopia is a space (or place) that is constructed within the framework of society and its institutions, but which nurtures resistance against the same society that created it. Heterotopias are, according to Foucault, 'sorts of places that are outside all places, although they are actually localisable'.[46] Foucault divides heterotopias into two categories: crisis heterotopias (which I will not discuss further) and heterotopias of deviation that are more relevant to the theme discussed here.

The lyrics may be read as being concerned with temporary (chronic) heterotopias of deviation: the space of deviation created and experienced on the supporter bus, and *placeless places*⁴⁷ like McDonald's along the motorway, the truck-stop during a 'piss-break', or the ferry between Rödby and Puttgarden; or when a large group of supporters 'conquer' a pub, a town or, say, Copenhagen's Town Hall Square during an 'invasion'. Spaces or places that normally have one or a few relatively well-defined meanings and functions, spaces taken for granted, not open for questioning. However, through the appearance, interaction and performance⁴⁸ of the supporters on tour, manifest in the lyrics of the song 'Crazy Hooligans', many of the carnivalesque aspects of supporter culture are joined together in transforming such spaces into temporary heterotopias of deviation. The supporters provoke frightened looks on the faces of families at an invaded McDonald's, or looks of loathing and fear in businessmen travelling on the high-speed train when the alcohol is uncorked in time for the train departure at 8am; but it is mostly for fun, and there is rarely any evil intent other than simply 'having a laugh'.⁴⁹ This behaviour entails an aesthetic view of violence and the hooligan: it's a staging of the prejudices regarding supporters/hooligans that already exists in the mind of the general public. The threat of violence in the lyrics of the AIK Troubadour's 'Crazy Hooligans' is precisely that, a type of play, almost self-ironical, a form of symbolic violence.

This is in line with what Bakhtin and historians such as Peter Burke⁵⁰ and Emmanuel Le Roy Ladurie⁵¹ tell us about traditional carnivals, when performances may involve symbolic acts of violence such as the armed marches through towns organised by the medieval guilds. These authors emphasise the conservative function of carnivals as a form of outlet through which to release tension, and where relations and power struggles (symbolically) are temporarily overthrown. However, the status quo ultimately remains. The carnival is thus a phenomenon that is conservative and revolutionary at the same time. Peter Burke claims that:

> At all events, in Europe between 1500 and 1800 rituals of revolt did coexist with serious questioning of the social, political and religious order, and the one sometimes turned into the other. Protest was expressed in ritualised forms, but the ritual was not always sufficient to contain the protest. The wine barrel sometimes blew its top.⁵²

Nevertheless, as stated above, sometimes 'the wine barrel blows its top'. A carnival turns into a carnival simply because people accept it as one and (preferably) join in. Its meaning is a function of the interaction between actors and onlookers. But what if the onlookers misinterpret the actors? What if the onlookers misinterpret the values as being repugnant or the cussing among carnival participants as taking place in 'real' social space? What if the temporarily constructed space of a heterotopia of deviation is interpreted as being a revolutionary reality and the onlookers consist of policemen or security officials? The aesthetic, symbolic violence that is dramatised may, unfortunately, turn into revolution and repression if onlookers are unable to realise that it is often simply a question of aesthetics, symbolism and playing with violence in the temporary heterotopia of deviation made up of supporter trips domestically and abroad, something the AIK Troubadour captures so well in his partly self-ironical lyrics. The aesthetic hooligan is a self-ironical figure. It is not the 'real', organised hooligan that the AIK Troubadour sings about, but rather the carnival participant.

Supporter rock: mistletoe on the football and supporter movement's tree-trunk

In this chapter I have tried to present an original description of some artists that belong to a genre we may label 'supporter rock'. Through the reading of the lyrics of the three bands/artists studied, my objective has been to identify some shared traits: the supporter lifestyle, love, joy, masculinity, alcohol consumption, the construction of the feminine and devaluation of the Other, the urban/rural binary and so on. But differences are evident too. Apart from the apparent stylistic and musical differences, several special emphases appear in the respective supporter rock artists' lyrics. I believe they can be analysed and understood by relating these to aspects of the long history of the supported clubs or the history, mythology and practices of the supporter clubs' cultures since their formation in the mid-1970s. For example, the strong emphasis on the local and topophilia in Coca Carola's Djurgården lyrics is a reaction to the club's peripatetic history over the last 100 years and is an attempt at (re-)creating locality in the inner-city of Stockholm. The resistance to commercialisation and commodification in Bajen Death Cult's Hammarby lyrics must be understood in relation to the club now being partly owned by American sport capitalists – in contradiction to the self-image of supporters and club mythology as 'working-class' and 'bohemian'. The ironic self-staging of the hooligan in the AIK Troubadour's lyrics is less connected to the club supported but can also be understood as a reference to the early days of the supporter club, Black Army, who in late 1970s and 1980s was possibly the largest, most unruly and violent of the three team's supporter clubs (at least according to the Black Army's own self-narrative and in the eyes of the general public). But it is only remotely related to the Swedish hooligan/casual scene in real life.

I have no space here to give a more in-depth analysis of the subject of supporter rock either in Sweden or internationally. I am content with establishing the fact that this is a phenomenon on the borderline between rock music, sport and society, between identity construction and reproduction, between commercialism and the upholding of a more or less constructed authenticity, between revolution and conservatism, between carnival excess and social repression. The genre, of course, is disparate. In this chapter I have attempted to illustrate this in my choice of artists. They differ greatly, but all exist in symbiosis with their football clubs and, even more so, with the clubs' supporters. Consequently, two of the artists in particular – Bajen Death Cult and the AIK Troubadour – become something like mistletoe. Mistletoe is a parasite that grows on a host tree and eventually develops enough green leaves to be able to absorb carbon dioxide from the air, but still gets its nourishment from the host tree. A somewhat evil-spirited plant, one might say, but fun to watch when one encounters it on rare occasions.

Notes

1 A longer version of this chapter has previously been published in Swedish in the Swedish internet journal *Idrottsforum.org*. I wish to thank two of my colleagues at Växjö University: Ramona Anttonen for assistance in translating parts of the text and ice hockey historian Tobias Stark for comments on an early draft of the chapter.

2 In this chapter I focus on the three bands/artists most well-known and/or first in the genre with connection to these three clubs. Two of them have since officially stopped performing: Coca Carola in November 2004 (see note 25) and AIK Troubadour in 2006. There are other active bands within the supporter rock genre connected with all three clubs (and some other clubs in the country) such as Sektion B, Djurgårdsgitarristen, Martin Ahlqvist, Bajenrabinen, Sjuttisju, Guliganbandet, Typiskt Västkustskt and Blå Combo to name a few.

3 The emotional attachment to a football club and existing supporter cultures may be an important aspect of, and 'tool' in, the construction of social identities and self-identities of individuals and groups, but I leave those dimensions out here.

4 J. Bale, 'The place of "place" in the cultural studies of sports', *Progress in Human Geography*, 121, 1988, 519.

5 A. Tapp and J. Clowes, 'From "carefree casuals" to "professional wanderers" – segmentation possibilities for football supporters', *European Journal of Marketing*, 36, 2000, 1256.

6 R. Giulianotti and R. Robertson, 'The globalization of football: a study in the glocalization of the "serious life"', *The British Journal of Sociology*, 55, 2004, 551.

7 Ibid., 549; see also R. Giulianotti and R. Robertson, 'Glocalization, globalization and migration: the case of Scottish football supporters in North America', *International Sociology*, 21, 2006, 171–176.

8 B. J. Pine and J. Gilmore, *The Experience Economy – Work is Theatre and Every Business a Stage*, New York: Harvard Business School Publishing, 1999.

9 I. Rein, P. Kotler and B. Shields, *The Elusive Fan. Reinventing Sports in a Crowded Marketplace*, New York: McGraw-Hill, 2006, especially pp. 220–222.

10 See for example: R. Giulianotti and G. Armstrong, 'Avenues of contestation: football hooligans running and ruling urban spaces', *Social Anthropology*, 10, 2002, 211–238.

11 T. Andersson, *Kung Fotboll. Den Svenska Fotbollens Kulturhistoria från 1800-Talets Slut till 1950*, Stockholm/Stehag: Brutus Östlings bokförlag Symposion, 2002.

12 There exists larger, established firms connected with a few other clubs too, mainly IFK Göteborg, Helsingborgs IF and GAIS. A few other football, ice hockey and bandy clubs also have smaller and/or less well-established hooligan groups within their supporter cultures.

13 'Cheering section' refers to the Swedish word 'klack'. Klack is a shorter form of the word 'hejar-klack' which originally referred to a relatively unique Swedish phenomenon: spectators singing songs or chanting in an organised fashion, where a hired 'hejarklacksledare' (cheer leader), who was often a male celebrity of some sort, led the spectators' chanting and singing at club and international matches from the 1920s to the early 1960s. 'Klack' nowadays refer to sections of spectators standing and singing/chanting and/or travelling to and performing at away games.

14 Västerås SK, GAIS (Gothenburg) and IFK Göteborg in football; Färjestad (Karlstad), Brynäs (Gävle), Södertälje and Vita Hästen (Norrköping) in ice hockey. Some

of these were covered by the media, for example Brynäs–Djurgården in the spring of 1982, whereas some went rather unnoticed.

15 Giulianotti and Armstrong, 'Avenues of contestation', 212.

16 Giulianotti and Robertson, 'The globalization of football', 553; Rein, Kotler and Shields, *The Elusive Fan*, pp. 23–25.

17 Mainly by S. Redhead, *Post-Fandom and the Millennial Blues: The Transformation of Soccer Culture*, London: Routledge, 1997; C. Long and J. Williams, 'Football and music cultures in Liverpool', *Esporte e Sociedade*, 1, 2005, 1–43. Online, available at: www.lazer.eefd.ufrj.br/espsoc. See also B. Carrington, '"Football's Coming Home" but whose home? And do we want it? Nation, football and the politics of exclusion', in A. Brown (ed.), *Fanatics! Power, Identity and Fandom in Football*, London: Routledge, 1998, pp. 101–123; K. MacLeod, '"We are the Champions": masculinities, sport and popular music', *Popular Music and Society*, 29, 2006, 531–547.

18 The Cockney Rejects have since reformed, split and reformed again in 1999. As late as 2006 they released a new version of the 1980 hit single 'I'm Forever Blowing Bubbles' in connection with the FA Cup Final that West Ham had reached.

19 G. Bushell, 'The story of oi', 2001. Online, available at: www.garry-bushell.co.uk/oi/index.asp; J. Turner with G. Bushell, *Cockney Reject*, London: John Blake Publishing, 2005, pp. 157–187.

20 www.dth.de.

21 Long and Williams, 'Football and music cultures in Liverpool', 16–22.

22 www.charlieandthebhoys.co.uk/index.htm.

23 www.beatbutchers.se/cocas.htm and www.myspace.com/cocacarola.

24 www.beatbutchers.com/coca-historia.htm.

25 However, as recently as before the 2006 home derby against Hammarby, I saw Coca Carola perform for Djurgården supporters on the back of a lorry outside Råsunda Stadium. They performed under the name 'The Sophias', referring to the stand with the most devoted supporters at the Stockholm Stadium.

26 Giulianotti and Armstrong, 'Avenues of contestation', 213. See also J. Fiske, *Power Plays, Power Works*, London: Verso, 1993.

27 J. Bale, 'Virtual fandoms: futurescapes of football', in A. Brown (ed.), *Fanatics! Power, Identity and Fandom in Football*, London: Routledge, 1998, p. 271.

28 M. Foucault, 'Different spaces', in *Essential works of Foucault, 1954–1984*, Vol. 2, London: Penguin, 2000, pp. 175–186.

29 'Bajen' is slang for Hammarby. 'Bajare' or (more unusual) 'Hammarbajare' is slang for a Hammarby supporter. AIK and Djurgården supporters often use the term 'brajare' instead, meaning 'pot junkies' in a degrading manner.

30 www.bajendeathcult.se.

31 T. Andersson, *Kung Fotboll*; H. Hognestad, 'Viking and farmer armies: the Stavanger–Bryne Norwegian football rivalry', in G. Armstrong and R. Giulianotti (eds), *Fear and Loathing in World Football*, Oxford: Berg, 2001, pp. 159–172, 275.

32 Personal correspondence with the band.

33 www.ultraboys.se.

34 Pine and Gilmore, *The Experience Economy*.

35 www.trubaduren.nu. Black and yellow are the colours of AIK.

36 'Gnagare' is slang for an AIK supporter and sometimes also for a member/player of the club. Gnagare means rodent in Swedish. AIK supporters are generally called 'råttor' (rats) or 'råttjävlar' (fucking rats) by Djurgården and Hammarby supporters.

37 www.trubaduren.nu/sidor/historia.html.

38 All three Stockholm clubs attract some supporters from all over the country and all have more or less formal supporter groups throughout Sweden.

39 www.trubaduren.nu/Sidor/nyheter.html.

40 'BA's battalions' meaning supporter club Black Army's battalions.

41 www.blackarmy.se.

42 Quoted in M. Bernard-Donals, 'Knowing the subaltern: Bakhtin, carnival and the other voice of the human sciences', in M. Mayerfield Bell and M. Gardiner (eds), *Bakhtin and the Human Sciences*, London: Sage, 1998, p. 120.
43 A. van Gennep, *The Rites of Passage*, London: Routledge and Kegan Paul, 1909/1960; V. Turner, *The Ritual Process. Structure and Anti-Structure*, Chicago: Aldine de Gruyter, 1969/1995.
44 D. Porsfelt, 'Management trainee – möten med förhinder', Doctoral thesis, Human Work Sciences, Industrial Work Environment, Luleå University of Technology, 2001, 24.
45 Foucault, 'Different spaces', pp. 175–185.
46 Ibid., p. 178.
47 E. C. Relph, *Place and Placelessness*, London: Prion, 1976, pp. 79–121.
48 E. Goffman, *The Presentation of Self in Everyday Life*, New York: Doubleday/Anchor, 1959.
49 P. E. Willis, *Learning to Labour: How Working Class Kids get Working Class Jobs*, Aldershot: Gower, 1977.
50 P. Burke, *Popular Culture in Early Modern Europe*, Aldershot: Scolar, 1994.
51 E. Le Roy Ladurie, *Carnival in Romans: A People's Uprising at Romans 1579–1580*, Harmondsworth: Penguin, 1981.
52 Burke, *Popular Culture in Early Modern Europe*, p. 203.

12 'Uíbh Fhalí, how I miss you with your heather scented air'
Music, locality and the Gaelic Athletic Association in Ireland

Mike Cronin

Ireland is well known and highly regarded for its music. As the then *Taoiseach* (Prime Minister) Bertie Ahern stated in 1998:

> music and writing have always played a central role in the social and cultural life of Ireland. Not only is music a source of entertainment, but it is an effective way of recording Irish history and communicating its stories widely throughout the country and the world.[1]

When the traditional musician, and cornerstone of the Clancy Brothers, Tommy Makem died in 2007, his importance was acknowledged globally as his fame had stretched far beyond his homeplace of Keady, County Armagh. The President of Ireland, Mary MacAleese, declared Makem, 'the consummate musician and a superb ambassador for his native land's culture and history'.[2] What Makem represented, in addition to his musical and compositional excellence, was the use of Irish forms of music and tradition that were at once generic, in that they could be appreciated by all, but also geographically specific in that they spoke to, and of, Irish locality. His best-known songs, such as 'The Town Of Ballybay' and 'Farewell To Carlingford' spoke of an Irish obsession during the long decades of emigration (which only ceased in the 1990s): the need to locate oneself within the familiar confines and images of the local. In arguing for the identity-forming and locating nature of music Martin Stokes argued that, 'music is very clearly very much part of modern life and our understanding of it, articulating our knowledge of other peoples, places, times and things, and ourselves in relation to them'.[3]

One of the major engines that led to traditional Irish music flourishing across the nations of the Irish diaspora was that the form, its airs and performances used music and lyrics to re-imagine landscapes and places from across the 32 counties of Ireland. That said, we have to acknowledge that the very idea of a single, all-encompassing form of traditional music is problematic and that the various forms and styles that are included in the canon suggest different meanings of Irishness. While traditional Irish music does have clear historical roots and the lineage between past and present remains strong due to the rich folklore culture of the music and the constant back referencing of time-honoured tunes and performers, the invocation of traditional music as a symbol for a singular Irish identity also brings into question its authenticity. As Colin Graham has explained, in the context of the debate surrounding the authenticity of Ireland as it appears in various forms of cultural production, there is a long-standing and contemporaneous process by which 'Ireland becomes "Ireland", a "cited", quoted version of itself which is both excessive and phantasmal'.[4] Traditional music has been part of this process, and there has always been a danger that traditional music appears not as something that is an authentic version of Irishness, but rather a pastiche that functions as a shorthand note for national identity and all that entails. This conundrum was recognised by Gerry Smyth who identifies two forms of traditional music, one 'which pits elegiac Paddy Sad (think misty mountains, low whistles and slow airs) against Paddy Mad (think smoky pubs and diddley-eye jigs and reels) in a constant battle for the meaning of Irishness'.[5] The two versions of traditional music have long been in competition, and in the wake of the Celtic Tiger and the ensuing creation of a globally consumed 'Celtic Cool', the associated imagery of both forms was once more exported around the world.[6] The debate over what is meant by traditional music, and the questions relating to authenticity and how this informs ideas of Irishness are central to this chapter.

In the 1980s and 1990s, when there was an upsurge in the popularity of Irish music inspired by, but not necessarily rooted in, the traditional forms, major bands achieving chart success also reinforced notions of locality that have been a long-standing feature of Irish music and lyrics. For instance, the Pogues' (perhaps the band best personifying Smyth's 'Paddy Mad') perennial Christmas hit, 'The Fairytale Of New York', locates an Irish man across the Atlantic, but the band of the New York Police Department, featured in the song, play the music of 'Galway Bay'. Such a specific re-imagining of 'home' adds additional pain to the ignominies of the warring couple of the song. 'Galway Bay' reminds them that they are not in Ireland, but are cut adrift on the cold streets of New York.[7] The power of music to locate and re-locate people is centrally important here. As Tia DeNora notes,

> music moves through time; it is a temporal medium. This is the first reason why it is a powerful *aide-mémoire*. Like an article of clothing or an aroma, music is part of the material and aesthetic environment in which it was once playing, in which the past, now an artefact of memory and its constitution, was at once present.[8]

Essentially music is a tool which allows individuals to travel to places and spaces, through their pasts and in their present.

The central concept of home, of being from a place and having a locality, is at the heart of Irish identity, and as such, appears as a regular idea in various forms of cultural production. Music has, because of its ability to be carried across oceans, sustained forms of Irish identity and locality even when they are displaced. The 1990s collection, *Bringing It All Back Home* was a recording that brought together various artists from the wider Irish diaspora to perform songs about their links with Ireland.[9] Many of the songs, such as 'Nothing but the Same Old Story', bemoaned the experience of the emigrant and positioned the new home (in this case America) as alien and negative, while valorising Ireland as familiar and positive. Other songs, including 'Kilkelly' and 'Sonny', depict the local and would have driven those hearing the songs while overseas to imagine and reconnect with what they had left behind.

The need to connect with the local through music is not solely the concern of the Irish diaspora. Songs and music have long been crafted that embrace the stories, legends and heroes of the local that were to be performed and consumed by people in Ireland so that they could celebrate home. This is due, in part, to a long history of local and civic pride (competition and rivalry) between localities in Ireland that was heightened and sustained by the parish system used by the Catholic Church. Indeed, one recent commentator has argued that, despite the regular listing of Ireland as the most globalised country in the world, the country actually remains a bastion of localised ties, feelings and identities.[10] That is an argument that is endorsed in this chapter. Not only has Ireland, as has been discussed so far, produced a rich, indigenous music tradition that celebrates the local, it has also been the home of one of the strongest and most localised forms of sport in the western world.

The chapter will argue that the Gaelic Athletic Association (GAA), which was formed in 1884 to resist the spread of British sports across Ireland, used the parish, county and provincial structures of the country to develop a highly localised form of sporting expression. In turn, as will be shown, this sense of local sporting identity has found expression in the music and songs of the GAA. In this case, music and sport are closely tied together, building on the oral, folk and musical traditions of Ireland so that the songs and music of the GAA function as a reservoir of sporting folk memory and as the celebration of the local.

Sport is a central concern here, and in this Ireland differs from many western nations. The games of the GAA, namely hurling and Gaelic football, are the most popular in Ireland and outstrip football and rugby in terms of support and participation. While provincial rugby has flourished in the years since professionalism, the main media focus is on the matches of the Heineken Cup, in which interest has been heightened given the success of Munster in recent years. Football, which had a high point in support during the World Cups of 1990, 1994 and 2002, has recently been in the doldrums and the domestic game struggles for support and media attention. There is more interest in the Premier League and its Irish players and managers than there is in the League of Ireland.[11] The GAA is different to rugby and football, not only because it is the most popular, but because it remains a strictly amateur game. Since its foundation in 1884, the GAA has seen itself as counterweight to what its founders believed were the degenerate practices associated with British sport. Although attitudes have changed during the period of the 1990s economic boom in the Republic of Ireland and as a result of the peace process in Northern Ireland, the issue of amateurism, while debated, remains sacrosanct. It is clear that while the ending of rule 21 in 2000 (which banned members of the British security forces and police from joining the GAA), the temporary suspension of rule 42 (which had banned foreign games from being played on GAA pitches but was relaxed in 2006 to allow football and rugby to be played at Croke Park while Lansdowne Road was rebuilt) and the attendance of the Northern Irish sports minister at a GAA game have all transformed the Association, its bedrock beliefs that underpin its success remain unaltered.[12]

Without professionalism the GAA has remained a strong agent of local identity. Players can only play for their parish and their county and cannot, unless their circumstances are exceptional, move. This means that the players and their identities, like those of the supporters, are rooted in the places they were born and live. Such local ties that are engendered by the GAA in Ireland are one of the key tools in sustaining an Irish identity in a period when the country has changed profoundly due to a booming economy (for the first time in the history of modern Ireland), the collapse of church authority, a transformation in sectarian identities that had been central to the period of the troubles and a huge inward migration that has, in the space of ten years, brought the number of non-Irish living on the island to approximately 12 per cent. The local nature of the game has also been acknowledged as an important agency in introducing the 'New Irish' (those immigrants who have arrived in the country during the economic boom) to their communities and providing them with a ready-made identity.[13] This process has been highlighted by the positive integration of players with a foreign parent into the top echelons of the GAA, namely Jason Sherlock (a Dublin footballer) and Seán Óg Ó hAilpín (a Cork hurler), both of whom are popular with fans for embodying the identity and guile of their counties.[14]

The local nature of Gaelic games and their ties to the community are a by-product of the original organisational structure of the GAA. In 1884, the founders of the GAA made the decision that the structure of the Association would be the Catholic parish. This tied the GAA in with the Church (essential for its success as a national movement), but also created a ready-made playing structure. At present there are over 3,000 parish clubs across the 32 counties of Ireland, and they are often the social hub of the locality. The GAA accounts for 42 per cent of all volunteering in Ireland, and this revolves around coaching, working in the clubhouse, staging social and fundraising events and so on.[15] Active membership of the GAA, which covers both genders and all ages, is currently estimated to total over 850,000 people (over 20 per cent of the population). The GAA is at the heart of local life. Social identity is constructed around clubs, parishes and counties. It is built on a collective folk memory of games from the past, former heroes and local rivalries. It embraces geography and location, embodies the community through the players that make the representative sides and identifies players and supporters alike through the materiality of club and county jerseys. In 2001 the Bank of Ireland ran its most successful advertising campaign in support of its sponsorship of the GAA's annual football championship. The campaign, which adapted J. F. Kennedy's famous plea, demanded of GAA supporters: 'Ask not what your *county* [my emphasis] can do for you.' This line encapsulated perfectly the nature of GAA support and participation and its ties to the local. The decision to follow the GAA is not necessarily one of choice, rather it is a product of a historical context and the accident of local birth.[16] The GAA then, is one of the most significant mainstays of localised and community identities in Ireland.

Given the importance of the GAA in Irish society, and the common linkage between sport and music that lies at the heart of this collection, it is perhaps unsurprising that the Association has a rich musical tradition. These songs and music are the products not only of the sport–music nexus, but also feed off the rich and long-standing history of traditional music, oral culture, folklore and balladeering in Ireland. The recent debates in Irish sport over the choice and use of national anthems offer a good starting point for understanding the significance of songs in Irish (and other nations') life. Since the formation of an independent Irish state (now the Irish Republic) in 1921, there have been two national anthems on the island: 'God Save the Queen' for Northern Ireland and 'Amhrán na bhFiann' ('A Soldier's Song') for the Irish Republic. However, sporting organisations did not follow the simple division of Ireland along the border. While football does have two Associations and honours each separate anthem, Gaelic Games organises across all 32 counties and plays 'Amhrán na bhFiann' before all its games, even in Northern Ireland. The situation in rugby is more complex. The Irish Rugby Football Union (IRFU) organises across all 32 counties, but draws its players from both the Catholic (nationalist) and Protestant (unionist) communities. When games are played in the Irish Republic, the players stand for 'Amhrán na bhFiann', but when overseas they use an apolitical anthem, 'Ireland's Call', written specifically for the rugby team in 1995. Anthems should be straightforward affairs, symbolising as they do, the nation in song and verse. However, when the idea of the nation is contested, this creates problems. In an arena such as international sport, which is now one of the most common venues for the playing of national anthems, such songs can be as divisive as they are communal. Unionists in Northern Ireland have long complained that the GAA only represents its own community and is not prepared to reach out to them. They argue that while all GAA matches in Northern Ireland are played under the Irish tricolour and with the singing of 'Amhrán na bhFiann', they will always feel alienated from the Association. In practice there is little appetite for the GAA amongst Northern Protestants, and the argument seems to be an example of the cross-community problematisation of perceived sectarian symbolism within a new Northern Ireland engaged in a working peace process. In rugby the argument is far more complex. As many Protestants play and support rugby, and have represented Ireland at international level, the singing of 'Amhrán na bhFiann' does challenge them. They stand to play at the highest level and have to honour an anthem of a foreign country sang in a language (Irish) that few, if any of them, understand. There has been a sustained campaign in recent years to remove 'Amhrán na bhFiann' from matches played in Dublin, but this has come to nothing. Likewise, with the rebuilding of Lansdowne Road there have been further questions raised. In 2007 it was decided that a World Cup warm-up game would be played at Ravenhill in Belfast. This was the first time that Ireland had played an international match in Northern Ireland since 1954, a game which was nearly abandoned because of arguments amongst the Irish players over which anthem should be sung.[17] Under IRFU rules the 2007 game was considered to be outside of the Irish Republic, and as a result only 'Ireland's Call' would be sung. Unionists complained bitterly, arguing that because many of the team were from Northern Ireland, 'God Save the Queen' should be played. The Ulster Unionist Member of the Legislative Assembly, Michael McGimpsey argued: 'The Irish rugby team is an all-Ireland team with players from across Northern Ireland. It is only right and proper therefore that for international fixtures in Belfast our national anthem is played.'[18] The divisive nature of competing anthems on the island of Ireland, in the context of sporting bodies which operate across borders, demonstrates how important musical moments are in defining a sense of identity and locality. Such songs and music can act, as in the case of anthems, to both include and exclude people from any given community.

For the GAA, the playing of 'Amhrán na bhFiann' does not present problems as it speaks to an all-Ireland identity that is enshrined in the constitution of the organisation. The GAA, while making positive strides to open its doors to the 'New Irish' and the Protestant community, does not consider itself as representing anything other than an Irish national identity. The GAA is a successful and long-standing cultural nationalist organisation, and as such its use of anthems, and more generally songs and music, seeks only to speak to itself and its own constituency. It is not concerned with producing a musical repertoire to be consumed outside the Association. The songs that will be discussed here use a series of references and styles that speak to the insider, those who are knowing and who relate to the sense of community and identity that is at once being promoted but, perhaps more importantly, being sustained across the generations. As such, the music and songs of the GAA can be seen as authentic. They build on the historic roots of traditional music and speak to an Irishness that is based on solid and long-standing local and community identities.

Many sporting teams across the world have a piece of music or a song that is associated with them. Celtic in football and Munster in rugby both claim 'The Fields Of Athenry' as their own, the Boston Red Sox have adopted the 2004 version of 'Tessie' that was recorded by the Dropkick Murphys, and various representative English sides in different sports have become accustomed to the strains of 'Jerusalem' accompanying their on-field efforts. The same is true in Gaelic games: each parish and county has its own song. However, I would argue that in Gaelic games the range of music and songs available to followers of the game, their repertoire, is far larger and more sophisticated than would be the case, for example, in English football. While it is true that much commercially released music and many songs about or featuring Gaelic games have been a common feature of recent years,[19] commercial music is not our concern here. However, many of their themes and ideas mirror those that appear in the songs sung by followers of Gaelic games. What is at the heart of the analysis here is music and song that is based on a traditional oral and musical culture. These represent, as their historic linkages are strong and their sense of place and person paramount, an authenticity of Irish identity. There are four main themes in the music and songs that relate to the GAA: locality, history, players and matches.

Each of the counties in Ireland has a song that is related to its GAA team. In Cork this is 'The Banks of my Own Lovely Lee', in Dublin 'Molly Malone', for Kerry 'The Rose of Tralee', in Sligo 'The Isle of Innisfree' and in Offaly 'The Offaly Rover'.[20] The majority of the county songs relate to place and do not refer to Gaelic games. This is an important distinction as they are songs to be sung by supporters at matches and in other social situations where they gather. Many of the songs are traditional and are based around long-standing airs. 'The Offaly Rover', to take just one example, demonstrates the traditions of the county song. The song offers a journey around the county from the perspective of a narrator, the rover, who has emigrated. The words of the song combine an appreciation of the geography of the county (its places), its topography (natural beauty), its people (various professions) and its traditions (singing and story-telling). The rover proclaims his sense of loss on being separated from home by invoking, 'Uíbh Fhailí, how I miss you with your heather scented air', and acknowledging the perpetual pull that home has on its people even when they are absent: 'Silently the peaceful Brosna calls your sons from far and near.' The idea of community and a shared folklore is central to the song. The final verse asks that we 'pile the Brown turf high upon the fire and bring the keg in from the barn'. Such conviviality of atmosphere will lead to an exchange of shared history between the rover and others, namely that 'the blacksmith sing his rebel song and the poacher tell his yarn'. The whole song posits a sense of identity and affiliation that is inescapable. Affiliation to county is a product of birth, and one that cannot be changed whatever the circumstances. Such affiliation to county, a central component in the success of the GAA, binds people to place. Even the rover, far away, pledges that 'to that faithful county dear, I shall return someday'. Similar sentiments of a desire and a longing to return home are also present in the 'Isle of Innisfree', 'Oh, Innisfree, my island, I'm returning from wasted years across the wintry sea. And when I come back to my own dear Ireland, I'll rest a while beside you, *gradh mochroidhe*.'[21] Equally the Cork song, 'The Banks of my Own Lovely Lee', positions an emigrant ('my home far away') longing for his native Cork. If return were possible (and as many of these county songs have nineteenth-century roots, such return was unlikely), then the emigrant dreams of being 'there with the friends I love best' so that he could, even in death ('my last crimson drop be for thee, to moisten the grass of my forefathers' grave') be home and lay 'on the banks of my own lovely Lee'.

That county songs, which have been adopted by GAA fans as anthems, do not refer to sport is significant. It gives primacy, as these are the best-known and most often performed songs, to the centrality of geographical belonging. An understanding, and a public announcement of place through song, unites people from across the county and proclaims, irrespective of their setting, the ties that bind them to the homeplace.

Clearly such county songs build on tradition, and many of the verses and airs have their roots in the song-collecting renaissance of the late eighteenth and nineteenth century. Those who follow the GAA have performed a similar feat, in that songs detailing events from the GAA's history have been remembered, passed down from generation to generation and recorded. A significant propor-tion of these songs detail matches and events from the first decades of the GAA, and locate themselves in an emergent sporting culture that was resisting the dominance (both political and cultural) of the colonial British. Such histor-ical songs are valuable as they demonstrate how parish and county rivalries, again a bedrock in the success of the GAA, were formed. The recording of such rivalries inscribes them with significant meaning, and the repetition of the song recreates not only the historical moment, but also the rivalry which continues to the present.

A good example of a historical song, which was uncovered by Jimmy Smyth from the Irish Folklore Collection, is 'The Kickers of Lios na Caolbhaí'.[22] The songs recounts a match of Gaelic football played in county Kerry on 4 March 1888, only four years after the foundation of the GAA. The match was a chal-lenge match, which would have been a common way of organising games before the advent of regular leagues and cup tournaments, and brought together Camp from the eastern end of the Dingle peninsula against Lios na Caolbhaí (Lis-nakealwee) from the western end. The song records the sporting prowess of the men from Lios na Caolbhaí ('no better or bolder in Ireland were seen, for wrestling or gaoling or taking a spree') and locates the match as a return fixture: 'for some sham beating they [Camp] gave us long 'go'. In the song many players are named and their professions mentioned. One significant player would even-tually find fame as an Antarctic explorer, Tom Crean. The match was not to be his finest hour:

> There was a blacksmith from Camp, they called him Tom Crean
> He wanted like Cearbhall to make a cat with two tails.
> Before half the game was over he had to retreat,
> And got sticking plaster and screw in his teeth.

The mention of Crean, while an interesting historical footnote, is more inter-esting for the use of folklore to contextualise his playing style. Cearbhall is a ref-erence to 'the legendary poet and sportsman Cearbhall Ó Dálaigh who – according to folklore – carved a cat with two tails in stone as his trademark'.[23] That a song from the late nineteenth century contains complex references to an individual from folklore (and there are three other incidences in the song) speaks volumes about the strength of oral culture at the time, and acknowledges that the GAA and its players understood the impulses of the cultural revival that linked their modern incarnation with the Irish heroes of old. The song also contains contemporary references. Pat Hoare, 'the champion from Lios na

Caolbhaí' is positioned, because of his strength and skill as being able to 'challenge John L for a round in the ring'. This is a reference to John L. Sullivan, heavy-weight champion of the period. The contemporary conditions of Kerry, a poor rural county, also lend a sadness to the song. It tells of Jim O'Rourke, 'the prince of the field' who 'is now going to leave, to earn his living far over the sea. But whether in New York or Boston or in far Tennessee, He'll be fondly remembered in Lios na Caolbhaí.' The song, one which was carried in the memories of people until the 1930s, offers a powerful recording of a local challenge match in the early years of the GAA. It encapsulates the idea of locality and belonging while also recording players and contextualising them in both folklore and contemporary realities.

Songs about players are one of the most dominant themes in the musical pantheon of the GAA. One of the most poignant relates to the famous Cavan footballer, John Joe O'Reilly. John Joe, as he was known, was born in Killeshandra and played for Cavan from 1937 until 1952. He captained the county to two all-Ireland championships, including the only final ever played outside Ireland, the 1947 Cavan–Kerry game that was staged in New York. O'Reilly died in 1952, when only 34, and the song is a lament to his memory. The narrator of the song is told of John Joe's death as he walks home. He sings that 'John Joe O'Reilly has left us behind. He was called by the good Lord to his faithful and kind, He brought him to Heaven, that proud land to show; A true son of Breffni is the gallant John Joe.' O'Reilly is valorised as the quintessential hero of Cavan. Not only a great athlete ('None could compare with our sportsman the Gallant John Joe'), a popular man ('He made many friends, though his life it was short') but most centrally an embodiment of the county ('In each corner of Breifne there's sorrow and pain, Such a true-hearted sportsman we'll ne'er see again'). The role that John Joe played in the New York final is also recalled, as is his captaincy the following year that brought Cavan back-to-back championships:

> He led Cavan to victory on that memorable day,
> In the final against Kerry in New York far away.
> The next year in Croke Park when our boys beat Mayo,
> Once again they were led by the gallant John Joe.

The song was composed by Tommy Gilronan from John Joe's homeplace of Killeshandra, and is performed to the traditional air of 'The Gay Galtee Mountains'. Not only does the song perform the function of memorialising Cavan's greatest footballer and lamenting his loss, it brings singer and audience into the world that John Joe lived in. It talks of his birthplace, his embodiment of county and his legendary exploits on the field. The fact that the song is still regularly performed and is known to all GAA supporters in Cavan, more than half a century after John Joe's death, is testament to the power of song and music in sustaining and remembering the local hero much loved by the community. As Cavan has enjoyed little on-field success since the 1950s (due to the combined effects of emigration, economic stagnation and the toll of tuberculosis), the ongoing embrace of John Joe signifies the importance of successful local heroes to a county devoid of contemporary victories.

The final category of songs to consider here are those that recall great matches. A more contemporary song, 'Team Spirit Eighty-Two' recalls the victory of the Offaly footballers over Kerry in 1982. The match was significant as the Kerry team, regularly listed as one of the greatest ever, was striving for a record-breaking fifth successive title. Offaly won the game in the dying minutes after a late goal by Séamus Darby. Written by Bernie Robinson and performed to the air of 'Slattery's Mounted Foot', the song is still to be heard when Offaly supporters gather. It begins by acknowledging how great, in the history of Offaly, the victory was:

> You'll read in history's pages of great deeds that have been done,
> The countless records that are made, the battles lost and won,
> But there's one page of glory sets all Offaly's hearts aglow
> 'Tis how they shattered Kerry's dream, five titles in a row!

The victory is contextualised in biblical terms, and offers hope to all minor counties who feel they can never reach the highest pinnacle. The song offers

> a moral for all counties great and small,
> As to how the weak can muster strength, and how the mighty fall;
> As encouragement to underdogs, it was the greatest thing,
> Since David slew Goliath with a pebble from a sling!

The song lists every single play in its course and locates each of them in terms of their parish ('There'll ever be an honoured spot, for Brendan, Mick and Séan, As long as there's a green field round their native Ferbane!'). Like many other songs, there is a folklore aspect. Martin Furlong, one of the most active players on the pitch that day, is named as the one 'to man the Bearna Baoil'. This is actually a line from the Irish national anthem, but refers to the Bearna Baoil (the 'gap of danger') which appears regularly in Irish folklore as a place where heroes have stood, since time began, to defend their people. This posits Furlong not only as a sporting hero, but as a defender of his people, the people of Offaly. The majority of songs that record great matches, be they at parish or county level, follow the same basic course. Players are named and their localities listed. Their heroic deeds are recorded and folklore is invoked so as to compare their feats with the heroes of old. The songs offer a mix of place and history. They produce a seamless link between the heroism recorded in ancient tales and found again in the period of the cultural revival, and hark back to an age before British colonialism. In doing so the songs embrace the very resistance to British culture that lies at the heart of the GAA's historic mission.

What then do we make of the music and songs of the GAA? What is clear is that the GAA has a rich and varied musical culture. While only representative examples of the main themes have been used here, Jimmy Smyth's collection, produced in 2007, features over 250 songs from across the island, and this, by his own admission, is only a sample.[24] The songs and music of the GAA spring from the specific history of the Association. Founded in 1884 to preserve Gaelic sporting culture and resist the advance of British games, the GAA allied itself with the broader impulses of the cultural revival that was centred on the belief that historic Irish culture was centrally important in the construction of Irish identity. This cultural identity was based around the re-imagining of a pre-British culture, and involved the preservation and support of the Irish language, folklore, art and sport. It was an essentially historic rediscovery of Ireland, and sought to link identity with ideals of place, community and shared ancient pasts. That the GAA was at the forefront of a movement that created an Irish identity is vitally important, and it is a role it maintains to this day. By rooting itself, through the parish and county system, in local and community identities, the GAA celebrates an 'authentic' sense of being Irish. In its songs and music the GAA invokes the past, records the great games and players and constantly re-inscribes the concept of being local. This is an organic locality that is a product of birth and history; it ties players and supporters (wherever they may be) to their roots. In using forms of traditional Irish music and historic airs, the songs of the GAA express the mission of the cultural revival by constantly returning to tradition and folklore. The songs and music may be about contemporary sporting figures and events, but they are praised in terms of the past. The songs and music of the GAA have an essential role to play in recording the local, embracing it, and through performance and re-performance, celebrating it.

Notes

1 Quoted in Gerry Smyth, *Noisy Island. A Short History of Irish Popular Music*, Cork: Cork University Press, 2005, p. 2.
2 *The Connection*, 18 January 2008.
3 Martin Stokes, 'Introduction', in Martin Stokes (ed.), *Ethnicity, Identity and Music: The Musical Construction of Place*, Oxford: Berg, 1994, p. 3.
4 Colin Graham, *Deconstructing Ireland. Identity, Theory, Culture*, Edinburgh: Edinburgh University Press, 2001, p. ix.
5 Gerry Smyth, 'The isle is full of noises: music in contemporary Ireland', *Irish Studies Review*, 12, 1, 2004, 4–5.
6 For a discussion of how a consumable and highly fashionable Irishness was exported around the globe in the late twentieth century, see Diane Negra (ed.), *The Irish in Us. Irishness, Performativity and Popular Culture*, Durham: Duke University Press, 2007.
7 For a discussion of the celebratory role of nostalgia in 'The Fairytale of New York' see Joe Cleary, 'A fairytale steeped in truth', *Irish Times*, 16 December 2006; see also Joe Cleary, *Outrageous Fortune: Capital and Culture in Modern Ireland*, Dublin: Field Day Publications, 2007.
8 Tia DeNora, 'Music and self-identity', in Andy Bennett, Barry Shank and Jason Tonybee (eds), *The Popular Music Studies Reader*, London: Routledge, 2006, p. 144.
9 Bob Dylan, *Bringing It All Back Home*, Valley Entertainment, 1998.

10 See Tom Inglis, *Global Ireland: Same Difference*, London: Routledge, 2008.
11 In the 2007–2008 season, the interest in Sunderland FC, managed by Roy Keane and owned by a consortium headed by Niall Quinn, led to that team being seen as the Irish representative in the Premier League. This led the two leading daily broadsheet newspapers to place permanent reporters in Sunderland, and every week the *Irish Times* features a 'Letter from Sunderland'.
12 In January 2008 the Democratic Unionist Minister, Edwin Poots attended his first ever GAA game when Down played Donegal. He arrived after the playing of the Irish national anthem, 'Amhrán na bhFiann', and so side-stepped the controversy of a 'foreign' anthem being played on British soil. Despite the positive reaction to the event, Poots remains critical of what he sees as the political stance of the GAA. See *Irish Times*, 26 January 2008.
13 For further details on the 'New Irish' and sporting identities, see Mike Cronin, David Doyle and Liam O'Callaghan, 'Foreign fields and foreigners on the field: Irish sport, emigration, immigration and inclusion since the nineteenth century', *International Journal for the History of Sport*, 25, 9, 2008.
14 The legendary GAA commentator, Mícheál Ó Muircheartaigh, in reference to Seán Óg Ó hAilpín once noted: 'Sean Óg Ó hAilpín.... His father is from Fermanagh, his mother is from Fiji – neither a hurling stronghold.'
15 See Liam Delaney and Tony Fahey, *The Social and Economic Value of Sport in Ireland*, Dublin: ESRI, 2005.
16 For a discussion of local identities as they have been captured in recent GAA-related advertising, see Mike Cronin, '"It's for the glamour": masculinity, nationhood and amateurism in contemporary projections of the Gaelic Athletic Association', in Wanda Balzano, Anne Mulhall and Moynagh Sullivan (eds), *Irish Postmodernisms and Popular Culture*, Basingstoke, Palgrave, 2007, pp. 39–54.
17 Vic Rigby, 'The riddle of Ravenhill: Ireland's last rugby international in Belfast', unpublished paper presented at the third annual Sports History Ireland conference, Centre for Irish Studies, NUI Galway, February 2007.
18 'God Save the Queen ruled out at rugby international'. Online, available at: www.rugby.ie/news/story/?jp=KFCWMHCWCW (accessed 22 August 2006).
19 For a discussion of the Folk Footballers, and their album, *The First Fifteen*, which related entirely to the Galway Gaelic football team, see Mike Cronin, 'Beyond sectarianism: sport and Irish culture', in Liam Harte and Yvonne Whelan (eds), *Ireland Beyond Boundaries. Mapping Irish Studies in the Twenty-First Century*, London: Pluto, 2007, pp. 215–238.
20 A full list of county songs can be found on the An Fear Rua website: www.anfear-rua.com/story.asp?id=1004.
21 *Gradh mochroidhe* – Irish, meaning: 'love of my heart'.
22 The Irish Folklore Commission was a government-sponsored initiative that began in the 1920s and aimed to preserve Ireland's folk and oral traditions. It specifically concentrated on the Irish-speaking population of the west of Ireland. Many of those who were interviewed in the 1920s and 1930s had been born in the mid-nineteenth century. It is likely that this song was recorded by the Commission in the later 1920s. The song is one of many documented by Jimmy Smyth. See Jimmy Smyth, *In Praise of Heroes. Ballads and Poems of the GAA*, Dublin: Geography Publications, 2007, pp. 335–337.
23 Ibid., p. 38.
24 Ibid.

13 'This thing goes beyond the boundary'

Cricket, calypso, the Caribbean and their heroes

Claire Westall

Sport and music are both examples of popular culture and mass entertainment often performed by skilled practitioners exhibiting modes of aesthetic physicality. Although Adorno attacked their commodification by the 'culture industry', there is, as this volume demonstrates, more to be said about their interrelation than his rejection of sport and popular music indicates (though contemporary examples of their meeting ground may also point to the pertinence of his critique of the hegemonic flattening of cultural forms).[1] When we think of the coexistence of cricket and music, the subject of this chapter, we may think historically of a number of cricketing musicians, like Sir Thomas Beecham, or examples of musical cricketers and cricket commentators, most famously Sir Neville Cardus, or cricket-inspired music and song, including those sung for or about public schools.[2] We might perhaps turn to David Rayvern Allen's *A Song for Cricket* (1981) which pulls together a large number of cricket-inspired ditties. Today, we may even bring to mind the sounds of the Barmy Army, that band of journeying England cricket supporters who seek to rally their team with chants of 'Come On England', renditions of songs like 'Jerusalem', and their own creative treats punning on the names of players and their most distinctive characteristics.[3] Along similar lines, we could consider the relatively recent tendency, particularly in shortened one-day and Twenty20 versions of the game, to have fast, pumping pop tunes crashing out of speakers during brief interludes in the action, due largely to Sky's repackaging of the sport, cricket's need for TV revenues and its hope for larger and younger crowds. It seems quite likely that an English audience will also bring to mind the run of signature tunes that have introduced cricket coverage on TV and radio. In 2007, the year the cricket World Cup would be held in the Caribbean for the first time, Sky Sports was using 10cc's hit 'Dreadlock Holiday', with its catchy refrain 'I don't like cricket, oh no, I love it', despite the song describing the intimidatory theft of a tourist's jewellery by a local (read 'black') Caribbean man. In 2006 Channel Five's brief hold on the game brought Noll Shannon's 'Shine' to speak for its tone of optimistic anticipation.[4] Between 1999 and 2005 Channel Four's award-winning reinvigoration of televised cricket made Lou Bega's version of 'Mambo No. 5' synonymous with the game. And, before all of these, the BBC had, for more than 30 years, used Booker T and the MGs' 'Soul Limbo' (also known as

'Soul Dressing') as the musical lynchpin of its cricket coverage both on TV and on the radio with *Test Match Special*.

Excluding the Australian interruption of Noll Shannon, what we notice from these theme tune examples is that the promotion of cricket in the British media, and sometimes farther afield, often draws on the idea of a Caribbean 'flavour'. The music used may not come from the region – 10cc were an English band singing about holidays in Jamaica on their *Bloody Tourists* (1978) album, Booker T & the MGs were a mixed-race American soul group from Tennessee and Bega is a German citizen of Sicilian and Ugandan parentage whose time in Miami brought him to the Latin rhythms of 'Mambo No. 5', a remake of Pérez Prado's 1952 track of the same name – and it may only imitate or allude to the musical impulses of the Caribbean, even in its broadest geographical sense. Nevertheless, by employing these tracks, programme makers overlay English and international cricket with what they see as the unique vibrancy of Caribbean cricket, music and carnival culture. Mike Marqusee makes the argument in *Anyone But England* (1994):

> Ironically, the musical theme used by BBC television to introduce its cricket coverage, Booker T's 'Soul Dressing', with its heavy syncopation and hint of steel drums, invokes the spirit of Caribbean carnival. Much loved by fans as a harbinger of cricket, this song of summer has become the anthem of the English national game. It is clear that in West Indies cricket English people find a joy and confidence absent from the English scene. The angry old men ranting about bouncers, slow over rates and bad behaviour speak for a minority.[5]

Marqusee pinpoints the ironic gap between the public appreciation of musical tunes evoking a carnivalesque experience and the institutional attitude within English cricket towards the pace attack of the West Indies in the 1970s (as well as afterwards) that was underpinned by racial stereotypes and entrenched opinions about appropriate cricketing behaviour and crowd decorum. For Marqusee, the English audience finds its own expression of 'joy and confidence' in the seeming evocation of the postcolonial refashioning of cricket connected with the Caribbean. Making a related and insightful argument, Tim Crabbe and Steven Wagg have described the contradiction between marketing cricket as a carnival event while banning instruments, banners and face masks (generally the elements of celebratory abandon that constitute carnival) from grounds, as occurred during the 1999 World Cup in England. They contend that 'the English cricket establishment had hoped to procure a "carnival" on their own terms, carefully circumscribed by a set of detailed prohibitions ... prohibitions [which], in turn, emanated from a racism that dominated public discourse in Britain'.[6] Such a disjuncture between a carnival/calypso sales pitch and the absence of an enabling environment returned to haunt the game at the 2007 World Cup when the intensely marketed appeal of 'carnival' and 'calypso-cricket' was undercut by reports of a lack of atmosphere in the new, oversized and decidedly corporate stadiums that were built for the tournament but failed to reflect the region's historical ties to the game. The overall effect of the spatial organisation of the stadiums, the approach to food and drink, the advanced ticket sales and high ticket prices was to alienate local supporters – those very fans who had been sold to the world as the bastions of the cricket carnival.

In the context of this appropriation of Caribbean culture used to package cricket as a global product for international consumption, this discussion considers the relationship between cricket and music, specifically calypso music, in the Anglophone cricketing area of the Caribbean basin.[7] These two notable cultural forms have existed, and continue to exist, as intersecting and overlapping practices used to articulate the complex socio-political tensions of the region, particularly its struggles with forms of colonialism, new and old. They also share styles of masculine performance that are bound to the search for, and investment in, an individual male hero. This chapter first presents the connections between these two modes of popular 'play', their relation to carnival and their expressions of masculinity, emphasising the history and influence of calypso. It then moves to identify a number of calypsos and calypso-related songs and poems which depict cricket and cricketing heroes in order to illustrate how repeated metaphors and motifs of heroic cricketing action are seen as a means of postcolonial compensation and improvement for the people. It argues that calypsos about cricket are most often praise-orientated pieces which are indicative of the region's attempts to negotiate a successful union between 'the one' and 'the many', between island independence and regional collectivity, by glorifying a single, and sometimes poignantly isolated, male hero. Finally, it briefly draws attention to the cricket music of David Rudder and the official songs of the World Cup which were used to represent the region on the world stage.

'Cricket and calypso belong together'

These were the words of Curtly Ambrose, the West Indian fast-bowling legend, when he was interviewed in Antigua, his home island, as part of the BBC's long-running travel programme *Holiday* (aired 12 January 2004 on BBC One). He and Richie Richardson, his friend and former captain, were filmed playing with their band The Big Bad Dread and the Bald Head. When asked about the connection between cricket and music Ambrose moved away from the reggae styling of his own group to describe how cricket and calypso are bound together in the Caribbean. His comments worked on two levels. First, especially given the nature of the programme, they registered at the level of cliché where calypso and cricket are compressed into the oft-cited phrase 'calypso-cricket'. This slogan is the basis of many media headlines and is sold to tourists as the summation of Caribbean culture. Second, they also registered at the level of historical and cultural appreciation as he quietly signalled the intersection of cricket and calypso as forms of socio-political dissent. This discussion is sensitive to the void that can be the 'calypso-cricket' cliché and seeks instead to attend to cricket and calypso as densely encoded and interrelated examples of what Geertz, following Bentham, labelled 'deep play'.[8] For this is the way that cricket in the Caribbean – with the game's well-documented links with slavery, British imperialism, anti-imperialism, nationalism and regional collectivisation and competition – must be read, as evinced by C. L. R. James' classic work *Beyond a Boundary* (1963) and, more recently, by the cricket writings of Beckles, Birbalsingh, Sandiford and Frank Manning in his investigation of Bermuda's cricketing festivals.[9] It is also the manner in which calypso's past and continuing import has been studied by Warner (1983), Rohlehr (1990), Hill (1993), Regis (1999) and others.[10]

In a broad sense, calypso is a type of popular music using complex polyrhythmic structures and which developed principally in Trinidad and Tobago, though it is also found on other islands despite V. S. Naipaul declaring that 'no song composed outside Trinidad is a calypso'.[11] Like the uncertain origins of the word 'cricket', the term 'calypso' has a confused back story. Reflecting Trinidad's mixed history, Keith Warner usefully summarises the potential sources of calypso as:

1   the carib word 'carieto', meaning joyous song;
2   the French patois 'carrousseux' from the French 'carrousse', meaning a drinking party;
3   the Spanish word 'caliso', used for a topical song in St Lucia;
4   'careso', a similar type of song from the Virgin Islands; and
5   the West African term 'kaiso', a corruption of 'kaito' as an expression of approval, which is sometimes used instead of calypso.[12]

While the Roaring Lion (Rafael de Leon) has emphasised calypso's debt to the French *ballade*, numerous other commentators have insisted upon the influence of African traditions, specifically noting calypso's proximity to slave songs, its reliance upon call and response and its use of theatrical satire to critique leaders.[13] Traditionally, calypso is a medium of folk news, social commentary and political critique as well as a feast of gossip and satirical humour conveyed in a witty, combative style called picong which builds upon excessive flattery or mockery and insults and, wherever possible, is performed extempore. It is through the use of linguistic 'play' as 'symbolic action' that calypso, according to Phillips, reframes social, political and historical situations so as to enable listeners to find a new perspective and to think differently.[14] Historically, calypsonians, predominantly but not exclusively men, have been charged with keeping the local population informed of significant communal and international events, including sporting ones, and with maintaining an engaged critical stance on behalf of the people. As the calypsonian Mighty Duke (Kelvin Pope) says, calypso is an 'editorial in song'.[15] Though calypso's development can be traced back into the eighteenth century at least, it was after Emancipation in the 1830s that calypso, along with carnival, took on its recognisable form, sharing with carnival a commitment to freedom, individuality, masquerade and subversion. From the 1920s it was performed in tents patronised by and associated with black and creole working-class men. In *Beyond a Boundary* James describes how he was banned from attending these tents by his puritan mother who believed that 'calypso was a matter for ne'er-do-wells' and that 'the calypso tent was the road to hell'.[16] During and after the Second World War calypso became a repository for attacks against colonialism – against Britain, the old Massa, and America, the new neo-colonial presence – and spread internationally as migrant calypsonians, like Lord Kitchener (Aldwyn Roberts) and Lord Beginner (Egbert Moore), travelled to Britain and America (where Harry Belafonte was championing the genre).[17] In more recent decades, calypso has mutated into, merged with or touched various musical genres including pan, chutney, rapso and soca – a term said to have been coined in the 1970s by Lord Shorty to describe the meeting of calypso and Indian rhythms, but which is now commonly taken to mean upbeat, dance or party tunes that have de-emphasised calypso's traditional lyrical content and critical commentary.[18] In both its older and newer forms, calypso continues to be an important part of the competitive engagements of the carnival season with the annual Calypso Monarch and Road March Competitions.[19]

Importantly, calypso descends from the boastful speeches and songs used by male chantwels (also chantwells) or chantuelles in the post-Emancipation period. These figures would accompany a calinda (also kalinda) stick-fighting band and act as their spokesman, entertainer and issuer of challenges. They were revered as possessors of 'the word' and would use it to heap heroic praise on their own batonier and insults, ridicule or even *obeah* (folk magic) on their opponents. Calypso, Rohlehr explains, 'grew out of this milieu of confrontation and mastery, of violent self-assertiveness and rhetorical force'. According to Warner, the calypsonian's compositions, relying upon verbal dexterity and linguistic competencies, constitute oral poetry. For Rohlehr, it was 'a predominantly male mode, whose themes are manhood and the identity of the individual with the group'.[20] Consequently, the calypsonian is connected with the articulation of heroic, warrior-like combative endeavours, their public incitement and depiction, and is the negotiator between singular heroic acts and communal self-confidence.

Beckles has claimed that slavery meant the capture and suppression of 'defeated male warriors' who then had to be 'kept' and 'kept down' and, as a consequence, notions of black masculinity in the Caribbean have sought to recover, resurrect or re-establish ways for black men to become warriors.[21] Rohlehr has demonstrated that calypso became an important way of imagining and investigating masculinity. In 'I Lawa: masculinity in Trinidad and Tobago calypso', he examines at some length the figure of the warrior-hero as descended from the stick fight, tracing his evolution into the popular heroes of calypso and cricket, among numerous other activities, and arguing that this archetypal figure has affected the way men have been culturally understood in Trinidad. He writes:

The Warrior-Hero of the stickfight devolved not only into the sportsman/boxer/athlete/footballer/cricketer, or the lover/sagaboy/cocksman/phallic hero/sexual athlete, or the singer/artist/popular performer, but, as politics developed, into the figure of the rebel, the political leader, the man-in-power.[22]

Analysing this warrior persona, Rohlehr draws attention to the repeated appearance of sport in calypso, most notably the cluster of calypsos about boxers like Joe Louis and Muhammed Ali that emerged with the rise in Black consciousness, and the cycle of cricket calypsos 'celebrating cricket and eulogising cricketers as warriors and emblems of Caribbean masculinity' that has developed since the 1920s.[23] Yet, he also outlines the methods used by male calypsonians to create their reputation-based mask of masculinity – based on strength, skill, virility, dominance, verbal dexterity and style – and their comedic exposure of this mask as a mask, their ironic representation of their own social, economic, political or sexual impotence and hence emasculation. That is, he documents the calypsonian's ability to both 'elevate and deflate the ideal of phallocentric masculinity' where 'phallus worship is largely a mask worn by calypsonians because of tradition but equally mocked by them because of its disconnections from reality'.[24] It is such a layered approach to the gender facades and entanglements of calypso that is proffered by the best practitioners.

Taking up the issue of Caribbean masculinity and 'play', Richard Burton, in *Afro-Creole: Power, Opposition and Play* (1997), argues that forms of Afro-Creole 'play', specifically including the three Cs of carnival, calypso and cricket, articulate oppositional attitudes to the dominant or dominating system, an 'anti' position as it were, but one that by continuing to maintain an internal dialectic of compliance and dissent fails to destroy or move beyond that very system. His assertion that such 'play' therefore does not offer politically profitable resistance is in contrast to that of Beckles and Rohlehr, who contend that change has already been achieved in some ways because of these cultural practices, and closer to Orlando Patterson's contention in 'The ritual of cricket' that cricket is intrinsically bound to its imperial past and therefore cannot be decolonised.[25] Following the lead of Abrahams and Wilson, Burton claims that these types of activities are organised by the dialectic of inside/respectability/yard/women and outside/reputation/street/man that structures Caribbean experience.[26] Moving to creolised cricket, he suggests that the game embodies two traditions, namely, the 'play up and play the game' ethos of nineteenth-century Englishness as it was exported to the islands (associated with inside/respectability) and the exuberant performativity of 'play' that characterises the African legacies residing within the Caribbean (associated with outside/reputation). He identifies the Caribbean elements of this construction as emerging from 'street values' (aggression, bravado, etc.) expressed in calypso, arguing that the fast bowling of West Indian players is part of the reputation-based assertion of masculinity found in calypso/street culture and that the flamboyant and aggressive stroke play of West Indies batsman historically emerges from the style of the batonier in the stick fight.[27] Douglas Midgett deems Burton's links between cricket and stick fighting as 'fanciful', yet while he may be right in adopting a cautionary, even critical tone toward Burton's easy layering of binaries, the association of the cricketer with the heroic stick fighter and the strength of masculine virtues connected to him have often been used in the depictions of cricket in calypso and literature.[28]

Cricket heroes in calypso

In *The Middle Passage* (1962), his travel book about his first return trip to the Caribbean after a decade away, V. S. Naipaul offers his view of Trinidad, remembering that when he was a boy 'the cricketer was our only hero-figure' and proclaiming that 'it is only in calypso that the Trinidadian touches reality'.[29] However, he condemns local writers who, he feels, are pandering to the wishes of the 'insecure' to be 'heroically portrayed' and thereby defined.[30] Taking up this nexus of heroism, cricket, calypso and representation in *The Development of West Indies Cricket* (1998), Beckles sets out the cultural and aesthetic links between cricket and the game's presentation in calypso and literature. He articulates the aesthetic and politically resistant commonalities between these depictions and the performative mass of the cricket crowd, highlighting the carnivalesque characters of King Dyall and Gravey as theatrical performers who bring the crowd, the players and the culture of carnival closer together.[31] In 'Music, literature and West Indian cricket values', Rohlehr provides a more expansive survey of cricket's appearance in calypso and literature, dividing his discussion into five historical periods which, given the breadth, quality and influence of his discussion, are worth revisiting.[32]

First, according to Rohlehr, the 'Learie Constantine era' after 1923 saw a number of songs in praise of this great all-rounder, including Beginner's 1928 dedication to Constantine, which is accredited as the first calypso to praise a West Indies cricket hero and carried the lines 'Learie Constantine/That old pal of mine'. The era also saw 'Learie Constantine' by Lord Caresser, which sat alongside Eric Roach's sonnet 'To Learie' in 1939.[33] The era also provided several 'documentary' calypsos describing tours and debating selection issues, e.g. 'Bad Selection' (1928) by Beginner, 'MCC vs West Indies' (1930) by Railway Douglas, and 'International Tournament: 1937' (1937) by Atilla the Hun. Second, the 1950s, with the first West Indies series win in England, brought the defining and canonical 'Victory Test Match' (1950) by Beginner with 'Those two little pals of mine', but also Kitchener's less well-known 'Kitch's Cricket Calypso' depicting the same event and King Radio's 'We want Ramadhin on the Ball' (1951). Mighty Spoiler also gave us 'Picking Sense from Nonsense' (1955) as he sought to unpick the reasons for the West Indies' 4–1 defeat to Australia in 1951. This period also wrought the greatest literary references to the game with Sam Selvon's 'The cricket match' (1956), Errol John's play *Moon on a Rainbow Shawl* (1958), V. S. Naipaul's *Miguel Street* (1959) and George Lamming's *Season of Adventure* (1960) all drawing upon it. It is also the period Kamau Brathwaite's 'Rites' and Bruce St John's poem 'Cricket' look back upon. Third, 'Independence and Transition 1962–1975' grants us Kitchener's 'The Cricket Song' (1964) celebrating the 1963 series win in England, his 'Cricket Champions' (1967) and Sparrow's 'Sir Garfield Sobers' (1966) which, as Rohlehr suggests, is crafted to praise the entire team rather than merely Sobers, as the title would imply, and lacks the 'insular bias' of island favouritism which has so plagued West Indies cricket. The period runs quiet toward its conclusion with the exception of Relator's dedication to 'Gavaskar' (1972) which criticises the West Indies through its very praise of the master Indian batsman. However, fourth, 'The Great Revival 1974–1994' captures the spirit of success and achievement that characterised the West Indies team under Clive Lloyd and Vivian Richards with Maestro's 'World Cup' (1976) and Short Shirt's 'Vivian Richards' (1976). Rohlehr closes by discussing the 'Era of Dominance', a section that overlaps with the 'Great Revival' chronologically but which he uses to move toward the contemporary issues of the game's professionalisation and commodification, as in Sparrows' 'Kerry Packer' (1978). Rohlehr also discusses the changing fortunes of the West Indies team, captured by David Rudder's 'Rally Round the West Indies' (1987) and the political significance of the post-apartheid emergence of South Africa in 'Maestro Born Again' and MBA's 'Beyond a Boundary' (1993), a calypso that calls upon Rudder's use of James' phrase to insist on the importance of the race issues surrounding the 1992 South Africa–West Indies series.

While space does not permit a full engagement with the insightful interpretive readings Rohlehr grants us, it is important to recognise the repeated patterns his survey highlights. It illustrates how strongly focused on the male hero cricketing calypsos have been – singling out players like Constantine, Griffith, Hall, Holding, Sobers, Kanhai, Lloyd and Richards, to name but a few – and how, almost as a consequence, criticism of lesser mortals, players and selectors alike, has been used as a scapegoating technique (e.g. Rohlehr suggests that in 'MCC vs West Indies' Douglas blames the bad selection of Joe Small as causing their collapse in the Second Test of 1930). When the team is hailed as a collective, as in 'Sir Garfield Sobers', this less usual occurrence is typically a sign of potential rather than achieved regional co-operation, improvement or possibility. It is a marker for what can be done off the field if the region were to operate as its cricket team have shown is possible. Consistently in the examples, cricketing excellence is a means of playing back to, and defeating, the old Massa while trying to negotiate with the present and increasingly looming economic shadow of the US, and the impact of the global market. The game is repeatedly described as a 'war' for the West Indies ('Cricket Champions'), with the crowd 'waiting for the kill' ('The Cricket Song'), especially against England, where victory is used to define a nation still under construction. Reiterating the moments of significance, Rohlehr outlines Midgett's article 'Cricket and calypso: cultural representation and social history in the West Indies', and brings socio-political pressure to bear on three pivotal cricketing and calypso moments: Kitchener's 'Victory Test Match' from 1950, Sparrow's 'Sir Garfield

Sobers' of 1965 and Rudder's 'Rally Round the West Indies' of 1987. His selection concentrates more on examples that are team-orientated, which slightly obscures the larger, hero-orientated tendency that is present in cricket calypsos but does indicate that important moments are collective ones. Midgett also effectively charts the mood changes across these periods, as the modest celebratory tones of Kitchener give way to Sparrow's verbose assertion that England must understand that they 'lost, you know you lost' which, in turn, alters to become the heartfelt appeal of Rudder to his people to unite in the face of adversity.[34]

From this long list of players and songs, I wish to turn to the example of Vivian Richards as seen in calypso, but also (scribal) poetry, to suggest how heroic cricketing performances are seen to offer potential postcolonial retribution and compensation for the people of the Caribbean. In 'World Cup' Maestro celebrates Richards' 'splendid fielding' and in 'Vivian Richards' Short Shirt praises his intense all-round contribution – as bowler, batsman and fielder – but plays up his batsmanship, both in its attacking certainty and defensive impenetrability. For Short Shirt, cricket is deemed Richard's vocation, 'his game', a calling beyond general comprehension that makes him Sobers' heir apparent. Richards is a 'man', a 'hunk of a man', and the calypsonian is adamant about the visibility of his masculine strength and the need for us to 'see' it. Short Shirt also emphasises Richards' intelligence, 'his mind', as well as his 'technical skill', refuting the 'calypso-cricket' image of a natural, carefree stroke-maker. Lacking any sense of fear, Richards' batting is a relentless assault on the opposition, 'again and again'. It is an act of wilful 'plundering', of postcolonial reclamation on behalf of those who watch on. Explosive like 'dynamite', Richards 'drives you', in a pun upon his forceful forward play, his ability to dictate and his historically informed push ahead. His movement and motion is counterpoised by the immobility of 'mid-on' at a 'standstill'. Here, the collective of postcolonial nations that the West Indies represent is dynamic, energetic and pressing, while its opposition, England (seemingly bound to its past), is staid and stationary, beaten by ability, pace and timing. The description of how 'the machine must run' is both a reference to the scoreboard and Richards' automaton-like determination until 'runs like rain', flowing with the alliteration of the line, enable him to reach a century. This watery rejuvenation prompts Rohlehr to read Richards as the 'revitalized Hero' of batsmanship taking on 'the mantle of Weekes, Walcott, Kanhai and Sobers' in order to explode the oppressive bind of the region's history of slavery.[35] An elderly James also saw Richards as a 'super batsman', one of an elite who can 'dominate all kinds of attacks under diverse circumstances', suggesting that Richards 'can be ranked with great batsmen of any time'.[36] It is as the 'super batsman', even super man, that Richards is portrayed in calypso and poetry which view him as a warrior, a conqueror in battle violently defeating England and overturning the imperial racial order of cricket. Poems like Ian MacDonald's 'Massa Day Done', 'Viv' by Faustin Charles and 'Conquest' by Howard Fergus all focus on Richards as 'batsman-hero', as Charles names him, and have clearly been influenced by the tradition of praise-calypsos about cricketers.[37] They challenge Richards' reputation, particularly in the English media, of arrogance by supporting Richards' sense of his own worth while also playing upon the idea of his masculine bravado, as in the 'Vivian Richards' calypso.

In all of these pieces there is a strong sense of what Paul Gilroy termed the 'slave sublime', as the unspeakable terrors of slavery are re-articulated in the violently aesthetic batting of Richards. Although Gilroy explores the primary example of music as the mode in which there is a 'centrality of terror in stimulating black creativity and cultural production', we can transpose this onto the physical articulation of this terrorising performance in cricket and its musical or literary representation, especially given the game's loaded imperial legacy and postcolonial backlash which reached its peak in Richards (both in his professional performances and the personal convictions he brought to the pitch).[38] Richards is cast as the prophet of transformation, expressing and combating the brutalities of the past through his cricketing performance. This is shown as MacDonald builds to a climatic end that claims Richards' vast political and healing power: 'Something hurt he bad you could see/as if heself alone could end we slavery!' Richards is thought to be able to end the collective pain of the Caribbean alone, ending their long enslavement and oppression by defeating or overturning the colonial cricketing order. He represents the rebellious spirit of protest of his time and enacts Fanon's sense of the violence of decolonisation. There is, however, a seeming confusion of history in that Emancipation and Independence have been achieved or granted, yet it is up to Richards to cut the people free and end slavery, to end the so far unending oppression. From the outset there is a feeling of the underlying conditionality of this possibility, that Richards' innings 'could' change life but, by implication, may not and this opens the potential of individual and collective failure or of his individual failure leading to the people's collective demise (as was so famously presented in Edward Braithwaite's poem 'Rites' where the failure of Clyde Walcott left the masses impotent, defeated). This is reinforced by the conditionality of Richards' ability to 'end slavery'; the 'could' works at a number of levels: implying that he could have ended slavery if he had been present in that period; that he believes his cricketing performance can end the ongoing slavery of present neo-colonial conditions; or that his pain is caused by their slavery and his belief that he can end it (though in reality this may not be the case). Consequently, in Gilroy's terms, Richards is a messiah of the 'politics of fulfilment', he is both the future fulfilment that previous generations left unaccomplished and a sign that there is still much to do for and by the people.[39] Yet by relying upon him and him alone, these poems and Short Shirt's calypso isolate him from that of his team, his home and their collective potential at the moment of their greatest triumphs.

Both Rohlehr and Midgett draw their discussions to a close before the mid-1990s, only gesturing toward the place of Brian Lara in Caribbean music, but the isolation of the cricketing hero, especially as batsman, has taken on greater import in recent years, with Lara's individual talent being cast against the repeated failures of his team. Due to Lara's unique position in West Indies and world cricket, a large number of calypsos and poems have been written in praise of him since 1994. In terms of poetry, Jean 'Binta' Breeze, Howard Fergus, Paul Keens-Douglas and a number of others have all crafted pieces in commemoration of the 'Prince of Port of Spain'. These poets not only draw on the style of calypso to present their hero but sometimes refer to Caribbean music and actual calypsos. For example, in 'Song for Lara' Breeze draws on Rudder's 'Rally Round the West Indies' to identify the versatility of Caribbean musical forms, especially of calypso, of the slow rhythmic play which the crowd can soon turn 'extempo'. By calling on Rudder, Breeze intertextually references the struggles facing the West Indies and Rudder's call for the region to stand behind their team, though she nevertheless concentrates on Lara's successes.[40] Calypso, pan and soca tracks about Lara have included 'Lash dem Lara' by Alexander de Great, 'Signal for Lara' by Superblue and 'Four Lara Four' by de Fosto, all marking his remarkable personal achievements of 1994, while Rootsman's 'Lara' rang out around the Caribbean in 2004 when Lara's record-breaking Test score of 400 not out was captured by de Fosto in his sequel 'He Strikes Again' and 'Lara Again' by Alston Becket Cyrus. Like the poetic pieces, 'Lash dem Lara' claims that there is a 're-writing of history with this one special man' through his batting reversion of the 'lash'. Rootsman carnival release, 'West Indies Forever' (2004), also known as 'Lara', claims that it is the 'Windies forever' but focuses explicitly upon Lara as the 'brightest star' and 'father figure' who can lead the young crop of talent 'back to the top', as if this single hero can be charged with reclaiming the glory and success of past generations on behalf of the region. In 'West Indies Now and Forever' (2004), Alison Hinds, the 'Queen of Soca', begins with the declaration that she will 'support the West Indies forever' but moves to focus upon the bowling attack directed at Lara, 'they giving him bouncers', before calling upon him and his team to 'turn it round/turn it round'. Another track called 'West Indies Forever' (2004) but by Gino McKoy claims that the 'West Indies we will reign again' and refers to Lara as 'Emperor'. However, having singled Lara out McKoy offers a roll-call of player's names, asking them all to contribute, to 'give me something', to the collective cause as heroes-in-waiting. In all of these examples, criticism of Lara is deflected or refuted in order to solely praise the heroic master, even if the team are recognised as lacking. While this may be understandable given their celebratory nature and Lara's world records, it seems to belie the controversy that surrounds his career, especially in his role as captain, and does little to attend to the crisis of West Indies cricket. The closest we come to a critical position is offered by Paul Keens-Douglas in 'Lara Fans' as he wisely demands the improvement, not of Lara, but of his 'fans', those fanatics who concentrate upon their hero at the expense of the rest of the team.[41] His call for genuine collective endeavours, beyond those of individual men, is a call of hope for the still-awaited united nation.

It is perhaps the trajectory of David Rudder's cricket music over the last 20 years that most clearly expresses the recent, overlapping journey of calypso and cricket. Rudder's *The Cricket Chronicles* (2007), released to coincide with the

World Cup, brings together his key cricket tracks, including 'Rally Round the West Indies', first released on the hit album *Haiti* (1989) and altered for the 1999 World Cup. This, Rudder's most famous cricket track, laments the passing of the high-point of West Indies cricket glory and attempts, as the title signals, to 'rally' the Caribbean community. It is, as Midgett describes it, 'a calypso of the 1980s and 1990s'.[42] Rudder sings of the change of guard with 'old generals' like Lloyd retired and Michael Holding, 'a warrior', falling 'in the heat of the battle'. Yet his tone is optimistic, perhaps rightly so given its time, as he appeals to his fellow islanders to relinquish their cynicism, their rivalries and culture of blame because 'pretty soon the runs are going to flow like water' and 'little keys can open mighty doors'. Many of its ideas and lyrical constructions are reformulated in 'Here Comes ... the West Indies' (1994), released on an album of the same name with its cover displaying a broad-rimmed, maroon West Indies cricket hat, as Rudder more forcefully celebrates the appearance of the West Indies on the cricketing and international stage. Rudder's 'Legacy', on the *Lyrics Man* (1995) album, coincided with the descent of West Indies cricket into failure, pay disputes and an ongoing leadership crisis just as Brian Lara was establishing himself as one of the best ever batsmen. With its title referring to 'history, heritage, struggle and achievement', Rohlehr describes Rudder's track 'Legacy' as celebrating 'masculinity in kingship' through its praise of West Indies batsmen, culminating in Lara, as 'heroes whose achievements challenge the old colonial order of authoritarian control and undermine the ancient stereotypes and fixed negative assumptions about the potential of the Caribbean man'.[43] However, it is in 'Cricket (Its Over)', a new recording in 2007, that we can detect a considerable shift in Rudder's tone. The song repeatedly evokes the passing of cricket, and even Rudder's underlying optimism that the game will return seems strained. Eerily, the song describes an after-match situation, when 'the crowds are gone and the arenas stand so silent', when 'every run, every rising ball is now a memory'. The past action lingers but less as a nostalgic association and more immediately as a mournful loss, an absence caused by a lack, a gap, a failure to be. 'This game, the bloody game' still defines its people through its associations with colonial violence and anticolonial/postcolonial rebellion, but the frustration it brings as a 'bloody game' is mounting. Cricket in the Caribbean is 'a torture, a beautiful torture', but its absence marks the worrying emptiness or hole in Rudder's hopeful posture in the face of the surrounding globalising forces.

Rudder did not compose the official 2007 World Cup anthem. The official song was 'The Game of Love and Unity' by Shaggy (a Jamaican), Ruppee (a Barbadian) and Faye-Ann Lyons-Alvarez (a Trinidadian), an up-beat, high-tempo dancehall-style track set to appeal to ready-made British and American markets where artists like Sean Paul (who had his own 'West Indies Cricket' track) already had a sizeable chart presence. The lyrics of 'The Game Of Love and Unity' draw upon ideas and phrases about coming together that are commonly used in the Caribbean (especially as derived from the carnival slogan 'all o' we is one') but mobilise them to address the world as a single, coherent and equally welcome set of visitors rather than to demand Caribbean integration. The song fails to reflect the importance, complexity or competitive agenda held within the game and instead replaces these essential features – so significant to cricket's place in the postcolonial world – with the notion that 'the rules and aim remain the same' (as if the shift from colonial to postcolonial, from English dominance to English defeat, had not taken place at all). What is usually an appeal to the Caribbean region to act together has been turned into a call to everyone and all nations, removing any sense of historical conflict or opposition and working to erase the unsavoury past the game holds within itself. While Rudder sings of 'Twenty two yards of truth' in 'Lifted', it seems that the historical realities of cricket in the Caribbean were obfuscated for the sake of mass, global appeal during the World Cup. The official anthem featured on *Caribbean Party: Official 2007 Cricket World Cup* along with other tracks expressing obvious attempts to patch over the harsh socio-political realities of the moment and the disastrous predicament of West Indies cricket (lyrics such as 'Come on, come on everybody, everything's all right' in 'Caribbean Party' by Morgan Heritage and 'Smile, just smile, never let them see you cry' in 'Smile' by Junior Kelly). However, in their own way, such glocal, amnesia-inducing appeals also suggest that these cultural forms, cricket and Caribbean music, still go far beyond their own boundaries.

Notes

1 See Theodor Adorno, *The Culture Industry: Selected Essays on Mass Culture* (edited by J. M. Bernstein), London: Routledge, 2001, pp. 86–91, for his assessment of sport where he states 'sport itself is not "play" but ritual in which the subjected celebrate their subjection' (p. 89).

2 This is exactly what Philip Scowcroft does in 'The interface between sport and music', 'Sport and light music' and 'Cricket and music'. See www.musicweb-international.com/classrev/2001/Jan01/Sport_and_Music.htm.

3 The Barmy Army acquired their name in the mid-1990s when Sky TV commentators used the phrase 'barmy' and the Australian media took it up during the 1994–1995 tour to describe England supporters who insisted on spending large sums of money travelling to support their team despite England's dismal performances. They are constantly looking for new members, including musicians and people to write new songs. See www.barmyarmy.com.

4 Noll Shannon had been the runner-up in *Australian Idol* in 2003, reinforcing the interdependence and commercial overlapping of pop and television.

5 Mike Marqusee, *Anyone But England. Cricket and the National Malaise*, London: Verso, 1994, p. 151.

6 Crabb and Wagg, '"A carnival of cricket?": the Cricket World Cup, "race" and the politics of carnival' in S. Wagg (ed.), *Cricket and National Identity in the Postcolonial Age: Following On*, London: Routledge, 2005, p. 219. They also note the irony of selling the tournament as a calypso event, with stereotypical images of 'West Indians' in vibrant coloured shirts, when the tournament's success in England was set to rely upon the Asian and British-Asian cricket supporters who have constituted a much larger group than Afro-Caribbean supporters in recent years.

7 It is noteworthy that throughout this discussion the 'West Indies' and 'West Indian' will only refer to the cricket team and its players, while 'Caribbean' will be used to

describe the social, cultural and geographical Anglophone Caribbean region instead of the largely outdated 'West Indian'. While the Caribbean is larger and more diverse than this would imply, 'Caribbean' is used for terminological clarity and consistency.

8 See Clifford Geertz, *The Interpretation of Cultures: Selected Essays*, London: Fontana Press, 1993, where, in his famous chapter 'Deep play: notes on the Balinese cockfight', he describes 'deep play' as play where the stakes are so dangerously high for the participants that their act of 'play' must be read for its 'thick' relation to its cultural surroundings and historic moment.

9 See Hilary McD. Beckles, *The Development of West Indies Cricket: Volume 1. The Age of Nationalism* and *Volume 2. The Age of Globalization*, London: Pluto, 1998; Frank Birbalsingh, *The Rise of Westindian Cricket: From Colony to Nation*, Antigua: Hansib, 1996; Keith A. P. Sandiford, *Cricket Nurseries of Colonial Barbados: The Elite Schools, 1865–1966*, Jamaica: University of West Indies Press, 1998. Also, Frank E. Manning, 'Celebrating cricket: the symbolic construction of Caribbean politics', in Hilary McD. Beckles and Brian Stoddart (eds), *Liberation Cricket: West Indies Cricket Culture*, Manchester: Manchester University Press, 1995, pp. 269–289.

10 For readings of calypso's prominent cultural position within Trindadian culture see Hollis Liverpool, *Kaiso and Society*, Virgin Islands: Virgin Islands Commission on Youth, 1986; Raymond Quevedo, *Atilla's Kaiso: A Short History of Trinidad Calypso*, Trindad: University of West Indies Press, 1983; Louis Regis, *The Political Calypso: True Opposition in Trinidad and Tobago 1962–1987*, Barbados: University of West Indies Press, c.1999; Gordon Rohlehr, *Calypso & Society in Pre-Independence Trinidad*, Trinidad: G. Rolehr, 1990; Keith Q. Warner, *The Trinidad Calypso: A Study of the Calypso as Oral Literature*, London: Heinemann, 1983. For considerations of the interrelation of calypso and carnival see John Cowley, *Carnival, Canboulay and Calypso: Traditions in the Making*, Cambridge: Cambridge University Press, 1996; Donald R. Hill, *Calypso Calaloo: Early Carnival Music in Trinidad*, Gainesville: University of Florida Press, 1993.

11 V. S. Naipaul, *The Middle Passage*, London: Picador, 2001, p. 66.

12 Warner, *The Trinidad Calypso*, p. 8.

13 See Roaring Lion, *Calypso from France to Trinidad: 800 Years of History*, Trinidad: n.p., 1988, p. 28. In contrast, Rohlehr's substantial and authoritative work, *Calypso and Society in Pre-independence Trinidad*, is productively sensitive to the multilayered influences that have contributed to the formation of calypso.

14 See E. M. Phillips, 'Recognising the language of calypso as "symbolic action" in resolving conflict in the Republic of Trinidad and Tobago', *Caribbean Quarterly* 52,1, 2006, 53–73.

15 Liverpool, *Kaiso and Society*, Introduction.

16 C. L. R. James, *Beyond a Boundary*, London: Serpents Tail, 2000, p. 16.

17 For a discussion of the impact of Kitchener in England see Hugh Hodges, 'Kitchener invades England: the London calypsos of Aldwyn Roberts', *Wasafiri: The Transnational Journal of International Writing*, 45, 2005, 24–30.

18 Most recent studies of calypso explore its relationship to soca, but for an analysis of the rhythmic similarities and difference between the two see Shannon Dudley, 'Judging "by the beat": calypso versus soca', *Ethnomusicology*, 40, 2, 1996, 269–298.

19 For a discussion of the particular forms of music associated with carnival, especially more contemporary examples, see Shannon Dudley, *Carnival Music in Trinidad: Experiencing Music, Expressing Culture*, Oxford: Oxford University Press, 2004.

20 Rohlehr, *Calypso in Pre-independence Trinidad*, p. 54.

21 Hilary McD. Beckles, 'Black masculinity in Caribbean slavery', in R. E. Reddock (ed.), *Interrogating Caribbean Masculinities: Theoretical and Empirical Analyses*, Jamaica: University of the West Indies, p. 228.

22 G. Rohlehr, 'I Lawa: the construction of masculinity in Trinidad and Tobago calypso', in R. E. Reddock (ed.), *Interrogating Caribbean Masculinities: Theoretical and Empirical Analyses*, Kingston, Jamaica: University of the West Indies, p. 274.

23 Ibid., pp. 208–211.
24 Ibid., pp. 219–220.
25 See O. Patterson, 'The ritual of cricket', in Hilary McD. Beckles and Brian Stoddart (eds), *Liberation Cricket: West Indies Cricket Culture*, Manchester: Manchester University Press, 1995, pp. 141–147.
26 See Richard Burton, *Afro-Creole: Power, Opposition and Play*, Ithaca and London: Cornell University Press, 1997, pp. 165–171. Donald Hill also uses this division to explain calypso in D. Hill, *Calypso Calaloo: Early Carnival Music in Trinidad*, Gainesville: University Press of Florida, 1993, pp. 22–43.
27 See Burton, *Afro-Creole*, pp. 179–187.
28 Douglas Midgett, 'Cricket and calypso: cultural representation and social history in the West Indies', *Sport and Society*, 6, 2–3, 2003, 265.
29 Naipaul, *The Middle Passage*, pp. 35, 66.
30 Ibid., p. 65.
31 Beckles, *The Development of West Indies Cricket. Volume 1*, p. 113.
32 For Rohlehr's full discussion see 'Music, literature and West Indian cricket values', in Hilary McD. Beckles (ed.), *An Area of Conquest: Popular Democracy and West Indies Cricket*, Jamaica: Ian Randle, 1994, pp. 55–102.
33 Beckles, *The Development of West Indies Cricket. Volume 1*, p. 108.
34 See Midgett, 'Cricket and calypso', 239–268.
35 Rohlehr, 'Music, literature and West Indian cricket values', p. 88.
36 Hilary McD. Beckles, 'Viv', in *A Spirit of Dominance: Cricket and Nationalism in West Indies Cricket – Essays in Honour of 'Viv' Richards on the 21st Anniversary of his First Debut*, Kingston: University of West Indies Press, 1998, p. 2.
37 See 'Massa Day Done' in Ian MacDonald, *Between Silence and Silence*, Leeds: Peepal Tree, 2003, pp. 87–88; 'Viv' in Faustin Charles, *Days and Nights in the Magic Forest*, London: Bogle-L'Ouverture, 1986, p. 43; and 'Conquest' in Howard Fergus, *Volcano Verses*, Leeds: Peepal Tree, 2003, pp. 59–60.
38 Gilroy, *The Black Atlantic: Modernity and Double Consciousness*, London: Verso, 2000, p. 131.
39 Ibid., 37.
40 See 'Song for Lara', in Jean 'Binta' Breeze, *On the Edge of the Island*, Newcastle-upon-Tyne: Bloodaxe, 1997, pp. 67–69.
41 See 'Lara Fans', in Paul Keens-Douglas, *Roll Call: Poetry and Short Stories by Paul Keens-Douglas*, Trinidad: Keensdee Production, 1997, pp. 8–9. Paul Keens-Douglas brought his cricket-related poems and performance pieces together on a single CD entitled 'Crick! ... Crack! ... Cricket!!'. Though Keens-Douglas is not a calypsonian per se he is certainly of the same tradition and demonstrates many of the stylistic elements calypso draws upon. His most famous poem is 'Tanti at de Oval', while in recent years he has engaged with the person and persona of Lara in 'Tanti Backin' Lara' and the poem 'Lara Fans', with its built-in critique of the singular focus upon Lara as a heroic saviour and the need for team and regional collectivity for a successful future.
42 Midgett, 'Cricket and calypso', 256.
43 Rohlehr, 'I Lawa', p. 211.

14 Bouts of Kiwi loyalty
Musical frames and televised sport

Malcolm MacLean

[Rock] cannot be reduced to ... its sonic register ... although we cannot ignore its musical textuality, its sonorial presence.... Moreover the identity, meaning, and effect of rock ... is always contextually produced. Rock's musical practices always already exist in specific and complex sets of relations that articulate their meanings and effects.[1]

To suggest that much contemporary experience of sport is mediated is not new. To claim that music plays an essential role in shaping the meaning of that mediated sport may seem novel. Analyses of broadcast media sport have tended to focus, among other things, on the visual (re)presentation of sports events,[2] the commentaries presented as part of those events[3] or the supposed negative effects of new technologies, including broadcast media, on sports participation. There is an underlying ahistorical aspect to policy and related debates about mediated sport. It is not as if this sport–media dynamic is all that new: Britain has had a vibrant sporting press since the late eighteenth century and for much of the time it has exhibited national characteristics. A sports press developed later in other countries, but moving pictures of sports events have been publicly shown since the 1890s.[4] Technological advances in the twentieth century led to debates about the impact of concurrent broadcast commentaries on attendances at matches: since at least 1926 the Football League (in England and Wales) has been trying to manage its relationship with broadcasting.[5] The economic and cultural intertwining of commercial sport and media industries as a sport–media complex has been the subject of extensive analysis by economists (both political and econometric), sociologists, historians, cultural studies based analysts, anthropologists and others. This chapter will not rehearse, rehash or reiterate their analyses: it will explore one way that we might start to think more creatively about this complex of industrial production by exploring the role of a television theme tune in the cultural production of televised sport. The chapter draws on a case study from New Zealand to explore the multiple ways that a theme tune accompanying televised rugby union broadcasts both delineated the show from those around it and embedded the sport in a specific socio-cultural context.

It is often the case that the things of which audiences are least aware are essential in shaping and directing the understanding of particular texts – Jane Austen's use of semicolons lead to the construction of sentences that have a particular flow, leading to a persuasive but conversational tone in her books. Likewise, theme music for or incidental music during a television show can become, and often is, an essential indicator of meaning and the intended terms of audience engagement. The use of Tina Turner's 'Simply the Best' as the theme to Channel Seven's Australian rugby league broadcasts during the 1980s and 1990s is seen as vital in repackaging the game in strongly nationalist terms as well as playing a part in revitalising Turner's career.[6] The BBC indicates the end of its Wimbledon coverage each year with a different piece of music to that which it uses at the end of the previous 13 days' broadcasts.[7] These musical pieces are not naïve space fillers and they are not devoid of meaning, they are an integral part of the broadcast text: as Grossberg notes in the opening quotation – their meanings and effects are articulated with musical forms that always already exist in specific and complex sets of relations. These relations are intratextual, intertextual and contextual – that is, the elements of the broadcast sporting practice are mutually interdependent and genre-based in shaping and creating meaning, and the localised socio-cultural meanings, status and value of the sport being broadcast are equally important in this meaning-making. A key, arguably *the* key, musical component of any sports broadcast is the theme music. It marks the beginning and the end of the broadcast, and in doing so it indicates that the material presented in between the musical moments is a particular television show and is seen by the producers and broadcasters as having a particular type of coherence. In doing so, the theme delineates the show from those around it and proclaims it as being of a certain type: that is, it frames the programme.

The literary frame

John Frow proposes an interpretation of the literary frame that sees it as a fluid, unstable and indeterminate component of a text.[8] His case is that all aesthetic objects have frames that are peculiar in each instance. Whereas we tend to see the frame of a piece of aesthetic work as its limit, delineating it from its context so that text and context are discrete, Frow argues that the frame should more usefully be seen as both a delimitation of the work and a bridge between text and context. More often than not there is more than one frame: a picture may be framed, but it may also hang within a gallery or museum and as such carry with it implications different to a framed painting in a suburban house. This multiple framing means that, 'we could think of the "edge" as [a piece of] work as a series of concentric waves in which the aesthetic space is enclosed'.[9] Whereas a frame may seem to be a fixed and solid barrier between text and context, Frow's argument is that this 'barrier', as well as being multiple-layered is more osmotic than impermeable. By permitting and preventing certain information and meaning flows across this barrier, the shape, character and form of the frame creates specific intended meanings, understandings and articulations between a text and its various contexts. This helps explain why the understood and intended meanings of texts change.

Frow's frame is neither and both inside and outside its text. In being concurrently a barrier and a bridge, the frame is a component of both the structure of the text and of the situation in which the text exists, with the effect that 'the text is closed and suspended'.[10] Because the frame is part of the text, the text itself signifies what it excludes: the television show theme music is an integral part of the show. This frame (a picture frame makes this obvious) is both an aesthetic space and the edge of aesthetic space; audiences see, hear or comprehend both text and non-text (the picture, the frame, the wall and the building within which it is located are both discrete and interconnected). As Frow suggests, 'the energy of the frame thus radiates in two directions simultaneously',[11] both allowing and conducting into the aesthetic area elements or traces of the excluded non-aesthetic area, meaning that the text becomes constructed by its limit. A literary frame should, therefore, be understood not as a thing but as a process; not as fixed but permeable, active and actively interpreted. As Jay and Miller note, a frame 'is the operation that allows for representation, for the appearance of what is and what it understands'.[12] Recognising the textual or literary frame is a key step in exploring meaning-making through, and with, music – as Grossberg argues, 'people respond neither to individual songs nor to individual performers, but to sounds and images within larger contexts and logics'.[13] The problem, especially in musical texts that are for the most part non-figurative and intrinsically abstract, is the near invisibility of the frame. Frow suggests that for the most part it is naturalised because we naturalise 'the artificial space of the aesthetic object'.[14] An essential step for analysts seeking to identify the means of interpellation of audiences is making the frame visible as the device linking a text to its larger 'contexts and logics'.

These frames are relatively easy to identify when exploring a literary or visual aesthetic, but much less obvious when considering an aural text. We can, for instance, in the case of literary and visual texts identify a material thing that indicates where and what the frame might be (indeed many visual texts have things called frames). In the case of a musical text, while there may be a beginning and an end, the frame itself is usually embedded. Musical codes and genre-linked expectations to a large extent shape meanings and our understanding of a piece of music. When those generic codes are disrupted, the music can become understood in different ways. Perhaps the most well-known piece of music by the Kronos Quartet, a San Francisco-based string quartet, is their version of 'Purple Haze' (originally by Jimi Hendrix).[15] There are no lyrics in the Kronos Quartet's version, but otherwise the only significant change is the instrumentation. I have used the piece for several years to explore with undergraduates notions of genre and textual difference, and note that first-time hearers' responses vary greatly: some laugh loudly when they first hear it, more are perplexed as if they know they know the tune but cannot place it; both are indications that a string quartet should not be playing a piece that is, to most listeners, classic 1960s rock. This chapter illustrates the musical framing of media sport by unpacking a single piece of music as both framed and as a frame – that is, to explore the content and form of the piece, and to consider its use in the sport mediascape of late 1970s New Zealand. In both its form and its use, the piece of music cites and invokes rugby union, hence a need to shift to a second zone of contextualisation – the cultural status of rugby union in New Zealand.

Cultural status of New Zealand rugby

To even pose a question about the cultural politics of rugby union in New Zealand during the 1970s is to explore the cultures of New Zealand masculinities, and in particular the type of masculinity Jock Phillips calls the 'hard man'.[16] Whether the 'hard man' actually existed is a different question – he was, and is, mythologised and functioned as an ideal type of New Zealand masculinity. Recent work by Greg Ryan suggests that the rugby union elements of the myth lacked a material basis; it was, however, a potent and pervasive myth.[17] The 'hard man' embodied a set of characteristics associated with the mythology of the idealised pioneer: he valued physical prowess, best seen in hard physical labour, as both strength and endurance; he was versatile and saw value in being a 'jack of all trades'; he could cope with physical adversity; he held little use for intellectual skills and book learning; and above all he existed in a culture Phillips describes as 'mateship'. Nineteenth- and early twentieth-century mateship was, and to an extent remains, homosocial but was seldom a passionate or enduring friendship: it tended to be intense but temporary. The myth holds that mates tended to ignore each other's class background and practiced a form of ritualistic egalitarianism. The male culture of mateship tended to be self-regulating – that is, the rules were enforced within the group – and exhibited many of the usual elements of cultural networks, including a distinctive language, widespread use of nicknames and widespread and often intense swearing (all of which signified a willingness to live without 'the genteel conformities of civilised life'[18]). This was an oral culture that emphasised songs and yarns – elaborate and often fanciful tales, but more often anecdotes that emphasised shared experiences – and placed great emphasis on the pub as a place of masculine camaraderie where status was earned by, in part, an ability to consume great quantities of alcohol.

Key elements of the cultural practices surrounding and incorporated into rugby union drew on these traits of mateship as adapted to the cultural life of the 'hard man'. Status in rugby union was, and to a large extent remains, the product of an agonic code as seen in the expectation to 'play through the pain'. Furthermore, rugby was resolutely homosocial and, although women were at times admitted to the club house, it remained a potently masculine space, and it is only recently that there has been a growth in the acceptance of women as players of the game, and even then 'women's rugby' is marked as different and inferior to 'rugby', where the men play a game normalised by its lack of gender-marking. In idealised rugby union all that matters is competence on the field: off-field status is not, in theory, a determinant of an ability to play, with the result that the mythology of the game is ritualistically egalitarian. In most respects rugby union was the apotheosis of several key forms of New Zealand masculinity during the period from at least the Second World War until the later 1970s, in that the unwritten rules of mythologised hard man mateship outlined the code of practice to which 'real' men in the rugby world were expected to comply.

During the 1970s, however, rugby's hold on the various codes of masculinity was weakening. There were emerging and significant new forms of entertainment such that rugby found itself in a new leisure market place. As with most cultural shifts of this kind, there is no smoking gun but there is clear evidence of a trend away from rugby union's near absolute dominance of male leisure spaces and of the cultural codes of the most widespread forms of masculinity. Clear and quantifiable evidence is difficult to secure, but by the end of the 1970s there are indications that fewer boys were playing rugby, and that attendances at major games were falling to the extent that in a number of stadiums such as Wellington's Athletic Park standing areas were replaced by ticketed seats. By 1985 the Accident Compensation Commission, a state agency providing forms of personal injury insurance, estimated that rugby and football had the same number of players, though as Bill Keane has argued, there appears to have been a significant flight to football in 1981 and 1982.[19]

Changes both in and beyond the game were highly likely to have contributed to the apparent decline in rugby's status. Since 1971, and through most of the decade, the All Blacks, New Zealand's national men's rugby team, were less successful internationally than they had been in the previous two decades and were therefore less able to mark, in an uncontested manner, national pride: a losing team is not much use as a sign of national prowess. Throughout the decade there was increasing attention given to rugby injuries, and widespread concern expressed about broken necks which seem to have become more common. In addition, it seems that rugby lost much of its cultural status because of its place at the centre of political turmoil. Since the beginning of the 1960s, with greater and growing intensity after 1970, there had been increasing public concern expressed about, and organised demonstrations against, the New Zealand Rugby Football Union's continuing sporting relations with South Africa.

It was not until 1976, however, that this seems to have a significant impact on rugby's status. Until that time the issue could be, and often was, presented as malcontent New Zealanders responding to a call by politically dubious black South African organisations that sought to overthrow a government of settler Europeans. Between June and August 1976 the All Blacks toured South Africa; this tour coincided with the Soweto rising and black-led mass protest. Pictures of the All Blacks in tear-gas clouds were seen alongside images of the South African police and army shooting at school children. The tour led directly to the boycott of the Montreal Olympic Games by teams representing 26 African,

South Asian and Caribbean states. In the space of a few months rugby union had shifted from being a source of pride (even if the national team did not win so often, it could recover) to a source of political controversy and humiliation. In 1979 and 1980, rugby union was a powerful but challenged marker of a significant and widespread form of New Zealand masculinity. It was in the context of New Zealand rugby's contested cultural standing that 'Give 'Em a Taste of Kiwi'[20] (hereafter 'GEATOK') became the theme tune to televised rugby, and thus articulated its complex of meanings to the public.

Framing 'GEATOK'

There are two axes along which the song must be explored: as a text in its own right, framed by the conventions of its genre; and as a frame, as the boundary of a piece of televised sport that derives its authority from the 'genre expectations it establishes'.[21] It is musically nondescript: a piece of late 1970s rock music with repetitive lyrics and an uninventive tune. That is, it could be any one of a thousand other pieces of music, and it is precisely this generic conformity that makes the tune so interesting – along with the specific words that make up the lyrics and the setting in which it was used.

The style is internationally dispersed: a hard-edged guitar with a driving beat while also being rhythmically repetitive and with slight syncopation, known in Australia and New Zealand as 'pub rock'. 'Pub rock', which may contain powerful traces of rhythm and blues, was paradoxically, primarily white-men's music: it was consciously and aggressively anti-disco and anti-'stadium rock'. Like so much in popular music studies, pub rock is relatively under-researched – in part because it is mainstream and does not seem to attract the types of resistive cultural politics seen in other musical forms. Histories of punk rock often imply that pub rock was one of the musical genres against which punk rebelled, although in the New Zealand setting Wade Churton is unusual in providing an explicit critique of the pub rock scene.[22]

The label comes in part from the relative paucity of music venues in Australia and New Zealand, with the result that during the 1970s and 1980s pubs provided a major venue for touring bands in small music markets. Playing the pub circuit was part of a music industry apprenticeship: 'New bands were expected to put the effort in and "pay their dues" to overcome considerable record company reticence, invariably by playing popular cover versions to hotel audiences on a recognised circuit.'[23] Some of these pubs were large 'beer barns' into which several hundred or more patrons could fit. As Walker notes, these 'punters wanted to hear something unpretentious and hard edged. It didn't have to be loud, fast, raw or brash, but that helped. Most importantly, it had to be music that got to the point.'[24] Many of Walker's adjectives fit 'GEATOK' – loud, raw, brash, unpretentious, hard-edged: it certainly is music that gets to the point. 'GEATOK', although recognisably 'pub rock', has an edge to it that could be linked to popular forms of 1960s and 1970s rhythm and blues as exemplified in Britain by Chickenshack or John Mayall's various groups, or in New Zealand by Midge Marsden.

In case that point is not obvious, the lyrics drive it home. This is men's music. It is the genre of the public bar. It was rarely heard in small neighbourhood bars. It invokes a set of icons and motifs that are important in notions of 'real man' masculinity. A 'classic' of New Zealand pub rock, Th' Dudes' 'Be Mine Tonight', invokes the ubiquitous joint ('Asian cigarettes' are the song's opening words), beer and bar-room flirtation that nearly 30 years after its release can still be guaranteed to get the patrons on the dance floor and singing along.[25] In a similar fashion, the lyrics of GEATOK summon up images of 'real men' doing iconically 'real men' things:

> With a flash of black
> The lightening pack
> We're out to change the score
> When the packs go down
> We're gonna run that town
> You'll know us by our roar.
>
> Give 'em a taste of kiwi
> Give 'em the kiwi guts
> Give 'em a taste of kiwi
> Give it no ifs or buts
> Give 'em a taste of kiwi
> Show 'em you're made of steel
> Give 'em a taste of kiwi
> Show 'em the way you feel
> Give 'em a taste of kiwi
> Get in and show your best
> Give 'em a taste of kiwi
> You're better then the rest.

The genre – pub rock – should not, however, be seen as politically or socially neutral – as just a bit of Saturday night entertainment. Graham Turner notes a trend in Australian rock music that was paralleled in New Zealand where 'the often masculinist, racist and reactionary discourses of ... pub rock became conflated with attempts to "champion the egalitarian, the unpretentious, the 'authentic'"'.[26] Pub rock was clearly 'articulated into the ... conservative reconfiguration of everyday life'.[27] Despite this trans-Tasman similarity, the late 1970s and early 1980s Australian setting – where some rock bands such as Midnight Oil and Aboriginal-based or linked bands such as Goanna and Coloured Stone that fit the pub rock style but not the politics – was not replicated in New Zealand where by the late 1970s these more progressive politics were more associated with an emerging roots reggae scene.[28] This era of cultural disruption and dislocation, of an influential counterculture, and of a rapid diversification of rock and other popular music styles, often by artists who eschewed commercial imperatives, gave impetus to discourses of pretentiousness and authenticity. Pub rock was one of the paths to authenticity, and with it a powerful spatial connection with 'hard man' masculinity: as Phillips notes, the pub was a central location for the development and maintenance of this set of masculine codes. It was, as Hey notes of England, a 'masculine republic'.[29] Not only was pub rock associated in several ways with this 'hard man' mode of masculinity, it was stylistically conservative as well. According to John Dix, 'New Zealand rock in the mid-'70s had been an insipid period, almost devoid of inspiration', and while the 'hotel scene had opened up ... most pub managers issued strict stipulations, stifling any originality a band may have had'.[30] In the cultural life of New Zealand in the mid-to-late 1970s, therefore, pub rock was associated with a social group that exercised considerable mundane social power and was, as Phillips had noted, coming under siege from challenges to, and changes in, the gender order, and was also a musical form that was stylistically conservative. Some analyses suggest that rock itself may be particularly identified with 'the white male subject [who controls] the heterogeneity of popular culture practice ... [through the] unchallenged superiority of "rock" to other musical forms'.[31] (This view is indirectly supported, although not in its specifically psychoanalytic form, by a number of scholarly and journalistic analyses.[32]) As such, pub rock's stylistic association with masculinist control and spatial association with men's space – the public bar – may well have resonated at a number of preter-conscious levels.

It is not just the musicological form and generic codes of 'GEATOK', the frame built into its form, that asserts its associations with 'hard man' masculinity. The song was released as a single in 1980, with the performers named as Black Bolt and the Silver Ferns accentuating the claims to All Black identification, to nation (the silver fern is unproblematically seen as a distinctive marker of the New Zealand sporting nation), and to the performance of superiority. A similar linkage may be seen in the lyrics, which explicitly invoke key traits and characteristics of 'hard man' masculinity. The notion of 'giving it to them' forms part of an idiomatic language of both victory and revenge, remembering that the All Blacks had suffered a slump in form throughout the 1970s. A central element of the self-defined and perceived 'New Zealand character' was that New Zealanders, especially the men, would not engage in self-promotion – in the words of one author of an outsiders' guide to New Zealanders (a popular form of writing from the 1950s to the 1970s): 'If the Kiwi has one fault it's modesty. He never blows his own trumpet.'[33] The reference in the lyrics to being 'the best' may therefore seem out of place – but it is important to note that the listeners or the team (it is not entirely clear to whom the song is addressed) are encouraged to 'get in and show your best'. This is not bluster of self-promotion, a claim that they are better than the rest, it is a call to irrevocable demonstration through practice of superiority and is consistent with the myth of the superiority of the (humble) New Zealand man.

Of course, these lyrics should not be taken too literally, and some are quite absurd. What, in the context of a rugby match, does it mean to claim that 'we're gonna run that town'? What is more, the sixth line points to a problem with pushing too far the use of metaphor: the kiwi as a quiet and shy bird – not so much of the 'mighty roar'. It is not the specific lyric that carries the message, but the affective response of the audience to the aural event. Cultural studies analysts often invoke the notion of affect used by psychologists to discuss emotional engagement.[34] In the case of 'GEATOK', the affective response presupposes that the All Blacks unproblematically stood in for and represented New Zealand, and in particular a specific set of New Zealand men. Despite claims to rural and labour force representativeness in composition, there is little evidence that the All Blacks were literally representative – but there is little doubt that they were figuratively and mythologically representative.[35] It is this mythical (in the sense used by Barthes[36]) representativeness that provides the basis for the affective engagement of the song, and that provides a key element of the frame that is hailed into existence by its musical structure.

'GEATOK' as frame

There is a second level of framing in the song that is derived from its initial televisual function of being the theme tune to televised rugby matches. Here it goes through a number of other changes in form and function. To begin with, although it retains its internal characteristics that provide it with a frame, it also articulates in a much more explicit way to other media texts and becomes the material form of a frame. In doing so it takes on a new function as a single and coherent text. As Frow notes,

> by delineating aesthetic space as an 'unreal' space (an 'imaginary garden with real toads in it'), the frame both neutralises direct referentiality and calls attention to the concentration of meaning within this space: the absence of immediate meaning creates an expectation of *total* meaning.[37]

The television event of a rugby match becomes a clearly demarcated televisual space where 'GEATOK' acts in a manner similar to a book cover: it lets in some ideas and approaches and excludes others; it legitimates some understandings and interpretations and denies the legitimacy, authenticity and veracity of others.

As a television theme tune 'GEATOK' retained its internal characteristics that called into existence a set of legitimate modes of textual understanding. At the same time it became part of the event that is televised rugby, where the frame 'signifies only the norm (the text as an aesthetic object and the normative expectations governing the reception of this object)'.[38] This latter framing function is vital for this sort of frame and textual analysis; 'GEATOK' as the frame is 'a sign of a *conventionally* guaranteed use of the text [that] cannot account for deviant function, i.e., for uses of the text which choose to ignore this norm'.[39] Aside from its role as shaper of interpretation and understanding, the musical frame of 'GEATOK' does two major things within the televisual text. As with every theme tune, it sets the mood for the programme that follows, and provides a leitmotif. It is, in a way, artificial to distinguish between the mood and the leitmotif in that the mood depends on the leitmotif: that is, the mood depends on the recurrent theme that is associated with a particular idea. In this case, this is the idea of rugby as a marker of the 'Kiwi hard man', but also to mark the televised game as entertainment. It is 'unreal' space. Frow's case that a literary frame both 'neutralises direct referentiality' and points to 'the concentration of meaning' means that a frame shifts an entertainment spectacle to a metaphorical level. In these functions, then, 'GEATOK' operates in a manner similar to the way that music associated with news broadcasts marks the show as a form of entertainment.[40]

This marking as entertainment is further intensified because the generic form of the music changes when the analytical focus shifts to consider its role in relation to the TV show it accompanied. It retains many of the characteristics of pub rock but may also be seen as an advertising jingle. The lyric lines are short, abrupt and repetitive: there is little doubt that viewers were being sold a product; the product appears to be both televised rugby and hard man masculinity. That one of the products is televised rugby is not in doubt; the song was the sport's theme tune on television. That the other is hard man masculinity may be seen clearly in both the pub rock style instrumentation and the composition itself. The generic codes of pub rock means that it links to a set of masculine characteristics in rock music including assertive, even aggressive, posturing akin to mild versions of the genital-accentuating poses of some forms of 1970s metal. To remove any doubt, the second half of each of the repetitive couplets: 'Give 'em the kiwi guts/Give it no ifs or buts/Show 'em you're made of steel/Show 'em the way you feel/Get in and show your best/You're better then the rest' are markers of a product being sold, of hard man masculinity. The call on the audience/players is to be visceral, to be uncompromising, to be hard, to demonstrate intense emotion and to show superiority through action. It is a call to an uncompromising drive to victory, and an assertion of hard man masculinity as legitimate and as the authentic way to be a 'Kiwi'.

There is another role that this song-as-jingle now plays, especially these rhyming lyrics. Noting Frow's case that the frame radiates in both direction and operates in an osmotic manner, letting through certain cultural traits, these couplets become signs of the gaps in the barrier tailored to let through (from game to context and from context to game) a set of characteristics. This is not Corinthian rugby, where playing is all that matters, this is rugby where victory is all that matters – and perhaps this is where 'running the town' becomes significant. A rugby victory becomes not just success over a team of opponents, but also over the place they represent: Gruneau and Whitson have suggested that the supporters of losing hockey teams riot to reassert their masculinity after it has been compromised by their team's loss.[41] The claim that 'we're gonna run that town' seems to suggest that in the wake of 'our' victory 'we' will be in control of the society from which the losers are drawn. At this stage there is a risk of reading too much into a line: its prime virtue and role seems to be that 'town' rhymes with 'down'. In the context of the song and shifting away from a constrained textual analysis for a moment, however, the author's intent becomes less significant than the way it is understood by its audiences. Here we have a song that praises the hard man version and virtues of rugby, and asserts the need for absolute victory through being uncompromising, through being 'made of steel', and through being the best: in such a context a celebration of dominance does not seem so out of place. There is little about this version of rugby that is gentlemanly, in the Corinthian sense.

These are bold claims for something that is little more than an advertising jingle, but it is hard to overstate the significance of music as leitmotif in television and film. In both media, music is often under-recognised by audiences as a mood-making part of the text, though from time to time film scores gain high levels of popularity and television themes are often invoked in nostalgic moments. In-text music, often referred to as incidental, is less noted yet probably plays a greater leitmotif role than the theme tune. During the fifth season of *Buffy the Vampire Slayer*, one episode, 'The Body' (5.16), deals with character responses to the death by natural causes of a major but second-tier character (the show is littered with supernatural deaths). It is a sparse, sombre and hollow episode and, uniquely in the seven series of the show, has no music except the theme tune, that is, no incidental music. This absence, unobserved by many well acquainted with the Buffy-verse, gives the show a level of rawness seldom experienced in popular television and makes it emotionally draining because the audience receives no clues about how to engage with the characters other than what they say and do.[42]

In its commercially released, 7-inch single version, 'GEATOK' incorporates its own piece of incidental music in the form of a rugby commentary between the first and second choruses. It sounds like, and may be, an actual piece of commentary from an All Black match – the players named were all in the team during the latter half of the 1970s. Frow, again, provides a useful way to understand this. As well as marking the match as a form of entertainment and in providing an osmotic barrier between the game and the non-game world in and around the sport mediascape, the song holds the game 'in a kind of suspension such that the framed word is, in Mikhail Bakhtin's terminology, a "represented word": the word represents itself, *cites* itself as a fictive word, a word which cannot be accepted directly'.[43] In this case, although the generic codes of GEATOK mark it as a type of music, as pub rock, the song also cites and fictionalises rugby commentary, raising expectations of the game about to be broadcast. The commentary provides a reminder of the team's prodigious, if erratic in the 1970s, try-scoring ability and of the fluidity of movement when that particular All Black back line was on form. Whether it is an actual piece of commentary, and which game it might be, is irrelevant: it sounds authentic. This apparent authenticity reveals a further ambiguity: the implied verisimilitude appears in the midst of a musical moment marking a television show that identified rugby as entertainment. The released record asserted the rugby as 'real', while at the same time occupying the 'unreal space' of a sport mediascape.

In being both 'real' and 'unreal' 'GEATOK' relied on rock's cultural marking as authentic, and on pub rock's deep-seated masculinity. Grossberg's emphasis on affect and on the articulations of the rock formation to other aspects of the socio-cultural condition means that he sees rock as

> a promise of a kind of salvation. If it does not define resistance, it does at least offer a kind of empowerment, allowing people to navigate their way through, and even to respond to their lived context. It is a way of making it through the day.[44]

The centrality of rugby to definition of a particular form of masculinity explicitly and implicitly invoked by 'GEATOK' both as a text and as textual frame meant that there was a large group of New Zealanders, not all of them men, who were interpellated as an audience. For much of this audience, the song's textual form articulated to important elements of their lived context. The song, and the theme tune, became the mechanism that allowed an articulation of the individual rugby match and the game in general to specific socio-culturally identifiable audiences. It asserted and culturally validated a specific version of New Zealand's hard man masculinity that was linked to a form of nationalism where the hard man produced victory. In doing so, it became a celebration of triumphalism. This is an awesome responsibility for a piece of music that in its longest form was a three-minute song – but like a book cover it shaped the meanings that could be ascribed to the televised rugby match while also allowing certain non-rugby cultural traces into the mediascape. 'GEATOK', when read through the lens provided by Frow's notion of the textual frame, is a 'pub rock' jingle that also served as an osmotic barrier encasing individual rugby matches as broadcast and rugby as an icon.

Notes

1 Lawrence Grossberg, *Dancing in Spite of Myself: Essays on Poplar Culture*, Durham: Duke University Press, 1997, pp. 109–110.
2 See for instance, Margaret Carlisle Duncan, Michael Messner, Linda Williams and Kerry Jensen, 'Gender stereotyping in televised sports' (edited by Wayne Williams), in Susan Birrell and Cheryl Coles (eds), *Women, Sport, and Culture*, Champaign, IL: Human Kinetics, 1994, pp. 249–272.
3 Brett Hutchins and Murray Phillips, 'Selling permissible violence: the commodification of Australian rugby league 1970–1995', *International Review of the Sociology of Sport*, 32, 1997, 161–176.
4 Dan Streible, 'Female spectators and the Corbett–Fitzsimmons fight film', in Todd Baker (ed.), *Out of Bounds: Sports, Media, and the Politics of Identity*, Bloomington, IN: Indiana University Press, 1997, pp. 16–47.
5 Matthew Taylor, *The Leaguers: The Making of Professional Football in England, 1900–1939*, Liverpool: Liverpool University Press, 2005, pp. 268–272.
6 Jim McKay and David Rowe, 'Field of soaps: Rupert V. Kerry as masculine melodrama', *Social Text*, 50, 1997, 69–86; Murray Phillips and Brett Hutchins, 'From independence to a reconstituted hegemony: rugby league and television in Australia', *Journal of Australian Studies*, 58, 1998, 134–147.
7 As an aside, the piece used would not be out of place at the *Last Night at the Proms*, suggesting Wimbledon's place in a vision of populist Englishness.

8 John Frow, 'The Literary Frame', *Journal of Aesthetic Education*, 16, 2, 1982, 25–30.
9 Ibid., 25.
10 Ibid., 27.
11 Ibid.
12 Gregory Jay and David Miller, 'The role of theory in the study of literature?', in Gregory Jay and David Miller (eds), *After Strange Texts: The Role of Theory in the Study of Literature*, Alabama: University of Alabama Press, 1985, p. 6.
13 Grossberg, *Dancing in Spite of Myself*, p. 106.
14 Frow, 'The Literary Frame', 29.
15 Kronos Quartet, 'Purple Haze', from *Kronos Quartet: Sculthorpe, Sallinen, Glass, Nancarrow, Hendrix*, Nonesuch Records, 1986.
16 J. O. C. Phillips, *A Man's Country? The Image of the Pakeha Male – A History*, (revised edition), Auckland: Penguin Books, 1996.
17 Greg Ryan, 'Rural myth and urban actuality: the anatomy of All Black and New Zealand rugby 1884–1938', *New Zealand Journal of History*, 35, 1, 2001, 45–69.
18 Phillips, *A Man's Country?*, p. 32.
19 Bill Keane, '"Ex-pats" and "poofters" rebuild the nation: 1982, Kiwi culture and the All Whites on the road to Spain', in Brad Patterson (ed.), *Sport, Society and Culture in New Zealand*, Wellington: Stout Research Centre, 1999, pp. 49–60.
20 D'Arcy MacManus, Masius and Murray Grindlay, 'Give 'Em a Taste of Kiwi', EMI Records, 1980.
21 Frow, 'The Literary Frame', 27.
22 Wade Ronald Churton, *Have you Checked the Children? Punk and Post-punk Music in New Zealand, 1977–1981*, Christchurch: Put Your Foot Down Publishing, 1999.
23 Ibid., p. 6.
24 Walker Clinton, 'The roar from the back room: The rise of "pub rock"', in *Juice/Powerhouse Museum Special Issue: Real Wild Child*, Sydney: Powerhouse Museum, 1994, p. 14.
25 Dave Dobbyn, 'Be Mine Tonight' (Th' Dudes), Key Records, 1978.
26 Quoted in Tony Mitchell, *Popular Music and Local Identity: Rock, Pop and Rap in Europe and Oceania*, London: Leicester University Press, 1996, p. 209.
27 Grossberg, *Dancing in Spite of Myself*, p. 101.
28 John Castles, 'Tjungaringanyi: Aboriginal rock (1971–91)', in Philip Hayward (ed.), *Sound Alliances: Indigenous Peoples, Cultural Politics and Popular Music in the Pacific*, London: Cassell, 1998, pp. 11–25; Tony Mitchell, 'He Waiata Na Aotearoa: Maori and Pacific Islander music in Aotearoa/New Zealand', in Philip Hayward (ed.), *Sound Alliances: Indigenous Peoples, Cultural Politics and Popular Music in the Pacific*, London: Cassell, 1998, pp. 26–44; McKenzie Wark, 'Homage to Catatonia: culture, politics and midnight oil', in John Frow and Meghan Morris (eds), *Australian Cultural Studies: A Reader*, Urbana: University of Illinois Press, 1993, pp. 105–116.
29 Valerie Hey, *Patriarchy and Pub Culture*, London: Tavistock Publications, 1986.
30 John Dix, *Stranded in Paradise: New Zealand Rock 'n' Roll 1955–1988*, Wellington: Paradise Publications, 1988, p. 191.
31 Dave Laing, 'Rock anxieties and new music networks', in Angela McRobbie (ed.), *Back to Reality: Social Experience and Cultural Studies*, Manchester: Manchester University Press, 1997, p. 120.
32 See Sheila Whitely (ed.), *Sexing the Groove: Popular Music and Gender*, London: Routledge, 1997; Liz Evans, *Women, Sex and Rock and Roll in Their Own Words*, London: Pandora, 1994, especially interviews with Kim Gordon (pp. 165–183) and Kat Bjelland Gray (pp. 57–73).
33 Austin Mitchell, *The Half-gallon Quarter-acre Pavlova Paradise*, Christchurch: Whitcombe and Tombs, 1972, p. 17.
34 Lawrence Grossberg, *We Gotta Get Out of This Place: Popular Conservatism and Postmodern Culture*, New York: Routledge, 1992; Lawrence Grossberg, 'Is there a fan in

the house: the affective sensibility of fandom', in Lisa Lewis (ed.), *The Adoring Audience: Fan Culture and Popular Culture*, London: Routledge, 1992, pp. 50–65; Grossberg, *Dancing in Spite of Myself*, pp. 29–121.

35 Chris Laidlaw, *Rights of Passage: Beyond the New Zealand Identity Crisis*, Auckland: Hodder Moa Beckett, 1999; Phillips, *A Man's Country?*; Ryan, 'Rural myth and urban actuality'.

36 Roland Barthes, 'Myth today', in *Mythologies*, London: Vintage, 1993, pp. 109–159.

37 Frow, 'The Literary Frame', 27.

38 Ibid., 28.

39 Ibid.

40 Neil Postman, *Amusing Ourselves to Death: Public Discourse in the Age of Show Business*, New York: Penguin, 1985, pp. 102–103.

41 Richard Gruneau and David Whitson, *Hockey Night in Canada: Sport, Identities and Cultural Politics*, Toronto: Garamond Press, 1993, p. 69.

42 Joss Weedon, 'The Body', *Buffy the Vampire Slayer*, series 5, episode 16, 2000.

43 Frow, 'The Literary Frame', 26.

44 Grossberg, *Dancing in Spite of Myself*, p. 115.

Selected bibliography

Adorno, T., 'Bürgerliche oper', *Klangfiguren, Musikalische Schrifeten, I*, Berlin-Frankfurt/Main: Suhrkamp, 1959.
——, *Philosophy of Modern Music*, trans. A. G. Mitchell and W. Blomster, New York: Seabury, 1973.
——, *Introduction to the Sociology of Music*, trans. E. A. Ashby, New York: Seabury, 1976.
——, *Minima Moralia: Reflections from Damaged Life*, trans. E. F. N. Jephcott, London: Verso, 1978.
——, *Prisms*, trans. S. and S. Weber, Cambridge, MA: Harvard University Press, 1981.
——, *The Culture Industry: Selected Essays on Mass Culture* (edited by J. M. Bernstein), London: Routledge, 2001.
Allen, D. R., *A Song for Cricket*, London: Pelham Books, 1981.
Anderson, B., *Imagined Communities: Reflections on the Origin and Spread of Nationalism*, London: Verso, 1983.
Andersson, T., *Kung Fotboll. Den Svenska Fotbollens Kulturhistoria från 1800-talets Slut till 1950*, Stockholm/Stehag: Brutus Östlings bokförlag Symposion, 2002.
Anshel M. H. and D. Q. Marisi, 'Effects of music and rhythm on physical performance', *Research Quarterly*, 49, 1978, 109–113.
Arlott, J. (ed.), *The Oxford Companion to Sport & Games*, Oxford: Oxford University Press, 1975.
——, *Arlott on Cricket* (edited by D. R. Allen), London: Collins, 1984.
Attali, J., *Noise: The Political Economy of Music*, trans. Brian Massumi, Manchester: Manchester University Press, 1985.
Back, L., T. Crabbe and J. Solomos, *The Changing Face of Football*, Oxford: Berg, 2001.
Bacon, C., T. Myers and C. I. Karageorghis, 'Effect of movement–music synchrony and tempo on exercise oxygen consumption', (under review).
Bale, J., 'The place of "place" in the cultural studies of sports', *Progress in Human Geography*, 1988, 12, 507–524.
——, *Sport, Space and the City*, London: Routledge, 1993.
——, *Landscapes of Modern Sport*, London: Leicester University Press, 1994.
——, 'Virtual fandoms: futurescapes of football', in A. Brown (ed.), *Fanatics! Power, Identity and Fandom in Football*, London: Routledge, 1998.
——, *Running Cultures*, London: Routledge, 2004.
Ballantine, C., *Music and its Social Meanings*, New York: Gordon and Breach Science Publishers, 1984.
Bandura, A., *Social Foundations of Thought and Action*, Englewood Cliffs, NJ: Prentice-Hall, 1986, p. 47.

Bányai, E. I., 'On the technique of hypnosis and ecstasy: an exceptional psychophysio-logical approach', in Mihály Hoppál (ed.), *Shamanism in Eurasia*. Göttingen: Herodot, 1984, pp. 174–183.

Bargh, J. A., 'Auto-motives: pre-conscious determinants of thoughts and behavior', in E. T. Higgins and R. M. Sorrentino (eds), *Handbook of Motivation and Cognition*, Vol. 2, New York: Guildford, 1990, pp. 93–130.

Barker, J. R. V., *The Tournament in England 1100–1400*, Woodbridge: Boydell & Breer, 1986.

Barney, R. and M. Heinne (eds), *Cultural Imperialism in Action: Critiques in the Global Olympic Trust*, London, Ontario: International Centre for Olympic Studies, 2006.

Barthes, R., *Mythologies*, London: Vintage, 1993.

Beckles, H. McD., *The Development of West Indies Cricket: Volume 1. The Age of National-ism*, London: Pluto, 1998.

——, (ed.), *A Spirit of Dominance: Cricket and Nationalism in West Indies Cricket – Essays in Honour of 'Viv' Richards on the 21st Anniversary of his First Debut*, Kingston: Univer-sity of West Indies Press, 1998.

——, 'Class, ethnicity, nation and notions of masculinity: Black masculinity in Caribbean slavery', in Rhoda E. Reddock (ed.), *Interrogating Caribbean Masculinities: Theoretical and Empirical Analyses*, Jamaica: University of the West Indies Press, 2004.

Beckles, H. McD. and Brian Stoddart (eds), *Liberation Cricket: West Indies Cricket Culture*, Manchester: Manchester University Press, 1995.

Belezkaja, W. B., 'Mythos oder wirklichkeit?', *Sowjetunion Heute*, 2, 1988, 26–28.

Berlyne, D. E., *Aesthetics and Psychobiology*, New York: Appleton Century Crofts, 1971.

Bernard-Donals, M., 'Knowing the subaltern: Bakhtin, carnival and the other voice of the human sciences', in M. Mayerfield Bell and M. Gardiner (eds), *Bakhtin and the Human Sciences*, London: Sage, 1998.

Berridge, K. C. and J. Wilbarger, 'Unconscious affective reactions to masked happy versus angry faces influence consumption behaviour and judgments of value', *Person-ality and Social Psychology Bulletin*, 31, 2005, 121–135.

Birbalsingh, F., *The Rise of Westindian Cricket: From Colony to Nation*, Antigua: Hansib, 1996.

Birbalsingh, F. and C. Shiwcharan, *Indo-Westindian Cricket*, Antigua: Hansib, 1988.

Bishop, D. T., C. I. Karageorghis and G. Loizou, 'A grounded theory of young tennis players' use of music to manipulate emotional state', *Journal of Sport & Exercise Psy-chology*, 29, 2007, 584–607.

Blackmore, S., *Consciousness: An Introduction*, New York: Oxford University Press, 2003.

Bloch, C., *Flow og Stress. Stemninger og Følelseskultur i Hverdagslivet*, Frederiksberg: Sam-fundslitteratur, 2001.

Blood, A. J., R. J. Zatorre, P. Bermudez and A. C. Evans, 'Emotional responses to pleas-ant and unpleasant music correlate with activity in paralimbic brain regions', *Nature Neuroscience*, 2, 1999, 382–387.

Böhme, G., *Atmosphäre. Essays zur neuen Ästhetik*, Frankfurt/Main: Suhrkamp, 1995.

Bonny, H. L., 'Music the language of immediacy', *Arts in Psychotherapy*, 14, 1987, 255–261.

Boo, M., *The Story of Figure Skating*, New York: William Morrow and Company, 1998.

Borden, I., *Skateboarding, Space and the City. Architecture and the Body*, Oxford: Berg, 2001.

Born, G. and D. Hesmondhalgh (eds), *Western Music and its Others: Difference, Representation and Appropriation in Music*, London: University of California Press, 2000.

Bradley, I., *Abide With Me: The World of Victorian Hymns*, London: SCM Press Ltd, 1997.

Breeze, J. 'Binta', *On the Edge of the Island*, Newcastle-upon-Tyne: Bloodaxe, 1997.

Bremner, J., *Shit Ground No Fans. It's by Far the Greatest Football Songbook the World has Ever Seen . . .*, London: Bantam Press, 2004.

Brown, A. (ed.), *Fanatics! Power, Identity and Fandom in Football*, London: Routledge, 1998.

Brown, D., 'Revisiting the discourse of art, beauty and sport from the 1906 consultative conference for the arts, literature and sport', *Olympika: The International Journal of Olympic Studies*, 5, 1996, 1–14.

Brown, P., 'An enquiry into the origins and nature of tempo behaviour: II. Experimental work', *Psychology of Music*, 9, 1979, 32–43.

Browne, D., *Amped. How Big Air, Big Dollars and a New Generation took Sports to the Extreme*, New York and London: Bloomsbury, 2005.

Bukafzer, M., *Music in the Baroque Era*, New York: Norton, 1947.

Burgess, K., *The Challenge of Labour: Shaping British Society*, London: Croon Helm, 1980.

Burke, P., *Popular Culture in Early Modern Europe*, Aldershot: Scolar, 1994.

Burkhardt, J., 'Vom Handlungstheater zum modernen Stimmungsprinzip', in August Nitschke (ed.), *Verhaltenswandel in der Industriellen Revolution*, Stuttgart: Kohlhammer, pp. 49–56.

Burton, R. D. E., *Afro-Creole: Power, Opposition and Play in the Caribbean*, New York: Cornell University Press, 1997.

Butler, R. J., *Sport Psychology in Action*, Oxford: Butterworth-Heinemann, 1996.

Cannon, W. B., 'The James-Lange theory of emotions: a critical examination and an alternative theory', *American Journal of Psychology*, 39, 1927, 106–124.

Carducci, G., 'Pietro Metatstasio', in *Prose di Giosue Carducci MDCCCLIX–MCMIII*, Bologna: Nicola Zanichelli, 1907, pp. 903–904.

Carrington, B., '"Football's Coming Home" but whose home? And do we want it? Nation, football and the politics of exclusion', in Adam Brown (ed.), *Fanatics! Power, Identity and Fandom in Football*, London: Routledge, 1998.

Castles, J., 'Tjungaringanyi: Aboriginal rock (1971–91)', in Philip Hayward (ed.), *Sound Alliances: Indigenous Peoples, Cultural Politics and Popular Music in the Pacific*, London: Cassell, 1998, pp. 11–25.

Charles, F., *Days and Nights in the Magic Forest*, London: Bogle-L'Ouverture, 1986.

Churton, W. R., *Have You Checked the Children? Punk and Post-punk Music in New Zealand, 1977–1981*, Christchurch: Put Your Foot Down Publishing, 1999.

Clark, T., '"I'm Scunthorpe 'til I die": constructing and (re)negotiating identity through the terrace chant', *Soccer and Society*, 7, 4, 2006, 492–507.

Clarke, E. F., 'Music and psychology', in M. Clayton, T. Herbert and R. Middleton (eds), *The Cultural Study of Music: A Critical Introduction*, London: Routledge, 2003, pp. 119–120.

Clarke, P., *Hope and Glory: Britain 1900–1990*, London: Penguin Books, 1996.

Clayton, M., T. Herbert and R. Middleton, *The Cultural Study of Music: A Critical Introduction*, London: Routledge, 2003.

Clément, C., *Opera, or the Undoing of Women*, trans. Betsy Wing, Minneapolis: University of Minnesota Press, 1988.

Clerici, G., *500 Jahre Tennis. Vom Spiel der Könige zum Milliarden- Dollargeschäft*, trans. Ulrich Kaiser, Berlin: Ullstein, 1987.

Clowe, J. G. and B. J. Cross, 'Individual and social motivation in Australian sport', in T. Morris and J. Summers (eds), *Sport Psychology, Theory and Application and Issues*, Australia: John Wiley & Sons, 1995, pp. 90–121.

Cohn, N., *Awopbopaloobop Alopbamboom*, London: Paladin, 1969.

Connor, S., *Postmodernist Culture: An Introduction to Theories of the Contemporary*, Oxford: Blackwell, 1989.

Copeland, B. L. and B. D. Franks, 'Effects of types and intensities of background music on treadmill endurance', *The Journal of Sports Medicine and Physical Fitness*, 31, 1991, 100–103.

Copley-Graves, L., *Figure Skating History: The Evolution of Dance on Ice*, Columbus, OH: Platoro Press, 1992.

Corbin, A., *Time, Desire and Horror: Towards a History of the Senses*, trans. Jean Birrell, Oxford: Polity Press, 1995.

——, *The Foul and the Fragrant: Odor and the French Social Imagination*, trans. Miriam L Kochan, Cambridge, MA: Harvard University Press, 1998.

——, *Village Bells: The Culture of the Senses in the Nineteenth-Century French Countryside*, trans. Martin Thom, New York: Columbia University Press, 1998.

Coubertin, P. de, *Olympism – Selected Writings*, Lausanne: International Olympic Committee, 2000.

Cowley, John, *Carnival, Canboulay and Calypso: Traditions in the Making*, Cambridge: Cambridge University Press, 1996.

Crabbe, T. and S. Wagg, '"A carnival of cricket?": the Cricket World Cup, "race" and the politics of carnival' in S. Wagg (ed.), *Cricket and National Identity in the Postcolonial Age: Following On*, London: Routledge, 2005.

Critchley, M., 'Musicogenic epilepsi', *Brain*, 60, 1937, 13–27.

Crolley, L. and D. Hand, *Football, Europe and the Press*, London: Frank Cass, 2002.

Cronin, M., 'Beyond sectarianism: sport and Irish culture', in Liam Harte and Yvonne Whelan (eds), *Ireland Beyond Boundaries. Mapping Irish Studies in the Twenty-First Century*, London: Pluto, 2007, pp. 215–238.

Damasio, A., *The Feeling of What Happens: Body, Emotion and the Making of Consciousness*, London: Vintage, 2000.

Darwin, C., *The Expression of the Emotions in Man and animals*, Chicago: University of Chicago Press, 1998/1872.

Deci, E. L. and R. M. Ryan, *Intrinsic Motivation and Self-determination in Human Behaviour*, New York: Plenum Publishing Co., 1985.

DeNora, T., *Music in Everyday Life*, Cambridge: Cambridge University Press, 2000.

——, 'Music and self-identity', in Andy Bennett, Barry Shank and Jason Tonybee (eds), *The Popular Music Studies Reader*, London: Routledge, 2006, pp. 119–120.

Dix, J., *Stranded in Paradise: New Zealand Rock 'n' Roll 1955–1988*, Wellington: Paradise Publications, 1988.

Dudley, S., 'Judging "by the beat": calypso versus soca', *Ethnomusicology*, 40, 2, 1996, 269–298.

——, *Carnival Music in Trinidad: Experiencing Music, Expressing Culture*, Oxford: Oxford University Press, 2004.

Duncan, M. C., M. Messner, L. Williams, K. Jensen and W. Williams, 'Gender stereotyping in televised sports', in S. Birrell and C. Coles (eds), *Women, Sport, and Culture*, Champaign, IL: Human Kinetics, 1994, pp. 249–272.

Eagleton, T., *The Ideology of the Aesthetic*, Oxford: Blackwell, 1990.

Edworthy, J. and H. Waring, 'The effects of music tempo and loudness level on treadmill exercise', *Ergonomics*, 49, 2006, 1597–1610.

Ehrard, J. and P. Viallaneix (eds), *Les Fêtes de la Révolution. Colloque de Clermont Ferrand 1974*, Paris: Société des Études Robbespierristes, 1977.

Elliott, D., S. Carr and D. Savage, 'Effects of motivational music on work output and affective responses during sub-maximal cycling of a standardized perceived intensity', *Journal of Sport Behavior*, 27, 2004, 134–147.

Eichberg, H., *Leistung, Spannung, Geschwindigkeit. Sport und Tanz im gesellschaftlichen Wandel des 18./19. Jahrhunderts*, Stuttgart: Klett-Cotta, 1978.

——, *The People of Democracy. Understanding Self-determination on the Basis of Body and Movement*, Århus: Klim, 2004.

Eichberg, H. and B. Vestergård Madsen, *Idræt som Fest. Bogen om Landsstævnet*, Århus: Klim, 2006.

Eichberg, H., J. Kosiewicz and K. Obodyńsky (eds), *Sport for All as a Form of Education*, Rzeszów: University of Rzeszów, 2007.

Evans, L., *Women, Sex and Rock and Roll in Their Own Words*, London: Pandora, 1994.

Eyerman, R. and A. Jamison, *Music and Social Movements. Mobilizing Traditions in the 20th Century*, Cambridge: Cambridge University Press, 1998.

Farnsworth, P. R., *The Social Psychology of Music*, Iowa: Iowa State University Press, 1969.

Fergus, H., *Volcano Verses*, Leeds: Peepal Tree, 2003.

Fichard, R. F., *Handbuch des Lawn-Tennis Spieles*, Baden-Baden: Emil Sommermeyer, 1887.

Fischer-Lichte, E., *Theatre, Sacrifice, Ritual. Exploring Forms of Political Theatre*, London: Routledge, 2005.

Fiske, J., *Power Plays, Power Works*, London: Verso, 1993.

Foucault, M., *The History of Sexuality*, New York: Vintage Books, 1980.

——, 'Different spaces', in *Essential works of Foucault, 1954–1984. Vol. 2, Aesthetics, Method and Epistemology*, London: Penguin, 2000.

Frijda, N. H., *The Emotions*, New York: Cambridge University Press, 1986.

Frith, S., 'Music and identity', in S. Hall and P. du Gay (eds), *Questions of Cultural Identity*, London: Sage, 1996, p. 109.

Frow, J., 'The literary frame', *Journal of Aesthetic Education*, 16, 2, 1982, 25–30.

Fucilla, J. (trans.), *Three Melodramas by Pietro Metastasio*, Lexington: University Press of Kentucky, 1981.

Gabrielsson, A., 'Emotions in strong experiences with music', in P. Juslin and J. A. Sloboda (eds), *Music and Emotion: Theory and Research*, Oxford: Oxford University Press, 2001, pp. 431–449.

Garland, H. J., *Henry Francis Lyte and the Story of 'Abide With Me'*, Manchester: Torch Publishing Company, n.d.

Geertz, C., *The Interpretation of Cultures: Selected Essays*, London: Fontana Press, 1993.

Gennep, A. van, *The Rites of Passage*, London: Routledge and Kegan Paul, 1960.

Gillmeister, H., 'The origin of European ball games: a re-evaluation and linguistic analysis', *Stadion*, 7, 1981, 19–51.

——, 'Tennis bei olympischen spielen (1896–1924)', *Stadion*, 11, 1985, 193–262.

——, 'Den skriftliga utmanigen i de gotländska bollspelen. Dess kulturella och historiska innebörd', in *Idrott Historia och Samhälle. Svenska Idrottshistoriska Föreningens Årsskrift*, Helsingborg: Schmidts Bogtryckeri, 1988, pp. 21–41.

——, *Kulturgeschichte des Tennis*, Munich: Wilhelm Fink Verlag, 1990.

Gilroy, P., *The Black Atlantic: Modernity and Double Consciousness*, London: Verso, 2000.

Giulianotti, R. and G. Armstrong, 'Avenues of contestation. Football hooligans running and ruling urban spaces', *Social Anthropology*, 10, 2002, 211–238.

Giulianotti, R. and R. Robertson, 'The globalization of football: a study in the glocalization of the "serious life"', *The British Journal of Sociology*, 55, 2004, 545–568.

——, 'Glocalization, globalization and migration. The case of Scottish football supporters in North America', *International Sociology*, 21, 2006, 171–198.

Gluch, P. D., 'The use of music in preparing for sport performance', *Contemporary Thought*, 2, 1993, 33–53.

Goffman, E., *The Presentation of Self in Everyday Life*, New York: Doubleday/Anchor, 1959.

Graham, C., *Deconstructing Ireland. Identity, Theory, Culture*, Edinburgh: Edinburgh University Press, 2001.

Gregory, A., *The Silence of Memory: Armistice Day 1919–1946*, Oxford: Berg, 1994.

Griffiths, P., *A Concise History of Modern Music from Debussy to Boulez*, London: Thames and Hudson, 1978.

Grossberg, L., *We Gotta get Out of This Place: Popular Conservatism and Postmodern Culture*, New York: Routledge, 1992.

——, *Dancing in Spite of Myself: Essays on Popular Culture*, Durham: Duke University Press, 1997.

Gruneau, R. and D. Whitson, *Hockey Night in Canada: Sport, Identities and Cultural Politics*, Toronto: Garamond Press, 1993.

Guegold, W., *100 Years of Olympic Music: Music and Musicians of the Modern Olympic Games 1896–1996*, Mantua, OH: Golden Clef, 1996.

Hailey, C. (ed.), *Arnold Schoenberg 1874–1951. Eine Interaktive Multimediale Ausstellung*, Venice: Marsilio Editioni, 1996.

Halliwell, W., 'Providing sport psychology consulting services in professional hockey', *The Sport Psychologist*, 4, 1990, 369–377.

Hanin, Y. L. (ed.), *Emotions in Sport*, Champaign, IL: Human Kinetics, 2000.

Hardy, L., G. Jones and D. Gould, *Understanding Psychological Preparation for Sport: Theory and Practice of Elite Performers*, Chichester, UK: John Wiley, 1996.

Hargreaves, D. J. and A. C. North, 'The functions of music in everyday life: redefining the social in music psychology', *Psychology of Music*, 27, 1999, 84–95.

Hauschild, T., *Magie und Macht in Italien. Über Frauenzauber, Kirche und Politik*, Gifkendorf: Merlin, 2002.

Hernandez-Peon, R., 'The efferent control of afferent signals entering the central nervous system', *Annals of New York Academy of Science*, 89, 1961, 866–882.

Hewston, R., A. M. Lane, C. I. Karageorghis and A. M. Nevill, 'The effectiveness of music as a strategy to regulate mood [Abstract]', *Journal of Sports Sciences*, 22, 2005, 181–182.

Hey, V., *Patriarchy and Pub Culture*, London: Tavistock, 1986.

Hill, D. R., *Calypso Calaloo: Early Carnival Music in Trinidad*, Gainesville: University of Florida Press, 1993.

Hill, J., '"Rite of Spring": cup finals and community in the North of England', in Jeff Hill and Jack Williams (eds), *Sport and Identity in the North of England*, Keele: Keele University Press, 1996, pp. 85–112.

——, 'Cocks, cats, caps and cups: a semiotic approach to sport and national identity', *Culture, Sport, Society*, 2, 2, 1999, 1–21.

——, *Sport and the Literary Imagination*, Oxford: Peter Lang, 2006.

Hillyard, G. W., *Forty Years of First-Class Lawn Tennis*, London: Williams & Norgate, 1924.

Hines, J. R., *Figure Skating: A History*, Urbana and Chicago, IL: University of Illinois Press, 2006.

Hodges, H., 'Kitchener invades England: the london calypsos of Aldwyn Roberts', *Wasafiri: The Transnational Journal of International Writing*, 45, 2005, 24–30.

Hognestad, H., 'Viking and farmer armies: the Stavanger–Bryne Norwegian football rivalry', in G. Armstrong, and R. Giulianotti (eds), *Fear and Loathing in World Football*, Oxford: Berg, 2001.

Höhne, E., 'Music and sport', *Olympic Review*, 141–142, 1979, 437–439.

Holt, R., *Sport and Society in Modern France*, London: Macmillan, 1981.

Homer, *Odyssey*, trans. A. T. Murray, Cambridge, MA: Harvard University Press, 1919.

Howard, D., 'Measuring the tuning accuracy of thousands singing in unison: an English Premier Football League table of fans' singing tunefulness', in *Logopedics Phoniatrics Vocology*, 29, 2004, 77–83.

Hughes, M. and R. Stradling, *The English Musical Renaissance 1840–1940: Constructing a National Music*, Manchester: Manchester University Press, 1993.

Humphreys, D., 'Snowboarders: bodies out of control and in conflict', *Sporting Traditions*, 13, 5, 1996, 3–23.

Hutchins, B. and M. Phillips, 'Selling permissible violence: the commodification of Australian Rugby League 1970–1995', *International Review of the Sociology of Sport*, 32, 1997, 161–176.

Inglis, T., *Global Ireland: Same Difference*, London: Routledge, 2008.

Ives, J. C., W. F. Straub and G. A. Shelley, 'Enhancing athletic performance using digital video in consulting', *Journal of Applied Sport Psychology*, 14, 2002, 237–245.

James, C. L. R., *Beyond a Boundary*, London: Serpents Tail, 2000.

James, W., 'What is an emotion?' *Mind*, 9, 1884, 188–205.

Jay, G. and D. Miller, 'The role of theory in the study of literature?', in G. Jay and D. Miller (eds), *After Strange Texts: The Role of Theory in the Study of Literature*, University, AL: University of Alabama Press, 1985, pp. 1–28.

Johnson, T. A., *Baseball and the Music of Charles Ives*, Lanham, Maryland: Scarecrow Press, 2004.

Jones, C. and S. Fleming, ' "I'd rather wear a turban than a rose": a case study of the ethics of chanting', *Race Ethnicity and Education*, 10, 4, 2007, 401–414.

Jones, M. V. and R. D. Mace, 'Relationship between emotional state and performance during international field hockey matches', *Perceptual and Motor Skills*, 90, 2000, 691.

Karageorghis, C. I., 'The magic of music in movement', *Sport and Medicine Today*, 5, 2001, 38–41.

Karageorghis, C. I. and P. C. Terry, 'The psychophysical effects of music in sport and exercise: a review', *Journal of Sport Behavior*, 20, 1997, 54–68.

Karageorghis, C. I., K. M. Drew and P. C. Terry, 'Effects of pretest stimulative and sedative music on grip strength', *Perceptual and Motor Skills*, 83, 1996, 1347–1352.

Karageorghis, C. I., D. L. Priest, P. C. Terry, N. L. D. Chatzisarantis and A. M. Lane, 'Redesign and initial validation of an instrument to assess the motivational qualities of music in exercise: the Brunel Music Rating Inventory-2', *Journal of Sports Sciences*, 24, 2006, 899–909.

Karageorghis, C. I., P. C. Terry and A. M. Lane, 'Development and initial validation of an instrument to assess the motivational qualities of music in exercise and sport: the Brunel Music Rating Inventory', *Journal of Sports Sciences*, 17, 1, 1999, 713–724.

Keane, B., ' "Ex-pats" and "poofters" rebuild the nation: 1982, Kiwi culture and the all whites on the road to Spain', in B. Patterson (ed.), *Sport, Society and Culture in New Zealand*, Wellington: Stout Research Centre, 1999, pp. 49–60.

Keens-Douglas, P., *Roll Call: Poetry and Short Stories by Paul Keens-Douglas*, Trinidad: Keensdee Productions, 1997.

Kern, S., *The Culture of Time and Space*, London: Weidenfeld and Nicolson, 1983.

Kiisk, H., *Körsången i Estland*, Stockholm: Estniska Nationalfonden, 1967.

King, A., *Memorials of the Great War in Britain: The Symbolism and Politics of Remembrance*, Oxford: Berg, 1998.

Krebs, H.-D., 'Sport and music: an uncommon partnership', *Olympic Review*, 37, 2001.

Kuhn, H., *Defining a Nation in Song. Danish Patriotic Songs in Songbooks of the Period 1832–1870*, Copenhagen: Reitzel, 1990.

Laban, R. von, *A Vision of Dynamic Space*, London and Philadelphia: Falmer, 1984.

Lafranchi, P., C. Eisenberg, T. Mason and A. Wahl, *100 Years of Football: The Fifa Centennial Book*, London: Weidenfeld and Nicolson, 2004.

Laidlaw, C., *Rights of Passage: Beyond the New Zealand Identity Crisis*, Auckland: Hodder Moa Beckett, 1999.

Laing, D., 'Rock anxieties and new music networks', in Angela McRobbie (ed.), *Back to Reality: Social Experience and Cultural Studies*, Manchester: Manchester University Press, 1997, pp. 116–132.

Lambert, C., *Music Ho! A Study of Music in Decline*, London: Faber and Faber, 1937/1934.

Lanzillo, J. J., K. L. Burke, A. B. Joyner and C. J. Hardy, 'The effects of music on the intensity and direction of pre-competitive cognitive and somatic state anxiety and state self-confidence in collegiate athletes', *International Sports Journal*, 5, 2001,

Lazarus, R. S., *Emotion and Adaptation*, New York: Oxford University Press, 1991.

Leavitt, J., J. Young and D. Connelly, 'The effects of videotape highlights on state self-confidence', *Journal of Applied Research in Coaching and Athletics*, 4, 1989, 225–232.

LeBlanc, A., 'An interactive theory of music preference', *Journal of Music Therapy*, 19, 1982, 28–45.

Le Roy, L. E., *Carnival in Romans: A People's Uprising at Romans 1579–1580*, Harmondsworth: Penguin, 1981.

Levesque, C. and L. G. Palletier, 'On the investigation of primed and chronic autonomous and heteronomous motivational orientations', *Personality and Social Psychology Bulletin*, 29, 2003, 1570–1584.

Lewis, I. M., *Ecstatic Religion. A Study in Shamanism and Spirit Possession*, London and New York: Routledge, 1989.

Lewis, W., 'The credentials of the painter', in P. Edwards (ed.), *Creatures of Habit and Creatures of Change: Essays on Art, Literature and Culture 1914–1956*, Santa Rosa: Black Sparrow Press, pp. 66–76.

Lim, H., G. Atkinson, M. Eubank and C. I. Karageorghis, 'The effect of timing exposure on performance, perceived exertion and psychological affect during a 10-km cycling time trial', in T. Reilly and G. Atkinson (eds), *Sixth International Conference on Sport, Leisure and Ergonomics*, Liverpool, UK: The Ergonomics Society, November 2007, p. 46.

Littlejohn, D., *The Ultimate Art: Essays Around and About Opera*, Berkeley, CA: University of California Press, 1992.

Loizou, G. and C. I. Karageorghis, 'The circumplex model of affect: A bi-cultural study', *Journal of Sports Sciences*, 25, 2007, 316.

Long, C. and J. Williams, 'Football and music cultures in Liverpool', *Esporte e Sociedade*, 1, 2005, 1–43.

Longhurst, B., 'Popular Music and Society', *Texts and Meanings*, Cambridge: Polity Press, 1995.

Lucaccini, L. F. and L. H. Kreit, 'Music', in W. P. Morgan (ed.), *Ergogenic Aids and Muscular Performance*, New York: Academic Press, 1972, pp. 240–245.

Lumpkin, A., *Woman's Tennis. A Historical Documentary of the Players and Their Game*, New York: The Whitson Publishing Company, 1981.

McClary, S., *Feminine Endings: Music, Gender and Sexuality*, Minneapolis: University of Minnesota Press, 1991.

MacDonald, I., *Between Silence and Silence*, Leeds: Peepal Tree, 2003.

McKay, J. and D. Rowe, 'Field of soaps: Rupert V. Kerry as masculine melodrama', *Social Text*, 50, 1997, 69–86.

McLeod, K., '"We are the Champions": masculinities, sports and popular music', *Popular Music and Society*, 29, 2006, 531–547.

McNamee, M., 'Hubris, humility, and humilation: vice and virtue in sporting communities' *Journal of the Philosophy of Sport*, 29, 1, 2002, 38–53.

——, 'Schadenfreude in sport: envy, justice and self-esteem', *Journal of the Philosophy of Sport*, 30, 1, 2003, 1–16.

Madsen, B. V., *Oplysning i Bevægelse. Kultur, Krop og Demokrati i den Folkelige Gymnastik*, Århus: Klim, 2003.

Maier, C. S., *Recasting Bourgeois Europe: Stabilization in France, Germany, and Italy in the Decade After World War One*, Princeton, NJ: Princeton University Press, 1974.

Malm, K., *Fyra Musikkulturer. Tanzania, Tunisien, Sverige och Trinidad*, Stockholm: Almqvist & Wiksell, 1981.

Marqusee, M., *Anyone but England: Cricket and the National Malaise*, London: Verso, 1994.

——, *Redemption Song. Muhammad Ali and the Spirit of the Sixties*, London: Verso, 1999.

Mason, T., *Association Football and English Society, 1863–1915*, Brighton: Harvester, 1980.

Mayerfield Bell, M. and M. Gardiner (eds), *Bakhtin and the Human Sciences*, London: Sage, 1998.

Melly, G., *Revolt into Style. The Pop Arts in Britain*, Harmondsworth: Penguin, 1970.

Menon, V. and D. J. Levitin, 'The rewards of music listening: response and physiological connectivity of the mesolimbic system', *NeuroImage*, 28, 2005, 175–184.

Merriam, A., *The Anthropology of Music*, Chicago: Northwestern University Press, 1964.

Michel, W. and H. U. Wanner, 'Einfuss der musik auf die sportliche leistung [Effect of music on sports performance]', *Schweizerische Zeitschrift für Sportmedizin*, 23, 1975, 141–159.

Midgett, D., 'Cricket and calypso: cultural representations and social history in the West Indies', *Sport and Society*, 6, 2–3, 2003, 239–268.

Mihaly, C., *Beyond Boredom and Anxiety. The Experience of Play in Work and Games*, San Francisco: Jossey-Bass, 1975.

Mihule, J., *Martinů: Osud Skladatele*, Prague: Charles University Press, 2002.

Mitchell, A., *The Half-gallon Quarter-acre Pavlova Paradise: An Introduction to the Wonderful People, the Fulfilling Lifestyle and the Fascinating Spectacles which will Greet the Interested British Immigrant on his Arrival in New Zealand, a Land Believed by Many to be the Fairest Jewel in the British Crown; the Whole being Communicated in the Form of Twelve Letters to a new Settler*, Christchurch: Whitcombe and Tombs, 1972.

Mitchell, T., *Popular Music and Local Identity: Rock, Pop and Rap in Europe and Oceania*, London: Leicester University Press, 1996.

Moorhouse, H. F., 'One state, several countries: soccer and nationality in a "United" Kingdom', in J. A. Mangan (ed.), *Tribal Identities. Nationalism, Europe, Sport*, London: Frank Cass, 2002.

Morris, D., *The Soccer Tribe*, London: Jonathan Cape, 1981.

Mott, M. M., 'A bibliography of song sheets. Sport and recreations in American Popular songs (part 2)', *Notes*, 7, 4, 1950, 522–561.

——, 'A bibliography of song sheets. Sport and recreation in American popular songs (part 3)', *Notes*, 9, 1, 1951, 33–62.

Mulhern, F., *The Moment of Scrutiny*, London: New Left Books, 1979.

Naipaul, V. S., *The Middle Passage*, London: Picador, 2001.

Negra, D. (ed.), *The Irish in Us. Irishness, Performativity and Popular Culture*, Durham: Duke University Press, 2007.

Neher, A., 'A physiological explanation of unusual behaviour in ceremonies involving drums', *Human Biology*, 34, 1962, 151–160.

Neville, D., 'Metastasio and the image of majesty in the Austrio-Italian baroque', in Shearer West (ed.), *Italian Culture in Northern Europe in the Eighteenth Century*, Cambridge: Cambridge University Press, 1999, pp. 140–158.

Newson, R., 'Music to your ears?', *When Saturday Comes*, 110, 1996.

Nisbett, R. E. and T. D. Wilson, 'Telling more than we can know: verbal reports on mental processes', *Psychological Review*, 84, 1977, 231–259.

Nolte, C. E., *The Sokol in the Czech Lands to 1914: Training for the Nation*, Basingstoke: Palgrave, 2002.

Nørretranders, T., *The User Illusion: Cutting Consciousness Down to Size*, New York: Penguin, 1991.

North, A. C. and D. J. Hargreaves, 'The musical milieu: studies of listening in everyday life', *The Psychologist*, 10, 1997, 309–312.

Nowlis, V. and H. H. Nowlis, 'The description and analysis of mood', *Annals of the New York Academy of Sciences*, 65, 1956, 345–355.

Oriard, M., 'Professional football as a cultural myth', *Journal of American Culture*, 4, 3, 1981, 27–41.

Page, M., *The Power of Chi. An Introduction to Chinese Mysticism and Philosophy*, Wellingborough: Aquarian, 1988.

Panksepp, J., 'The basics of basic emotion', in P. Ekman and R. J. Davidson (eds), *The Nature of Emotion: Fundamental Questions*, New York: Oxford University Press, 1994, pp. 20–24.

Pates, J., C. I. Karageorghis, R. Fryer and I. Maynard, 'Effects of asynchronous music on flow states and shooting performance among netball players', *Psychology of Sport and Exercise*, 4, 2003, 413–427.

Pawson, T., *100 Years of the FA Cup: The Centenary History*, London: William Heinemann, 1972.

Pearce, K. A., 'Effects of different types of music on physical strength', *Perceptual and Motor Skills*, 53, 1981, 351–352.

Perloff, N., *Art and the Everyday: Popular Entertainment and the Circle of Erik Satie*, Oxford: Clarendon Press, 1991.

Phillips, E. M., 'Recognising the language of calypso as "symbolic action" in resolving conflict in the Republic of Trinidad and Tobago', *Caribbean Quarterly*, 52, 1, 2006, 53–73.

Phillips, J. O. C., *A Man's Country? The Image of the Pakeha Male – A History*, revised edition, Auckland: Penguin Books, 1996.

Phillips, M. G. and B. Hutchins 'From independence to a reconstituted hegemony: Rugby League and television in Australia', *Journal of Australian Studies*, 58, 1998, 134–147.

Pine, B. J. and J. Gilmore, *The Experience Economy – Work is Theatre and Every Business a Stage*, New York: Harvard Business School Publishing, 1999.

Plowright, F., 'Record attempts', in 'Football memorabilia special', *When Saturday Comes*, 227, 2006.

Porsfelt, D., *Management Trainee – Möten med Förhinder*, Doctoral thesis, Human Work Sciences, Industrial Work Environment, Luleå University of Technology, 2001.

Porteous, D., *Environmental Aesthetics: Ideas, Politics and Planning*, London: Routledge, 1994.

Porter, R. (ed.), *Myths of the English*, Cambridge: Polity Press, 1992.

Postman, N., *Amusing Ourselves to Death: Public Discourse in the Age of Show Business*, New York: Penguin, 1985.

Prince, R. (ed.), *Trance and Possession States*, Montreal: R. M. Bucke Memorial Society, 1968.

Prunières, H., *L'Opéra Italien en France Avant Lulli*, Paris: Champion, 1913.

Pujol, T. J. and M. E. Langenfeld, 'Influence of music on Wingate anaerobic test performance', *Perceptual and Motor Skills*, 88, 1999, 292–296.

Quevedo, R., *Atilla's Kaiso: A Short History of Trinidad Calypso*, Trindad: University of the West Indies Press, 1983.

Ramnarine, T. K., *Creating their Own Space: The Development of an Indian–Caribbean Musical Tradition*, Jamaica: University of the West Indies Press, 2001.

Redhead, S., *Football with Attitude*, Manchester: Wordsmith, 1991.

——, (ed.), *The Passion and the Fashion. Football Fandom in the New Europe*, Aldershot: Averbury, 1993.

——, *Post Fandom and the Millennial Blues*, London: Routledge, 1997.

Regis, L., *The Political Calypso: True Opposition in Trinidad and Tobago 1962–1987*, Barbados: University of the West Indies Press, c.1999.

Reich, E. K., *Solskin og Lyn. Grundtvig og Hans Sang til Livet*, Copenhagen: Vartov, 2000.

Reilly, R., 'The sweet songs of soccer', *Sports Illustrated*, 104, 24, 12 June 2006.

Rein, I., P. Kotler and B. Shields, *The Elusive Fan. Reinventing Sports in a Crowded Marketplace*, New York: McGraw-Hill, 2006.

Reiss, T. J., *Music, Writing and Cultural Unity in the Caribbean*, Trenton, NJ: Africa World Press, 2005.

Relph, E. C., *Place and Placelessness*, London: Prion, 1976.

Rickard, N. S., 'Intense emotional responses to music: a test of the physiological arousal hypothesis', *Psychology of Music*, 2004, 32, 371–388.

'Roaring Lion', *Calypso from France to Trinidad: 800 Years of History*, Trinidad: n.p., 1988.

Roberts, G. C., *Advances in Motivation, in Sport and Exercise*, Champaign, IL: Human Kinetics, 2001.

Roessler, K. K., 'Sport and the psychology of pain', in S. Loland, B. Skirstad and I. Waddington (eds), *Pain and Injury in Sport. Social and Ethical Analysis*, New York and London: Routledge, 2006, pp. 34–48.

Rohlehr, G., *Calypso & Society in Pre-Independence Trinidad*, Trinidad: G. Rohlehr, 1990.

——, 'Music, literature and West Indian cricket values', in H. McD. Beckles (ed.), *An Area of Conquest: Popular Democracy and West Indies Cricket*, Jamaica: Ian Randle, 1994, pp. 55–102.

——, *A Scuffling of Islands: Essays on Calypso*, Trinidad: Lexicon, 2004.

Ross, A., *The Rest is Noise: Listening to the Twentieth Century*, London: Fourth Estate, 2008.

Rowe, D., *Popular Cultures. Rock Music, Sport and the Politics of Pleasure*, London: Sage, 1995.

Russell, D., 'Music and northern identity 1890–c.1965', in N. Kirk (ed.), *Northern Identities. Historical Interpretations of 'The North' and 'Northernness'*, Aldershot: Ashgate, 2000.

——, 'Abiding memories: the community singing movement and English social life in the 1920s', *Popular Music*, January, 2008.

Ryan, G., 'Rural myth and urban actuality: the anatomy of All Black and New Zealand Rugby 1884–1938', *New Zealand Journal of History*, 35, 1, 2001, 45–69.

Saarikallio, S. and J. Erkkila, 'The role of music in adolescents' mood regulation', *Psychology of Music* 35, 1, 2007, 88–109.

Sadie, S., (ed.), *The New Grove Dictionary of the Opera*, New York: Macmillan Press, 1992.

Šafránek, M., *Bohuslav Martinů: His Life and Works*, trans. R. Finlayson-Sambourová, London: Allan Wingate, 1961.

——, *Bohuslav Martinů: Život A Dílo*, Prague: Státni Hudební Vydavatelství, 1961.

Sandiford, K. A. P., *Cricket Nurseries of Colonial Barbados: The Elite Schools, 1865–1966*, Jamaica: University of the West Indies Press, 1998.

Sayer, D., *The Coasts of Bohemia: A Czech Cultural History*, Princeton: Princeton University Press, 1998.

Schachter, S. and J. Singer, 'Cognitive, social and physiological determinants of emotional state', *Psychological Review*, 69, 1962, 378–399.

Scherer, K. R., 'Which emotions can be induced by music? What are the underlying mechanisms? And how can we measure them?', *Journal of New Music Research*, 33, 2004, 239–251.

Scherer, K. R. and M. R. Zentner, 'Emotional effects of music: production rules', in P. Juslin and J. A. Sloboda (eds), *Music and Emotion: Theory and Research*, Oxford: Oxford University Press, 2001, pp. 361–392.

Schwab, H. W., '"Anyone for tennis". Anmerkungen zum Genre Tenniskomposition', in Marianne Sammer (ed.), *Leitmotive. Kulturgeschichtliche Studien zur Traditionsbildung (Festschrift für Dietz-Rüdiger Moser)*, Kallmünz: Verlag Michael Lassleben, 1999, pp. 457–483.

Seddon, P. J., *A Football Compendium. An Expert Guide to the Books, Films and the Music of Association Football*, Boston Spa, Wetherby: The British Library, 1999.

Segrave, J. O., 'Pietro Metastasio's L'Olimpiade and the survival of the Olympic idea in 18th century Europe', *Olympika: The International Journal of Olympic Studies*, 2005, 14, 1–28.

Shilling, C., *The Body in Culture, Technology and Society*, London: Sage, 2005.

Simpson, S. D. and C. I. Karageorghis, 'The effects of synchronous music on 400-m sprint performance', *Journal of Sports Sciences*, 24, 2006, 1095–1102.

Sloboda, J. A., 'Music structure and emotional response: some empirical findings', *Psychology of Music*, 19, 1991, 110–120.

Smith, D. and G. Williams, *Fields of Praise: The Official History of the Welsh Rugby Union 1881–1981*, Cardiff: University of Wales Press, 1981.

Smoll, F. L. and R. W. Schultz, 'Relationships among measures of preferred tempo and motor rhythm', *Perceptual and Motor Skills*, 46, 1978, 883–894.

Smyth, G., *Noisy Island. A Short History of Irish Popular Music*, Cork: Cork University Press, 2005.

Snyder, E., 'Responses to musical selections and sport: an auditory elicitation approach', *Sociology of Sport Journal*, 10, 2, 1993, 168–182.

Spratt, G. K., *The Music of Arthur Honegger*, Cork: Cork University Press, 1987.

Stamp, G., *The Memorial to the Missing of the Somme*, London: Profile Books, 2006.

Stanton, R., *The Forgotten Olympic Art Competitions: The Story of the Olympic Art Competitions of the 20th Century*, Victoria, Canada: Trafford, 2000.

Stokes, M. (ed.), *Ethnicity, Identity and Music: The Musical Construction of Place*, Oxford: Berg, 1994.

Streible, D., 'Female spectators and the Corbett–Fitzsimmons fight film', in T. Baker (ed.), *Out of Bounds: Sports, Media, and the Politics of Identity*, Bloomington, IN: Indiana University Press, 1997, pp. 16–47.

Szabo, A., A. Small and M. Leigh, 'The effects of slow- and fast-rhythm classical music on progressive cycling to physical exhaustion', *Journal of Sports Medicine and Physical Fitness*, 39, 1999, 220–225.

Szmedra, L. and D. W. Bacharach, 'Effect of music on perceived exertion, plasma lactate, norepinephrine and cardiovascular hemodynamics during treadmill running', *International Journal of Sports Medicine*, 19, 1998, 32–37.

Tapp, A. and J. Clowes, 'From "carefree casuals" to "professional wanderers" – segmentation possibilities for football supporters', *European Journal of Marketing*, 36, 2000, 1248–1269.

Taylor, M., *The Leaguers: The Making of Professional Football in England, 1900–1939*, Liverpool: Liverpool University Press, 2005.

G. Tenenbaum, R. Lidor, N. Lavyan, K. Morrow, S. Tonnel, A. Gershgoren, J. Meis and M. Johnson, 'The effect of music type on running perseverance and coping with effort sensations', *Psychology of Sport and Exercise*, 5, 2004, 89–109.

Terry, P. C. and C. I. Karageorghis, 'Psychophysical effects of music in sport and exercise: an update on theory, research and application', in M. Katsikitis (ed.), *Proceedings of the Joint Conference of the Australian and Psychological Society and the New Zealand Psychological Society*, Melbourne: Australian Psychological Society, 2006, pp. 415–419.

Thackray, R. M., *Music and Physical Education*, London: Bell, 1958.

Thayer, R. E., *The Biopsychology of Mood and Arousal*, Oxford: Oxford University Press, 1989.

Turner, J. and G. Bushell, *From Ritual to Theatre*, New York: PAJ, 1996.

——, *Cockney Reject*, London: John Blake Publishing, 2005.

Turner, V., *The Ritual Process. Structure and Anti-Structure*, Chicago: Aldine de Gruyter, 1995.

Uppal, A. K. and U. Datta, 'Cardiorespiratory response of junior high school girls to exercise performed with and without music', *Journal of Physical Education and Sport Science*, 2, 1990, 52–56.

Vallas, L., *Achille Claude Debussy*, trans. Kurt Lamerdin, Potsdam: Athenaion, 1944.

Vallerand, R. J. and C. M. Blanchard, 'The study of emotion in sport and exercise: historical, definitional, and conceptual perspectives', in Y. L. Hanin, *Emotions in Sport*, pp. 3–37.

Vallerand, R. J., C. M. Blanchard, L. G. Pelletier, M. Blais, N. M. Briere, C. Senecal and E. F. Vallieres, 'The academic motivational scale: a measure of intrinsic, extrinsic and amotivation in education', *Educational and Psychological Measurement*, 52, 1992, 1003–1019.

Walker, C., 'The roar from the back room: The rise of "pub rock"', in *Juice/Powerhouse Museum Special Issue: Real Wild Child*, Sydney: Powerhouse Museum, 1994, p. 14.

Wark, M., '"Homage to Catatonia": culture, politics and midnight oil', in J. Frow and M. Morris (eds), *Australian Cultural Studies: A Reader*, Urbana: University of Illinois Press, 1993, pp. 105–116.

Warner, K. Q., *The Trinidad Calypso: A Study of the Calypso as Oral Literature*, London: Heineman, 1983.

Watson, J. R., *The English Hymn: A Critical and Historical Study*, Oxford: Oxford University Press, 1997.

Whitcomb, I., *After the Ball*, Harmondsworth: Penguin, 1972.

White, A. and L. Hardy, 'Use of different imagery perspectives on the learning and performance of different motor skills', *British Journal of Psychology*, 86, 1995, 191–216.

Whitely, S. (ed.), *Sexing the Groove: Popular Music and Gender*, London: Routledge, 1997.

Williams, A. M. and A. Grant, 'Training perceptual skills in sport', *International Journal of Sport Psychology*, 30, 1999, 194–220.

Williams, J., '"Kopites", "scallies" and Liverpool fan cultures: tales of triumph and disasters', in J. Williams, S. Hopkins and C. Long (eds), *Passing Rhythms. Liverpool FC and the Transformation of Football*, Oxford: Berg, 2001.

——, 'Rethinking sports fandom: the case of European soccer', *Leisure Studies*, 26, 2, 2007.

Willis, P. E., *Learning to Labour. How Working Class Kids get Working Class Jobs*, Aldershot: Gower, 1977.

Wilson, J. K., *L'Olympiade: Selected Eighteenth-Century Settings of Metastasio's Libretto*, PhD dissertation, Harvard University, 1982.

Wilson, R. M. F. and N. J. Davey, 'Musical beat influences corticospinal drive to ankle flexor and extensor muscles in man', *International Journal of Psychophysiology*, 44, 2002, 177.

Winkielman, P. and K. C. Berridge, 'Unconcious emotion', *Current Directions in Psychological Science*, 13, 2004, 120–123.

Winter, J., *Sites of Memory, Sites of Mourning: The Great War in European Cultural History*, Cambridge: Cambridge University Press, 1995.

Index